Microcomputer Interfacing

BRUCE A. ARTWICK

President
Sublogic Company
Urbana, Illinois

PRENTICE-HALL, INC., *Englewood Cliffs, New Jersey 07632*

Library of Congress Cataloging in Publication Data

Artwick, Bruce A.
    Microcomputer interfacing.

    Includes index.
      1. Microcomputers. 2. Microprocessors.
3. Computer interfaces. I. Title.
TK7888.3.A86   621.3819'58'3   79-16747
ISBN 0-13-580902-9
ISBN 0-13-580928-2 (limited paperback edition)

Editorial/production supervision and interior design by Gary Samartino
Cover design by Edsal Enterprises
Manufacturing buyer: Gordon Osbourne

Printed in the United States of America

10 9

PRENTICE-HALL INTERNATIONAL, INC., *London*
PRENTICE-HALL OF AUSTRALIA PTY. LIMITED, *Sydney*
PRENTICE-HALL OF CANADA, LTD., *Toronto*
PRENTICE-HALL OF INDIA PRIVATE LIMITED, *New Delhi*
PRENTICE-HALL OF JAPAN, INC., *Tokyo*
PRENTICE-HALL OF SOUTHEAST ASIA PTE. LTD., *Singapore*
WHITEHALL BOOKS LIMITED, *Wellington, New Zealand*

Contents

3 MEMORY 100

4 MICROCOMPUTER INPUT AND OUTPUT METHODS 144

8 INTERFACE LAYOUT
AND CONSTRUCTION

299

9 INTERFACE SOFTWARE DESIGN
AND IMPLEMENTATION

314

Preface

Assembling a microcomputer system, including the task of interfacing the components for specific system applications, is a matter of defining the system, selecting and matching the proper components, and ultimately building the system using acceptable design and construction techniques. The information needed to carry out these phases of the overall project, however, is currently available only from diverse sources such as manufacturers' specifications sheets, journal articles and industry papers, and textbooks that are often highly theoretical. Getting together enough useful data to build and interface a real nuts-and-bolts microcomputer system can be a major task in itself. My intention in writing this book has been to integrate into a single volume all the information necessary to conceptualize, select, mate and match, build, and interface microcomputer systems to most applications, thereby eliminating — or, at the very least, minimizing — the sometimes costly, usually erratic, and always time-consuming task of information gathering.

This text covers a wide range of topics. Advanced interface devices and methods are examined, of course; but in deference to the less technically skilled readers, basic facts often taken for granted are covered as well. This approach is intended to equalize the design starting point for all levels of reader.

Before delving deeply into a comprehensive comparison of microprocessors and interface components, we look at the capabilities of microcomputers through examples of some current systems and applications. The many forms of microcomputer — ranging from simple 4-bit, single-card controllers to complete multibit data processing systems — are evaluated, which sets the stage for your own conceptualization, without additional outside assistance, of the system that is "right" for your planned applications.

Troublefree interfacing depends on a good knowledge of the principles of microcomputer communications, or input/output. These principles are covered in particular detail in this book, along with up-to-date specifications and performance data on advanced interface devices such as CCD memories, one-chip microcomputers, monolithic multipliers, and analog-to-digital converters. And a section concerning the often ignored mechanical interface components such as stepping motors and relays, servos, and mechanical transducers will help you in real-world interfacing and control applications.

Interface design and construction techniques encompass a wide spectrum of "how to" data, from how to keep a transformer from vibrating loose in a microcomputer chassis to how to "design" noise problems out of high-performance ECL microprocessor systems. These and other procedures are presented with a strong emphasis on optimization, performance, and reliability.

A concluding section is devoted to the all-important software development task; this information describes what is necessary to develop various software entities for a range of microcomputer applications.

The discussions presented in this book are not simple comparisons of specifications and model numbers; instead, components and interfacing methods are examined and analyzed in terms of what these devices and techniques can do for you the user and how to use and get the best results from the components selected.

In addition to design and construction techniques, this book consolidates many industry standards previously available only from scattered sources, making this a valuable reference work as well as a hands-on design and construction guide.

BRUCE A. ARTWICK

1

The Microcomputer's Role in the Real World

The early 1970s marked the beginning of a revolution in the world of electronics: the microprocessor revolution. Although proponents heralded the development of the microprocessor as a large leap in the state of the art, this was more of an evolutionary development—a logical extension of the small-scale, medium-scale, and (by today's standards) the primitive, large-scale integration which preceded it. The first 4-bit microprocessors were not designed to function specifically as central processing units but rather as complex controllers.

The original designers of microprocessors were, in fact, quite puzzled over why anyone would want to use their FET-based microcontroller as a computer when more advanced bipolar minicomputers were readily available. The answer to this question was economics. For the first time, real computing power was available to everyone at a reasonable cost.

Gradually, the usefulness of microprocessors as central processing units was realized and more powerful 8-, 16-, and 32-bit units were developed. Today microprocessors are making significant inroads into the field of traditional computing. The distinctions between microcomputers and minicomputers are vanishing, and the coming years will witness the arrival of microprocessors with performance and complexity levels so high that such devices would have been inconceivable only a decade ago. Basically, better products will be available for less as microelectronics evolve.

Processor performance, instructions per second, word widths of 4, 8, or 16 bits, and floating-point operations per second are only one facet, however. The

1

science of using a microprocessor and efficiently integrating it into an overall system, commonly referred to as *interfacing,* is equally important yet frequently overlooked. The support circuitry and all the devices surrounding a microprocessor cost more, take up more space, have more critical environmental constraints, and draw more power than the microprocessor in nearly every case and should be given very high priority in the design of a system. Careful consideration of a system's interface requirements during the design phase and adherence to defined design rules will result in a clean, highly reliable design that makes use of all the advanced features microprocessors have to offer.

This chapter touches on some of the advantages of microcomputer-based information and control systems and will aid you in determining whether a microcomputer-based design is desirable in your application. The economic advantages are stressed, and a few actual implementations are examined from a performance and interface standpoint to give you an idea of what you have to look forward to if you choose to go the *micro* route for your computing application.

PREREQUISITE TERMINOLOGY

Any discussion in a technical field tends to lose some of its substance if the terminology is not explicitly understood by all participants. The comparatively recent phenomenon of a multiplicity of writers assigning a multiplicity of meanings to a limited lexicon of terms only compounds the problem. Also, the microcomputer field is notorious for its overabundance of acronyms and buzzwords. These problems point to the need for a cleared-away starting point. A glossary is provided at the end of the text to help make some sense out of microcomputer jargon but it is important to define a few of the most basic terms at the outset.

The terms microcomputer, minicomputer, microcontroller, microprocessor, and mainframe are but a few of those terms which are but loosely defined, and their definitions seem to keep changing as people abuse them. In this text, definitions derived from a composite of the accepted industry terminology are used.

A *mainframe* is a very large computer system, typically for business-related data processing or advanced scientific computations. A mainframe requires a staff of support personnel and handles many peripheral devices such as line printers, card readers, magnetic tape units, disks, and terminals. An IBM 3033 system or Control Data 6600 would be considered a mainframe; a personal computer packed full of boards driving dual floppy disks and a terminal would not be.

A *microcomputer* is a fully operational computer system built around a microprocessor. Included in the microcomputer are memory, clocks, and interfaces. A personal computer with a CPU card, a few memory boards, a power supply, and interfaces would constitute a microcomputer.

A *microprocessor* consists of one or more large-scale integrated (LSI) circuits designed to work as a sequential computational or control unit by executing a predefined or user-defined set of instructions contained in a memory.

A *minicomputer* is a small computer with the central processing unit built from small- or medium-scale integrated circuits (SSI or MSI) or from discrete parts. Included as part of a minicomputer are the associated memory and interface modules. A minicomputer does not require a large support staff and can even be turned off when you're not using it. Digital Equipment Corporation's PDP-11/35 is a minicomputer.

A *microcontroller* is a module consisting of a microprocessor, memory, and interfaces used for control applications. A card which controls the stoplights at a street corner, if built with a microprocessor, would be considered a microcontroller.

MICROCOMPUTERS AND MICROCONTROLLERS

You may be able to reap big savings and increase a system's performance and reliability by replacing some logic with or by building a whole system around a microprocessor; but you may also end up facing big problems. It's therefore wise to get familiar with the characteristics of microprocessors before you start a project. The idea is to cash in on all the advantages and dodge all the pitfalls.

LSI Traits

Microprocessors, by their very LSI nature, tend to bring all the advantages and disadvantages of large-scale integration to a system.

Overall system package count is decreased. Much of the data storage, arithmetic, and interface logic previously constructed with discrete MSI or SSI parts are incorporated into one central unit. Package count reductions translate into system size and weight savings.

Logic complexity on a gate-for-gate basis typically increases. A microprocessor is a multipurpose programmable device and has many features that won't get used in a given application. Since microprocessors cannot ordinarily be modified, they cannot be optimized to the user's requirements as discrete logic can. Nonoptimizability and programmability are the primary causes of the increased logical complexity.

Despite the increase in logical complexity, the use of microprocessors and other LSI devices decreases overall power consumption. Small driving currents and low parasitic capacitances on the LSI chip provide a dramatic power-per-gate savings as well as increased speed–power products.

LSI devices also increase system reliability, mostly because of mechanical factors. Highly reliable one-piece metallization layers and end-to-end transistor and resistor junctions on the LSI chip replace mechanically connected and soldered discrete components. As a result, LSI components are less sensitive to mechanical shock and fatigue and more tolerant of poor environmental conditions.

Finally, microprocessors and other LSI components can greatly reduce system costs. One inexpensive microprocessor can replace a large number of SSI, MSI, and discrete-component devices and thus save a sizable amount of parts alone; but more often than not the greatest cost savings are realized from indirect savings in other areas. Circuit board size and complexity reductions save on materials and layout costs. Because most of a system's large parallel data buses can reside on the microprocessor chip, the expensive task of parallel-bus circuit board layout is greatly reduced. More of a system's functions can be crammed into the space of a single circuit module, thereby reducing the module and connector count as well as the enclosure size and complexity. All of these savings contribute to the reduction of overall system costs.

Computer Traits

Just as a microprocessor assumes the LSI advantages and disadvantages of its LSI construction, it takes on the traits of a computer due to its processor-like architecture. This statement may seem obvious, but it's important to take a close look at these computer traits. In many applications they can be more harmful than helpful.

Microprocessors, like computers, are programmable devices and are versatile in function. This feature tends to make microprocessor-based systems easily reconfigurable and able to perform complex tasks in a step-by-step manner. Many of a system's complex functions thus need not be implemented in special-purpose system hardware. Complex hardware development effort is considerably reduced as the burden is shifted to the system software.

Don't think that the programming will be an inconsequential matter, however. Algorithm and program development are costly and time-consuming. Depending on the situation, a program can cost as much as $200 per line of debugged code. The true advantage lies in the fact that programming is usually less costly than building the equivalent hardware.

Like most large computers, microprocessors are Von Neumann in character: they execute one instruction after another in a predefined sequence to implement a given task. This type of machine has demonstrated its usefulness for problem solving, but the limitation that only one instruction can be executed at one time may lead to some serious consequences when constructing a control system. When multiple events must be examined or initiated at precisely the same time, a microprocessor falls short of the goal. An illustrative example is the case of a microprocessor-based inertial navigation system.

Assume that an aircraft's inertial navigation system outputs navigational reference data at a rate of one sample per millisecond. Among the navigational data are three bytes of data containing degrees, minutes, and seconds of longitude. The navigational processor (in this case the candidate for a microprocessor application) is required to sample these and other data and plot the aircraft's position on a display device. The three bytes of data must be sampled simultaneously by the processor if accurate results are to be obtained. If they are not, the microprocessor may take the degrees from one sample and the minutes and seconds from the next, resulting in an erroneous input. A sampling error occurring at the transition between 120°, 59', 59" and 121°, 0', 0" could result in an input of 120°, 0', 0". This constitutes an error of 59', 59", approximately 70 miles at the equator.

There are two possible solutions to this problem. The microcomputer could sample a status line indicating that the navigational data will be stable for a known period of time and proceed to sample data during the safe window, or external registers could be used to simultaneously capture all three bytes of data. In either case additional hardware would be required, turning the microprocessor into just another part in a component system.

Microprocessor manufacturers have realized the need for simultaneous event processing and have built interface chips to aid microprocessors in performing simultaneous tasks.

Data Processing Ability

Microprocessors are appearing in more and more small-business and scientific computers. How do microprocessors stack up against highly developed MSI- and SSI-based CPUs?

In regards to computer architecture or processing power, microprocessors are nothing new; in fact, in most cases their computer architecture is crude. There's not much being done on microcomputers which hasn't or couldn't have been done 20 years ago on larger minicomputers or mainframes; however, it now costs three orders of magnitude less to do it. Add to this the fact that a microcomputer of similar complexity is extraordinarily reliable. The cost-and-service element has therefore disappeared, allowing computers to find their way into tasks where they were not economically feasible before.

There are three primary factors hindering even wider business and scientific microcomputing use: the high cost of software development, inherently low processor speed, and the continuing high cost of peripherals.

As with any computer system, microcomputers need a software support base for data processing, business, or scientific applications. Editors, assemblers, high-order languages, and application packages take time and money to develop; and unlike microprocessor prices, software costs are constantly rising. What makes matters worse is that new microprocessors are being introduced constantly. Only a few "start-from-scratch" microprocessors currently have large software support bases (notably the 8080 and 6800 series). One approach taken by manufacturers to alleviate the software support problem is to simply not "start from scratch," but rather pattern a microprocessor around a current minicomputer's instruction set, making that microcomputer totally software compatible with an existing machine. Digital Equipment Corporation's LSI-11, Data General's *Micro Nova* and Texas Instrument's 9900 are notable examples of this approach. It's quite ironic that much of the software for these microcomputers was written in the 1960s, before microprocessors were even invented, dispelling the "software follows hardware" myth to some extent.

The software support base problem has actually hindered the introduction of more efficient and architecturally more advanced microprocessors. Software upward compatibility has become a matter of prime importance when introducing new processors. The Intel 8086 and Motorola 68000 are being called the "new generation of microprocessors," yet many of the old inefficient instructions and architectural traits are still present.

The computer world seems to have a never-ending hunger for more computing power. Mainframes and minicomputers have been increasing in performance, and programming languages as well as programs themselves have come to rely on brute-force processing power and large quantities of memory to mask program complexity and inefficiency.

When comparing minicomputers and mainframes to microcomputers on a processing-speed basis, micros will be seen to be about 20 years behind. Advanced technology is beginning to close this gap, however. Memory in microcomputer systems is also very limited when compared to large machines. Because of these factors, computer programmers have to take a large leap backward in their programming methods when confronted with a micro system. For most microcomputers, hand-optimized assembly language is still being used extensively (and expensively).

Microcomputer system software is rapidly coming of age. High-order languages which compile very time- and memory-efficient codes such as Intel's PL/M and Zilog's PL/Z are gaining wide acceptance in the field. But interface and peripheral costs tend to detract from a microcomputer's desirability in business and scientific applications. Although a microcomputer-based central processing unit is a relatively inexpensive investment, the peripherals it drives are quite costly. A typical small-business processing system, for example, requires a CPU ($1500 for a micro—three times that for mini); but it may also require:

- Console terminal—$1500
- Printer—$4000
- Two disks (floppy)—$2000
- Appropriate mounting hardware—$1000
- System and business software—$4000

A microcomputer CPU only costs a third of what a minicomputer would cost. It is also much less powerful; but if the less expensive machine can handle the task, the savings initially seem worthwhile. Once all the peripherals have been taken into account, however, the microcomputer-based system doesn't appear altogether advantageous. A minicomputer can give double or triple the performance of the microcomputer and only costs about 15% more on the system level. The peripheral cost remains the same whether you opt for a mini or a micro.

This situation can be changed by the introduction of inexpensive peripherals. Reducing peripheral costs, however, is not an easy task because of the expense of the mechanical components. Printers and disks are two examples of highly mechanical peripherals. Fortunately, microprocessors can replace much of this mechanical hardware. Volume production will also bring mechanical costs down.

New Product Applicability

The small size and low power requirements of microprocessors are creating a few new forms of information processing systems. The long-dreamed-of desktop computers are now available at very low cost. The whole personal computing concept is based around these small computers.

Intelligent peripherals which are in most respects small, dedicated information processing systems are coming into common use. Intelligent peripherals usually contain a microprocessor to handle data formatting and communication from the computer system to the peripheral device. Internal functions such as offline editing and formatting in intelligent terminal are also performed.

Advanced microcomputer games are also small information processing systems made economically possible by the microprocessor.

All of the advantages and disadvantages of microcomputer-based information and control systems just described are not only due to the microprocessor chip itself; all the circuitry surrounding the processor, driving the peripherals, sensing the inputs, and channeling the outputs play a part in making a microcomputer a usable system.

INTERFACES

Interfacing is defined as the mating of one component in a system to another to form a totally operational unit. Since a microprocessor standing alone is essentially useless, extensive interfacing is required to build a usable product. In this section we examine some of the typical interfaces found in a microcomputer system.

Microcomputer systems vary in size and configuration. With the new one-chip microcomputers it is possible to build a complete system from just one LSI

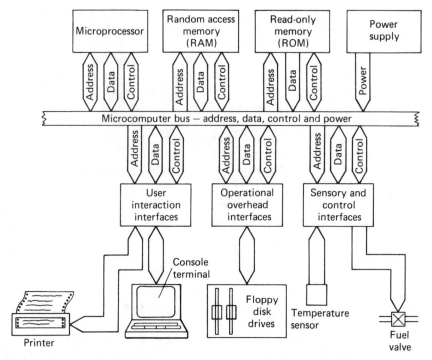

Figure 1-1   A typical microcomputer system and its interfaces.

chip and a few discrete parts, but the most common microcomputer systems consist of considerably more. A microprocessor chip, memory chips, and a few I/O interfaces are usually included. Figure 1-1 illustrates a typical microcomputer system. The microprocessor executes programs out of read-only and random-access memories (ROMs and RAMs) and takes user commands and sensory inputs through the three interfaces.

The interfaces have been broken into four basic categories: operational overhead, user-interaction, sensory, and control.

Operational Overhead Interfaces

Operational overhead interfaces are those interface components necessary to make a processor function on the most basic level. This class includes data and address bus drivers, bus receivers, and the clock circuit surrounding the microprocessor. Larger interface items such as those for memory and data storage devices would also fall into this category.

Figure 1-2 further defines the contents of the microprocessor block of Fig. 1-1. A clock circuit, bus drivers, and bus receivers have been used to connect the microprocessor to the system bus. Bus drivers are amplifiers used to increase the driving power of a microprocessor's data and control lines. The very

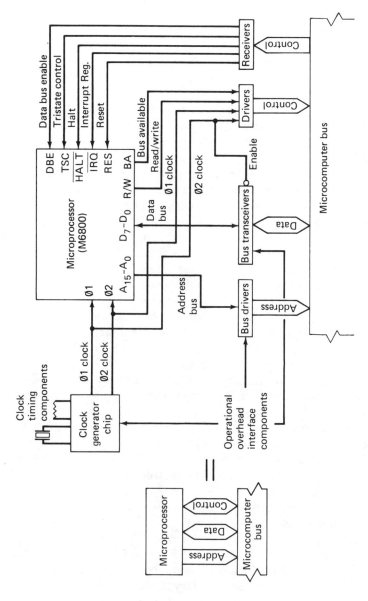

Figure 1-2 A typical microcomputer system's microprocessor interfaces.

9

common MOS microprocessors available today are capable of supplying only a few milliamperes of drive current on each of their many output lines (8 data lines, 16 address lines, and 8 control lines on the 6800). The thermal dissipation from all of these drivers would be too high if more powerful onboard drivers were built into the chip. The internal driving capability of some microprocessors, however, is adequate to drive a small number of interface and memory ICs directly without using external bus drivers. Complete little systems and controllers can thus be built with few parts. This ability is one of the Motorola 6800's big selling points. Even with the 6800, though, bus drivers are needed for large systems that use a high amount of memory or interfaces; and nearly every 6800-based data-processing microcomputer system uses them just to be on the safe side.

Bus receivers perform three functions: bus load reducing, bus filtering, and impedance matching. Data, address, and control buses are relatively long and are subject to noticeable transmission-line effects (signal attenuation, noise pickup, waveform alteration, and so on). Interfaces on the buses act as stubs and reflection points and can cause ringing and noise generation due to termination impedance mismatch. In mainframe systems the "backplane ringing" can become so bad that active terminators and even ferrite beads must be placed on the indiviudal bus lines to filter the noise. Bus receivers usually use hysteresis to increase their noise immunity.

With the exception of the one-chip microcomputers that have built-in RAM and ROM, microprocessors require external memory and associated interface components. Figures 1-3 and 1-4 expand on the ROM and RAM blocks in Figure 1-1. Bus receivers are used on the memory address lines to reduce microcomputer bus loading. Bus drivers are used on the memory ICs because, like the microprocessor, memory elements cannot be used to drive too many loads.

At this point I must digress for one moment to discuss form. The lowercase letter k is the symbol for kilo in the International System of Units (SI)—and kilo means *thousand*. In microcomputer usage k more commonly stands for 1024; the value 2 raised to the 10th power. In this text, a capital letter K with no space is used to represent this value.

Memory modules, especially those built with many small RAMs, have large numbers of memory ICs with their address lines wired in parallel. A 16K × 8-bit RAM module would put 128 (16 × 8) loads on each address line if 1K × 1-bit RAMs were used. An equivalent RAM module built with 16K × 1-bit RAMs would only put eight loads on the processor address, data, and control lines. As this example shows, larger-memory ICs help reduce interface circuitry by reducing the amount of bus loads. Wide-word-width memory ICs such as Motorola's 6810 (128 × 8-bit organization) can reduce or eliminate the need for memory interface circuits in very small systems in which small amounts of memory are required. This IC features a full 128 bytes of data yet presents only one load to each address and data line.

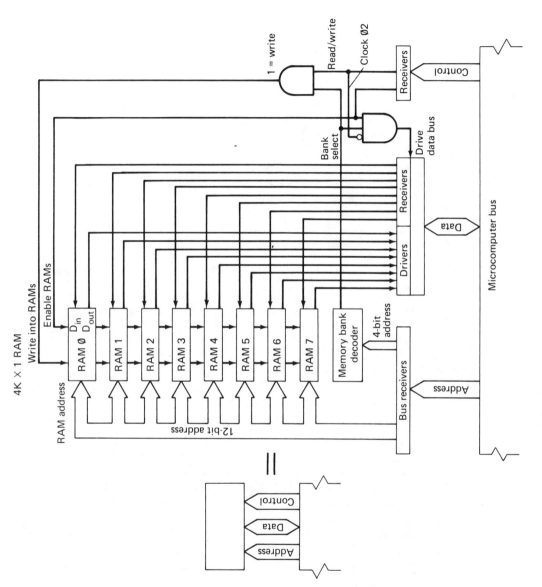

Figure 1-3 A typical microcomputer's RAM interfaces.

11

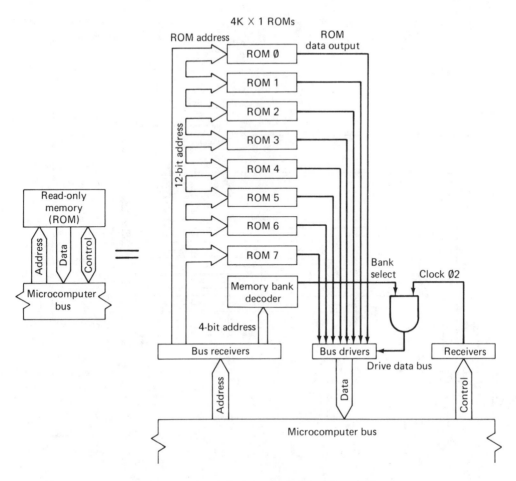

Figure 1-4 A typical microcomputer's ROM interfaces.

Memory control lines usually require interface circuitry also. Static RAMs require just a read–write line and possibly a chip select line driver. Dynamic RAMs require much more. Chip enable, row select, column select, and write enable are often present, and the timings on these signals are not always straightforward. In many cases, high-voltage MOS drivers are required to drive the chip enable lines. Modern dynamic RAMs demand less critical timing and voltage levels than earlier designs.

Read-only memory interfacing is very much like RAM interfacing. Receivers on the address lines and drivers on the data lines are used. No receivers on the data lines are necessary, however, since by definition no data is ever written into a ROM.

Field programmable ROMs, such as the ultraviolet-erasable programmable ROMs (EPROMS) and electrically erasable ROMs, sometimes require write interface circuitry if in-circuit programming is required. Since PROMs require unusual programming voltage levels to insure that normal signals don't modify the PROM's contents, interfacing circuits become more complex. Again, high-voltage drivers are required in the PROM interface.

Semiconductor RAMs and ROMs are the most common memories used in microcomputers. In certain applications, however, magnetic core memory is used to store data. Core memory is one of the most difficult storage media to interface.

A core plane consists of thousands of small magnetic donuts strung into a square grid with driving wires. By selectively applying current to the driving wires, magnetic fields can be built up and collapsed. Ones and zeros are defined by the magnetic fields. A very minute sense current is induced in a sense wire (which strings through all the cores) when a field collapses. By monitoring the collapsing fields, ones and zeros can be detected.

There are problems that make it difficult to interface core memory. High currents (several amperes) for short periods (fractions of microseconds) are required to drive the grid lines; thus necessitating the use of special drive transistors. Very small-current sensing is required for the sense wire, so amplifiers must be used. Finally, reading out of core is destructive; that is, the memory contents are destroyed with the collapse of the magnetic fields. If provisions for rewriting are not included in the CPU, special interface circuitry must be provided to rewrite the data back into memory.

When interfacing core memory to a microcomputer system, one very rarely has to deal with the core plane itself. Core is almost exclusively sold in modular form with all the critical interface components (current drivers, sense amplifiers, and write-after-read circuitry) included. These modules can be treated as regular RAMs. Semiconductor RAMs also have a critical array of data storage cells that require special interfacing, but the user never has to interface directly to them because onchip interfaces (again, drivers and sense amplifiers) do the job.

Interfaces that control external mass memory systems, such as magnetic tapes, disks, and floppy disks, can also be grouped under the *operational overhead* category. These devices usually have their own controllers built into them to handle the mechanical sequencing required. Interfacing them to a microprocessor bus is simply a matter of building a serial or parallel data communication interface to send commands and data and retrieve status and data. The specifics of parallel and serial data communications channels and complex controllers are covered in detail later in this text.

User-Interaction Interfaces

User-interaction interfaces are those circuits required to send and receive user-specified data to and from a processing system. This interface class includes computer terminal interfaces, keyboard interfaces, graphic-device interfaces, and voice recognition and synthesis interfaces.

People and computers work with totally different languages; large and complex devices are required to convert from one to another. Basically, two things must be converted: representation and presentation speed. The *representation* conversion task has traditionally been assigned to the computer peripheral, while *presentation speed* conversion has been assigned to the CPU. The standard teletypewriter or computer terminal is a good example of this. The user enters data through the keyboard (a mechanical-to-electrical interface). The data is converted to the American Standard Code for Information Interchange (ASCII) and is sent to the CPU in the computer's form of representation: a string of ones and zeros. The processor and its associated interfaces use either interrupts or *software wait* loops to synchronize the processing with the user's data entry rate, thus performing the presentation speed conversion.

Communication in the other direction is similar. The processor sends characters to the printer at the fastest rate the unit can handle, using software wait loops or interrupts. The ASCII is converted back into mechanical motion, and the data is printed at the terminal.

Since people can only accept data at a very slow rate with relation to the computer's processing speed, serial interfaces are commonly used to drive peripherals. Breaking the multibit ASCII down and sending it to the processor a bit at a time cuts the communication line size down to three basic signals: serial transmit data, serial receive data, and a common ground. The EIA RS-232C interface standard is the most commonly used serial standard and is specified to operate at up to 20,000 serial bits per second.

Many high-speed peripherals require a faster flow of data than a slow speed serial interface will allow. When faster transfer rates are required, designers usually resort to high-speed parallel interfaces. One example in which a parallel interface would be useful is the case of the high-speed line printer. This device is nonreal-time from the user's standpoint because the user does not react with the device while it is in operation. The computer listing is printed at a high rate and the user looks at it later. A parallel interface is used to supply the line printer with data at a rate which would exceed the RS-232C standard's limit.

Because many lines must go to a peripheral when a parallel interface is being used, the complete controller is not always built into the peripheral. An interface card which plugs into the CPU often contains much of the control circuitry for the peripheral. When parallel data transfers are used, the data going across the parallel lines does not have to be in the ASCII format, so the designer usually decides which lines he is going to use for communication with the peripheral. Although this approach to parallel interfaces improves efficiency and package size in some cases, it has one major drawback: nonstandardization. There are a few parallel interface standards such as the NTDS military standard, but no parallel standard has gained as wide an acceptance as the RS-232C serial standard. The result, of course, is a unique interface card for every processor with which the peripheral will be interfaced.

Graphic devices, such as raster-scan display terminals, will frequently be interfaced to a system that uses a parallel interface. People seem capable of grasping large amounts of graphic information very quickly, therefore high data transfer rates to the display device are necessary. Again, custom parallel interfaces are the most common type. Some microcomputer graphic display units are simple enough so the whole display unit's circuitry, as well as the interface components, can fit on one plug-in module. The result is a single video output line that goes from the display unit module in the computer to the video monitor on which the generated images are displayed.

Figure 1-5 illustrates a simple serial RS-232C interface to an interactive terminal (an interactive terminal is one usable by the operator for computer intercommunication). Drivers and receivers are used to buffer the microcomputer bus. An *asynchronous communication interface adapter* (ACIA) converts the microcomputer's parallel bus data into a serial format, and RS-232C drivers and receivers are used to generate the proper voltage levels. The rate at which data is sent to and from the terminal is determined by the rate at which serial data is shifted out of the ACIA. The baud-rate generator produces a clock waveform to precisely control the serial shift rate. Typical serial data transfer rates for serial communications range from 110 to 19,200 bits per second.

Some of the other user-interactive peripherals are joysticks, light pens, keypads, and LED indicators (these are covered in detail in later chapters).

Sensory Interfaces

When dealing with strict scientific computing or business data processing, a central processing unit, operational overhead interfaces (including memory and disk interfaces), and a few user-interaction interfaces for computer terminals and line printers are usually sufficient to accomplish the task. Control systems are a different matter, however. Events in the real world must be monitored.

Sensory interfaces are those circuits required to monitor events in the real world and send the results to a microprocessor system. Pressure sensor, thermal sensor, flow-rate indicator, and tachometer interfaces are but a few of the interfaces that fall into this class.

The real world is an analog world. Temperature, pressure, and speed can assume an infinite range of values. The devices used to sense parameters like these are usually based on the electrical or mechanical response characteristics of a certain material to the given parameter. A thermistor, for example, ideally changes its resistance in a linear manner with a change in temperature. For a microcomputer to manipulate thermistor-sensed temperature information, an interface that converts resistance to a byte or two of data in the microprocessor is needed. The interface can be considered as two functional pieces: the resistance-to-digital-value converter and the digital-value-to-microprocessor-bus interface.

The process of changing the variable resistance to a variable digital value begins by using the thermistor's variable resistance characteristics to make a variable-voltage source. A simple two-resistor voltage-divider network, with

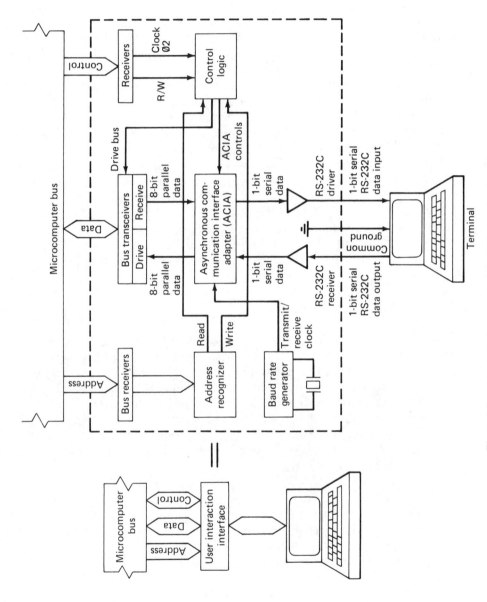

Figure 1-5 A typical microcomputer user-interaction interface.

16

one of the resistors being the thermistor, serves this purpose. The resulting temperature-dependent voltage can then be sent to an analog-to-digital (A/D) converter. This device takes the variable-voltage signal applied to the analog input and generates a word of data which represents this voltage. A/D converters are relatively complex pieces of hardware that have gained wide acceptance in the interfacing field due to their ability to match the analog world to the digital world.

The word generated by the A/D converter must then be sent to the microcomputer system. If the temperature sensor interface is far away from the processor and extremely rapid samplings are not required, converting the data word to a serial signal is desirable. The serial signal can then be sent to the microcomputer, converted back to a parallel data word, and put onto the microcomputer bus when the microprocessor requests it.

It may be possible to save parts by mounting the entire temperature-sensing interface including the A/D converter on one module at the microcomputer, thus avoiding long parallel lines or serial-to-parallel conversion. If the thermistor is at a distant location, however, a long analog signal line would be required. Analog lines are very susceptible to noise, especially when carrying very low-level signals, making this arrangement undesirable. In general, when analog sensors are being used, you should convert analog signals into digital signals as soon as possible and keep all analog lines well shielded to reduce noise levels.

Figure 1-6 shows the thermistor interface to a 6800-based typical microcomputer system. Other interfaces are simpler than the A/D converter just described. A mechanism that counts items as they pass on an assembly line and a sensor that detects an intruder by the breaking of a light beam are two cases in point. No analog-to-digital conversion is necessary as a simple one-bit sense signal presents adequate information.

In the case of the photoelectric assembly-line counter, the counting pulses may possess some noise due to the photoelectric circuit's response characteristics and uneven breaking of the beam. A filtering circuit may therefore be needed to prevent false counts. It may also be necessary to translate the circuit's voltage level to a level compatible with the microcomputer's logic family. A simple resistor dividing network or a resistor and voltage-limiting zener diode can be used if the photoelectric circuit puts out more voltage than necessary. If greater voltage levels are required, an amplifier circuit consisting of a few transistors or an operational amplifier is necessary. Once the pulse has been translated to the proper voltage level, a driver can send the pulse to the microcomputer where it can be sampled along with other single-bit signals.

Single-bit status lines can conveniently be sampled using one bit of a parallel-input-port interface. A software loop can repetitively sample (poll) the port and take appropriate action on the bit's status.

Sensory interfaces are often used in industrial control, computerized security systems, instrumentation, automotive electronics, and other fields. In these

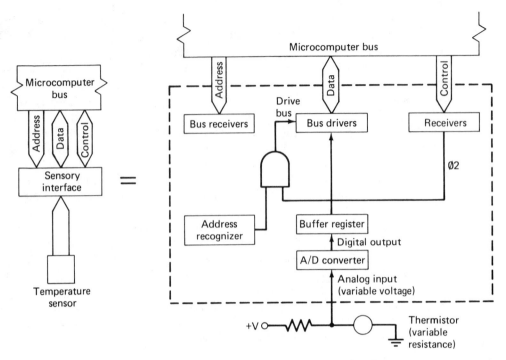

Figure 1-6   A typical microcomputer's sensory interface.

environments a microcomputer controller may be required to sense the status of many machines, each of which may be running on a different electrical circuit.

Vastly different voltage levels may be present on different machines, so the need for electrical isolation between sensors arises. The most common method of electrically isolating interfaces is to send the data from each machine through an optoisolator. This device consists of a light-emitting diode (LED) illuminating a phototransistor. Modulating the LED causes corresponding changes in the phototransistor, but because the only medium physically connecting them is the light beam, thousands of volts of electrical isolation is provided. Optoisolators increase interface complexity, however. Low-current output sensors require additional amplifiers to drive the LED, and amplifiers are sometimes required on the phototransistor side as well.

Control Interfaces

Once the sensor provides the status and the microcomputer decides what action is to be taken, a control interface is usually needed to carry out the action. Control interfaces take a microcomputer's milliampere-level data signals and convert them to the proper voltage and current levels to control real-world devices. The circuitry needed to drive a stepping motor on a machine tool, to activate a solenoid-controlled valve, or to illuminate a bank of stoplights falls into this interface category.

Microelectronics has made great progress in reducing the amount of current needed to perform logical functions. Internal currents in microprocessors are continually dropping as smaller, more advanced device technologies become available. These advances produce lower power, faster, and denser devices but take microcomputers further away from real-world signal levels. For example, a 1 μA (one microampere) signal within a microprocessor may have to be amplified by a factor of one hundred million to activate a large industrial motor. For this reason, control interfaces use a large variety of parts. Low-power parts like bus receivers and small transistors are used to take data from the microcomputer bus and perform preliminary formatting and amplification. Large transistors and solid-state relays (triacs, diacs, SCRs, and the like) are used to perform larger-current switching functions.

When a variable-voltage analog signal is required in a control system, digital-to-analog (D/A) converters are used. These devices mix and add current, depending on the value of the word specified at the digital input. The resulting analog voltage at the analog output is directly proportional to the value of the data word.

PRACTICAL MICROCOMPUTER APPLICATIONS

The following four examples of microprocessors in real-world systems are designed to give you more than a theoretical view of how microprocessors and their interfaces are used. The examples illustrate the applicability of the four interface classes and describe some of the problems encountered in accomplishing the interfacing task. Many new interface ideas and terms will be mentioned. These topics are treated at a greater depth in following chapters.

The Personal Computer System

One of the first things that comes to mind when microcomputers are mentioned is the personal or small-business computer system. Personal computers are small computers built around popular microprocessors (usually having a wide software support base) that sell for a relatively low price. These small systems usually include a CPU, 4K to 64K of memory, a console terminal, and a magnetic storage device such as a floppy disk. The central processing unit, console terminal, and magnetic data storage units sometimes come in separate enclosures, but the trend is toward integrated units with built-in keyboards, display generators, and floppy disks.

From an interface standpoint, personal computers are relatively simple devices. A few user-interaction interfaces control the keyboard, display generator, printer, and other interactive peripherals. Operational overhead interfaces usually include bus drivers and receivers on the CPU card, memory interfaces, and interfaces for the magnetic storage devices. The microprocessor's address, data, and control lines are fully buffered because personal computers are designed to be expandable, and each additional module adds extra loads to the microcomputer bus.

A personal computer's user-interaction interfaces are usually quite simple because data communication standards are often followed in the peripherals associated with the system. RS-232C serial interfaces or 20 mA current-loop interfaces with 110 to 9600 bit per second (bps) data transfer rates are used on most terminals.

A personal computer's memory is usually broken into memory blocks of 4K to 16K (4096 to 16384) bytes per block. Some blocks contain ROM for permanent storage of important programs and the system monitor program, and some blocks contain RAM for data and program read–write storage. Each memory block must have an address recognizer to determine if it is being addressed. Each memory module that plugs into the microcomputer bus must have bus receivers for the address lines, bus drivers and receivers for the data lines, and control components for the read–write and refresh logic.

The interfaces to nonstandard system peripherals are usually the most complicated interfaces within the personal computer system. A highspeed line printer and floppy disk controller are two cases in point. A floppy disk controller controls the transfer of data from a microprocessor to a slowly rotating flexible magnetic disk. The interface is actually a combination of an operational overhead, sensory, and control interface. Commands and data must be taken from the microcomputer bus. Sensors must determine the orientation of the spinning disk and the position of the disk head. The interface must then position the head to the proper disk track using a stepping motor or voice-coil movement and provide proper write current through the head to write onto the disk (or amplification to read from it).

Additional features such as "disk power-down" (automatic disk motor shut-down when data is not being accessed) also must be built into disk controllers. Due to this complexity, disk controllers typically approach 50% of the cost of a disk drive–interface system; they may cost even more than the central processing unit module in many personal computers. This situation is rapidly changing. LSI is currently doing to disk controllers what microprocessors did to computers. A few manufacturers already supply single-chip floppy disk controllers.

Figure 1-7 illustrates one of the first personal computer systems to gain wide popularity—the Southwest Technical Products 6800 system. This system is built around the 6800 microprocessor and follows Motorola's suggested designs very closely. A microcomputer bus features expandability of up to five memory cards or large peripherals. A smaller subset of the microcomputer bus can support up to eight interface cards in addition to the five full-size cards (Figure 1-8 depicts the bus structure and Fig. 1-9 shows the processor card and a small interface card).

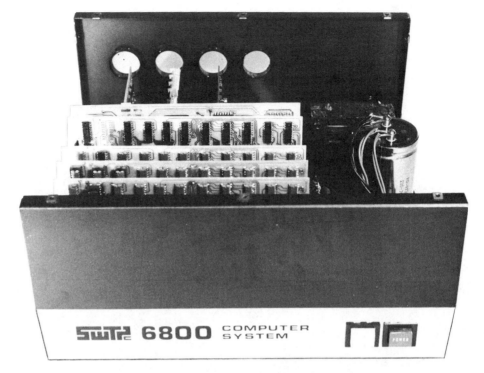

Figure 1-7   Southwest Technical Products' 6800-based personal computer system.

Figure 1-10 shows one of the most popular integrated personal computer systems—the *Apple II*. This system contains a complete processor, memory, and cassette interface all on one board. Eight small peripheral sockets are provided for device expansion. This personal computer is built around the 6502 microprocessor.

Intelligent Computer Terminals

Microprocessors are placing computing power in peripherals that previously needed complete *host computer* support. The "intelligent computer terminal" is a good example of this. Traditional "dumb" terminals accept serial data on an RS-232C or 20 mA current-loop line and put the appropriate characters on the display screen (assuming it is a video terminal). There may be a few crude cursor control commands such as cursor up, line feed, and carriage return. The terminal's keyboard sends characters to the host computer over a standard interface as they are typed by the user. Basically, this sort of terminal is the video equivalent of a standard teletypewriter terminal, or as personal computing hobbyists say, "a TV typewriter." File editing and simple calculations must always be done by the host computer using this kind of terminal.

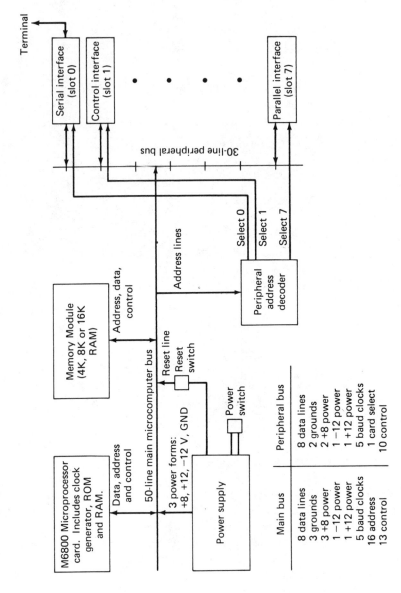

Figure 1-8 Southwest Technical Products' 6800 microcomputer bus structure.

Terminal

Serial interface (slot 0)

Control interface (slot 1)

Parallel interface (slot 7)

30-line peripheral bus

Select 0
Select 1
Select 7

Peripheral address decoder

Address lines

Memory Module (4K, 8K or 16K RAM)

Address, data, control

Reset line

Reset switch

Power switch

3 power forms: +8, +12, −12 V, GND

50-line main microcomputer bus

M6800 Microprocessor card. Includes clock generator, ROM and RAM.

Data, address and control

Power supply

Main bus	Peripheral bus
8 data lines	8 data lines
3 grounds	2 grounds
3 +8 power	2 +8 power
1 −12 power	1 −12 power
1 +12 power	1 +12 power
5 baud clocks	5 baud clocks
16 address	1 card select
13 control	10 control

22

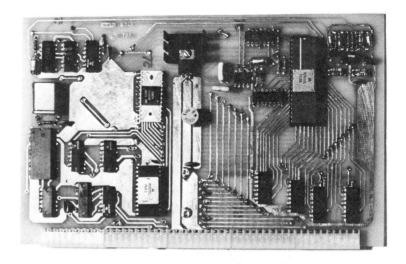

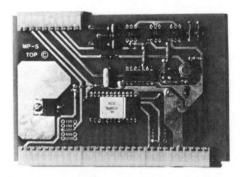

Figure 1-9   Southwest Technical Products' 6800 system processor and interface card.

By adding some intelligence (a small microcomputer, say) to the terminal, simple tasks like offline editing and text formatting can be performed. In addition, the terminal becomes user-configurable. User-defined data communication formats can be programmed, and certain special characters sent by the host computer can initiate very powerful processes within the terminal.

A graphic terminal's capabilities can be greatly enhanced using a built-in microcomputer. Complex graphic functions like zoom, line drawing, and shading can be performed totally by the terminal. An intelligent graphics terminal can perform tasks that, until recently, required a dedicated minicomputer with a video display terminal.

The Ramtek 6000 is an intelligent graphic terminal built around a Zilog Z80 8-bit microprocessor. It generates alphanumerics as well as graphics such as vectors, conics, and color shading. Alphanumeric, special function, and cursor

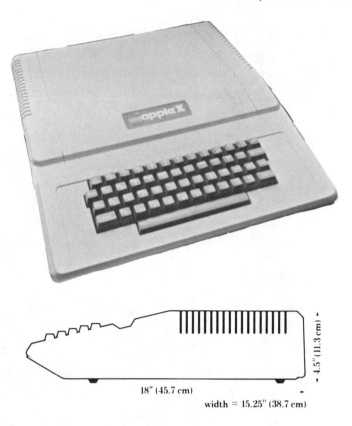

Figure 1-10   The Apple II personal computer system. (Courtesy Apple
Computer, Inc., Cupertino, Ca.)

control keyboards are provided. The graphics unit is a 256×512-bit dot matrix
raster-scan unit, with each dot corresponding to a bit in the built-in display
memory. Three 256×512 memory planes provide a 3-bit code for each screen
bit, allowing eight levels of shading or eight colors. Figure 1-11 shows the
Ramtek 6000.

Examination of the internal processor structure reveals that extensive interfacing is used to give this terminal its many capabilities. A Z80 microprocessor is interfaced to a common bus. From 4K to 16K bytes of RAM are used for
program storage and 16K to 28K of PROM hold the commonly used graphic
generation routines (vector, conic, plot, bar chart, and so on).

Data communication emulation programs are also stored in PROM. When
the system is turned on, it must be bootstrap-loaded; that is, an initial user-
interaction and terminal communication program must be executed, just as

Figure 1-11   One of Ramtek's 6000-series intelligent graphics terminals.
(Courtesy Ramtek Corporation.)

with a full-scale computer. The Ramtek 6000 executes a teletypewriter emulation program stored in PROM upon power-up, causing the terminal to act as a normal communications terminal until other instructions are given.

Three graphic memory planes are also interfaced to the microcomputer bus. Graphic memory planes are large banks of memory (256 × 512 bits in this case) that are continuously being read onto the terminal's display screen. Bits that are in the logic 1 state represent white dots on the display screen while bits in the logic 0 state represent black dots. By using three planes, bits on one plane can represent blue data, bits on another green data, and bits on the third plane red data. Complete color capability is the final result. Since the display memory must be continually read onto the screen, the microcomputer must insert data into the planes between rapidly occurring refresh read cycles. This is called memory access interleaving. Adding this capability to a memory takes a lot of extra interface components. To relieve the microprocessor of the burden of critical timing, the memory interface on the R6000 makes the two-port nature of the graphic memory planes transparent to the microcomputer system.

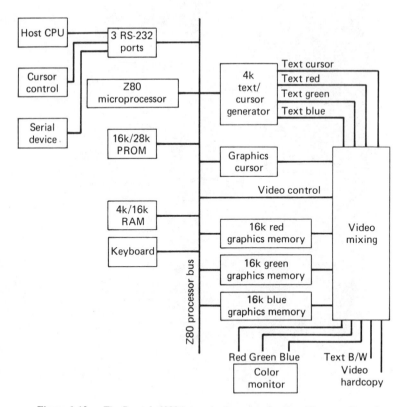

Figure 1-12   The Ramtek 6000 internal microcomputer bus. (Courtesy Ramtek Corporation.)

A separate display generator and video mixer are used in the R6000. Sending video data to a display screen at 6 megabits per second is simply too much of a job for a Z80 to handle; but it is simple enough for separate circuitry to perform. The display generator, however, must be interfaced to the microcomputer data bus to be properly controlled. The R6000 has a 4K data area in memory set aside as a text–cursor generator interface area. Simply writing into memory at these locations controls the display generator. Figure 1-12 shows the Ramtek 6000 bus structure.

Finally, communications interfaces are necessary to provide terminal communication to the outside world. The R6000 has three RS-232C I/O ports to perform this function. One port is used for terminal-to-host-computer communication and is selectable for 50 to 9600 baud (bits per second in this case) communication rates. Two additional ports allow for an optional cursor control device, such as a joystick, and an auxiliary serial device, such as a printer or graphic hard-copy unit.

Another interesting intelligent graphic terminal is Hewlett-Packard's 2648A shown in Fig. 1-13. This terminal features a 720×360-dot raster-scan bit map

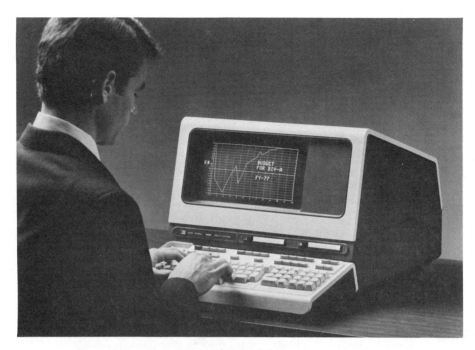

Figure 1-13   Hewlett-Packard's 2648A intelligent graphics terminal. (Courtesy Hewlett-Packard, Palo Alto, Ca.)

and HP's own microprocessor. The terminal has no color capabilities but its black-and-white capabilities are astounding. Extensive software provided with the terminal deserves most of the credit. Automatic plotting, rubberband line, patterned shading, text writing in any direction (including upside-down), and offline editing are just a few of its features. Additional hardware is interfaced to the microcomputer to perform computationally difficult tasks such as zoom and pan.

The Automotive Computer

Microcomputers have great potential in the field of automotive electronics. An automobile has so many functions to monitor and control that experts in the microprocessor marketing field feel that most new cars by the mid-1980s will have no less than three microprocessors, thus creating a market for some 100 million microprocessors per year. Not only will microcomputers be sold, however: sensors, controls, and interface parts will be in demand in even greater numbers.

The first application of automotive microcomputers will be in the engine control and pollution control areas. Automotive manufacturers already have experience in the areas of electronic carburetors, fuel injection, ignitions, and transmission systems, mostly due to development efforts aimed at pollution control. In many cases the sensors and controls are already there and the microprocessor and its interfaces are merely add-ons.

Automotive microprocessors are currently controlling carburetor and fuel injection systems, ignition systems (spark advance), and pollution systems (exhaust gas recirculation) on a trial basis. (The big three auto makers are currently using Motorola, Toshiba, Texas Instruments, RCA, and Intel microprocessors and interface components.)

The 1980s and '90s will see even greater acceptance of the microcomputer in automobiles, and the applications will not be limited to engine control. Everything from fuel economy measurements to navigation may be incorporated.

An interesting example of a futuristic microcomputer-based automotive system is the optional dashboard on the Cadillac *Seville:* the Trip Computer. This unit may not be representative of the common dashboard of the future, yet it presents possibilities for automotive applications of microprocessors: Cadillac's primary reason for introducing it is to gain engineering experience, as future microcomputer decisions can be made on the sales and service record of the Trip Computer.

The Trip Computer consists of five circuit modules: processor, sensory and control interface, power supply, speedometer, and digital clock. The unit replaces the conventional speedometer, fuel gages, and clock with two 2-digit displays, one 4-digit display, and a 12-button keypad. The displays are 100-volt gas-discharge displays whose brilliant orange is bright enough to overcome ambient light levels and avoid the obvious pitfalls of having red lights on the dashboard.

Not only does the microcomputer measure speed, time of day, fuel flow, and fuel levels; it also computes miles per gallon (average and instantaneous), driving range on remaining fuel, estimated arrival time, and engine speed and temperature.

The driver controls the Trip Computer by entering appropriate commands on the dashboard-mounted keypad.

All of the stated measurements and calculations are quite trivial for the Motorola M6800 microprocessor, once the data has reached the microcomputer. But many interfaces must be crossed first.

The speedometer and engine tachometer drives have rotation sensors, while the gas tank has a fuel-level sensor. The engine has a temperature sensor, and fuel flow is accurately measured by counting the modulated fuel injector's pulses. The microcomputer contains two standard one-chip interface ICs and a custom I/O and clock chip. Onchip high-voltage drivers are used to illuminate the gas-discharge display.

There are still a few problems to be overcome in automotive microelectronics. Dealer maintenance and production volume have to be considered. Reliability is another big problem. The automotive world is an extremely severe environment; shock and thermal resistance of parts must be high, and military-like specified parts are required. Microcomputers will find their way into more critical automotive areas, but only after the problems encountered in first-generation hardware are solved. Figure 1-14 illustrates the functions of a future automotive microcomputer system.

Machine Tool Control

Personal computers, the latest graphic terminals, and computerized games are widely talked about topics in the microcomputer field, but not much is said about the ways in which microprocessors are revolutionizing industry. In regard to interfaces, the industrial microelectronics field presents some of the biggest challenges—especially in the way of sensory and control interfaces. As the final example of microprocessor applications, let's look at a micro-computer-controlled machine tool and its interfaces.

Microcomputers are currently being used in heavy machine tools to perform control and sensory functions. The cost advantages offered by the microprocessor allow extra precision and additional features to be added. A metal forming press brake equipped with an M6800 microprocessor-based monitor and control system is one of this new breed of machinery.

The machine operates as follows: A piece of sheet metal is inserted horizontally into the machine and positioned accurately with a gage that determines the exact position. A hydraulic press then forces the sheet into a die, where it is bent into the desired sheet-metal part.

This is a fairly unsophisticated machine operation. Two events must be monitored and controlled: the positioning of the sheet metal and the movement of the hydraulic press. The positioning of the sheet metal is monitored using odometers. A rotary encoder is used to sense the hydraulic press movement. Odometers and rotary encoders are electromechanical sensors that produce bidirectional square waves indicating movement. Sensory interfaces must convert the encoded pulses into a digital word the microprocessor system can use. Pulse-encoder logic and a parallel-bus interface handle the task nicely. Figure 1-15 illustrates the microprocessor controller for this machine.

Once the microcomputer has the metal and press position information, it computes the remaining distance to move the metal, the press velocity, and acceleration. Because the microprocessor runs at a 1 MHz clock rate, the computations can be done in real-time while the machine is in operation. Using the sensed and computed values, the microprocessor decides how much farther to move the metal and press and proceeds to control the metal-moving motors and hydraulic press. Control interfaces are required in this case. A motor switching circuit, a D/A converter, and an electrically controlled hydraulic valve are used.

The user-interaction interface consists of a keyboard and 40-character alphanumeric display on which piece-part information can be entered. Program parameters include metal positioning information, press speed, and stop data.

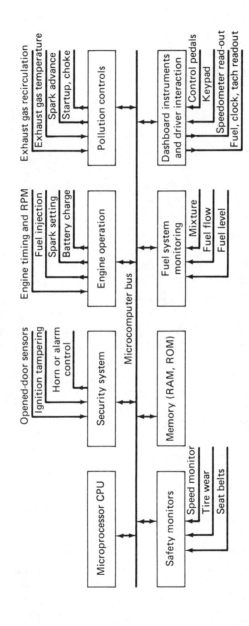

Figure 1-14 Possible functions of a future automotive microcomputer system.

30

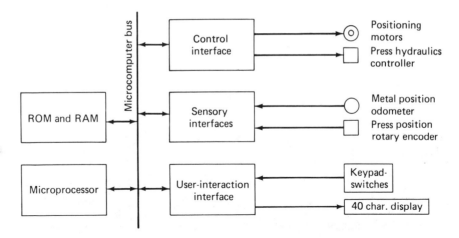

Figure 1-15   A microprocessor-based machine tool controller.

A keyboard interface for data entry and a display interface to drive the 40-character display are used.

The microcomputer and its associated interfaces have proved to be a good economic tradeoff on this machine. More accurate control (eight times the accuracy of a manually controlled machine) increases the machine's production efficiency and salability, while the elimination of manual controls and gages cuts costs.

2 Selecting the Right Microprocessor

Microcomputers come in many shapes and sizes. On the low end are the bare-bones microprocessors that can't function as microcomputers without extensive support circuitry. At the other end, complete microcomputer systems with built-in memory, keyboards, floppy disks, and other peripherals are available. In between are the one-card microcomputers with moderate memory and interface cirucitry all on one printed circuit card, multicard system construction sets, and one-chip microcomputers that require nearly no support circuitry at all. A successful microcomputer-based design requires the selection of the right microcomputer for the task.

This chapter covers all of the above-mentioned forms of microcomputers, but some basic concepts must be dealt with first.

HOW THE PROCESSOR AFFECTS THE SYSTEM

Since the microprocessor is the central element in a microcomputer-based system, its characteristics have a great effect on surrounding circuitry and interface design. The complexity and design philosophy of the microprocessor determines how many support devices will be required. A one-chip microcomputer with onboard RAM, ROM, clock, and serial interface, for example, reduces the chip count to a much lower number than that of a similar simple microprocessor with independent support chips.

Certain microcomputers are better suited to certain tasks. In an application where extensive I/O interfacing but very little data processing is required, an I/O oriented microprocessor such as the F8 can reduce the complexity of the interfaces. In an application in which a large amount of computing is performed, a computationally powerful microprocessor like the Zilog Z8000 can eliminate the need for external processing elements such as multipliers and floating-point arithmetic units.

Microprocessor selection affects system power dissipation. A bipolar microprocessor is a high-speed bipolar device, so all of its system overhead interfaces must also be high-speed bipolar devices. A whole system built with bipolar devices (integrated NPN and PNP transistors) will have considerably higher power dissipation than a CMOS system (integrated FETs) built around a CMOS microprocessor. The watchword is speed–power product. As a general rule, the faster and more complex the processor, the more power it draws.

The complexity and size of circuit boards and connectors are also affected by the microprocessor choice. A 4-bit microprocessor requires half the data lines of an 8-bit unit. The IC package is also smaller and has fewer pins. A smaller circuit board with less connectors is thus possible using the smaller processor.

The choice of microprocessor affects system cost. An expensive microprocessor may indeed replace enough external interface components, circuit boards, and I/O pins to reduce the overall cost of a system.

There are many other system factors affected by microprocessor choice, and it is up to you to determine which characteristics are desirable in your system and which microprocessor will best fit the specifications.

WHAT TO STRIVE FOR
IN SYSTEM DESIGN

Anyone building a microcomputer system has certain specifications and specific goals which must be met; but there are certain universal characteristics that are desirable in any system: high reliability, low power dissipation, small size, easy serviceability, and low cost. System decisions should be based on all of these characteristics — not just cost. In many cases, especially industrial and military designs, reliability and serviceability are of paramount importance.

It is also desirable to "design in" expandability. A system always seems to grow or have higher demands placed on it from the time it leaves the drawing board to the time it goes into production. Microcomputers offer an excellent opportunity for expandability. Additional interfaces can be added easily to a microcomputer bus, and the software can be modified if provisions are made for expansion.

EVALUATING SYSTEM REQUIREMENTS

The best starting point in determining the proper microprocessor for a system application is the evaluation of the system requirements. There is no simple step-by-step approach that will work under all circumstances; rather, the requirements must be considered and weighed against each other to arrive at the proper decision.

Consider the Task

You should consider what kind of task you are performing—a computational data processing task or a control task. There are certain microprocessors that are designed to be computer-like and others that are meant to be used as controllers. The microprocessor characteristics section will point these out. The use of a computing-oriented microprocessor in a control application is likely to increase control interface complexity while providing computational overkill. This sort of unbalanced system would definitely work, but it would be more complex, take up more space and power, and be less reliable than a system built around a control-oriented device.

A system's function should be evaluated through an unbiased eye. There are many fine discrete, SSI, MSI, and nonmicroprocessor LSI parts available for general and special-purpose applications. These parts should be considered with the system specifications in mind. Microprocessors are general-purpose devices. A device designed for a specific task can usually perform the task faster and with less power consumption and complexity than a microcomputer. The universal asynchronous receiver/transmitter (UART) is a good example of a very specialized LSI part. This device receives and sends a serial bit stream and performs serial-to-parallel and parallel-to-serial conversion. Used for data transmission, the UART is typically a 40-pin package that draws very little power. A UART's task could easily be handled by a microprocessor with ROM, a small scratchpad RAM, a parallel interface, and a clock circuit. A close examination of this implementation, however, reveals that four times the number of parts and nearly ten times the power is required to perform the same task using the microprocessor. This is hardly a good application for a micro-computer, although it would *seem* to be if you didn't know of the existence of the UART. When evaluating system requirements it is wise to search through available literature for specialized devices to fill your specific applications.

Reliability

Reliability may be another reason to avoid microcomputer implementations of logic in some situations. Microprocessors can be used to cost-effectively replace large discrete gating networks, but in critical applications, adherence to discrete gating may be the wiser choice.

Microcomputers are computers and they can "crash" (get out of the control program). A glitch on the power supply could cause this to happen. It would be nice if we could think of microcomputers as ideal devices, but in the real world we must consider nonideal situations. A combinatorial gating network has no states and is therefore self-recovering after a glitch (as long as the inputs remain the same). A device with states (flip-flops or memory cells) has a high probability of changing states when a glitch comes along, and microprocessors are just full of flip-flops and memory cells.

Performance Requirements

Another factor to evaluate is system performance requirements. The microcomputer must be able to perform the system's task in a given length of time. When choosing a microprocessor, an adequate *processing power* margin for expansion should be allowed. Microprocessor-based systems are somewhat less versatile in performance expandability than corresponding discrete-component implementations. If a microprocessor is being pushed to its computational limits and the need for more computing power arises, there are two alternatives: speed up the software if it isn't already optimized, or switch to a higher-performance microprocessor. A system built with discrete components is much easier to add capability to incrementally.

There are, of course, exotic alternatives to a totally new processor if you should wind up short on computing power. Add-on circuits and multiple processors may be used; but unless these are "clean" additions and not "patchwork fixes," they shouldn't be used. An example of a clean addition is an auxiliary multiplier added to a processor bus to help a microprocessor in a heavily multiply-weighted task. An example of a patchwork fix is speeding up at the processor clock to just beyond the microprocessor's performance limits and hoping for the best.

Microprocessor Loading

Sizings should be performed before a system is built to estimate processing needs. Once a candidate microprocessor is chosen, crude software that is very similar to the real task's software should be written. This initial sizing software doesn't have to be perfect and fully debugged because its purpose is to give a general idea of the processor's loading and not to correctly accomplish the task. You may use the interface software section of this text or appropriate material from other books to aid you in writing the software. After all the sizing programs have been written, the program's execution time can be estimated.

A good processor loading at the preliminary system design is about 50%. In other words, if a function must be executed in 10 ms, a microprocessor *task execution time* of 5 ms is desirable. This leaves an adequate margin for errors in initial task sizings and for some future expansion. If the loading approaches 75% or more, chances are that the microprocessor will be overloaded by the time the design is actually built. A more powerful microprocessor or discrete logic, which can handle some of the tasks, is definitely in order.

If the microprocessor is only 20% loaded, it might pay to consider a smaller, less complex microprocessor that is more reliable and less power-hungry. Or examine the possibility of the microprocessor taking over even more of the system's task, thereby eliminating discrete conponents.

The 50% loading criterion is just a general rule. Specific applications may dictate alternative loadings. A widely expandable general-purpose data processing system, for instance, will require greater expandability and thus lighter loading. For general-purpose data processing systems you may not even know what the system is going to be used for. In this case the processing capabilities can be anything you choose.

Other Considerations

An overall system block diagram helps in the evaluation process. The processor, discrete logic, interfaces, and peripherals can be specified as black boxes in the system block diagram as Fig. 2-1 illustrates.

All the system's physical characteristics should enter into the system evaluation process. Power consumption, thermal dissipation, and second-sourcing should all be considered if they have been specified.

Once the most likely microprocessor candidate has been chosen, preliminary hardware designs, source programs, object programs, and a prototype system can be built.

The proper evaluation of system requirements will be a somewhat difficult iterative process but the result will be a well balanced and cost-effective system.

IMPORTANT MICROPROCESSOR CHARACTERISTICS

Microprocessor choice greatly affects overall system characteristics, so it is important to understand the microprocessor you're working with and to be able to identify the important characteristics during the system evaluation stage.

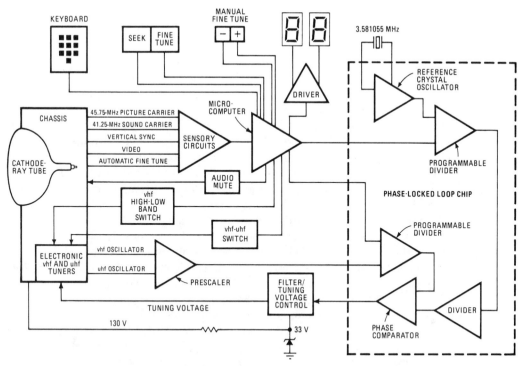

Figure 2-1 A sample block diagram for system evaluation. (Courtesy Signetics Corporation, Sunnyvale, Ca.)

The microcomputer field is currently on the steep end of the learning curve; things are changing so rapidly that any book attempting to give you a good overall picture of the devices in the field is obsolete by the time it reaches the press. This section is therefore designed to aid you in identifying important microprocessor characteristics for yourself. Current manufacturer's specification sheets should be consulted for up-to-date specifics. A few examples of microprocessors are presented and analyzed; these analysis techniques can then be applied to products currently on the market.

Microprocessor Purpose

Microprocessor purpose is a nebulous "parameter" that can't always be addressed in a specification sheet or data catalog; however, it is probably the most important consideration in choosing a microprocessor for a system.

Microprocessors are general-purpose devices that can perform almost any task if given enough external support circuitry and processing time; but they have designed-in features that make them better suited to certain applications. The two major purposes are electronic data processing (EDP) and control. In this context, EDP refers to tasks requiring extensive arithmetic operations. But a control application may indeed require some EDP, making an EDP-type microprocessor well suited to the task.

A microprocessor's purpose can be judged by looking at such characteristics as bit width, instruction set, and support hardware and software.

The very narrow word width of 4 bits is indicative of a controller. Arithmetic and ASCII character manipulation are difficult to implement using such a narrow word, and quadruple-precision arithmetic is necessary to represent even a comparatively small number like 23,754. On the other hand, a 4-bit word width would prove adequate for many control applications. Up to 16 traffic lights can be represented by a 4-bit code, for example.

Microcomputers with broader word widths usually indicate an EDP orientation. The LSI-11, MicroNova, and TMS 9900 are examples of microprocessors with 16-bit word widths. These processors are actually derived from minicomputers and are used extensively in EDP applications.

A microprocessors instruction set gives a clue to its purpose. An instruction set that won't allow arithmetic shifts and does not accommodate *twos' complement* arithmetic is not well suited to EDP tasks. The 8-bit Intel 8080, for example, only handles unsigned numbers, doesn't perform arithmetic shifts, and lacks complete arithmetic branch capabilities. This microprocessor was initially intended to be an enhanced version of the 8008 microcontroller, and its instruction set reveals the controller-like traits. Since so many people were trying to use the 8080 as a data processor, Zilog capitalized on the situation and included many arithmetic shifts and arithmetic overflow detection in the firm's Z80, an 8080 upgrade. The Z80 thus has more of an EDP character than the 8080, which is also reflected by the name Zilog has given the part—the *Z80 CPU*.

Support hardware and software lend more evidence to the purpose of a microprocessor. A simple controller chip such as the TMS 1000 will not have a broad range of support chips such as floppy disk controllers, memory mapping units, and one-chip modems because a controller won't require this kind of support. The Intel 8086, an EDP-oriented microprocessor, has a broad base of EDP-type hardware and software support, thus showing its purpose.

Microprocessor Bit Width

A microprocessor's bit width is defined as the number of parallel lines contained in the data bus. The bit width has a great effect on system capability and complexity.

Data and instructions are usually stored in a memory as wide as the bit width of the processor. The advantage of a microcomputer with a wide word-width is that the microcomputer can handle a much wider range of arithmetic values before resorting to inefficient multiple-precision arithmetic. It can also have a much larger set of single-word instructions. The results of having these features are higher memory bit widths, wider data buses and connectors, and usually wider bit widths on the interfaces tied to the bus.

A 4 K memory for a 16-bit microcomputer takes twice as many RAMs as that of a 4 K memory for an 8-bit machine. It is wise to keep the bit width as low as is reasonably possible in an application because parts counts, especially in the memory area, are much lower for narrow-bit-width machines.

As pointed out in the previous subsection, microprocessors with 4-bit word widths are almost exclusively designed for control applications. The 8-bit microprocessor can be designed for either EDP or control, but in most cases it is designed to be general-purpose enough for both. Double-precision arithmetic is fairly efficient on these devices, and 16 bits of precision is adequate for most EDP work. Microprocessors with 16-bit word widths are almost exclusively used for data processing in which more than just control functions are required.

Bit-Slicing

Some microprocessors, notably the high-speed bipolar types, are *bit-sliced*. Large-bit-width microcomputers can be built from a few 4- or 8-bit processor "slices."

Bit-slicing, especially with 4-bit elements, is primarily used for thermal reasons. Bipolar LSI circuits draw a lot of current and tend to run hot. A 16-bit or even an 8-bit processor would generate too much heat for a single package to dissipate.

Bit-sliced processors are usually more like LSI building blocks than self-contained processors with strictly defined I/O protocols and instruction sets. You can choose the desired microcomputer bit width and even instruction execution method by varying the number of bit slices and changing the control ROM that contains a microprogram for the control sequence.

Bit-sliced microprocessors are used in custom, high-performance applications. Due to the bit-sliced microprocessor's versatility, systems built with them can be made to emulate more common computers efficiently. Bit-sliced microprocessors are therefore being used extensively in the construction of minicomputers.

Processing Speed

Processing speed is the rate at which a microprocessor executes the *application* program, and this depends on three basic specifications: the clock rate of the microprocessor, the number of cycles required to execute a given instruction, and the instruction repertoire itself. To see the significance of these factors and the manner in which they interrelate, we must have a common understanding of the terms and their functional contributions.

Processor Clock Rate.   The clock rate is defined as the frequency of the clock input to the microprocessor—the number of clock pulses produced per second. Since the clock is the governor of all timed operations within a system, it follows that a high-rate clock permits more operations to be performed within a given period; but a high-rate clock coupled with low-rate peripherals translates to interface complexities.

Acquisition/Execution Rate.   The acquisition and execution rate of a microprocessor may be expressed in microcycles—the number of cycles or operational steps required to perform a given instruction. A microcycle consists of one or more clock cycles. Most MOS microprocessors require many microcycles to execute one instruction. Typically, one microcycle might be used to fetch the instruction, one or two more might be used for data access, and several more for the actual execution operation of the acquired instruction. The number of microcycles required by an instruction is affected by the addressing mode and the instruction complexity. A simple add, for example, may take 14 microcycles, while a *multiply* would take 52 on the TMS 9900 16-bit microcomputer.

Instruction Repertoire.   The kinds of instructions a microprocessor can execute determine its suitability to a task. Instructions should be evaluated on the basis of what they can do, not how many there are.

The number of instructions a microprocessor can perform might be a very misleading number, because every manufacturer has his own way of counting instructions. Intel, for example, counts *move immediate register* and *move immediate memory* as two instructions for the 8080 microprocessor, while Motorola counts *load accumulator immediate* and *load accumulator extended* as two addressing modes for the same instruction. Although the 8080 has more instructions than the 6800, the 6800 has many more real instructions than the 8080 *if all the addressing modes are counted.*

A microprocessor's instruction set should be oriented toward the kind of processing you are performing. In a *controller* application, particular attention should be paid to I/O instructions. In a *data* processing application, the data manipulation instructions (arithmetic shifts, twos' complement instructions, and arithmetic branches) should weigh heavily in the choice.

Determining System Speed.   A true measure of how fast a program will perform a given task is how much time it takes to execute a total program. This figure is the number of clock cycles needed to execute a program multiplied by the microprocessor clock rate.

Microprocessors go about executing programs in different ways. Some employ a high-speed clock and use many small operations (notably the TMS 9900, 8080 and Z80). Others employ a low-speed clock but use a small number of powerful operations (the M6800 and 6500 microprocessors). The *load high and low direct* instruction on the 8080 and the *load index register extended* instruction on the 6800 serve exactly the same function; they each load a 16-bit register that serves as both a general-purpose register and an index register. The 8080 requires 16 clock cycles versus 5 clock cycles for the 6800 to execute this instruction. A 6800 with a 1 MHz clock rate executes the instruction in two-thirds the time required by the 8080 wih its 2 MHz clock.

It is obvious from the above information that clock speed alone is not a valid indicator of system performance. Clock speeds can be directly compared only when dealing with the same processor. A 2 MHz 6502 has exactly twice the performance speed of a 1 MHz 6502. In all other cases, performance estimates and comparisons must be based on task sizings.

The applicability of an instruction set to a given form of processing also determines performance. If a microcomputer's task is to check parity on incoming signals, a branch-on-parity-even instruction can save a whole subroutine of bit-manipulation instructions, and execution time will be greatly reduced. Once again, however, only a sizing will tell how well a microprocessor will perform.

Power Dissipation

In power-critical systems, a microprocessor's power dissipation becomes a major concern. Power dissipation is governed by device technology, device complexity, and in many cases clock speed.

Wide-word-width microprocessors require extra complexity to handle the wide data paths, so they draw more power than narrow-word-width devices of the same technology.

High-speed bipolar microprocessors draw the most power of all. Medium power dissipation can be expected from NMOS and PMOS microprocessors, while CMOS microprocessors draw the least.

The clock rate itself affects the power dissipation of most microprocessors (excluding microprocessors based on emitter-coupled logic technology). The slower the clock rate, the less power the processor draws. The RCA 1802 microprocessor, which employs CMOS technology, is a good example of a clock rate's effect on power dissipation. If a very limited amount of processing is required, a relatively slow clock rate of 10 kHz can be used, thereby cutting power dissipation from 60 mW at 1 MHz to 5 mW at 10 kHz.

New device technologies such as *silicon on sapphire* (SOS) promise to decrease microprocessor power consumption and at the same time improve speed–power products. The latest manufacturer specification sheets should be used to find the power dissipation of these parts.

Interrupt Capability

Temporarily diverting execution of a program to a small task that requires immediate attention may be required in your application. A microprocessor with good interrupt capabilities should be chosen if this requirement is to be met.

Priority interrupt systems let multiple devices interrupt a processor simultaneously, automatically determining which task should be executed first. A separate LSI device is usually required to perform this task. The Intel 8259 priority interrupt control unit (PICU) is one such element.

DMA Capability

Direct memory access is the name applied to the operation when a device other than the processor is capable of accessing (reading or writing) directly into memory by temporarily taking over the microcomputer bus. This feature is good for large block data transfers and relieves the microprocessor of the burden of executing a data transfer program.

DMA transfers are much faster than program-controlled data transfers. If your system requires many high-speed data accesses by external devices, it is imperative to select a processor with DMA capability.

Many microprocessor chip sets include a DMA controller support chip. These chips can substantially reduce DMA interface complexity and simplify the system design task. The Intel 8257 DMA controller is a common DMA support IC. It supports up to four DMA channels simultaneously and contains all the circuitry necessary to take control of the 8080 bus and perform the data transfer.

Decimal Arithmetic

It is often desirable to store data in user-interactive systems as binary-coded-decimal (BCD) digits rather than multiple-precision bytes. Time-wasting and memory-consuming decimal-to-binary and binary-to-decimal conversions can be avoided in these cases.

Many microprocessors have instructions that perform BCD arithmetic on 4-bit BCD numbers packed two per 8-bit byte. The M6800's *decimal arithmetic adjust* (DAA) instruction is an example. If BCD arithmetic is required in your application, the microprocessor you choose should have a DAA-type instruction.

Second-Sourcing

It is always more desirable to work with a microprocessor type that is manufactured by two or more independent companies than with a part that is unique to one company. The second source can back up the primary supplier when back-order problems arise; and should one manufacturer decide to stop producing the device, availability from the other maker cushions the impact.

Another advantage to second-sourced microprocessors is the obvious benefit resulting from competition. Because more than one manufacturer is competing for the same market, the only way for a manufacturer to distinguish his product is by supplying a broader line of support chips and higher performance than the competitor. In the end, the consumer wins and the prize is threefold: a wide range of support chips, wide performance-range selection, and lower prices.

Cost

The cost of a system is one of the highest-priority items, especially in the consumer market; but when evaluating the cost of a microprocessor, the cost estimate should include the whole system and not just the microprocessor. Current price sheets from the microprocessor manufacturer should always be used because prices change so rapidly (and drastically) in this field.

Software Support

Software generation is a costly proposition, and it is not uncommon for software development costs to outrun hardware costs. For this reason, microprocessors with a large software support base are very desirable. Editors, assemblers, and high-order languages help speed development of a microprocessor system. The level of software support is less critical for small controller-type microprocessors intended only to run small control programs.

Load-Driving Capability

A microprocessor's technology will largely determine what voltage levels and drive currents are available at the microprocessors output pins. These characteristics determine how much support circuitry will be needed to incorporate the microprocessor into a system.

Many MOS microprocessors claim TTL compatibility. This statement is misleading, because usually only one or two standard TTL loads can be driven. In some cases only one low-power TTL load is drivable. To drive many TTL loads, buffers must be incorporated on most MOS microprocessors.

Some microprocessor chip sets are designed to eliminate the need for buffers in minimal system configurations by offering a wide range of memory and support chips that present only a light load to the processor's buses. The M6800 chip set is a good example. Up to eight devices can be driven on a nonbuffered bus. Well thought out schemes like this can save interface parts in a minimal system.

Bipolar microprocessors can usually drive many loads that are themselves based on the technology of which they are built. The Texas Instruments 74S481 bipolar microprocessor supplies 10 mA of drive current to its address lines; this is enough current to drive six standard TTL loads.

Architecture Philosophy

Microprocessors, like large computers, have many architectural forms. Two types of machines that are currently popular are the *register-oriented* machines like the 8086, Z8000, and RCA 1800 series and the *memory-oriented* machines such as the 6800, 6500, and 9900 series.

Stack operating capability is another architectural feature found on many microprocessors. Architectural features tend to simplify certain tasks. A stack is useful when many subroutines are to be performed.

Memory-oriented processing is helpful when working with large data bases in memory. Once again, the instruction set will describe what the processor architecture is capable of and sizings will tell how efficiently it is performing your task.

MICROPROCESSOR EVALUATION EXAMPLES

Up to this point, microprocessor characteristics have been described in general terms. In this section we get down to some specific examples. Descriptions and evaluations of a few common microprocessors are presented. No attempt has been made to cover all microprocessors, since new and more advanced microprocessors are constantly entering the market. By evaluating microprocessor specification sheets and all the latest literature in a way similar to what is presented here, you can pick the best device for your task at any time.

The TMS 1000 Family

With the proliferation of low-cost 8-, 12-, and 16-bit microprocessors, we might be inclined to think that 4-bit microprocessors are obsolete and undesirable in any application. This isn't the case. It's true that some 4-bit processors such as the Intel 4040 have been pushed aside by technology, but in the midst of 8- and 16-bit microprocessor development, some very viable third-generation 4-bit control-oriented microprocessors came into being. The TMS 1000 family is a good example.

Purpose.   The TMS 1000 series of one-chip microcomputers is made by Texas Instruments and second-sourced by Motorola. It is a family of about 35 microprocessors aimed at the industrial and consumer control applications market.

Features.   The TMS 1000 chip's complement of capabilities reflects its 4-bit control nature. TMS 1000 series microprocessors have 2048 8-bit bytes of ROM

44

and 124 4-bit "nybbles" of RAM built onto the chip. Some of the earliest versions have only 1024 bytes and 64 nybbles of ROM and RAM.

As with most 4-bit microprocessors, the instruction word size is 8 bits (the Toshiba T3444 is an exception to the 8-bit instruction rule—it has 4-bit instructions) and the data word width is 4 bits. Program execution is performed strictly out of ROM and no provisions for external ROM or RAM have been made. No external address bus is needed, freeing valuable I/O pins to perform the chip's control functions. Figure 2-2 shows the TMS 1000.

The TMS 1000 has 54 basic instructions that are oriented toward control applications. Because the processor has separate program and data memories that can't interchange data, strange instructions like A9ACC (add 9 to the accumulator) are a large percentage of the 54. Obviously, this type of processor could immediately be eliminated from further consideration in applications requiring extensive data processing.

Interface Capabilities.   The TMS 1000 series microprocessors come in 28- and 40-pin packages (a 64-pin evaluation model also exists), and their interfacing characteristics depend on the package size.

The 28-pin models have 4-bit data input buses, 8-bit data output buses, and 10 program-controlled control outputs. Data on the input lines (K lines) can be read into the processor's accumulator using the TKA (transfer K inputs to accumulator) instruction. Output can be performed by simply sending one control output bit to the device being controlled and strobing it using the SETR (set R output line) and RSTR (reset R output line) instructions. To send 8-bit data to a device, the 8 output lines can be set to the proper 8-bit value using the TDO (transfer data to output) instruction, and an R control line can be strobed to latch the data into a register at the controlled device.

Support.   The simple design, versatile I/O, and built-in RAM and ROM features of the TMS 1000 family of microprocessors make an extensive line of support chips unnecessary. Because no direct external access to memory is possible, a DMA chip doesn't make any sense. Three helpful support chips are available, however: 4 × 4 and 4 × 7 I/O expanders and a CPU-to-capacitive keyboard interface.

The TMS 1000 family's use in industry is constantly increasing and it has thus acquired a good software support base. An assembler, simulator, utility programs and even a high-level language are available. In addition, a few of the TMS 1000 series processors come preprogrammed to perform common functions.

Physical Characteristics.   Being a 4-bit economy model control processor, the TMS 1000 performance specifications are not exceptional. The clock frequency can range from 50 kHz to 1 MHz, and all instructions execute in 6 μs at 1 MHz.

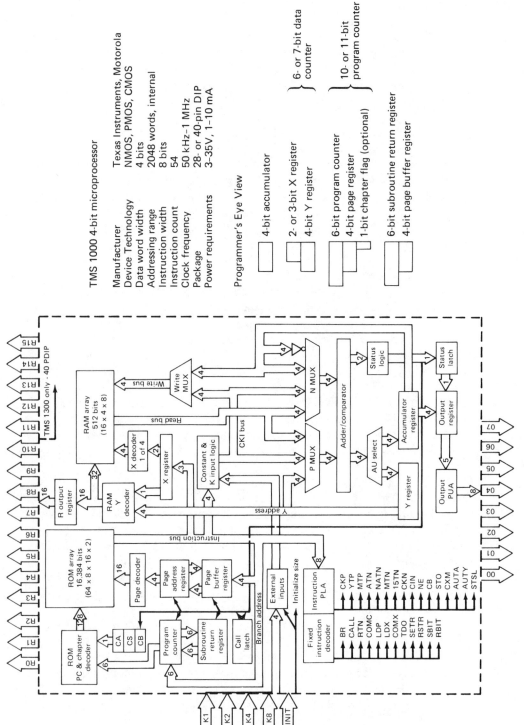

TMS 1000 4-bit microprocessor

Manufacturer	Texas Instruments, Motorola
Device Technology	NMOS, PMOS, CMOS
Data word width	4 bits
Addressing range	2048 words, internal
Instruction width	8 bits
Instruction count	54
Clock frequency	50 kHz–1 MHz
Package	28- or 40-pin DIP
Power requirements	3–35V, 1–10 mA

Programmer's Eye View

4-bit accumulator

2- or 3-bit X register
4-bit Y register

6-bit program counter
4-bit page register } 6- or 7-bit data counter
1-bit chapter flag (optional)

6-bit subroutine return register } 10- or 11-bit program counter
4-bit page buffer register

Figure 2-2 The TMS 1000 microprocessor. (Courtesy Texas Instruments, Inc., Dallas, Texas.)

46

This microprocessor family is available in several technologies for various applications. For relatively high-speed performance, NMOS and PMOS versions are available. A CMOS version from Motorola allows very low-power controllers (1 mA) to be built.

Probably the most noteworthy feature of the TMS 1000 series is its economy. A minimal system can be built with one part (an internal clock is also included in this processor chip), and at this writing it sells for less than $4.

The 8080 Family

The Intel 8080 was the first microprocessor to gain wide acceptance in the microcomputer field and did, in fact, help create the field. It is currently the most widely used microprocessor simply because it was first to reach the marketplace. This situation is rapidly changing as superior products such as the 8085 and Z80 are gaining in popularity.

The 8080, from an architectural and feature standpoint, is quite primitive, and improved processors are usually designed into new products; but due to its wide acceptance, multiple sources, and large line of support chips, the 8080 is here to stay.

Purpose. The 8080 instruction set reflects a control nature in this microprocessor. It is heavily loaded with data transfer instructions and has IN and OUT instructions for input and output control. Conditional jumps, subroutine calls, and subroutine returns (with parity even or odd jump instructions) are meant to be used to simplify data handling.

The 8080 has a few data processing characteristics, but some important features are missing. Some of the EDP-type instructions include the *add* and *subtract* instructions, the *double-precision add* instruction (although this feature is primarily intended for address manipulations), and the *decimal arithmetic adjust* instruction. Lacking are the arithmetic shift instructions, signed overflow detection, and the arithmetic conditional branch instructions such as *branch greater than or equal to*. These shortcomings could not be easily overcome because of a simple fact never mentioned in most manufacturers' literature: the 8080 is not designed to do signed *twos' complement* arithmetic. The modularity of the twos' complement numbering system makes many twos' complement operations work (adding −1 to 7 to get 6, for example), *but the 8080* has no way of telling if a result is negative or positive. A good example of this is the comparison of two numbers to see which is larger. A compare instruction followed by an examination of the overflow bit can be performed to compare a pair of twos' complement numbers. A set overflow bit means that the register being compared to the accumulator was greater than the accumulator value, *but only if the values were of like sign.* If the registers were of different sign, the set overflow bit would have just the opposite meaning. You must therefore manually keep track of the signs of numbers in the program. This involves additional software and execution time.

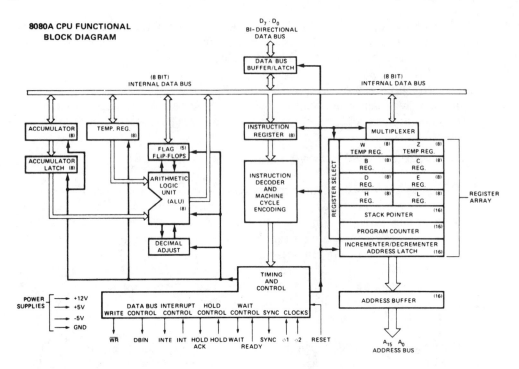

MCS-80 (8080 A) 8-bit Microprocessor   Programmer's Eye View

Manufacturer	Intel, AMD, and others
Device Technology	NMOS
Data word width	8 bits
Addressing range	65,536 words, external
Instruction width	8 bits
Instruction count	78
Clock frequency	0.5–4 MHz
Package	40-pin DIP or flatpack
Power requirements	12 V at 40 mA, 5 V at 60 mA, −5 V at 10 μA

	PSW	Program status word
	A	Primary accumulator
B	C	Secondary Accumulators/data counter
D	E	Secondary Accumulators/data counter
H	L	Secondary Accumulators/data counter
	SP	Stack pointer
	PC	Program counter

Figure 2-3   The Intel 8080 microprocessor. (Reprinted by permission of Intel Corporation, Copyright 1978.)

Features.   The 8080 has a register-oriented architecture containing six 8-bit registers that may be used individually or in pairs for 8- and 16-bit operations. An accumulator is provided to act as a primary working register. Figure 2-3 illustrates the 8080 microprocessor.

The 8080 is also capable of stack operations, as the instruction set of Fig. 2-4 indicates. A separate 16-bit stack pointer keeps track of the push-down stack that resides in the combined program and data memory. The stack is useful for implementing subroutines. Because subroutine return addresses are automatically pushed down onto the stack by the subroutine call, subroutine nesting is limited only by the amount of read–write memory a user has provided. This versatile feature makes more structured programs possible and lends itself to very complex control tasks and data processing.

All the 8080 features mentioned so far indicate that the 8080 is well suited for control tasks. The interrupt and DMA capabilities of this chip confirm the suspicion. An asynchronous *vectored interrupt* capability allows external devices operating through an 8080-series support chip (the 8259 priority interrupt controller), to interrupt program execution and vector the program to an appropriate service routine. Many devices can efficiently move data in and out of memory using the 8080's DMA capability and another support chip, the 8257 DMA controller.

It should be noted that the 8080 is really a 3-chip microprocessor—that is, it takes at least three chips or corresponding discrete hardware to build a useful microprocessor. In addition to the 8080, an 8224 clock generator–driver and an 8228 bidirectional bus driver are needed. Up-grades from the 8080 microprocessor have the functions of the two additional chips built into a single package.

Instructions. The 8080 has about 100 instructions. The exact count varies for each manufacturer due to the way instructions are counted, not because of differences between the microprocessors. Instructions vary from 1 to 3 bytes in length, depending on the addressing mode of the instruction. The instruction set is broken into seven primary groups. Figure 2-4 lists the instruction set.

Data transfer instructions move 8-bit data from register to register and also to memory. A few 16-bit data transfer instructions are provided as well. An interesting XCHG instruction swaps two specific register pairs (the D,E registers with the H,L registers). Two 16-bit transfer instructions (the LHLD and SHLD instructions) move data from a register pair to memory or from memory to a register pair, but these operations can only be performed on the H,L register pair. The I/O transfer instructions (IN and OUT) are provided for simple I/O handling.

Control instructions (there are six) are used. They are standard instructions and include the NOP (no operation), HLT (halt), and interrupt enabling and disabling instructions.

At first glance the 29 conditional and unconditional *branch* instructions seem to contain more branch capability than you would ever need. This is somewhat misleading for this instruction set because the 29 instructions only allow conditional branching on four conditions: carry, zero, sign, and parity. No combined conditional branches such as *branch if carry exclusive-ORed with sign* (more commonly called *branch less than*) are provided. This makes signed comparisons difficult.

Arithmetic instructions, like the transfer instructions, include 8- and 16-bit operations. The basic adds and subtracts are present and a *decimal arithmetic*

Op Code |7|6|5|4|3|2|1|0	No. of Bytes	Clock Cycles	Assembly Mnemonic	Instruction Description
DATA TRANSFER				
01dddsss	1	5	MOVr, r	Move register to register
01110sss	1	7	MOVm, r	Move register to memory
01ddd110	1	7	MOVr, m	Move memory to register
00ddd110	2	7	MVI, r	Move to register, immediate
00110110	2	10	MVI, m	Move to memory, immediate
00111010	3	13	LDA	Load Acc, direct
00001010	1	7	LDAX B	Load Acc, indirect via B & C
00011010	1	7	LDAX D	Load Acc, indirect via D & E
00101010	3	16	LHLD	Load H & L, direct
00100001	3	10	LXI H	Load H & L, immediate
00010001	3	10	LXI D	Load D & E, immediate
00000001	3	10	LXI B	Load B & C, immediate
00110001	3	10	LXI SP	Load stack pointer, immediate
00100010	3	16	SHLD	Store H & L, direct
00110010	3	13	STA	Store Acc, direct
00000010	1	7	STAX B	Store Acc, indirect via B & C
00010010	1	7	STAX D	Store Acc, indirect via D & E
11111001	1	5	SPHL	Transfer H & L to stack pointer
11101011	1	4	XCHG	Exchange D & E with H & L
11100011	1	18	XTHL	Exchange top of stack with H & L
11011011	2	10	IN	Input to Acc
11010011	2	10	OUT	Output from Acc
CONTROL				
01110110	1	7	HLT	Halt and enter wait state
00110111	1	4	STC	Set carry flag
00111111	1	4	CMC	Compliment carry flag
11111011	1	4	EI	Enable interrupts
11110011	1	4	DI	Disable interrupts
00000000	1	4	NOP	No operation
BRANCHING				
11000011	3	10	JMP	Jump unconditionally
11011010	3	10	JC	Jump on carry
11010010	3	10	JNC	Jump on no carry
11001010	3	10	JZ	Jump on zero
11000010	3	10	JNZ	Jump on not zero
11110010	3	10	JP	Jump on positive
11111010	3	10	JM	Jump on minus
11101010	3	10	JPE	Jump on parity even
11100010	3	10	JPO	Jump on parity odd
11001101	3	17	Call	Call unconditionally
11011100	3	17-11	CC	Call on carry
11010100	3	17-11	CNC	Call on no carry
11001100	3	17-11	CZ	Call on zero
11000100	3	17-11	CNZ	Call on not zero
11110100	3	17-11	CP	Call on positive
11111100	3	17-11	CM	Call on minus
11101100	3	17-11	CPE	Call on parity even
11100100	3	17-11	CPO	Call on parity odd
11001001	1	10	RET	Return unconditionally
11011000	1	11-5	RC	Return on carry
11010000	1	11-5	RNC	Return on no carry
11001000	1	11-5	RZ	Return on zero
11000000	1	11-5	RNZ	Return on not zero
11110000	1	11-5	RP	Return on positive
11111000	1	11-5	RM	Return on minus
11101000	1	11-5	RPE	Return on parity even
11100000	1	11-5	RPO	Return on parity odd
11101001	1	5	PCHL	Jump unconditionally, indirect via H & L
11vvv111	1	11	RST	Restart

Op Code |7|6|5|4|3|2|1|0	No. of Bytes	Clock Cycles	Assembly Mnemonic	Instruction Description
ARITHMETIC				
10000sss	1	4	ADDr	Add register to Acc
10001sss	1	4	ADCr	Add with carry register to Acc
10000110	1	7	ADDm	Add memory to Acc
10001110	1	7	ADCm	Add with carry memory to Acc
11000110	2	7	ADI	Add to Acc, immediate
11001110	2	7	ACI	Add with carry to Acc, immediate
00001001	1	10	DAD B	Double add B & C to H & L
00011001	1	10	DAD D	Double add D & E to H & L
00101001	1	10	DAD H	Double add H & L to H & L
00111001	1	10	DAD SP	Double add stack pointer to H & L
10010sss	1	4	SUBr	Subtract register from Acc
10011sss	1	4	SBBr	Subtract with borrow register from Acc
10010110	1	7	SUBm	Subtract memory from Acc
10011110	1	7	SBBm	Subtract with borrow memory from Acc
11010110	2	7	SUI	Subtract from Acc, immediate
11011110	2	7	SBI	Subtract with borrow from Acc, immediate
00100111	1	4	DAA	Decimal adjust Acc
STACK OPERATIONS				
11000101	1	11	PUSH B	Push registers B & C on stack
11010101	1	11	PUSH D	Push registers D & E on stack
11100101	1	11	PUSH H	Push registers H & L on stack
11110101	1	11	PUSH PSW	Push Acc and flags on stack
11000001	1	10	POP B	Pop registers B & C off stack
11010001	1	10	POP D	Pop registers D & E off stack
11100001	1	10	POP H	Pop registers H & L off stack
11110001	1	10	POP PSW	Pop Acc and flags off stack
LOGICAL				
10100sss	1	4	ANA r	And register with Acc
10100110	1	7	ANA m	And memory with Acc
11100110	2	7	ANI	And with Acc, immediate
10101sss	1	4	XRA r	Exclusive or register with Acc
10101110	1	7	XRA m	Exclusive Or memory with Acc
11101110	2	7	XRI	Exclusive Or with Acc, immediate
10110sss	1	4	ORA r	Inclusive Or register with Acc
10110110	1	7	ORA m	Inclusive Or memory with Acc
11110110	2	7	ORI	Inclusive Or with Acc, immediate
10111sss	1	4	CMP r	Compare register with Acc
10111110	1	7	CMP m	Compare memory with Acc
11111110	2	7	CPI	Compare with Acc, immediate
00101111	1	4	CMA	Compliment Acc
00000111	1	4	RLC	Rotate Acc left
00001111	1	4	RRC	Rotate Acc right
00010111	1	4	RAL	Rotate Acc left through carry
00011111	1	4	RAR	Rotate Acc right through carry
INCREMENT/DECREMENT				
00ddd100	1	5	INR r	Increment register
00110100	1	10	INR m	Increment memory
00000011	1	5	INX B	Increment extended B & C
00010011	1	5	INX D	Increment extended D & E
00100011	1	5	INX H	Increment extended H & L
00110011	1	5	INX SP	Increment stack pointer
00ddd101	1	5	DCR r	Decrement register
00110101	1	10	DCR m	Decrement memory
00001011	1	5	DCX B	Decrement extended B & C
00011011	1	5	DCX D	Decrement extended D & E
00101011	1	5	DCX H	Decrement extended H & L
00111011	1	5	DCX SP	Decrement stack pointer

Figure 2-4 The Advanced Micro Devices 9080 (8080) instruction set. (Copyright © 1978 Advanced Micro Devices, Inc. Reproduced with the permission of copyright owner.)

50

adjust instruction is included. Again, certain operations only apply to certain registers. Any register can be added to the accumulator, and memory can be added to the accumulator, but memory cannot be added to a register without first going through the accumulator. Two arithmetic instructions particularly suited to multiple-precision arithmetic are included: the *add with carry* and *subtract with borrow*.

Stack instructions work with 16-bit register pairs rather than individual registers. Pushing two registers onto the stack at once makes fast machine status saving possible.

Logical instructions are similar to the arithmetic operations except that only 8-bit logical operations are officially possible. One 16-bit logical operation, however, is possible—although this is not immediately apparent from the instruction set. By using the 16-bit *add* instruction, the H,L register pair can be added to itself, resulting in (H,L) × 2, or an arithmetic left shift. Many 8080 programmers use this trick, especially when working with double-precision numbers.

Increment/decrement instructions are provided for 12 discrete operations. Upon close examination we see that status flags are set for 8-bit register increments and decrements but no flags are set for 16-bit ones. This mode of operation was chosen so 8-bit data status would not be destroyed by address manipulation. Increments and decrements of 16-bits are typically employed when using indexed addressing through the H,L register pair. With the current status-setting method, the 8-bit arithmetic operations status can be saved while obtaining the next data byte through indexed addressing. This is particularly useful for multiple-precision arithmetic in which the carry from a least-significant *add* can be saved and added with the most-significant *add* through incremented index addressing. The main problem with the conditional status-setting arrangement is that it limits the double-precision capabilities of the 16-bit register pairs.

As you look at an instruction set, ask this question: *How easy is programming going to be with this instruction set?* On an assembly-language level, the 8080 takes a lot of getting used to and is difficult to program efficiently. The preponderance of registers, each with its own unique capabilities, creates this situation. When a programmer first tries to program the 8080 efficiently, he finds himself cornered into bad situations. He may want to store the B,C register pair directly into memory, but he'll find that only the H,L register pair has that capability. He may want to swap the D,E and B,C register pairs, but he'll find that only the H,L and D,E registers can be swapped. An 8080 programmer must be alert to all the 8080 register idiosyncrasies before efficient programming is possible. The use of a high-order language is one way of side-stepping this difficult learning process.

The 8080 has four basic addressing modes. *Direct-mode* addressing allows direct loading or storing of the accumulator or H,L register pair from the address specified in the two bytes following the instruction. The *immediate* addressing mode allows the loading of any register or register pair with the data following the instruction. *Implied* addressing is used in operations needing no memory reference (such as register-to-register transfers). *Indexed* addressing allows the contents of the D,E pair, the H,L pair, or the B,C register pair to be used as 16-bit pointers to the data being loaded or stored into memory. Autoincrement and autodecrement addressing on the stack pointer are also provided by the stack operations.

Interface Characteristics.   Data can be sent to and taken from interfaces in a few ways. The input and output instructions simply put an 8-bit device code on the 16-bit address bus (repeated in the upper and lower address bytes). The output instruction puts the present accumulator data on the data bus, and the input instruction clocks whatever is on the data bus into the accumulator. Status lines indicate when output and input operations are being performed. Devices on the bus can use these lines to load device registers or drive the data bus.

Because address lines and data lines are available outside the processor, memory-mapped I/O is also possible. By building an interface device that acts as a memory location at a certain address, data can be sent to that device simply by writing into the device's assigned memory location.

The 8080 control lines are configured for simple direct memory access interfacing. The processor can go into a *hold* state when a DMA device applies a signal to the 8080's *hold* line. The 8080 promptly disconnects itself from the bus, allowing the DMA device to take over address and data line controls and access memory directly.

Support.   The 8080 is currently one of the best supported microprocessors in regard to interface chips. Because eight manufacturers second-source the part, everything from DMA controllers to floppy disk controllers are available.

Software support is equally diversified. Editors, assemblers, and high-order languages are available. Intel's MDS software development system is the most popular means of developing 8080 software in industrial applications.

Physical Characteristics.   The 8080 is available in many clock speeds ranging from 1 to 4 MHz. Due to the intense competition in the 8080 market, prices are very low, but the fact that the 8224 and 8228 support chips are needed to make the 8080 operational adds significantly to this cost.

The 8080 is an NMOS microprocessor, requires three dc voltages for power, and dissipates about a watt. Again, clock speed and version make a big difference.

The 8085

The 8085 is an upgraded version of the 8080 that incorporates a built-in clock and system controller, thus eliminating the need for the two 8080 support chips (the 8224 clock generator and 8228 system controller). It is software compatible with the 8080 and contains two additional instructions.

A peripheral processor that is designed to operate as a slave to the 8080 or 8085 is a recent addition to the 8080 family. The 8041/8741 contains a processor, 1 K bytes of ROM, I/O ports, clock, and timer–counter. This part can be used with the 8080 to increase processing power or as a stand-alone processor.

The Z80

The Zilog Z80 is a greatly enhanced upgrade of the 8080. Enough similarity is maintained to allow 8080 programs to be used, and additional instructions (which correct the 8080's lack of arithmetic capability) are included in the instruction set. More than twice the number of internal registers are used, and two independent index registers enhance the addressing capabilities.

The hardware characteristics of the Z80 have also been improved. The system control functions of the 8228 and the clock functions of the 8224 have been built into the Z80, making it a one-package microprocessor. Only one power supply is required as opposed to the three required for the 8080. An additional nonmaskable interrupt line has also been added.

Purpose. The Z80 has enough features to qualify it as a true EDP-type microprocessor; but it has retained and even improved on the control characteristics of the 8080, making it an excellent controller as well. The Z80 has gained wide acceptance in both computing and control applications as a result of its dual-purpose nature.

Features. The Z80 is a register-oriented processor containing eighteen 8-bit registers and four 16-bit registers. Two accumulators and flag registers are also provided. Figure 2-5 illustrates the Z80 structure. A close look at the registers, however, reveal that only about half the registers can be used at any one time. The accumulator, flag, and registers B, C, D, E, H, and L in the main register set are mirrored as A', F', B', and so on in the alternate register set. An exchange instruction must be performed to select which set (main or alternate) is going to be used. This feature is useful for interrupt processing in which only one command is necessary to save the interrupted program's status, but it also means that the Z80's register set, at any given time, is about the same as the 8080's. Two totally new index registers have been added, however, and new indexed instructions support them.

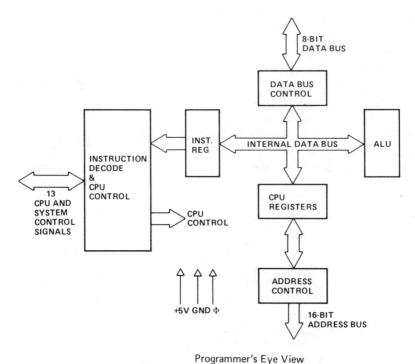

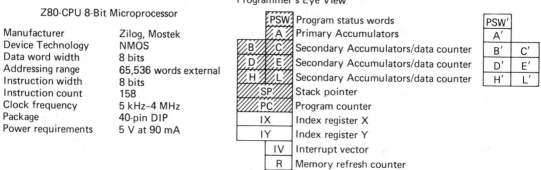

Shaded registers represent the 8080A subset.

Figure 2-5   The Zilog Z80 microprocessor. (Courtesy Zilog, Cupertino, Ca.)

Many additional instructions have been added, eliminating most of the 8080's arithmetic and data processing shortcomings. The first thing one notices when comparing the 8080 and Z80 instruction sets is that all the instruction names have been changed. This makes comparison difficult without a preliminary learning effort.

The basic additions to the instruction set include: arithmetic shifts, block transfer instructions, a loop control instruction, instructions specifying the new addressing modes, extended arithmetic operations (including a negate), and extended I/O instructions. On the surface this instruction set appears to be extremely powerful, but a few points should be noted. Many of the added arithmetic instructions decrease the amount of memory needed to represent an operation, since multiple instructions are no longer needed. But the single Z80 instruction execution time may actually be longer than the total of the 8080's multiple instructions. An arithmetic right shift is a good example of this. Using an RLC followed by two RAA instructions, an 8080 can perform the shift in 12 clock cycles. The Z80 has a single SRA (shift right arithmetic), but it takes up to 23 clock cycles to execute. In addition, most of the new Z80 instructions require a 2-byte representation, the first of which indicates that it is not an 8080 instruction.

The Z80 parity flag bit has a dual purpose. On logical operations such as AND it represents word parity, but on signed *twos' complement* operations it represents a twos' complement overflow. This is yet another enhancement to the Z80's signed arithmetic ability.

Interface Characteristics.   The IN and OUT instructions, memory-mapped I/O, and DMA are all used for I/O. From a software viewpoint, I/O is a bit simpler with the Z80 than 8080 since any register can be written to the output or loaded through the input instruction. The need for passing all the data through the accumulator has been eliminated. And block transfer I/O instructions simplify block I/O routines.

One very unique Z80 feature is its simultaneous I/O capability. On an 8080 input instruction, the 8-bit input address is output on the 8 least significant and the 8 most significant bits of the address; data is read into the accumulator over the data lines. The Z80, however, *outputs* the I/O address on the 8 low-order bits of the address bus, and *reads* the 8 data bus bits into the accumulator (or register). This allows you to output and input data to a device all in one operation. It's a very efficient and clever scheme. Figure 2-6 compares 8080 and Z80 I/O formats.

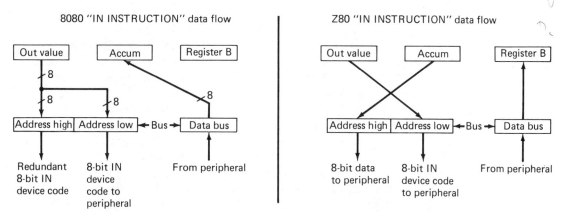

Figure 2-6   A comparison of 8080 and Z80 I/O methods.

The Z80 CPU has a dynamic RAM refresh capability that is worth reviewing if your design calls for dynamic RAMs and few parts. A *refresh* register and control circuitry interleave sequential memory *read* cycles between processor memory access cycles. The refresh operation is thus totally transparent to the user—unlike some computer refresh schemes that interrupt processing and execute a refresh routine (notably the LSI-11). This feature greatly simplifies the interfacing of dynamic RAMs to a Z80 system, as memory refresh logic is no longer needed on the interface.

Support.   The Z80 is similar to the 8080 so most of the 8080 software and many of the 8080 support ICs operate with it. In addition, Zilog, Mostek, and NEC all supply support chips and software designed for the Z80.

Physical Characteristics.   The Z80 is an NMOS microprocessor. It is available with clock speeds up to 4.5 MHz. It requires a single-phase square-wave clock and a single 5-volt power supply. It dissipates about 500 mW.

Other Z80 Family Members

Two additional processors are available in the Z80 family: a one-chip microcomputer with 96 bytes of RAM (called the Z8) and the computationally powerful Z8000 with built-in multiply and divide instructions.

The 6800 Family

The M6800 is another one of the most widely used microprocessors. This family of chips has design features that make it very desirable in control applications.

Purpose.   The M6800 microprocessor was designed to be a general-purpose central processing unit, featuring total twos' complement arithmetic as well as control capability. The 6800 therefore does very well in EDP-type applications.

The instruction set reflects the true computer-like design of the 6800. At first glance it looks very similar to that of Digital Equipment Corporation's PDP-11 minicomputer, the instruction set after which it was patterned. Many powerful arithmetic and comparison instructions are available. A wide variety of addressing modes add to the 6800's list of minicomputer traits.

Features.   The 6800 can be considered an advanced second-generation microprocessor or a very early third-generation model. Advanced features, such as a single 5-volt power supply, in addition to more primitive characteristics, such as the need for a two-phase clock, are both present.

The 6800 series of parts was, from its very beginning, designed to act as a functionally balanced microcomputer building-block set. The goal was to enable the construction of small controllers and computers with four or five parts plus a few discrete timing components—without the use of bus buffers. Straightforward software development was another goal.

The 6800 is memory-oriented and its architecture follows the philosophy of using a low-speed clock with many actions per clock cycle. Most 6800 instructions execute in 2, 3, or 4 clock cycles (versus 8 or 9 for the 8080). Data can be manipulated with two 8-bit accumulators, and a 16-bit index register is available for address manipulations. A direct addressing mode allows the lowest 256 bytes of processor memory to be accessed without supplying a full 16-bit address. This allows you to operate with a bank of 256 registers, which provides enough working storage to free you from having to plan a register data handling strategy.

A 16-bit stack pointer holds last-in–first-out data stored in external RAM (thereby "pointing" to the most recent push in the stack). Such external storage of nested instruction addresses simplifies subroutine calls and makes interrupt servicing a much easier proposition.

Although register strategy doesn't have to be planned, one thing that must be carefully planned is branching. The 6800 incorporates memory- and time-efficient relative conditional branching. An 8-bit offset is specified in the byte following the *conditional branching* instruction. If a branch condition is met, the offset will be added to the program counter and a branch will result. The only limiting factor is that branch distance is restricted to 127 bytes in either branch direction; no *extended conditional jump* instructions (specifying a 16-bit absolute jump address) exist. A single *unconditional extended jump* instruction is provided. You must therefore remember to either limit branching to a distance of 127 bytes or conditionally branch to an extended jump statement.

Branch relative to subroutine and *jump absolute to subroutine* instructions are included. The branch to subroutine, like the conditional branch statements, is limited to a subroutine branch distance of 127 bytes.

The 6800 instruction set's direct addressing mode and extensive conditional branch capabilities allow the majority of the instructions being performed to be one or two bytes long. This reduces memory requirements and decreases memory access, thereby increasing processor performance. These factors make the 6800 desirable in real-time application in which execution speed is important. Figure 2-7 shows the 6800 structure.

Interface Capability.   Like the PDP-11, the 6800 relies on memory-mapped I/O. No independent I/O channel or I/O instructions are provided. Device registers that act as memory locations must be provided. The advantage to this approach is that fewer processor control lines are required, so I/O programming is considerably simplified. With totally memory-mapped I/O, DMA peripherals can communicate directly with other devices as well as memory with no additional control lines or logic.

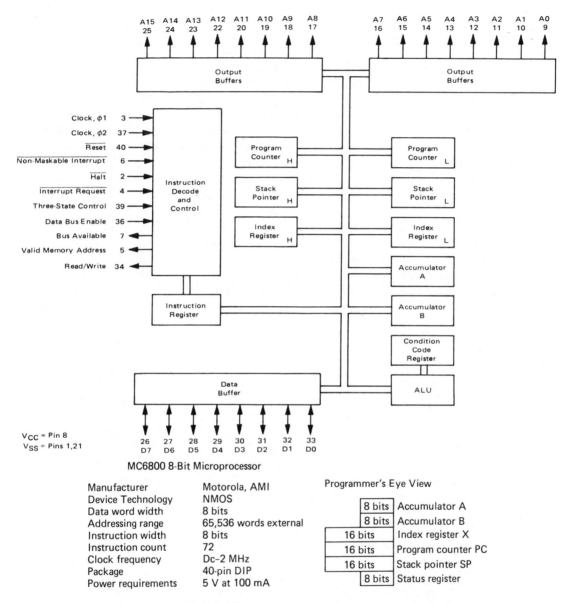

MC6800 8-Bit Microprocessor

Manufacturer	Motorola, AMI		
Device Technology	NMOS		
Data word width	8 bits		
Addressing range	65,536 words external		
Instruction width	8 bits		
Instruction count	72		
Clock frequency	Dc–2 MHz		
Package	40-pin DIP		
Power requirements	5 V at 100 mA		

Programmer's Eye View

8 bits	Accumulator A
8 bits	Accumulator B
16 bits	Index register X
16 bits	Program counter PC
16 bits	Stack pointer SP
8 bits	Status register

Figure 2-7   The Motorola M6800 microprocessor. (Courtesy Motorola Semiconductor Products, Phoenix, Arizona.)

The disadvantage of memory-mapped I/O is that every interface on the bus must be able to recognize its address and go through the strict memory I/O protocol. The 6800, however, avoids these pitfalls with a simple memory I/O protocol and by suggesting that you allocate the top 32K of the 64K address space to I/O devices. The most significant bit of the address (A15) thereby acts as an I/O bit and can be used along with a few other bits to distinguish between interfaces on the bus. This is a good solution for systems requiring less than 32K of memory. If more memory is required, you can use most of the 64K memory space for memory and use more complex 16-bit address recognizers, which wouldn't be too detrimental (in terms of added parts) to a very large system.

Support.   The 6800 has a wide range of support chips. Since 6800 series parts are designed to work as a functional building-block set, the interface parts have compatible control lines. Few discrete parts are needed to get a system going. As with the 8080 support chips, anything from simple serial interfaces to on-chip CRT and floppy disk controllers are available.

In terms of software, the 6800 is one of the best supported microprocessors. For initial circuit designs there are evaluation boards, and for software development there is the EXORciser system—a complete software development tool consisting of a terminal, floppy disks, PROM programmer, assembler, editor, and other development software.

Physical Characteristics.   The 6800 is available from six manufacturers in three basic speed ranges—1, 1.5, and 2 MHz. The 6800 requires only one 5-volt power supply and dissipates about half a watt of power. Commercial, industrial, and military versions are available.

The bus driving capabilities of the 6800 are adequate to support up to six 6800-series support devices without the need for a bus extender or additional drivers.

Other 6800 Family Members

The 6802, a truly third-generation version of the 6800, features an onchip clock plus 128 bytes of internal RAM that can be used as the stack. Just two chips (the 6802 and 6848 ROM–I/O–timer) can constitute a complete small system, as Fig. 2-8 illustrates.

The 6809 is an enhanced upgrade of the 6800 and features 16-bit operations and powerful data processing instructions like multiply and divide.

The 6500 Family

The 6500 series of microprocessors are direct descendants of Motorola 6800 technology. The MOS Technology people, however, took a somewhat different approach than Zilog did with the Z80 in enhancing an existing processor. The 6500 and 6800 microprocessors have similar architectures and instruction sets, but the 6502's instruction set has no upward compatibility with the 6800 as does the Z80 with the 8080. Although many identical-in-name-and-function instructions are used, the operation codes (or *opcodes,* as they're commonly called) are totally different. A 6800 program cannot run on a 6502 without major revision.

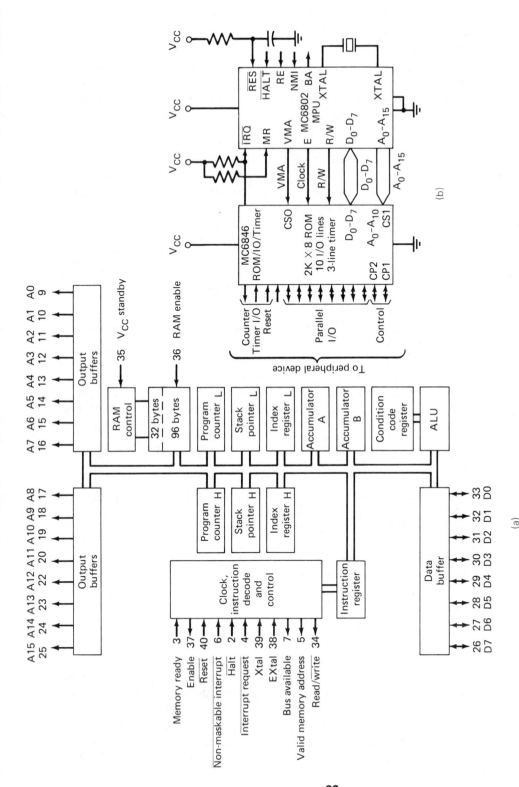

Figure 2-8 The 6802 and its application in a complete two-chip system. (a) 6802 microprocessor. (b) Complete microcomputer built with just two parts. (Courtesy Motorola Semiconductor Products, Phoenix, Arizona.)

60

Purpose.   Not surprisingly, the 6502 also shares a common purpose with the 6800. It's a general-purpose CPU featuring twos' complement arithmetic as well as control capabilities and therefore performs very well in data processing. One of the original design goals of the 6500 series was to reduce the cost of microprocessors. At the time it was introduced, microprocessors of this type were selling for about $100. Although the 6502 offered substantial savings then, the costs of microprocessors on the whole has dropped enough to make the cost benefit negligible.

Features.   We focus here on the features of the most common microprocessor in the 6500 family—the 6502. Architecturally, the 6502 uses a slow clock with many operations per clock cycle. Most operations execute in 2 or 3 clock cycles. It is a memory-oriented machine with only one accumulator (as opposed to the 6800's dual accumulators) and features two 8-bit index registers whose values are used to form index offsets. Figure 2-9 shows the 6502.

Stack capabilities are provided, but stack size is limited to 256 words because of the 8-bit stack pointer. The location of the 256-byte stack is always assumed to be 0100_{16} to $01FF_{16}$. For control applications—and indeed even in general-purpose processing—a stack size of 256 is usually adequate unless subroutines are nested very deeply or you happen to be a stack-oriented programmer.

In the addressing department, the 6502 has one mode that neither the 8080 or 6800 series has—indirect addressing. An indirect instruction consists of two bytes: one opcode byte and one offset byte that helps form a 16-bit address. The value of the 16-bit address represents the storage location where the data can be found.

Interface Methods.   The 6500-series processors use an I/O philosophy that is nearly identical to the 6800's. Memory-mapped I/O and DMA are the major features of these microprocessors. The fact that the 6500's most commonly used interface chip, the 6520 PIA, is identical and interchangeable with the 6800-series peripheral interface adapter (the 6820 PIA) says a lot about the I/O similarities of these processors.

One important thing should be noted about the DMA capabilities of the 6500 series. The address and data buses cannot be disabled separately, and there is no *halt* state. DMA can be handled by interleaving CPU processing and processing *wait* states. Since the 6500 series microprocessors are not well suited to DMA operations, it would be wise to choose the 6800 instead of the 6502 in applications requiring extensive DMA.

Support.   The 6502 is fairly well supported in both hardware and software areas. A few dedicated 6502 support chips, including the 6520 PIA and 6522 PIA plus two timers, are available, and many of the 6800-series support chips will work with the 6502 with little or no external matching circuitry.

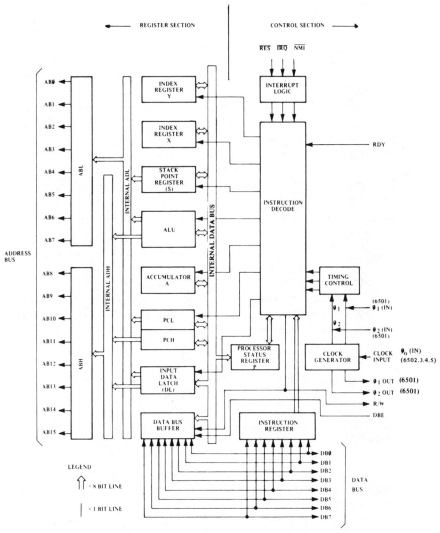

NOTE: 1. CLOCK GENERATOR IS NOT INCLUDED ON MCS6501.
2. ADDRESSING CAPABILITY AND CONTROL OPTIONS VARY WITH
EACH OF THE MCS650X PRODUCTS.

MCS 6502 8-Bit Microprocessor

Manufacturer	MOS Technology
Device Technology	NMOS
Data word width	8 bits
Addressing range	65,536 words
Instruction width	8 bits
Instruction count	56
Clock frequency	20 kHz–2 MHz
Package	40-pin DIP
Power requirements	5 V at 140 mA

Programmer's Eye View

8 bits	Accumulator A
8 bits	Index register X
8 bits	Index register Y
16 bits	Program counter PC
8 bits	Stack pointer SP
8 bits	Status register

Figure 2-9   The MOS Technology 6502 microprocessor. (Courtesy MOS Technology, Norristown, Pa.)

62

The 6502 has no software commonality with the 6800, but a good software support base has been developed by 6502 manufacturers and users. Editors, assemblers, cross assemblers, a math package, and even a FORTRAN compiler are available.

Hardware prototyping is supported by the KIM-1 and TIM microcomputer cards. Software development is supported by MOS Technology's MD2 650 development terminal and Rockwell's *System 65*, which features dual floppy disks.

Physical Characteristics.   The 6502 is available from three manufacturers in 1 or 2 MHz clock versions. It requires a single 5-volt power supply and dissipates about 750 mW of power. An onboard clock is included on many of the 6500-series microprocessors. The 6500 processors equipped with internal clocks output both phase 1 and phase 2 clock signals for timing uses by memory and interfaces.

Other 6500 Family Members

MOS Technology has chosen to expand the 6500 series of microprocessors horizontally instead of vertically. The 6500 is available in 10 versions, some with 40 pins and some with only 28 pins. Various memory addressing and control signal options are available.

SPECIAL-PURPOSE MICROPROCESSORS

So far we've discussed only the most popular microprocessors. The 8080, Z80, 6800, and 6502 clearly predominate in the microcomputer market. There are, however, many specialized microprocessors currently being used in applications in which certain features peculiar to a specialized microprocessor are desirable. In some cases this specialized feature may be power dissipation while in others it might be I/O versatility, high processing throughput, or multiply and divide capability.

The following paragraphs spotlight a few of the more common specialized microprocessors and describe the key features that make these devices desirable in special-purpose applications.

An I/O-Oriented Microprocessor: The F8

The Fairchild F8 microcomputer is well suited for use in I/O intensive applications. Unlike the single-chip 8085 and 6802, the F8 requires at least two chips to make a minimal system. These ICs are not merely bit-slice chips; they are separate operational pieces of the overall F8 architecture. This form of partitioning allows you to build a microcomputer or microcontroller in a customized I/O configuration.

The main chip in the F8 family is the 3850 CPU. Like most CPUs, this device contains an 8-bit arithmetic logic unit, control unit, and system bus interfaces for input and output. The CPU even contains a 64-byte scratchpad RAM and clock generator. These features were quite advanced and unique to the F8 when it was first introduced, before the advent of one-chip microcomputers. Figure 2-10 shows the 3850 CPU.

The main difference between the F8 and standard 8085- and 6800-type microprocessors is that the 3850 CPU has no program counter, data counter, or stack pointer on the CPU chip. These counters are instead placed on the interface and memory chips and are therefore duplicated many times if many memory and I/O chips are used. Six bytes of the scratchpad RAM are set aside to store program-counter and data-pointer addresses. The addresses are sent out to the memories over the I/O channels instead of the more common address bus.

The distributed addressing characteristics of the F8 give this micro family its good I/O capabilities. Because no 16-bit address bus is needed for a program address, many pins are freed for I/O use. The 16 pins on the CPU chip are divided into two 8-bit I/O ports.

Because all memory units have their own program counters and address registers, which all clock simultaneously, it would seem that many memory conflicts would arise. But this is avoided by assigning a unique addressing space in memory to each device.

Other chips in the F8 family include the 3851 1K ROM and I/O timer, the 3852 and 3853 dynamic and static memory interfaces, the 3854 DMA control unit, the 3861 peripheral I/O and timer chip, and a few other ROMs.

Mostek, an F8 second-source manufacturer, has produced the 3870, which is a complete single-chip microcomputer version of the F8. The 3870 not only includes the standard 3850 CPU but features a 2K ROM, lower power consumption (350 mW versus 700 mW for the 3850), a single 5-volt power supply (the +12 V supply has been eliminated), and a per-chip cost of less than $10 (in "quantity" buys).

The F8 has found wide use in the field of video games due to the large number of input interfaces (joysticks, switches, and control paddles) and output interfaces (video displays, score counters, and flashing lights) that seem to be the hallmark of electronic games. In these applications, the F8's specialized feature—its versatile I/O capability—has helped reduce interface complexity and cost.

A Low-Power Microprocessor:
The 1802 COSMAC

Power dissipation is not usually a top-priority item in the design of a microcomputer. Most microprocessors only draw a watt or two of power; the power consumption of the memories and interface components overshadows the mi-

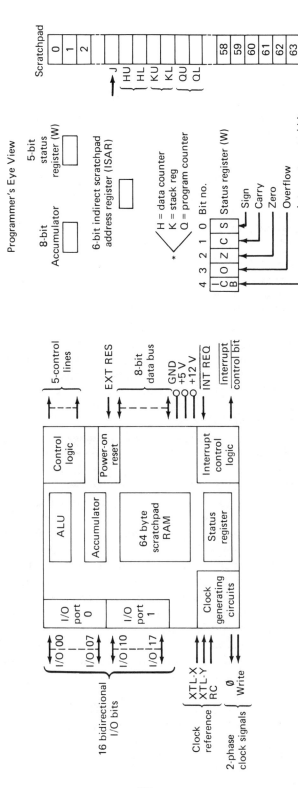

Figure 2-10 The Fairchild 3850 F8 CPU. (Courtesy Fairchild Camera and Instrument Corporation, Mountain View, Ca.)

croprocessor power draw. In the microcomputer field there is, however, one route left open to people who need a system that consumes a very small amount of power; that route is the COSMAC CMOS microprocessor supported by CMOS RAMs and CMOS interface circuitry. The COSMAC's low power dissipation has made it one of the most popular of the available special-feature microprocessors.

The COSMAC has a fairly primitive architecture, which is better suited to low-end controller applications than data processing tasks. The architecture is based on sixteen 16-bit general-purpose registers that are referenced by three 4-bit pointer registers. The registers can be designated as data pointers, program counters, I/O, or general-purpose registers by the programmer. This versatility allows you to set aside a few program counters for subroutine use. Figure 2-11 shows the COSMAC's architecture.

Three of the sixteen registers—R0, R1, and R2—are allocated for special functions. The R0 register is used as a transfer address register during DMA operations. When an external device references memory directly in the DMA mode, it steals one machine cycle and stores or fetches data from the address specified by R0. The R0 register is automatically incremented after a DMA transfer, leaving R0 pointing to the next data location. This unique built-in transfer address register cuts down significantly on the amount of hardware required to implement a DMA interface. No external 16-bit transfer address register or address bus driving circuitry is required, as it would be in a standard DMA interface.

More hardware savings can be realized in interrupt-driven I/O application when using the COSMAC. In most computers' interrupt-driven I/O systems, the interrupting peripheral's interface requests that the processor interrupt its current program and temporarily transfer control to an I/O program handling that peripheral's data communication. The interface then drives the microprocessor's data or address bus (depending on the microprocessor) with the address of the I/O program so the processor knows where to jump to execute the program and "service the peripheral." A set of bus drivers are needed to put this jump address on the bus. The COSMAC eliminates the need for this set of drivers by defining register R1 as the interrupt jump address.

The final dedicated register, R2, serves as a subroutine status-storing stack pointer. The COSMAC stack feature is not very powerful, however, and cannot be used to process data in general-purpose processing applications.

The actual power consumption of the COSMAC depends heavily on clock rate, power supply voltage, and even on the instruction being performed. As Fig. 2-12 illustrates, power consumption can be as low as 600 μW or as high as 5 mW.

The 1802 COSMAC is used extensively in battery-powered processors and portable equipment in which low thermal dissipation is required. Being a CMOS device, the COSMAC is very immune to electrical noise and input voltage variations.

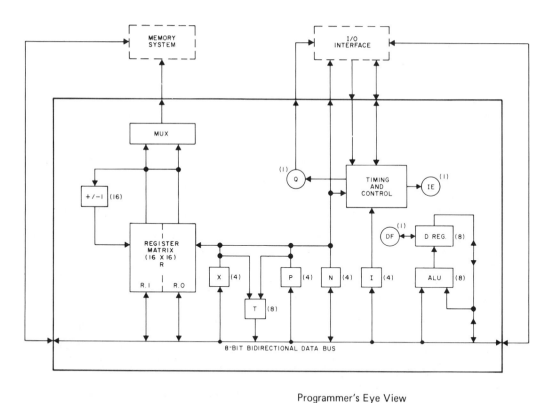

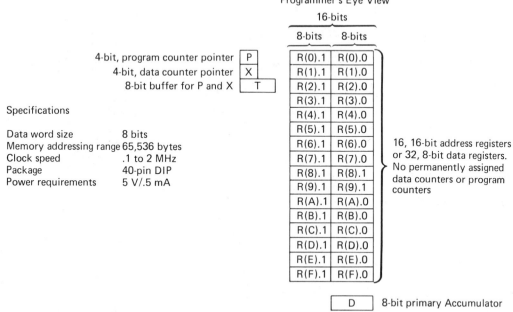

Programmer's Eye View

16-bits

8-bits	8-bits
R(0).1	R(0).0
R(1).1	R(1).0
R(2).1	R(2).0
R(3).1	R(3).0
R(4).1	R(4).0
R(5).1	R(5).0
R(6).1	R(6).0
R(7).1	R(7).0
R(8).1	R(8).1
R(9).1	R(9).1
R(A).1	R(A).0
R(B).1	R(B).0
R(C).1	R(C).0
R(D).1	R(D).0
R(E).1	R(E).0
R(F).1	R(F).0

4-bit, program counter pointer [P]
4-bit, data counter pointer [X]
8-bit buffer for P and X [T]

16, 16-bit address registers or 32, 8-bit data registers. No permanently assigned data counters or program counters

Specifications

Data word size	8 bits
Memory addressing range	65,536 bytes
Clock speed	.1 to 2 MHz
Package	40-pin DIP
Power requirements	5 V/.5 mA

[D] 8-bit primary Accumulator

Figure 2-11 The 1802 COSMAC's power dissipation characteristics. (Courtesy RCA Solid State, Somerville, N.J.)

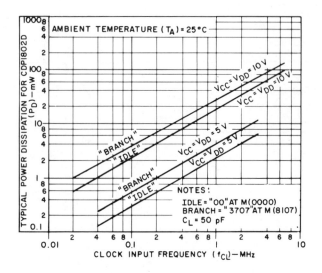

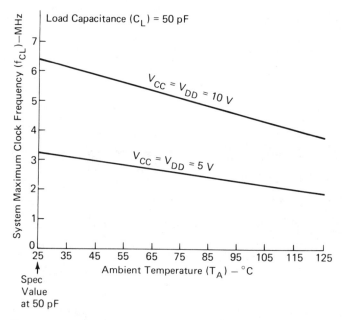

Typical power dissipation as a function of clock frequency for BRANCH instruction and IDLE instruction for CDP1802D.

Typical maximum clock frequency as a function of temperature.

Figure 2-12 The RCA 1802 COSMAC CMOS microprocessor. (Courtesy RCA Solid State, Somerville, N.J.)

Software support for the 1802 includes a resident and cross assembler, a simulator, a firmware debug package, and a floppy-disk-based development system. A high-level interpretive language is also available.

COSMAC hardware support includes the 1852 8-bit I/O port, 1854 CMOS UART and many other CMOS LSI parts that are part of RCA's extensive CMOS line.

The COSMAC microprocessor has been available in one form or another (the older 1801 COSMAC was a two-chip set) for many years, and to this day remains the only CMOS 8-bit microprocessor. For extremely low-power processing applications, the COSMAC is the only choice.

HIGH-PERFORMANCE MICROPROCESSORS

Some applications have one general requirement: the need for vast amounts of processing power. Data processing and scientific computing that require many arithmetic operations (including multiplication and division) are cases in point. A few years ago, only a minicomputer or mainframe could have efficiently handled these large processing tasks, but today's LSI technology allows the fabrication of microprocessors that perform as fast or faster than the minicomputers of a few years back. These powerful processors are usually 16-bit devices, many of which are built around minicomputer instruction sets in order to maintain software compatibility with existing program libraries.

The first two 16-bit upward-compatible microcomputers to enter the market were the Digital Equipment Corporation LSI-11 and the Texas Instruments TMS 9900, patterned after the PDP-11 and TI 990 series minicomputers. Since the introduction of these two microprocessors, other manufacturers have followed suit in concept. Table 2-1 lists a few of the current microprocessors and the minicomputers with which they maintain a compatibility with regard to instruction sets.

While the minicomputer-like microcomputers bring near-mini performance down to the micro level, a new generation of powerful 16-bit microcomputers

Table 2-1 Upward-Compatible Microcomputers

Microprocessor Part Number	Manufacturer	Compatible Minicomputer
TMS9900	Texas Instruments	TI's 990 series
IM6100	Intersil	Digital Equipment Corporation PDP-8
LS1-11	Digital Equipment	Digital Equipment Corporation PDP-11
9440	Fairchild Semicon	Data General Nova
mN601	Data General	Data General Nova
MCP-1600	Western Digital	Similar to DEC PDP-11

has evolved from the common 8-bit microprocessors. Extended and enhanced 16-bit versions of existing 8-bit microprocessors are now being introduced. The Motorola 6809 and 68000, Intel 8086, and Zilog Z8000, fall into this category.

A few representatives from both high-performance 16-bit categories will now be examined. Many experts feel that these processors will replace simple 8-bit micros and even minicomputers in many areas in the near future, so you should be familiar with these high-performance devices.

The TMS 9900 Family

One of the first 16-bit one-chip microprocessors was Texas Instruments' TMS 9900. Unlike the Digital Equipment Corporation LSI-11, which comes as a three-chip set, the TMS 9900 is one large chip in a 64-pin package. Figure 2-13 shows the primary physical characteristics.

Purpose.   The TMS 9900 was initially intended to be a central processing unit that could successfully compete with minicomputers in scientific applications. It is definitely intended to be a "data processing" type of microprocessor and would be considered overkill in all but the most complex controller applications.

Features.   The TMS 9900 is a 16-bit NMOS microprocessor that runs with a maximum clock rate of 3 MHz (four clock phases are required). The architecture follows the philosophy of high-speed clock with many small operations per cycle. A simple add operation takes 14 to 30 clock cycles, depending on the addressing mode. The TMS 9900 isn't very fast with simple character-manipulating operations, and this is attributable to the number of cycles it takes to perform simple operations.

The TMS 9900 is a memory-oriented machine whose structure consists of a program counter, status register, and workspace pointer. The work-space-register concept employed in the TMS 9900 is quite interesting: Instead of having a bank of general-purpose registers like the 8080 and COSMAC—or even dual sets of registers like the Z80—the device uses 16 memory locations for its working registers. The location of these registers in memory is determined by the workspace pointer. Once the workspace pointer is set to the proper location in memory, the 16 memory locations beyond the pointer can be referenced with simple 4-bit offsets that can be thought of as register labels (0_{16}–F_{16}). The workspace registers allow great flexibility in subroutine nesting and interrupt processing, since saving the machine's registers is simply a matter of changing and restoring the workspace pointer and using a fresh block of 16 registers in the interrupt service routine or subroutine.

The TMS 9900's memory structure reflects its lineage from the world of large computers. For its sophisticated minicomputer-like interrupt system, many of the lowest and highest memory locations are reserved for initialization trap vectors and interrupt service vectors.

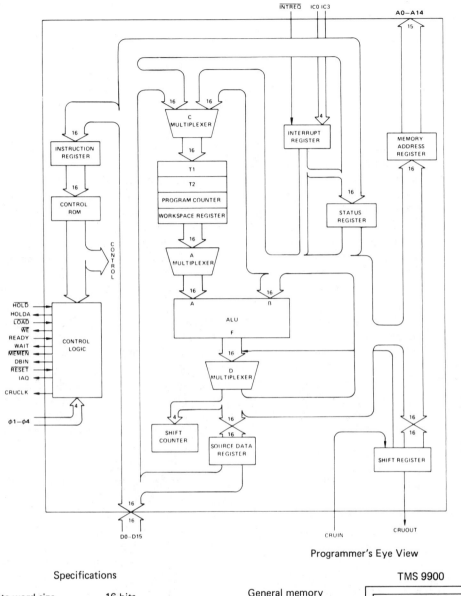

Programmer's Eye View

Specifications

Data word size	16 bits
Memory address range	32,768 bytes
Clock speed	500 kHz to 4 MHz
Package	64-pin DIP
Power requirements	5 V/75 mA
	12 V/40 mA
	−5 V/0.1 mA

Figure 2-13 The Texas Instruments TMS 9900 microprocessor. (Courtesy Texas Instruments, Inc., Dallas, Texas.)

Although the TMS 9900 doesn't transfer or add words very quickly, there are two features that drastically increase its throughput in arithmetic applications: its 16-bit precision and its built-in multiply and divide capability. A 16-bit multiply or divide takes about 400 microseconds using inline code (no loop counting) on a 4 MHz Z80, and it takes only 18 to 42 microseconds on the TMS 9900.

Interface Characteristics.   Three I/O methods are used in the TMS 9900: memory-mapped I/O, DMA I/O, and communication register unit or CRU register transfer I/O. Memory-mapped I/O and DMA transfer operations are quite standard and are similar in operation to the 6800's I/O scheme, but the CRU transfer, which is unique to the TMS 9900, deserves a closer examination.

Texas Instruments reasoned that board layout and parallel-data-bus complexity could be reduced if some sort of serial data transfer capability was incorporated into the microprocessor. In addition to being able to read or write a bit-stream of data, TI wanted the TMS 9900 to be able to selectively control the bits it was sending and receiving. The solution to these problems was the CRU system.

A serial input line (CRUIN), a serial output line (CRUOUT) and a synchronizing clock (CRUCLK) are provided, as shown in Fig. 2-14. Serially shifting n bits of a word stored at memory location x is simply a matter of invoking the LDCR X, N instruction (load CRU register with n bits from location x). As the specified bits are serially shifted out the CRUOUT output line, the addresses on the address lines are constantly incremented. The first address on the address lines in this transfer sequence is specified by workspace register 12. The incrementing address lines can thus be used to multiplex the serial bits out to different locations using an external multiplexer. Figure 2-14 gives an example of an address-driven multiplexing CRU application.

The CRU I/O concept can indeed cut down on interface complexity in some cases, but the CRU method of I/O transfers hasn't been accepted and isn't being incorporated in other microprocessors. A reason may be that it is a difficult concept to grasp unless you've worked with CRU transfers before.

Interrupt-driven I/O is easily handled by the 16-level priority-interrupt system. The TMS 9900 has fairly simple and straightforward electrical interface characteristics. Address, data, and control information flow on a 16-bit address bus, a 16-bit data bus, and a 15-bit control bus. TMS 9900 inputs are high impedance and reduce loading on the internal bus drivers. The need for bus drivers and receiver chips is thereby eliminated in small systems, but larger systems require many bus drivers due to the wide 16-bit data bus. With more than 32 lines to buffer at each peripheral interface, interface "component counts" rise rapidly.

A 4-phase clock must be generated for the TMS 9900. A TIM 9904 is available to perform this task, but it means that another interface part is added to the system.

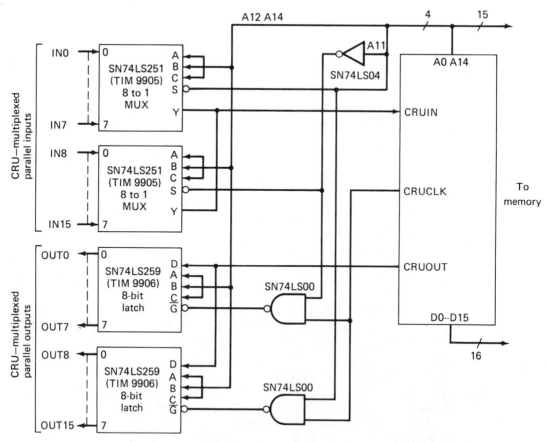

Figure 2-14   The TMS 9900's CRU input and output system. (Courtesy Texas Instruments, Inc., Dallas, Texas.)

Support.   A 9901 programmable interface chip, a 9902 asynchronous interface chip, and the 9904 clock driver help support the TMS 9900 on the hardware level.

Software support for the microprocessor is no problem. Because it is patterned after the TMS 990 minicomputer's instruction set, assemblers, editors, FORTRAN, BASIC and even a program library are available to all users. A high-order language called PL/9900 eases real-time programming tasks.

Other 9900 Family Members.   The 9900 comes in an I²L version called the SBP-9900. A single-phase 4 MHz clock is required, and performance is increased since I²L is a bipolar device technology.

A down-sized 8-bit-data-bus version of the TMS 9900, called the TMS 9980, is also available. This part comes in a 40-pin package, is cheaper than the TMS 9900, and is better suited to controller-type applications.

The MC6809

Motorola has taken the enhanced 8-bit microcomputer approach in entering the mid-performance 16-bit microprocessor market. By extending the existing 6800 instruction set, increasing the number of memory addressing modes, adding true 16-bit arithmetic capabilities, and providing an 8- by 8-bit multiply instruction, the 6809 has become a powerful processor that is well suited for complex data processing tasks.

Features. The MC6809 is designed to operate in both 8-bit and 16-bit modes. A complete set of 8-bit instructions with mnemonics identical to those for the 6800 is incorporated. Although object code cannot be transferred directly from the 6800 due to the different opcodes, old 6800 source programs will run if assembled with a 6809 assembler. And they will run more efficiently as a result of architectural improvements.

Because the 6800-series microprocessors are memory-oriented, the 6809 has been designed to operate more efficiently in memory-intensive data processing modes.

Figure 2-15 illustrates the MC6809's architecture and enhanced instructions. When comparing the MC6809 to the 6800, the increase in the number of registers becomes obvious. A user stack pointer, an additional index register, and a direct page register have been added. It is interesting to note that Motorola stuck to its dual-accumulator architecture philosophy. The new registers are not data-manipulation or general-purpose in nature but are rather enhancements to the processor control and addressing capabilities.

One of the biggest complaints programmers had about the 6800 was its total absence of long conditional branches. Only short (127-byte) relative branches were possible. This situation is totally remedied in the MC6809. A full complement of long branch instructions is now available. This improvement is in keeping with Motorola's philosophy: "make it easy to program." Table 2-2 shows the new 16-bit instructions.

The 6800 microcomputer has always been looked on as an 8-bit PDP-11. The instruction set is very similar, and extensive addressing capabilities are present in both machines. The MC6809 moves one step closer to the full addressing capabilities of the PDP-11 with the introduction of autoincrement addressing. This mode is very valuable when sequentially indexing through data because no index updating commands are required. Table 2-3 presents the new addressing modes; note that autoincrement by one *and* by two are available for both 8-bit and 16-bit operating modes.

One final feature that is new to the MC6809 is the SYNC instruction. Executing this instruction stops processing and causes the processor to wait until it receives an external interrupt before resuming its operation. This feature is said to be useful for synchronizing software to events in the real world, but it will also find use in synchronizing many processors in a multiprocessor system.

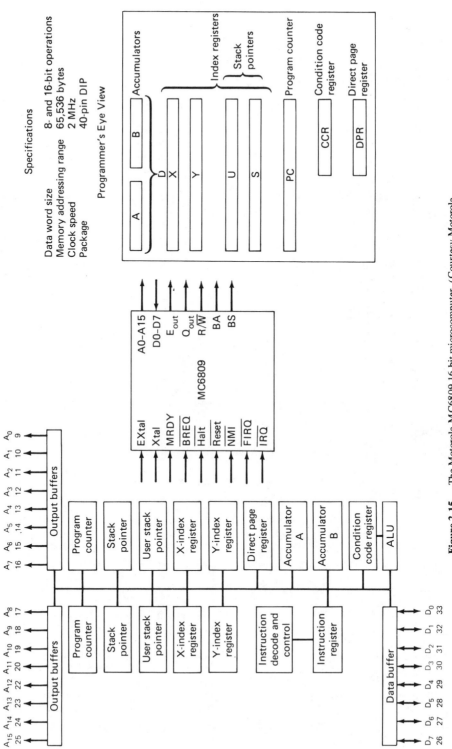

Figure 2-15 The Motorola MC6809 16-bit microcomputer. (Courtesy Motorola Semiconductor Products, Phoenix, Arizona.)

75

Table 2-2   The Motorola 6809's 16-bit Instructions

Instruction	Description
ADDD	Add memory to D accumulator
SUBD	Subtract memory from D accumulator
LDD	Load D accumulator from memory
STD	Store D accumulator to memory
CMPD	Compare D accumulator with memory
LDX, LDY, LDS, LDU	Load pointer register from memory
STX, STY, STS, STU	Store pointer register to memory
CMPX, CMPY, CMPU, CMPS	Compare pointer register with memory
LEAX, LEAY, LEAU, LEAS	Load effective address into index register
SEX	Sign Extend D accumulator
TFR register, register	Transfer register to register
EXG register, register	Exchange register to register
PSHS (register) $^7_1$	Push register(s) onto hardware stack
PSHU (register) $^7_1$	Push register(s) onto user stack
PULS (register) $^7_1$	Pull register(s) from hardware stack
PULU (register) $^7_1$	Pull register(s) from user stack

Table 2-3   The Motorola 6809 Indexed Addressing Modes

Mode	Effective Address (EA)	Description
,R	EA = R	Indexed with zero offset
[O, R]	EA = [R]	Indexed with zero offset indirect
,R+	EA = R; R+ 1 → R	Autoincrement by 1
,R++	EA = R; R+ 2 → R	Autoincrement by 2
[,R++]	EA = [R]; R+ 2 → R	Autoincrement by 2 indirect
,−R	R−1 → R;EA =R	Autodecrement by 1
,−−R	R−2 → R;EA =R	Autodecrement by 2
[,−−R]	R−2 → R;EA =[R]	Autodecrement by 2 indirect
N,R	EA = R+N	Indexed with signed N as offset (N = 5,.8, or 16 bits)
[N,R]	EA = [R+N]	Indexed with signed N as offset indirect (N = 5, 8, or 16 bits)
A,R	EA = R+A	Indexed with signed accumulator A as offset
[A,R]	EA = [R+A]	Indexed with signed accumulator A as offset indirect
B,R	EA = R+B	Indexed with signed accumulator B as offset
[B,R]	EA = [R+B]	Indexed with signed accumulator B as offset indirect
D,R	EA = R+D	Indexed with accumulator D as offset
[D,R]	EA = [R+D]	Indexed with accumulator D as offset indirect

R = X, Y, U, or S register

76

Interface Characteristics.   The MC6809 uses the same memory-mapped I/O methods employed on the 6800, 6801, and 6802 microprocessors. The external pinout of the 40-pin device is in fact nearly identical to the 6802; two pins are assigned as crystal inputs, since the 6809 has a built-in clock to which an outboard quartz crystal can be connected.

Support.   The wide selection of 6800 peripheral chips will all work with the MC6809. A unique assembler that handles 6800 assembler source code as well as all the new MC6809 instructions is also available. The EXORciser development system is also compatible with the new MC6809.

The 8086

Intel took the same approach as Motorola when it entered the market with its 16-bit high-performance microcomputer. By enhancing and upgrading an existing processor, the 8080, Intel managed to create one of the highest performance microprocessors available today. The objectives of the 8086 design were to provide up to ten times the performance of the 8080A while maintaining software compatibility at the assembly-language level. These goals were met by improving and expanding the 8080 architecture and by employing a new device technology.

The 8086 is the first microprocessor on the market to use the new silicon-gate short channel HMOS process. This process makes the 8086 faster as well as more reliable than a similar product fabricated from regular NMOS.

Features.   The 8080 was primarily a controller. Signed arithmetic, arithmetic-conditional branching, and arithmetic shifts were not possible. All of these problems have been eliminated on the 8086. A complete set of 8- by 16-bit signed or unsigned arithmetic operations including both 8-bit and 16-bit multiplies are available (remember, the 6809 only had an 8-bit multiply).

The 8086 has an expanded register set, also. Figure 2-16 illustrates the new registers. The general-purpose working registers of the 8080 (H, L, B, C, D) are retained but are now the A, B, C, and D 16-bit registers. Base pointer, source index, and destination index registers add to the indexed addressing capabilities of the 8086, and a whole block of relocation registers has been provided to support the 8086's automatic software relocation feature. The 8086 can address up to 1 million bytes as 64K pieces with a 20-bit address generated using the relocation feature.

The 8080 is much less sophisticated than the 6800 and 6502 in the way it handles instruction fetching and execution. The 8080 waits until it needs instructions before fetching them and finally executing them, while the 6800 and 6502 fetch instructions ahead of time and have them ready when the processor needs them. This form of instruction lookahead overlaps computations with memory operations (the next instruction is fetched while the current instruction

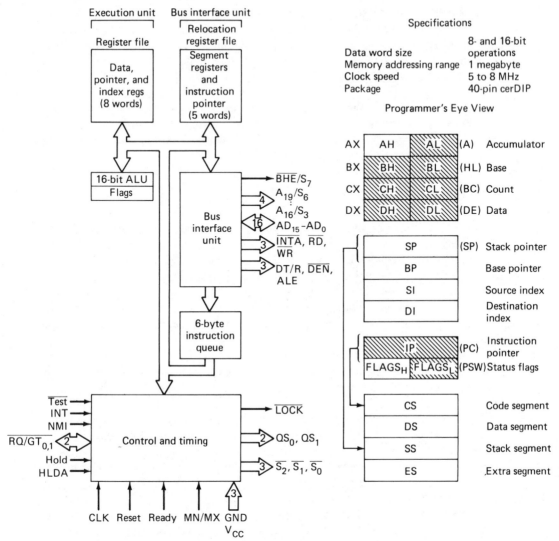

Figure 2-16   Intel's 8086 16-bit microprocessor. (Reprinted by permission of Intel Corporation, Copyright 1978)

is being executed). Instruction lookahead has been successfully used on large computers for many years. The 8086 does incorporate an instruction lookahead feature, which helps increase its operating speed.

The 8086 is actually two processors in one package. The *bus interface unit* (BIU) handles instruction fetching and maintains a queue of six instructions. In other words, the 8086 looks ahead by six instructions and uses nonmemory access cycles to keep the instruction queue full. The instructions are actually executed by the *instruction execution unit* (IEU), which performs the typical microprocessor instruction tasks; but instead of fetching instructions from memory, it fetches them from the instruction queue.

The six-instruction queue has a few big advantages other than the inherent speedup of processing due to instruction fetch–execution overlap. Since instructions are stored in the queue, the processor is not slowed down by DMA operations (at least not by light DMA transfers). A direct memory access by another device on the bus won't delay the fetching of an instruction by the IEU, because the EIU gets its instructions from the instruction queue rather than from memory. When the DMA operation is finished, the BIU "hurries" to fill the instruction queue, which has been depleted by the lack of memory-to-queue fetches. By optimizing memory use in this way, the 8086 makes the most out of the memory's maximum throughput rate (memory bandwidth).

Intel has gone to great lengths to make the 8086 easy to program and easier for a compiler to generate code for. A complete set of string-manipulation instructions result in simplified text and list processing in business data processing applications, and the dual index registers and stack pointer make modular and stack-oriented compiled programs easy to implement. Relative addressing is also included for software simplicity and for object-code reduction.

Interface Characteristics. The 8086 comes in a 40-pin ceramic dual-inline package (40-pin cerDIP) and interfaces to I/O devices in the same way as the 8080. Intel has again reverted to the three-package-microprocessor concept. As in the case of the 8080, a clock generator chip (8284 in this case) and a bipolar bus controller (8288) are needed to make the 8086 into a reasonable system. (The 8288 can be omitted in minimal configurations, however.)

Support. Support software for the 8086 is well thought out, and anyone owning Intel's MDS 8080-based development system will have no trouble developing 8086 programs. By using a new assembler, old 8080 source code can be compiled into new 8086 object code, and all the new instructions can be used on new programs.

The new ASM86 8086 assembler is one of the finest assemblers available in the microprocessor field and offers a comprehensive macro facility, piece-by-piece modular assembly, and absolute or relocatable object-code generation.

Physical Characteristics. The HMOS device technology has given the 8086 state-of-the-art specifications. The 8086 contains 29,000 transistors, runs on a single 5-volt power supply, and has a clock rate of 5 to 8 MHz (depending on the part version). Memory cycle time is 500 ns for the 8 MHz part, which makes the use of a high-performance RAM (such as Intel's matching HMOS 2147 4K RAM) imperative.

The Z8000

Zilog took a unique approach in the development of a high-performance 16-bit microprocessor. Unlike most manufacturers, who took either a minicomputer and scaled it down or a simple 8-bit microprocessor and enhanced it, Zilog started from scratch and took a no-holds-barred approach to processing power. By taking all the advanced design features of large minicomputers and mainframes, (notably the DEC PDP-11 and IBM 370) the company produced a very powerful microprocessor: the Z8000. The Z8000 is, in fact, the first microprocessor aimed at the high-end minicomputer market rather than the low-end market of micros that "approach minicomputer performance." A Z8000 microprocessor running at a mere 4 MHz provides twice to five times the performance of a Digital Equipment Corporation PDP-11/35 and even outperforms the PDP-11/45 in many applications.

Features. The Z8000 is in no way compatible at the assembly or compiler language level with the Z80; the advanced architecture ruled out any similarities. Instead, the Z8000 has a repertoire of 110 unique instructions that include powerful macroinstructions such as block searches and string manipulations.

The Z8000 has an interesting memory addressing scheme. Zilog realized that many users would be perfectly satisfied with a 16-bit address field, while some specialized applications would require a much larger addressing space. Therefore, the Z8000 comes in two configurations: a 40-pin version is available for 16-bit addressing, and a 48-pin version can be used when up to 48 megabytes of memory are required (a segmented 24-bit address is used to accomplish the task). Even the fastest-moving memory technologies will have trouble surpassing this memory addressing range.

Support. Zilog supplies unique support and application software for the Z8000. Compilers for BASIC, COBOL and FORTRAN are planned. A lower-level programming language called PL/Z is also available for the Z8000.

BIT-SLICED MICROPROCESSORS

Over the years, large computers and other large digital devices have advanced from one technology to another. The original mechanical and vacuum-tube logic designs were replaced by transistor equivalents. Small-scale integrated circuits then entered the picture.

The first generation of SSI was introduced in 1965, when three to six gates were available on chips costing from $10 to $20 each. The 7400 series of logic elements made its debut a short time later, with gates and dual flip-flops being the most advanced element in the 7400 line.

In the late sixties and early seventies, device technology matured to the extent that counters, shift registers, and complete arithmetic units could be put onto a single chip. This second generation of integration, called medium-scale integration or MSI, caused packages to increase in size from 14 pins to 16 and 24 pins. The problem was no longer squeezing a few hundred gates onto a chip, but rather finding enough pins to bring the terminals of these gates out to the real world.

Up until the early seventies, bipolar logic (TTL, DTL, and ECL) dominated the picture. The early seventies marked a turning point in logic design. Metal-oxide semiconductor (MOS) technology developed to the point at which complete control units could be built on one large-scale integrated (LSI) circuit, and many slow-speed logic designs started using MOS microprocessors to replace the unnecessarily fast, power-consuming bipolar MSI logic. High-performance applications, however, were still being implemented with bipolar MSI.

While the MOS microprocessor advanced through approximately four generations of refinements, bipolar logic also advanced. More and more devices were put onto single chips, and more complex functional building blocks were used due to the limited number of input and output pins on a single package. These LSI bipolar functions finally became so complex that they began to resemble microprocessors. Microprogram sequencers began to be called control units and powerful register file/ALUs began to be called bit-sliced CPUs. In reality, the new bit-sliced microprocessors are just logical extensions of standard bipolar logic families. Two cases in point are the Texas Instruments 74481 series, which is an extension of the 7400 TTL line, and the Motorola 10800, which is an extension of the MECL 10000 series.

For high-performance applications, such as mainframes, high-level minicomputers, high-frequency instrumentation, and high-speed dedicated logic, bipolar logic is still the best in terms of pure performance. Bipolar MSI and the new bipolar bit-sliced microprocessors are currently being used in these applications.

One of the most popular bipolar bit-sliced microprocessors is the 2900, which we'll examine now. We'll look at what appears to be the most powerful microprocessor in existence, the ECL 10800, in the following section.

The 2900 Family

The Advanced Micro Devices (AMD) low-power Schottky TTL 2900 series is a family of LSI logical building blocks designed for use in high-performance applications. Instead of having a one-chip structure and a fixed instruction set like most 8-bit and 16-bit MOS microprocessors, the 2900 is totally user-configurable to implement any instruction set or logical design the user chooses.

The key word for the 2900 series is *microprogramming*. Advanced Micro Devices recommends that you use one to four 4-bit microprocessor data slices (2901s), a few microprogram sequencers (2909 or 2911s), and a microprogram memory in implementing a logic design. The resulting processor executes a user's program by fetching a user's instruction out of the real microcomputer memory and sequencing through a small microprogram in microprogram memory to move data around and toggle control lines. Instructions in the microprogram memory are called *microinstructions*. These instructions are not the typical instructions that you would find in a MOS microprocessor's instruction set, but rather are wide-word-width (20 to 70 bits wide) instructions with each bit in the word controlling a unique multiplexer, ALU, or register. By defining the words in the microprogram memory properly, a 2900 system can be made to execute instructions in the same way an 8080 or 6800, or for that matter a PDP-11 or IBM 370 does. With this sort of flexibility it is obvious why many manufacturers are using 2900 series parts to build their minicomputers: less parts and identical performance.

In regard to chip counts, the 2900 series microprocessors in no way compare to MOS microprocessors. It typically takes 30 to 40 parts to implement a simple 2900 series design. The reason is twofold: In order to retain flexibility, lower-level building blocks are used in the design. Secondly, 16-bit or even 8-bit arithmetic elements are not possible due to the amount of heat generated by the bipolar circuitry.

Features.   Due to the design-it-yourself nature of the 2900 series, it is hard to talk about instruction sets, branch capabilities, and the like. Figure 2-17 illustrates a 2901 microprocessor slice. The best way to examine its characteristics is to look at its function and clock rate.

The 2901 is built around a 16-word, 4-bit two-port RAM, a high-speed 4-bit ALU, and associated shifting, decoding, and multiplexing circuitry. Nine control lines (which are intended to be driven by a microinstruction word) control the RAM and ALU. Full lookahead inputs and outputs are provided on the built-in ALU, and a 2902 high-speed carry lookahead generator can be used to cascade up to four of the 4-bit slices together to make a 16-bit ALU. Banks of 16-bit ALUs can also be cascaded to make machines with even wider word widths of 32, 48, and 64 bits.

Basically, processing is performed by moving data around within the microprocessor slice using RAM and the Q register as temporary storage locations. Data can be processed by the ALU and sent back to the RAM, or it can be output through the DATA OUT port. It's often desirable to bring data in from the outside as well, so a direct DATA IN port has been provided.

The 2901's performance varies, depending on how many bit slices are cascaded together. A 64-bit (word width) machine will run slower than a 16-bit machine due to the added ALU propagation delay, but as a general rule the 2901 can be expected to clock at 7 to 10 MHz. To get an idea of what this

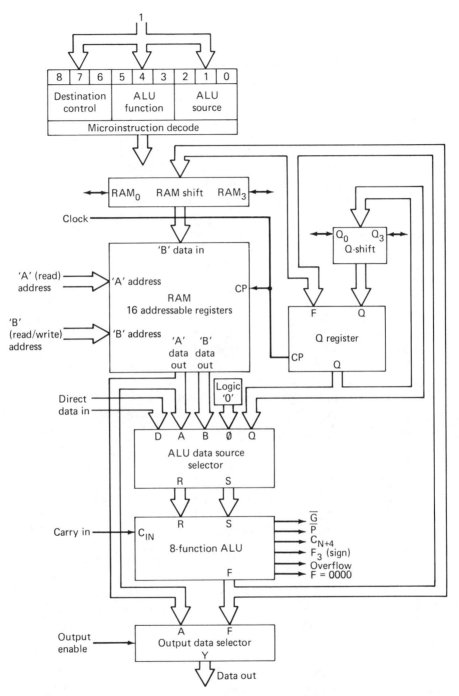

Figure 2-17   Advanced Micro Devices' 2901 bipolar microprocessor slice. (Copyright © 1978 Advanced Micro Devices, Inc. Reproduced with permission of copyright owner.)

means, performance-wise, compare the 2900's 110 ns add time to the 4 MHz Z80's 1 μs time. Bear in mind that 1μs is the equivalent of 1000 ns. Obviously, there's really no comparison.

Interface Characteristics.   Again, there is really no general well-defined way to interface to a 2900 microprocessor; you define your own interfaces. As with other bipolar designs, plenty of driving current (enough to drive about 10 other equivalent microprocessor loads) is available and little buffering is required. Figure 2-18 illustrates a 2900-based microcomputer. Notice how the I/O structure was set up. Independent bus interface registers are used to drive the data bus, and a 16-bit address bus is set up using four 2930 program control units. In this case the I/O protocol is determined by the microprogram memory contents. A similar I/O protocol and structure can be used for easy bus interfacing if you choose the 2900 for your high-performance design.

Support.   Assemblers, editors, and compilers are not available for the 2900, as no firm instruction set exists. Rather, an extensive hardware development system called *System 29* is available from AMD. Based on a 9080 (AMD's equivalent to the 8080), System 29 lets you develop and test your own designs on a software simulation and hardware breadboard basis. A universal assembler—which allows you to define the mnemonics and opcodes—is provided to accommodate almost any configuration we might come up with.

A hardware development kit called the Am2900K1 is also available as a learning and breadboarding aid.

Ancillary Devices.   In addition to the 2901 CPU, 2909–2911 microprogram sequencers, and 2902 lookahead units, the 2900 family features an interrupt expander (2913), vectored-interrupt controller (2914), and a one-by-two port register (2918). Other simpler interface components such as buffers and gates are given 2900-series designations also. All of the chips in AMD's extensive low-powered Schottky line are also compatible with 2900-series parts.

The latest addition to the 2900 family is the 2903. This unit does everything the 2901 does, but it also performs $n \times n$ multiplies in n clock cycles, divides, normalizes, and does double as well as single incrementing.

The 10800 Family

Ever since Motorola introduced its MECL 1 family of emitter-coupled logic (ECL) in the mid-sixties, competitive logic families such as TTL, MOS, and I²L have had trouble keeping up. On a pure performance basis there is still nothing that can touch the latest versions of ECL (Fairchild F100K subnanosecond logic). Large mainframes and scientific computers use ECL circuitry almost exclusively, and minicomputer makers are resorting to ECL designs to keep their CPUs competitive with the ever-threatening microprocessor. With this in mind, it is not surprising that the microprocessor with the highest processing performance is the ECL 10800 4-bit bit-sliced processor, and that Motorola, the leader in ECL technology (IBM may argue with this), introduced it.

The MC10800 is a 4-bit processor slice similar in function to the 2901 processor slice, except that it contains no register files. The user must provide an external register file. This allows the user to decide on how large a register file is necessary and doesn't limit him to 16 registers (as the 2901 does). Note that the register file is expandable in the improved 2903.

Features.   After considering the microprogram control and timing chips for the 10800 series (the 10800 uses microprogramming, too), it can be seen that the 10800 is better organized than the 2900. On the 2900 many discrete interface components were required to perform interface functions and generate an external bus (see Fig. 2-18). The 10800's support chips, however, work together in a "smoother" way and require fewer interface components. A small control memory, an MC10801 microprogram control unit, and a 10802 timing unit perform all the necessary control functions, while a dedicated memory interface chip, the MC10803, generates an external address and data bus. Figure 2-19 shows the 10800 and Fig. 2-20 illustrates a small system built out of these bit-sliced parts.

The basic ALU instruction execution time of the 10800 is 30 to 50 ns, which corresponds to a clock rate of 20 to 30 MHz. In wide-word applications, however, the clock must be run at 10 to 15 MHz to allow for ALU propagation delays. Like the 2901, the 10800 has a full carry–lookahead system.

The 10800 has one feature that no other bit-sliced processor has: it can work directly with BCD numbers. It uses a nines' complement adder circuit to simplify BCD calculations in the BCD mode.

Interface Characteristics.   As with the 2900 series, the user defines the interfaces to the 10800 microcomputer. All interface levels are ECL. Care must be taken in 10800 interfacing due to the frequencies of the signals involved. All lines must be treated as transmission lines and ECL-to-TTL level converters must be used to interface to any external TTL circuitry.

Physical Characteristics.   The 10800 parts come in 48-pin quad-inline packages (QUIL) for tight mounting configurations.

The 10800 runs on the standard -5.2 ECL power supply voltage and dissipates about 1.5 watts per 4-bit processor slice. Higher power consumption is the price we pay for speed.

Ancillary Devices.   In addition to the processor slice and its interface support chips, the 10800 series features a 5-bit ECL/TTL level translator (10804), a 32-× 9-bit register (10806) for building the register file, and a 16-bit programmable shifter (10808).

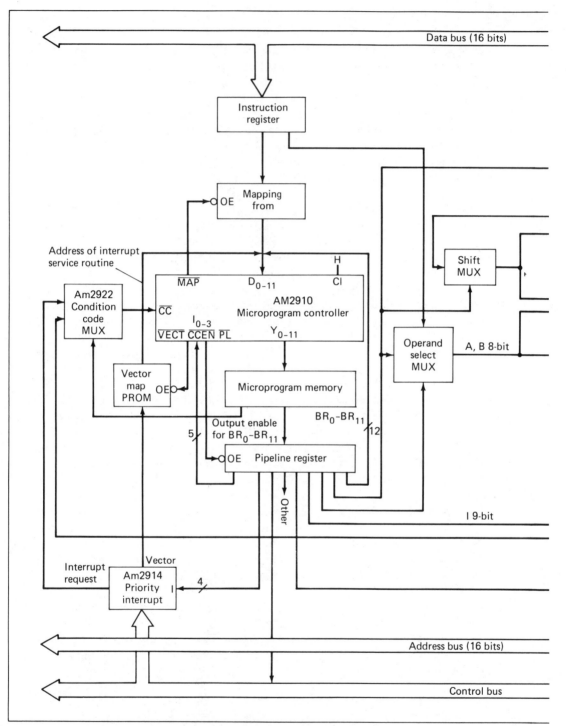

Figure 2-18   A complete microcomputer system built out of 2900-series parts. (Copyright © 1978 Advanced Micro Devices, Inc. Reproduced with permission of copyright owners.)

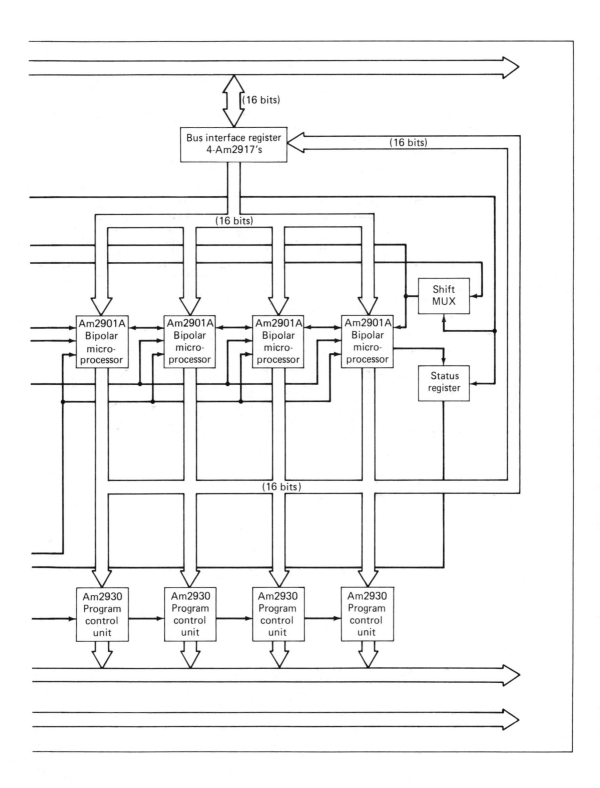

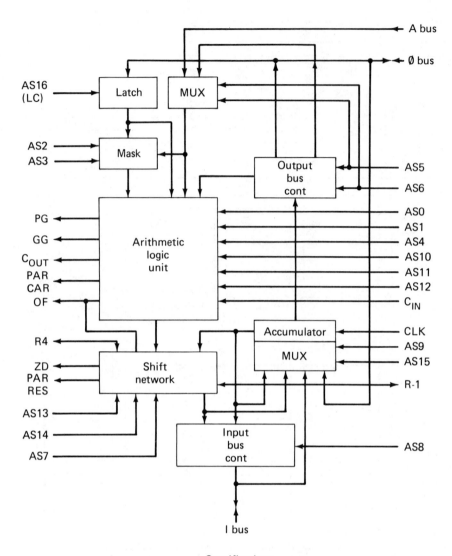

Specifications

Data word size	4 bits, bit-sliced
Memory address range	User determined
Clock speed	D¢ to 15 MHz
Package	48-pin QUIL
Power requirements	−5.2 V/240 mA
	−2.0 V/199 mA

Programmer's Eye View

User determined.

Figure 2-19 Motorola's 10800. (Courtesy Motorola Semiconductor Products, Phoenix, Arizona.)

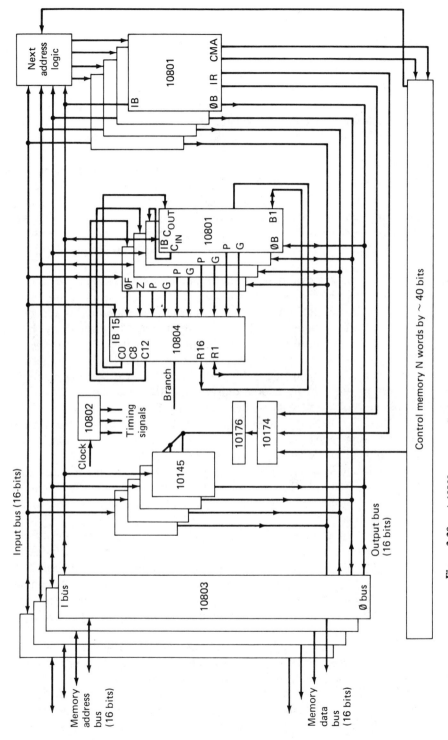

Figure 2-20 A 10800 system configuration. (Courtesy Motorola Semiconductor Products, Phoenix, Arizona.)

BUY OR BUILD?

We've been looking over a small sampling of current microprocessors, ranging from the small 4-bit TMS 1000 to the high-performance Z8000 and 10800. When choosing a microprocessor for your application, consult the up-to-date manufacturer's specification sheets, the latest electronics journals, and the *IC Update Master* for current parts and specifications, evaluating the parts in the manner used in the examples just given.

The microprocessor world is constantly changing, and more powerful, new devices will enter the scene in the next few years. What is on the market now is just a beginning. When very large-scale integration (VLSI) is mature enough to produce high-yield parts, some major breakthroughs in processing power and onboard memory will result. We can look forward to microprocessors with the processing power of a large mainframe along with 65K bytes of onboard memory.

When you are evaluating a microcomputer system, one question will inevitably arise: What form of microcomputer is best suited to my application? Starting from scratch with a logically selected microprocessor and a handful of interface parts is one way to set up a system, but it may not always be the most practical. Manufacturers have realized that many users have neither the time, desire, or resources to build a system from scratch, and they therefore offer completely assembled microcomputer boards and full-blown microcomputer systems to meet many user requirements. It's well worth considering these boards and full-sized systems before starting from scratch.

Table 2-4 lists the advantages and disadvantages of the various do-it-yourself approaches to a microcomputer system. Which method is best for your application depends primarily on the interface requirements, units to be produced, and your own (or your organization's) design and fabrication capabilities. By reading the upcoming descriptions of what is available in the three listed categories, and by using this table, you should be able to determine what you need.

Let's take an illustrative example of a design calling for a microcomputer. Assume that you want to build a word-processing electric typewriter for yourself, and you also intend to sell 40 or 50 of the units to local computer stores. The unit must be quite small (either built into the typewriter or contained in a small box that can sit beside the typewriter), and it must perform simple text-editing functions and a final dump function to type out the perfectly edited copy.

This is basically a simple data processing task. A typist can only type a few characters per second, so even the slowest of the data processing type of microprocessors would suffice in this application.

Table 2-4 reveals that the full-size system can immediately be eliminated from further consideration. The requirement states that the unit must fit inside the typewriter or in a small box beside it. Full-size systems come in fairly

Table 2-4 Micro System Do-It-Yourself Tradeoffs

Characteristic	Computer Form		
	Start from Scratch	One-Board Microcomputer	Full-Size System
Includes	Parts only,	Microprocessor, RAM, ROM, interfaces on a preassembled board.	Complete CPU and all memory and interfaces in a ready-to-plug-in form.
Advantages	Custom configurable; custom interfaces; most efficient for special tasks; cheapest for large-quantity production; small size.	Custom interfaces only; software available; less critical design at card edge; cheapest for few units; small size; prebuilt and tested; little labor involved.	No design labor costs; very little testing; complete software available; standard interfaces available; built and tested; no labor involved.
Disadvantages	Much labor involved; great design effort required; long lead time; must write most software; all system physical design must be done; unproven design: may have bugs.	Short lead times; limited selection of microporcessors; system physical design must be done.	Most hardware-expensive, least hardware-efficient; large physical size.
Special Considerations	This way is the best way to learn about microprocessors.	If you want to use a processor there is no board for, forget this approach.	Very good in large data processing tasks or other tasks of general-purpose nature.

large-sized boxes with card slots for expansion. The size constraint rules out the large system.

The start-from-scratch approach and the microcomputer single-board approach are left. Both methods seem to fit the design constraints. Interfacing the typewriter to the microcomputer will require a small user-interaction interface that will have to be designed and built in either case. There are two important factors which now enter into the decision. First, you have to get this product onto the computer store shelves before the competition saturates your market, and you have to be cost-competitive to avoid being aced out by others eyeing your market. If you are designing and building the units yourself, you have an enormous task to accomplish if you opt for the start-from-scratch approach. The microcomputer unit as well as the interface must be designed, built, debugged, and integrated. Software must be written for the word-processing task, and support software for your new microcomputer system design would be needed. The time constraint makes this approach generally unattractive.

If your company is building a limited-quantity project such as this, the profits gained on the sale of 50 units would not be large enough to finance a complete microcomputer and system software development program. In this case, the microcomputer board seems to be the best alternative. It offers a balance between development cost and getting your product completed in a reasonable length of time.

It is objective analysis like this that helps you to determine which microcomputer form is best suited to any given application. Consideration of the factors in Table 2-4 can help save you time and money in the production of your microcomputer product.

Starting From Scratch

If it turns out that designing and building a system from scratch is the best approach for meeting the system requirements, a large design and construction task lies ahead. The complexity of the task depends on the system requirements and the ease of interfacing to the chosen microprocessor.

Because the start-from-scratch method allows the greatest versatility in microcomputer function, the first step in the design is to determine exactly which functions will be performed by the microcomputer. Hardware that would normally come standard with a microcomputer board or full-sized system can be eliminated in the early design stages if it isn't needed. The expandability factor should be considered, however. A system will typically be asked to do more by the time it reaches actual production.

After you've determined the functional characteristics and drawn a block diagram of the system, you should decide on the actual interface methods to be implemented. The microcomputer input and output descriptions in this book explain the advantages of serial I/O, parallel I/O, DMA, and other interface methods. The devices being interfaced must be analyzed for their I/O transfer rates, handshaking requirements, and I/O data format. The proper interface parts for the job must be chosen.

One of the best ways to optimize the interface and processor design is to obtain all the manufacturers' (including the second-source manufacturer's) literature on the given microprocessor and see what form of I/O is typically used in the example implementations. In most cases these designs are generated by the microprocessor designers and their staffs, and the best designed-in I/O features of the processors are utilized.

While the microcomputer is being designed, a parallel software task should be taking place. The methods by which software will be developed, loaded into the microcomputer, and executed should be strictly defined. Software considerations should definitely influence the interface and microcomputer design. Certain types of interfaces, for example, may demand too much software overhead; as a consequence, a more autonomous interface may be in order.

The location of the interface and memory block in the memory map could decide whether you run existing support software on your design or write or rewrite all the support software yourself. Be sure to consider these facts.

Anyone developing a microcomputer from scratch should seriously consider buying or renting a development system for the chosen microprocessor. The initial cost or rental fee can easily be paid for with the savings of engineering time and money on the hardware and software development. Probably the biggest savings will be in the software development area.

A good development system comes with disk-based software, which usually includes an assembler and editor, a higher-order programming language such as PL/M or PL/Z, and a good operating system to keep all the programs neatly organized. The Motorola EXORciser system and the Intel MDS system are the two most often used development systems, but nearly every manufacturer offers one for its own chip.

One word of caution is in order concerning development systems. Some people believe that they can get by with a "hobbyist-type" microcomputer, such as one of the proliferating S-100 bus machines, as a development system. As the S-100 description in this book shows, compatibility between cards, unprofessional system design, and poor documentation can cause you to waste more time and money trying to keep the system operative than developing your product. If you are serious about developing a product, especially in the industrial or commercial market, use the professional equipment.

If you start from scratch, you will also be getting deeply involved in the physical design of the system. Circuit boards, power bus and clock distribution, thermal considerations, and backplane design will all have to be considered. Sections of this book will point out good physical and electrical design procedures. Manufacturers' literature should be consulted for device electrical and physical requirements.

The One-Board Microcomputer Approach

The past few years have seen the development of single-board microcomputers for original-equipment-manufacturer (OEM) applications. The big microprocessor companies take one of their microprocessors, 256 bytes to 16 K bytes of RAM (their RAM of course), a few kilobytes of ROM, some interface components, and put them all on a small ready-to-use card. Many of the low-end cards are intended for microcontroller applications (such as Intel's SBC 80/40), and many of the cards are meant to be the CPU section of a large microcomputer system (such as the 16-bit TMS 990/100M and DEC's KD11-F unit). Let's examine a low-end and a high-end one-board microcomputer.

The ISP-8C/100 SC/MP.   One of the first of the low-end microcomputer controller boards was the ISP-8C/100 by National Semiconductor. This board is better known as the SC/MP *CPU application module.* The ISP-8C is based on National's SC/MP chip. It is intended for end applications and prototyping, and comes on a circuit card that is 11 by 12.25 cm (4.37 × 4.825 in.).

It is therefore small enough to fit into tight quarters.

Figure 2-21 shows the SC/MP CPU application module. This module contains 512 bytes of user-programmable PROM, 256 bytes of RAM, and a handful of interface buffers and latches. The interface signals are brought out to a 72-pin edge connector that features a 16-bit address and data bus as well as discrete control lines. Like most one-board microcomputers, the ISP-8C can be expanded using its external bus.

National supplies separate RAM application modules and PROM application modules for memory expansion.

The CPU module runs on two power supplies (+5 and −12 V) and is self-initializing upon application of primary power.

Because the SC/MP is such a simple microprocessor, not much support software is available for it. In the kind of applications for which the SC/MP is intended (control functions), programming on the assembly-language level can easily be accomplished without extensive support.

The M68MM01A.   A good example of a one-board microcomputer that provides all of the processing and control functions required for a microcomputer-based system is the Motorola M68MM01A. As Fig. 2-22 shows, this unit contains:

- RS-232C serial input/output interface
- Two parallel I/O interfaces
- MC6800 microprocessor
- 1K of static RAM
- 4K of EAROM (electrically alterable PROM) of 8K of ROM
- Complete clock and bus interface circuitry

94

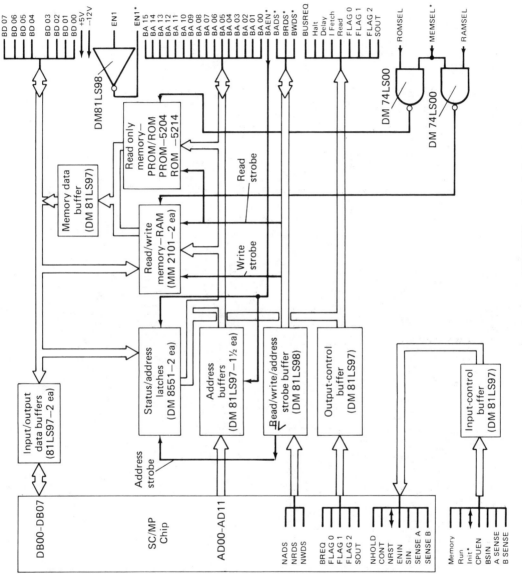

Figure 2-21 The National Semiconductor ISP-8C/100 one-board microcomputer. (Courtesy National Semiconductor, Santa Clara, Ca.)

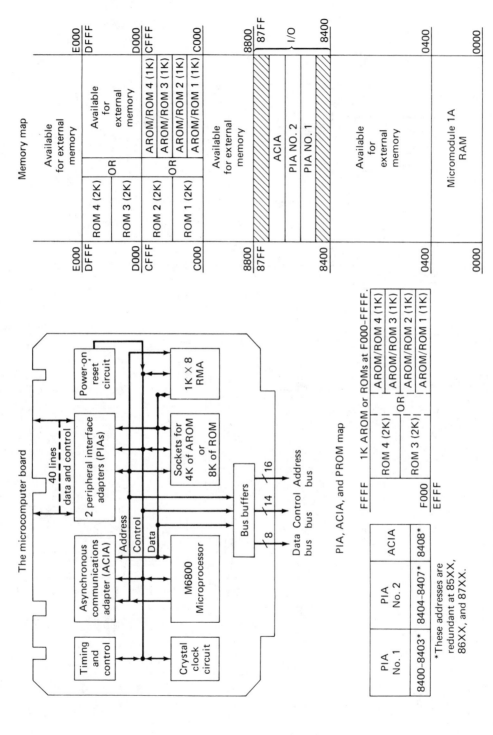

Figure 2-22 Motorola's M68MM01A one-board microcomputer. (Courtesy Motorola Semiconductor Products, Phoenix, Arizona.)

This module can be used to perform all the processing and I/O functions of a small system through the connectors at the top of the card; or it can be put into a card cage and expanded to a full 65K system through the well defined EXORciser bus at the bottom of the card.

The M68MM01A requires three supply voltages (+5, +12, and −12V), is 25 × 15.25 cm (9.75 × 6 in.), and has TTL-compatible signal levels at all I/O pins (except for the EIA RS-232C communication output).

This card enjoys all the hardware and software support of the 6800 family of microprocessors. The complete Motorola EXORciser development system, which includes all the programs and hardware needed to program the PROMs, can be used in the development effort.

Many of the one-card microcomputers have associated cards that may further reduce the design and construction effort. Analog I/O boards are available for most one-card microcomputers, and specialized boards such as CRT controllers, fast multipliers, and high-speed DMA interface boards are available for the more popular units.

If the one-card microcomputer seems to be the best approach for the task, the first step is to define the processing and memory requirements of the desired system. Microprocessor manufacturers should then be contacted to get the latest information on which kind of one-card microcomputers is available to match your specifications.

Finally, a prototyping package, which usually consists of a one-board microcomputer, prototyping board, card cage, programmable memory chips (if the unit uses PROMs), associated cabling, and documentation, should be purchased. Since most prototyping packages come with a system monitor program on a PROM, you can have the board operating within hours after receiving the prototyping kit. You can then get familiar with the system and begin the interface design and construction on the prototyping board.

Full-Size Microcomputer Systems

If a complete microcomputer system that fills all of your requirements already exists, it makes sense to use that system in your application. One area in which this is especially true is in the business data processing field. Complete systems with full complements of disk drives, terminals, and customized software are available from many microprocessor manufacturers as well as large computer companies such as IBM, DEC, and Computer Automation.

Full-size systems come with many options. Any given company will have a minimal-configuration system that is required to run the simplest software packages and optional peripherals and software to fit the customer's specific needs. Many of these options are specialized in nature. Array processors, A/D data acquisition units, and powerful graphics display devices can be obtained from the primary manufacturer or other companies that have built their businesses by supplying the specialized peripherals in many machine-compatible formats.

The Digital Equipment Corporation PDP-11 series of minicomputers has been a very successful product line. The PDP-11 minicomputer is available in a wide range of performances and memory configurations. At the low end of the PDP-11 series there is the PDP-11/04, which is a bare-bones processor that isn't much more powerful than an 8-bit microcomputer. At the high end there is the PDP-11/70, which is so large and powerful that it borders on mainframe performance.

Digital Equipment Corporation has successfully sold tens of thousands of PDP-11 full-size minicomputer systems and has built a large product line of peripherals, so it comes as no surprise that the microprocessor version of the PDP-11, the LSI-11, can also be bought in a nice packaged system form.

A complete business system can be pieced together from DEC's standard modules and peripherals. First, a CPU must be chosen. The PDP-11/03 is the natural choice. It is a combination of LSI-11 modules and accessories, including an H9270 backplane and card guides, an H780-H power supply, and 4K of RAM. The system comes packaged in a standard width enclosure and has room in the enclosure for up to six double-height interface modules. Optionally, the PDP-11/03-KA can be used as the CPU. This is basically the same as the CPU just described but includes a total of 16K of RAM instead of just 4K.

Secondly, the peripherals and appropriate interface modules for the system must be chosen. A console terminal and hard-copy device (in this case a slow-speed printer will do) are required, and the LA36 *DEC Writer II* seems to meet this requirement.

A magnetic data storage unit is required to store programs and records. The RXV11 dual floppy disk drives seem appropriate for this task. It is important to have two of any magnetic storage device since files will have to be copied and transferred from one disk or tape to another.

The peripheral interfaces must now be chosen. The console terminal/printer requires a serial interface. The DLV11 module is the standard LSI-11 serial interface card and fills this requirement. The floppy disk drive already comes with a plug-in controller card, so additional interfacing is not needed.

This completes the hardware selection, but a software package remains to be chosen. An operating system for the disk is required. The RT-11 operating system seems like a good choice, because the system is not going to be a multiuser, timesharing one.

The RT-11 operating system comes with an editor, assembler, system utilities, librarian, linker, and many other useful programs. Optional software such as FORTRAN, BASIC, and COBAL can be purchased for use under this system from DEC or independent software houses.

Finally, miscellaneous items can be selected. A mounting rack (to house the processor and disk) and communication cables (for the terminal) can be selected.

If the packaged system is the approach for you, a good starting point is to get a copy of the Digital Direct Sales Catalog, The Microcomputer Handbook, and The Peripheral Handbook—all from DEC. It would be wise to obtain literature from other microcomputer companies specializing in packaged systems as well. Once you have an idea of what you want, contact the manufacturer's representative. He will help you set up a system, and he will very probably give you a good "package deal." All the rules in dealing with salesmen should be followed in dealing with the representative. Buying a packaged system is like buying a car with many options; the price is *negotiable*.

CHAPTER

3

Memory

The very concept of sequential computing machines assumes that commands and data are being stored somewhere in the computing machine. Computer evolution has resulted in processors that can be divided into three functional pieces: the processor, the input/output unit, and the storage unit or memory. Because memory is such an integral part of computer systems, it has developed into a science in itself. Whole companies have been founded around computer memory devices, and memory technology is at least as complex as processor technology.

The microcomputer is basically no different from the large computer at the functional level. Data must be stored somewhere, and thus we have storage devices.

Most of today's microcomputers can be classified as cell-addressable single-memory machines. A cell-addressable memory is one that accepts a processor-issued address and returns a program or data word from the location in memory corresponding to that address. Most RAMs, ROMs, and other memory devices are cell-addressable.

The term *single-memory machine* refers to the way in which a processor accesses memory. A processor requires a sequence of commands or *program*, and it also requires data with which to operate. In the early days of computers two approaches were taken to this problem. The dual-memory approach provided a memory for the program and a separate memory for the data. The single-memory approach uses only one large memory containing both the program and the data. The advantage of the single-memory approach is that less hardware is required. Two separate memories and two memory addressing units are not required on a single-memory machine.

There is no universal form of memory that is suited to every data storage application. High-speed semiconductor memories store data reliably and allow fast data access times, but they also lose data at power-down, draw a lot of power, and are prohibitively expensive for storing huge blocks of data.

Magnetic tape, on the other hand, can store millions of bytes of data per dollar and doesn't lose its contents unless it is intentionally erased; but it is also extremely slow, must be sequentially accessed since it is one long strip of data, and requires a large piece of mechanical equipment—the transport mechanism—to be useful.

All this boils down to the fact that engineering tradeoffs must be made in a system and the proper memory and mass storage device must be used for the task at hand.

Many exotic memory devices have been designed, and many of them have been scrapped. The early days of memory technology produced mercury tank delay-line storage units, phase storage units or *paramatrons,* drum memories, and even a memory cathode-ray tube that could store millions of bytes of data on its face (the only problem was, you couldn't read it back!). These devices are interesting, but memory technology has finally stabilized to the point at which fast, reliable semiconductor memories and mechanical memories such as tape, disk, and core dominate the market. These common memories are the ones with which you will most likely be associated; these are the memories we will examine in this chapter.

MEMORY HIERARCHIES

Computer designers solve the problem of memory storage capacity versus memory speed and accessibility with *memory hierarchies.* The CPU section of a computer system typically uses a high-speed memory to temporarily store programs and data while it is being processed. This is a system's short-term memory or *working store.* Working stores usually range in size from a few bytes to a few tens of thousands of bytes in most microcomputer systems. This amount of working storage is enough to store the programs and data for most micro applications.

A few hundred thousand bytes of programs and data are accessed often enough in most applications to require a fairly quick storage unit to hold this data. Medium-term storage units serve this purpose. Disk drives, charge-coupled devices, and bubble memories work well as medium-term storage media.

Finally, huge blocks of data that will be referenced periodically require a bulk storage media. Magnetic tape and large disk packs are ideal for this long-term storage requirement. Long-term storage units are capable of storing hundreds of millions of bytes of data quite slowly but at a very low cost.

The three types of storage have been briefly outlined: short-term, medium-term and long-term storage. With today's diversified memory technology, ultrahigh-speed memories are available for use as fast working stores or short-term memories, but the price and power consumption of these memories make even a reasonable size working store out of the question. In high-performance processors, a fourth level is therefore added to the memory hierarchy: the *cache memory.*

A cache memory consists of a few hundred to a few thousand bytes of ultrahigh-performance memory that acts as a buffer between the processor and the large, fast, working store. Studies have shown that a few thousand words of high-performance memory, if operated properly, can make an entire low-performance working store look as though it's made from ultrahigh-performance memory (or at least about 80% as fast as the fast memory). Figure 3-1 illustrates a memory hierarchy and shows what devices are currently being used at what hierarchical level in the microcomputer field.

Memory hierarchies seem to be a simple answer to all data storage problems until you look at the software required to control a memory hierarchy. Data must be searched for and read-in from the long-term storage devices, put into the medium-term devices, and paged into the short-term memory as needed. After the data processing is complete, all the data has to be sent back down the hierarchy to the long-term storage devices.

Many large mainframe manufacturers have solved the hierarchy control software problem by using hardware to control hierarchical data transfers. The programmer pretends that the memory is nearly infinite in size and lets the hardware worry about paging and long-term storage control. This type of storage is called *virtual memory,* because it gives the appearance of one huge short-term memory.

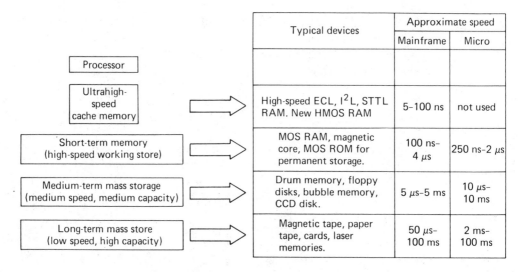

	Typical devices	Approximate speed	
		Mainframe	Micro
Processor			
Ultrahigh-speed cache memory	High-speed ECL, I^2L, STTL RAM. New HMOS RAM	5–100 ns	not used
Short-term memory (high-speed working store)	MOS RAM, magnetic core, MOS ROM for permanent storage.	100 ns– 4 μs	250 ns–2 μs
Medium-term mass storage (medium speed, medium capacity)	Drum memory, floppy disks, bubble memory, CCD disk.	5 μs–5 ms	10 μs– 10 ms
Long-term mass store (low speed, high capacity)	Magnetic tape, paper tape, cards, laser memories.	50 μs– 100 ms	2 ms– 100 ms

Figure 3-1   The components of memory hierarchies.

Microcomputers don't have hierarchy control problems to the same extent as mainframes. Because microprocessors are relatively slow, they cannot utilize a high-speed cache memory. And most microcomputers are not asked to handle hundreds of millions of bytes of data, so the long-term storage device is usually not necessary. Ordinarily, a medium-term storage device such as a floppy disk will do. This reduces the memory hierarchy down to two levels— the working store and the medium-term mass store. Because a two-level memory hierarchy does not require much control, virtual memory hasn't yet been needed or incorporated into any microprocessor; but, if the performance of processors keeps increasing, virtual memory may make its appearance on the microcomputer scene.

WORKING STORE

Of all the short-term working store media available today, semiconductor RAMs, ROMs, and magnetic core memories are the most common. Important characteristics of these storage units include fast access time and random-access capability.

Semiconductor RAM

A decade ago computers were totally dependent on magnetic core memory for their short-term memory needs. As semiconductor technology advanced, small 256-bit bipolar memory ICs became available for use in central processor units. As device technology improved, MOS entered the memory picture and 1K MOS RAMs were built. For the first time, semiconductor memory had the potential to surpass core memory on a cost and performance basis. Things have not been the same since. Today nearly every computer's main memory consists of semiconductor RAM, which comes in packages as large as 64K bits with access times as fast as a few nano-seconds.

The availability of RAM has also made the microcomputer possible. Without a low-cost, short-term memory, microprocessors have very little cost advantage over any other CPU.

A RAM consists of two functional blocks: the memory cell array and the peripheral interface circuitry. As Fig. 3-2 illustrates, a RAM must take in an address through a set of address lines and select the appropriate row and column corresponding to the addressed cell. The cell must be examined by the I/O circuitry and sent to the data output. This constitutes a *read* operation.

If data is being written into the cell array, the input data control unit must turn the addressed memory cell on or off to indicate a 0 or 1.

The memory cell array is the heart of the memory unit. It is usually a square matrix of individual one-bit memory elements arranged in rows and columns. Because the memory cell arrays are for the most part square, the capacity will tend to be an even power of 2. There are many 256, 1K, 4K, 16K,

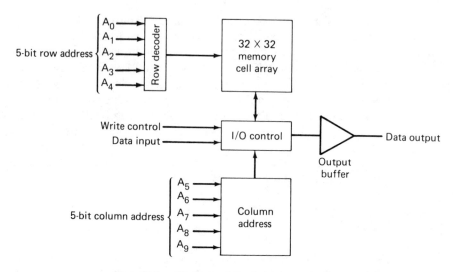

Figure 3-2   Memory peripheral circuitry and cells.

and now 64K RAMs — but very few 512, 2K, and 8K RAMs. Some companies make memories that are not integrally an "even power of 2," but many of these just contain two small even-power-of-2 arrays inside.

There are many approaches to the design of the individual memory cells. The most common are static flip-flop cells, transistor-base-charge dynamic cells, and pseudostatic charge-pumped cells.

The static memory cell is a two-transistor flip-flop, or bistable multivibrator. By activating either the right or left transistor, a 0 or a 1 can be represented. This data can be retained until an external current changes the flip-flop's state or until power is lost. The cell is called static because it can hold information indefinitely as long as it has power—there is no apparent change in the cell once it has been set.

The dynamic semiconductor memory cell consists of a single transistor. A current into the base of the transistor turns the stage on by building up a charge in the transistor base region. An *on* transistor represents a 1 while an *off* transistor represents a 0.

It may seem that the single-transistor dynamic cell is better than the static two-transistor cell in every way because it uses less parts, space, and power; but the dynamic cell has one big drawback: it must be refreshed. The term *dynamic* refers to the gradual change of state—a transistor can only hold a base charge for a few milliseconds before it leaks away. If the charge leaks away without being replenished, the stored data is lost.

To accomplish the replenishing or refreshing, refresh circuitry must be built into every dynamic RAM. The most common method used to refresh dynamic cells is to recharge every memory cell in a given row of a cell array whenever any element in that row is read. Most dynamic RAMs therefore require a read operation at least once every 2 ms. If this comes naturally in a processing task, great; if not, a time interval must be set aside to have the processor sequentially read through memory to refresh it every few milliseconds.

A pseudostatic memory cell is a memory cell that combines the advantages of the static and dynamic memory cells. Pseudostatic RAMs are basically dynamic RAMs with additional peripheral circuitry to periodically place an additional charge on all the transistors that are at a logic 1 level. These RAMs are called *charge-pumped* devices in reference to this additional charging circuitry. Pseudostatic RAMs have had some success in large mainframe computer memories, but the need for additional charge-interval clocks and strange voltage levels has kept these devices from becoming popular in the microcomputer field.

A RAMs peripheral circuitry consists of an address decoder that takes half of the memory address field and divides it into many single row-select lines, and a decoder that divides the other half of the field into many column-select lines. The current level used by the memory cells is very small, so low-current buffers and sense amplifiers must be incorporated to set, reset, and read memory cells. An output driver is also needed to drive the data output lines.

Dynamic RAMs often have an output latch as well as a driving buffer. Dynamic RAM timing can be very tricky on the memory-cell level, and a latch is used to catch the data as it becomes available in the read sequence.

Modern RAMs confine the complex timing to the chip level and provide circuitry to handle it. Onboard peripheral circuitry in many of today's RAMs is so complicated that it is almost a little processor in itself.

Because static RAMs require nearly twice as many transistors as dynamic RAMs, static RAMs always lag a step behind dynamic RAMs in memory size. Today's technology is bringing us 64K dynamic RAMs and 16K statics. By the time enough parts can be squeezed onto a chip to form a 64K static RAM, 256K dynamic RAMs should be making their appearance.

Important RAM Features.   Like microprocessors, RAMs have important features to watch for. The following paragraphs spotlight the more salient of these.

Memory type is the first characteristic to be considered. The static and dynamic memory types have already been discussed. It is important to determine which of these memory types is best suited for your application. Static memories are easier to interface because they don't have as many control lines associated with them. For small memory applications, static memory is usually the best choice. For large data stores (greater than 4K bytes) dynamic memory may save enough ICs and power to make its use worthwhile.

In some applications, such as display memory for a graphics terminal, dynamic memory is an ideal choice. In this and many other applications, the memory is constantly being read onto the screen, so special refresh intervals and additional circuitry are not required. Some microprocessors (the Z80 is a typical example) have built-in transparent refresh capabilities. Dynamic RAM use should be strongly considered for these kinds of microprocessors.

Memory size for a system must be determined by program sizing and through an analysis of data requirements. In systems requiring a large short-term memory, the large 16K and 64K RAMs should be used. In less complex systems, smaller and less costly (in terms of power and price) RAMs should be investigated.

Memory configuration (the way in which memories are organized) can play an important role in reducing the parts count in a memory system. The majority of the memories sold have one data input line and one data output line. A 16K memory with this sort of output is known as a 16K- by 1-bit (16K × 1) memory. To make an 8-bit word, eight of these memory packages must be used.

RAMs can also be bought in 1K- by 4-bit, 128- by 8-bit, and other multiple-I/O-bit configurations. These "wide" RAMs are particularly useful when a small amount of memory is required and the package count must be kept to a minimum. The only problem with multiple-I/O-bit RAMs are that they draw more power and take more I/O pins than standard RAMs of 1-bit width.

The power problem is caused by the need for more peripheral circuitry for the extra I/O lines (a RAM's peripheral circuitry usually draws much more power than the memory cell array) and cannot easily be solved.

The I/O pin problem has been solved to some extent by eliminating the dedicated data input and output lines found on a standard 1-bit-wide RAM. By bussing the memory's data lines, half the memory's data I/O pins are eliminated. The RAM becomes easily interfaceable to microprocessor buses using this method as well. Extra I/O pins are also freed simply because there are less address lines in a multiple-I/O-bit RAM.

Memory speed is another important consideration. Memory access time and memory cycle time are the two most common methods of measuring a memory's speed.

Access time is the period required for a memory to present valid data at the memory output pins after it receives a valid memory address. This figure tells you how fast one word can be read from memory. On many memories (most dynamic memories), byte after byte of data cannot be read at the single-byte access rate. Dynamic memories require a minimum amount of time for the internal sequencing circuitry to recover and reenter another read access cycle. *Read time* plus the *read recovery time* is collectively called the memory cycle time.

The importance of read access and read cycle time depends on the application. In a general processing system such as a business microcomputer, memory isn't accessed in a rapid byte-after-byte sequence. Access time is the most important consideration in this case. However, if a memory is going to be used as a fast operational store or input/output buffer, fast bursts of data may be required. In this case, cycle time will be the memory's limiting factor.

In applications in which memory cycle time is important, static RAMs offer some advantage over dynamic RAMs. A static RAM usually has no internal sequencing circuitry, so its access time is the same as its cycle time. The extra peripheral circuitry surrounding a dynamic cell array can slow memory cycle time down to twice the memory access time.

One word of caution is in order concerning memory speed. Memory speed is usually measured as a typical figure at the RAM's pins. The best performance that can be expected from a RAM is the maximum worst-case figure listed in the tables inside the manufacturer's specification sheet. The additional buffers and control circuitry on a microcomputer's memory cards must also be taken into consideration when determining memory speed. These delays can amount to a few hundred nanoseconds in some cases.

Device technology plays an important role in a RAM's characteristics. The standard TTL, NMOS, and RAMs are being rapidly replaced by I^2L, HMOS, VMOS, CMOS, and MNOS RAMs that offer higher performance, higher circuit densities, and lower prices than older RAMs. Table 3-1 lists most of the common memory device technologies on the market today and shows their advantages and disadvantages. Notice that many of the technologies have special features that are very desirable in a limited number of applications. The low-drain CMOS RAM, like the CMOS microprocessor (RCA 1802 COSMAC), is good in battery-powered applications, while the MNOS RAM has the property of *nonvolatility*—the retention of data even when power is switched off. The table gives a good idea of what to expect in the way of performance and features from today's RAMs.

Selecting a RAM

Manufacturer's literature should be consulted for the most recent memory specifications. The factors just discussed and the device characteristics should be kept in mind when looking at RAMs.

Let's look now at a few popular RAMs and see how to interface them to a microprocessor bus. The RAMs you select for your system can be interfaced in a similar manner.

A Simple Static RAM: the 2102. The 2102 is a somewhat obsolete 1K- by 1-bit (1K $\times$ 1) static RAM that helped build the microcomputer market in its earliest stages. Small 1K $\times$ 1 RAMs are rapidly being replaced by more efficient 4K and 16K devices, but the 2102 is a good example of a general-purpose static RAM.

Table 3-1 RAM Device Technology

Device Technology	Noted Trait	Advantage	Disadvantage
TTL and STTL bipolar	High speed, 20–40 ns access	Speed; TTL-compatible	Low Density; high power draw; expensive
ECL bipolar	Extremely fast, 5–30 ns	Speed; ECL-compatible	Low density; high power draw; expensive; no interfamily compatibility
I2L	Very fast, 50–150 ns	Speed; TTL-compatible relatively low power; quite dense packing	New technology; low availability
PMOS	Fairly dense but slow, 500–2000 ns	Inexpensive	Not TTL compatible; relatively slow speed
NMOS	Dense and relatively fast, 150–1500 ns	Inexpensive, TTL-compatible	Not fast enough for very high speed applications.
HMOS	Dense and fast, 50–250 ns	High density; low power; high speed	New technology; expensive
CMOS	Fairly dense and very low power	Low power	Expensive due to complex process.
MNOS	Fairly dense but quite slow	Nonvolatility	Expensive and slow
VMOS	Very dense and quite fast 100–500 ns	Best density of all RAMs candidate for 256K RAM	New technology; expensive

The 2102 is a TTL-compatible 1K NMOS memory with a data input line and a three-state (logic 0, logic 1, and a high-impedance floating state) data output line. The RAM comes in a 16-pin package.

Figure 3-3 shows the block diagram and timing relationships of the 2102 along with its important characteristics. Notice that there are 10 address lines to address a 1K memory space, a data input line, and a data output line. In addition, there are two control lines that are very typical of static RAMs: the read–write line and the chip enable line. The chip enable line is optional and is only used to turn the three-state output on or off (to the active or float states); therefore, the only real control line on the 2102 is the read–write line.

The timing diagram shows the simplicity of the static RAM timing. In the read cycle, data becomes valid at a time t_a after the address is submitted. This time, in nanoseconds, is the RAM's access and cycle time.

Writing is accomplished by submitting the write pulse (wp) on the read–write line for a minimum of t_{wp} ns. The address must be valid during the whole write pulse and even a little before and after it. These slight timing margins on both ends of the write pulse are called the address *setup* and *hold* times. All setup and hold times for the address as well as data must be strictly observed. If the address changes while the memory is being written into, all the memory locations that the address passes through while it is changing could be wiped out.

Interfacing the 2102 to a microprocessor is quite simple. The address lines are connected to the least significant ten bits of the microprocessor's address bus, as shown in Fig. 3-4. Because the microprocessor has 16 address lines, 6 of the lines are left over to address the total 64K memory space or the other 63 1K blocks of memory. A decoder is used to determine to which combination of 6 bits this 1K memory block will respond. In this case, it is block zero. The decoder simply *ANDS* the decoded *memory select* signal with the memory *read* signal (the phase 1 or Ø1 signal on the 6800) and enables the memory chips when they are properly addressed and a read is requested.

The read–write line is connected to the microprocessor's read–write output line so the processor can read or write at its discretion. Since so many address lines have to be driven (a total of 8 on each address line), buffers have to be used on the address lines.

A 256- by 4-Bit Static RAM: The 2101.   In a very small system requiring only 256 bytes of memory, there is no reason to use the 2102 1K RAM. It is too large (1K × 1) and it requires buffers to drive the address lines as described in the 2102 section.

The 256- by 8-bit memory requirement can be met using the 256- by 4-bit version of the 2102: the 2101. As Fig. 3-5 illustrates, this RAM has two fewer address lines than the 2102, because only 256 bytes are addressed. To accommodate the additional data I/O pins, a 22-pin package is used.

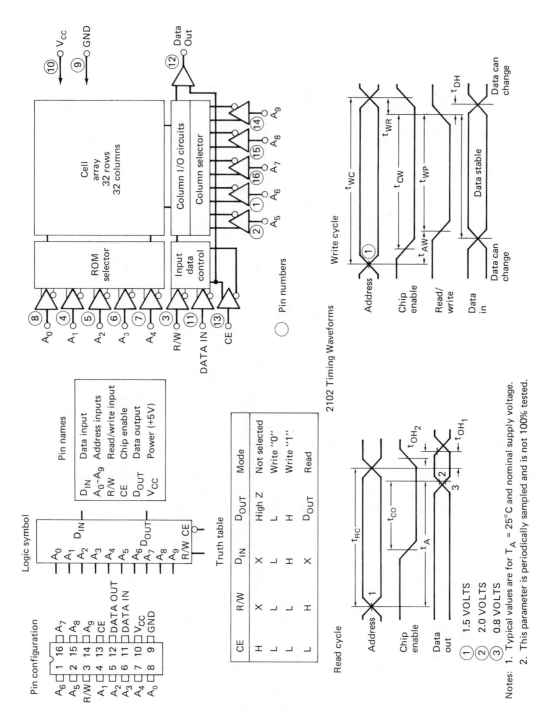

Figure 3-3 The 2102 1K- by 1-bit R.A.M. (Reprinted by permission of Intel Corporation, Copyright 1976.)

Notes: 1. Typical values are for $T_A = 25°C$ and nominal supply voltage.
2. This parameter is periodically sampled and is not 100% tested.

110

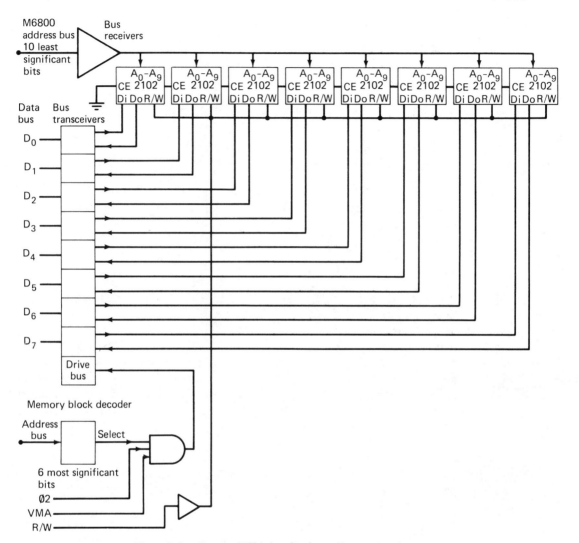

Figure 3-4   How the 2102 is interfaced to a microcomputer bus.

Using just two of these parts, a 256 × 8 memory may be built that places only two loads on the processor address lines. This memory is very well suited for such applications.

One interesting feature about the 2101 demands some discussion. Notice that two chip enable lines (actually a chip enable and an inverted chip enable) have been provided. In many RAMs and microcomputer interface components, multiple chip enable and inverted enables are added to a part if extra pins are left on the package. These multiple chip enable lines are useful when interfacing the part to an address bus, because they can be wired to act as decoders. For example, if you had a 9-bit address (capable of addressing 512 bytes), and you wanted to use two 2101s to fill the memory space, you could simply wire

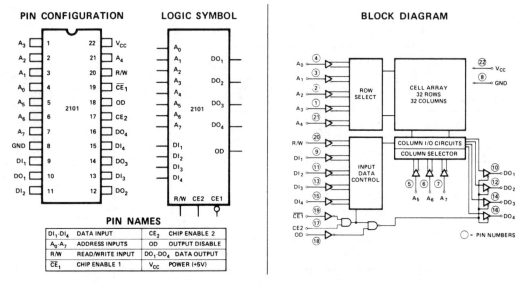

PIN CONFIGURATION   LOGIC SYMBOL   BLOCK DIAGRAM

PIN NAMES

DI$_1$-DI$_4$	DATA INPUT	CE$_2$	CHIP ENABLE 2
A$_0$-A$_7$	ADDRESS INPUTS	OD	OUTPUT DISABLE
R/W	READ/WRITE INPUT	DO$_1$-DO$_4$	DATA OUTPUT
$\overline{CE}_1$	CHIP ENABLE 1	V$_{CC}$	POWER (+5V)

Figure 3-5   The 2101: a 256- by 4-bit equivalent of the 2102 RAM. (Reprinted by permission of Intel Corporation, Copyright 1976.)

the ninth address bit to the chip enable input on one RAM (CE2) and to the inverted chip enable input on the other (CE1). The data inputs and outputs could then be tied to the processor bus. When the ninth bit was high (logic 1), one RAM would respond, and when it was low the other RAM would be enabled. This precludes the requirement for an address decoder in the memory interface circuitry. By using chip enables wisely, decoder and miscellaneous gate counts can be significantly reduced in a memory design.

A Simple Dynamic RAM: The 4K 2107.   The 2107 is a good example of a dynamic RAM with a standard 4K- by 1-bit configuration. The timing and addressing on this RAM is typical for most dynamic RAMs, at least on a functional level.

Figure 3-6 illustrates the block diagram and timing relationships of the 2107. Notice that the logic signals on the dynamic RAM are similar to those of the static RAM's, with one exception: a chip enable (CE) signal has been added. This signal initiates the internal memory accessing sequence required of the dynamic memory cells.

In dynamic memories, most of the timing signals are measured with relation to the CE signal or its equivalent. In the 2107 timing diagram, notice that the address must be stable during the rising edge of the CE signal. This edge causes data to be strobed into the row and column buffer registers. After the CE leading edge has occurred, and after a short stabilization period, the address can change because the access address is captured in the buffer registers.

After a short period (the read access time), read data becomes valid at the memory output pin. The data stays valid until the CE signal is dropped. The

PIN CONFIGURATION

LOGIC SYMBOL

BLOCK DIAGRAM

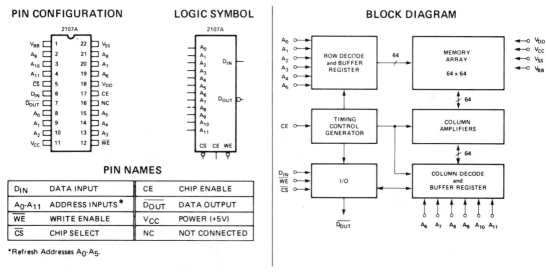

PIN NAMES

D_{IN}	DATA INPUT	CE	CHIP ENABLE
A_0-A_{11}	ADDRESS INPUTS*	$\overline{D_{OUT}}$	DATA OUTPUT
$\overline{WE}$	WRITE ENABLE	V_{CC}	POWER (+5V)
$\overline{CS}$	CHIP SELECT	NC	NOT CONNECTED

*Refresh Addresses A_0-A_5.

Read and Refresh Cycle

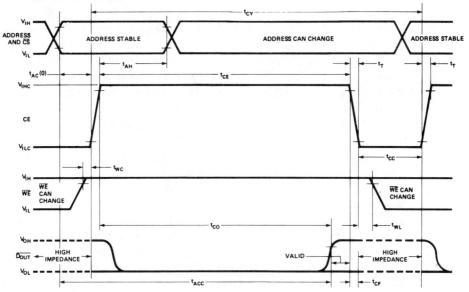

Figure 3-6   The 2107 4K- by 1-bit dynamic RAM. (Reprinted by permission of Intel Corporation, Copyright 1976.)

RAM's internal timing and control generator circuitry doesn't give the user much leeway in holding the CE signal high, however. The CE must be high for at least 280 ns but no more than 3000 ns. Unlike the static memory, with which you could hold an address and read the same byte of data for as long as you wanted, the 2107's memory requirements require that you catch the data in a small data-valid window of time.

The memory write cycle timing is very similar to the read cycle except that the write enable pulse must be generated. Again, this signal is timed relative to the CE signal that initiates the write sequence.

The 2107 was one of the first 4K dynamic RAMs and, like the first micro-processors, it lacks the sophisticated features of today's devices. Many of today's RAMs have holding latches at the data output so you don't have to time your system circuitry around the narrow read-access window.

Another primitive feature that is disappearing in today's RAMs is the highly capacitive, high-voltage (12 V) chip enable drive requirement. Intel spec-ifies that the CE signal shall rise to 12 V in a maximum of 50 ns. The high voltage and fast rise-time problem is compounded by the fact that most mem-ory systems will be using banks of 8 or 16 RAMs to form bytes of data. High-power MOS drivers must be used to parallel-drive the CE lines in order to meet the timing requirements.

An Advanced Dynamic RAM: The 4K 4027.   The Mostek 4027 is represen-tative of a state-of-the-art dynamic RAM. Very fast access and cycle times, data output buffering, and multiplexed address lines are featured.

To cut down on memory package size, the 4027 and other modern RAMs use multiplexed addressing. Instead of having a common chip enable line for the row and column address buffers, the row and column address lines are tied together and separate row and column address lines are provided. Only half the address pins are required, which allows for a 16-pin package. Figure 3-7 depicts the 4027. The row address select (RAS) and column address select (CAS) signals perform the multiplexing function.

Memory is read from the 4027 by first supplying a valid row address to the common address inputs and activating the RAS line. A valid column address is then supplied and CAS is activated to strobe-in the column address. After about 100 ns have elapsed, the read data is available in the output buffer and will stay there until the end of the next read cycle, when the most recently read data will take its place.

There are two features that aren't immediately apparent that allow you to build very fast memory systems out of 4027s. The first is the fact that the data stays valid in the output buffer well into the next read cycle. This allows the user's circuitry to take its time getting the data out of the memory and allows for wider timing margins. The second feature is that the memory's cycle time is longer than the sum of all the timing delays. This requires some explanation. On most dynamic memories the cycle time is simply the sum of all the smaller delays in the memory cycle (address setup, memory access, CE off time, and so on). For fast memory applications, the timing margins on all the critical memory timing signals have to be cut down to their absolute minimums to attain the maximum cycle throughput.

Mostek has arranged the timing and control circuitry on the 4027 so that all the critical timing signals can be above their specified minimums by a 20% or greater margin and still meet the minimum cycle time. This additional timing allowance makes the advertised minimum cycle time a realistic figure, because all the address, data, and control drivers' ''timing slop'' can be taken up by the 20% margins.

One final 4027 feature is the read and write cycles of the *page* mode. Most RAMs with multiplexed address lines allow you to operate in a page mode by submitting a row address and repeatedly submitting a long string of column addresses. Data can be taken from every column in a given row in a much shorter period of time using this mode.

The page feature is useful for fast sequential transfers, but it is even more valuable as a fast DMA cycle timing mode.

In order to speed refresh time, an exclusive *row address select* refresh mode has been provided. In this mode, the whole RAM can be refreshed by sequentially going through all the row addresses but not submitting any column address or CAS signal. Refreshing must be performed once every 2 ms.

The 16K Mostek 4116. The 4116 16K dynamic RAM has been cleverly designed to be an almost pin-for-pin replacement for the 4K 4027. By simply turning the 4027's chip select (CS) line into another address line, two additional multiplexed address bits were made available to access four times as much memory. Figure 3-8 illustrates the 4116.

RAM Implementation. A single RAM chip is fairly simple to work with. By following all the timing restrictions and physical parameters, we can get a RAM to work just as the specification sheet says it will. When we have to integrate hundreds of RAMs into a large memory module, however, problems arise. Address and control decoding and distribution networks are needed. Crosstalk between parallel memory data lines become a problem. Large current spikes caused by high-current chip enable lines start producing interference.

Before undertaking a large memory system design project, it is wise to study the memory interfacing requirements of the specific technology of choice. The memory manufacturers can supply such information in the form of notes and data sheets. A section in this book has also been set aside to go over memory system interfacing methods. This will also be helpful.

Content-Addressable Memory

A content-addressable memory (CAM) works like a cell-addressable memory in reverse. Data is supplied to the CAM and the address at which that data is stored is returned to the processor. At first glance, this sort of memory seems like a novelty item that could serve no useful purpose, but in certain kinds of processing, CAMs offer much higher performance than regular memories.

One of these applications is in programs requiring a lot of data sorting or searching. Instead of sequentially going through a cell-addressable memory, interrogating each location, you simply specify what you want to find and the

Functional Diagram

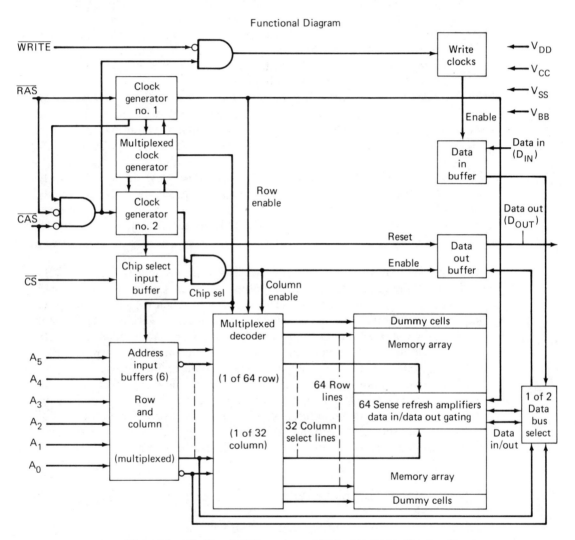

Figure 3-7 The Mostek 4027: an advanced 4K- by 1-bit RAM. (Courtesy Mostek Corporation, Carrollton, Texas.)

Pin Connections

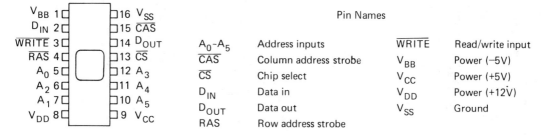

Pin Connections

V_{BB} 1		16 V_{SS}
D_{IN} 2		15 $\overline{CAS}$
$\overline{WRITE}$ 3		14 D_{OUT}
$\overline{RAS}$ 4		13 $\overline{CS}$
A_0 5		12 A_3
A_2 6		11 A_4
A_1 7		10 A_5
V_{DD} 8		9 V_{CC}

Pin Names

A_0-A_5	Address inputs		$\overline{WRITE}$	Read/write input
$\overline{CAS}$	Column address strobe		V_{BB}	Power (−5V)
$\overline{CS}$	Chip select		V_{CC}	Power (+5V)
D_{IN}	Data in		V_{DD}	Power (+12V)
D_{OUT}	Data out		V_{SS}	Ground
RAS	Row address strobe			

Read Cycle

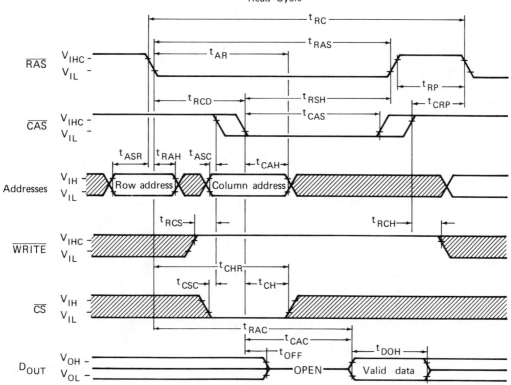

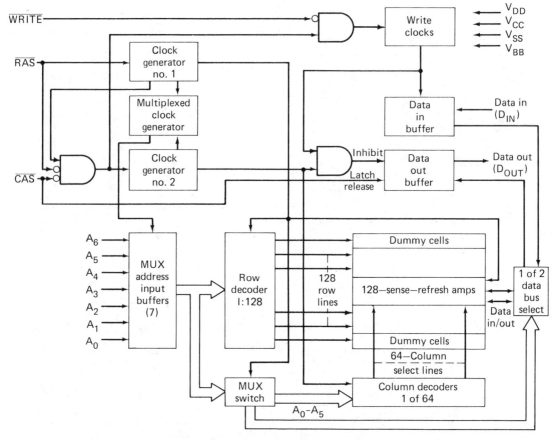

Figure 3-8   The Mostek 4116: an advanced 16K- by 1-bit RAM. (Courtesy Mostek Corporation, Carrollton, Texas.)

memory tells you where it is. Content-addressable memories are also being used in cell-addressable memory control units. Memory paging (the act of bringing in pieces of a program due to too small a processor memory) requires that the processor look to see if the page that the next instruction is on is already in memory. Checking each page takes a long time and uses up valuable processing time, so a CAM is used to store memory pages currently in memory. By simply asking the CAM if a given page is in memory, the processor can immediately determine if the page is there and where it is. This scheme is used in the associative lookaside buffers that control the cache memories on the *Amdahl 470 v7*.

Semiconductor ROM

It is sometimes desirable to have a nonvolatile memory store within a computer to hold often-run programs. If a program can be present at the moment a microcomputer is turned on, the need for program loading and the associated load delay times are eliminated. A permanent, nonvolatile program memory is also useful for storing a small program that has common system utility programs and an initialization program or a bootstrap program. Not many years back, full computer modules containing diode matrixes were used to store small permanent programs, but semiconductor memory technology now dominates the nonvolatile working storage field. Read-only memories (ROMs) and programmable read-only memories (PROMs) are the most popular nonvolatile storage devices. Many other names are given to nonvolatile semiconductor memories (EROMS, EPROMs, VROMS), but all of these devices fit into one of these two categories.

A ROM is similar in design to a RAM. A central array of memory cells is surrounded by peripheral circuitry that accesses the data stored in the array. The primary difference lies in the type of memory cells used in the cell array.

A ROM's data storage cells are designed to permanently store a 1 or a 0 even if power is turned off. This is accomplished by either selectively building 1- and 0-generating cells into the array at pre-defined memory locations or by building many identical 1-generating cells and burning out the cells that must be set to zero.

When the programming (setting of the 1 and 0 states) is done at the factory by altering the metallization mask on the memory chip itself, the end product is referred to as a mask-programmed ROM. When all the cells in a memory are originally one value and the user is given a means of programming the bits in the device to the values of his choosing (usually by using a high-voltage "programmer" that selectively blows small programming fuses on the chip), the memory is called a PROM.

Either device will permanently hold a program, but each device has its own unique advantages. A ROM requires only internal read circuitry to read the preprogrammed bits, and a PROM requires additional programming circuitry. Due to this extra circuitry and more complex fusible-PROM cell design, PROMs are not as dense as ROMs. The current-technology storage capacity of PROMs is about 50% that of ROMs.

Expense is the ROM's biggest drawback. A one-time mask setup charge of a few thousand dollars is required, and if a different program is ever needed, a new mask must be made. For large-volume applications, however, ROMs are a much less expensive proposition than PROMs because a ROM (excluding the one-time mask charge) is cheaper than a PROM.

The PROM's big advantage is, of course, its programmability. The one-time mask charge and the factory lead time can be avoided with PROMs.

Aside from the lack of write circuitry, the peripheral circuitry of the ROM or PROM is similar to that of the RAM. Decoders take an address and appropriately pick a memory cell to be examined. Sense amplifiers amplify the memory cell's small current and send the resulting data to the data outputs.

There are dynamic as well as static ROMs, but most designs today are of the static type. A dynamic ROM that must be periodically refreshed initially seems quite ridiculous. A ROM that essentially loses its data if not refreshed seems to violate the nonvolatility criterion that makes a ROM a ROM. The fact is, however, a dynamic ROM doesn't really lose its data if the cells aren't refreshed; it just starts reading them wrong until refreshing is resumed. A dynamic ROM is much like a dynamic RAM, except that the 1-generating transistors are permanently wired to stay in the conducting state. Charge must still be kept on the base region of the conducting transistors, so refreshing is necessary.

Dynamic ROMs were primarily used in applications in which refreshing came naturally, such as in a character generator of a display system. It is true that most of the dynamic ROMs have passed along the wayside, but they might return.

A Representative Bipolar Programmable ROM.   The first ROMs and PROMs to come into common use were small 64- and 256-bit high-speed bipolar devices. These chips found applications as large computer bootstrap storage units as well as combinatorial gating and other discrete logic replacements (in which the addresses act as gating inputs and the data acts as the desired resulting output). The DM 74S287 (made by National Semiconductor) is an example of an advanced version of these early bipolar PROMs.

The DM 74S287 is a 256 × 4 PROM built with Schottky-clamped TTL technology. It is quite fast (typically 35 ns from the time it receives an address to valid data output) and runs on a single supply voltage (+5 V).

Figure 3-9 illustrates the 74S287. Notice that the only controls on the PROM are the two lines that enable the tristate data output lines. Reading a location from memory is simply a matter of submitting the desired address at the address inputs and waiting for the data output.

Programming the PROM is not as simple a matter. The 74S287's memory cells consist of a four-transistor cell structure with a titanium–tungsten (Ti-W) fuse on the collector of the selecting transistor. By selecting the byte to be programmed with the address lines and properly sequencing the chip power, output, and enable lines to the high-voltage values shown in the programming waveforms, the fuse can be blown and the bit programmed to a logic 1 (high). Notice that the PROM contains all zeros before it is programmed.

The DM 74S287 was chosen for this example because of its advanced programming circuitry. On most fuse-programmable PROMs, the programming timing is very critical. Strange, slowly rising waveforms must be followed closely to program the PROM properly. Too fast a rise time will cause the programming fuse to blast apart and splatter beads of metal over adjacent circuitry, causing failures years after the programming. Too slow a rise time causes heating, with the result that the fuse will melt very slowly. Heat buildup from the slow melt causes thermal damage to the surrounding transistors.

National developed the *Tri-Safe* method to prevent poor programming caused by slow and fast rise times. By assigning the programming timing control function to an onboard programmer circuit, the PROM essentially programs itself at the optimum fuse blow rate.

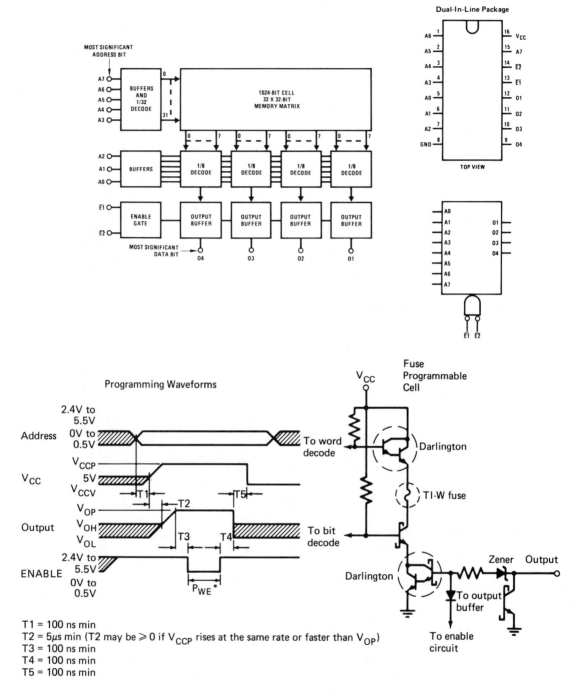

Figure 3-9 The National DM 74S287 256- by 4-bit programmable ROM. (Reprinted by permission of National Semiconductor Corporation, Santa Clara, Calif.)

Once a satisfactory PROM software program has been developed, an equivalent plug-in replaceable mask-programmed ROM, the DM 74S187, may be substituted in large-quantity applications.

A Representative Erasable PROM.   Like MOS RAMs, both MOS ROMs and PROMs have a higher number of bits per chip and a lower power dissipation per bit than bipolar devices; but unlike MOS RAMs, there is little similarity between the way most MOS and bipolar PROMs store their data. Instead of using fusible links to program MOS PROMs, charges are trapped in memory cells by applying a high-voltage programming pulse to the memory cell. These charges remain trapped, representing a logic 0, until an external high-energy source, such as ultraviolet light, is applied to the charged region (thus allowing the charge to leak away). This characteristic has been utilized in ultraviolet-erasable PROMs (EPROMS) and offers good PROM economy, because a program can be changed without purchasing a whole new PROM.

The 2708 family of EPROMs, which includes the $512 \times 8\ 2704$, the $1K \times 8$ 2708 and the $2K \times 8\ 2716$, is a good example of erasable, programmable, read-only memories. As Fig. 3-10 illustrates, the organization of the memory cells is very similar to that of the bipolar PROM. The 9-, 10-, or 11-bit address, depending on the PROM version, is submitted to the decoding circuitry, and a data word from the cell array is delivered on the data output pins.

The 2708's programming procedures are less critical than those of the bipolar PROM. Because no onchip fuse destruction takes place, there is little risk of damaging the silicon by applying bad programming signals. When unprogrammed, and after each erasure, all 4K, 8K, or 16K bits in the memory are in the logic 1 state. Zeros can be programmed into the PROM by raising the CS/WE input to +12 V, setting up valid address and data to be programmed, and applying a 0.1 to 1 ms 26 V programming pulse to the programming pin. A single pulse only partially programs the PROM, however. The whole program must be charged into the memory cells gradually and evenly over the whole surface of the silicon chip, so a programming loop that goes through and programs each byte about 100 times must be set up. Repeatedly programming the same memory byte is ineffective, because it violates the evenly distributed programming rule.

The only real caution to be observed in programming the 2708 is that of address changes while the programming pin is high. If an address changes before the falling edge of the CS/WE signal when it leaves the programming mode, random bits throughout the memory may be unintentionally programmed.

Interfacing the 2708 to a microcomputer system is very simple because it is designed to work with microcomputer buses. The address lines are connected to the microprocessor address bus and the data lines are connected to the data bus. The $1K \times 8$ configuration allows a 1-kilobyte memory to be implemented with just one chip. The chip select line can be controlled by circuitry that

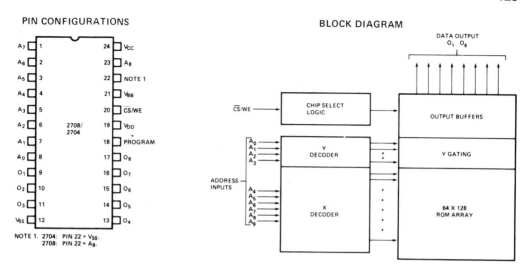

PIN CONFIGURATIONS

BLOCK DIAGRAM

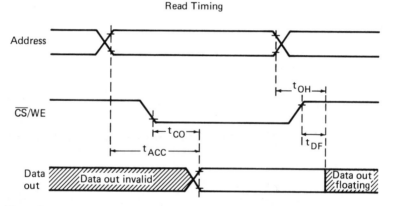

Read Timing

Figure 3-10 The Intel 2708 ultraviolet erasable PROM. (Reprinted by permission of Intel Corporation, Copyright 1976.)

decodes the specific 1K memory block in the microprocessor's address space this memory will be assigned to.

In production applications in which many of the same ROMs will be used, the 2708 can be substituted with the pin-equivalent 68308 or 2308 mask-programmed ROM.

Electrically Alterable ROMs. Electrically alterable ROMs are similar to EPROMs, but instead of requiring an ultraviolet source to erase them, an erasing voltage on the proper pin on the package can be used. A EAROM offers a price advantage, because an expensive quartz lid package (necessary for ultraviolet erasing on an EPROM) is not needed, and stray sunlight or X rays can't wipe out a program.

VMOS ROM.   New V-groove MOS ROMs, such as the American Microsystems (AMI) S4262, use new device technology to boost memory cell density as well as decrease access time. Current 64K MOS ROMs are bordering on the limit of practical silicon chip size. Because VMOS memory cells take up only half the space of standard MOS cells, this technology will be the most practical approach in upcoming 128K and 256K ROMs.

RAM/ROM.   A very interesting RAM/ROM is currently being developed and promises to be useful in many applications. The RAM/ROM acts as a regular RAM when power is stabilized. The difference is the way it "comes up." Most RAMs initially have a random pattern of logic 1s and 0s scattered throughout the memory array when power is first applied. This initial information is useless. The RAM/ROM can be programmed to initially have a program in it when power is first applied. After power-up, the device acts like a normal RAM that has just been loaded with a valid program. This chip has the potential for eliminating small dedicated bootstrap and utility ROMs from many microcomputer applications. The RAM/ROM can be used either as ROM or as an extension of normal RAM, thereby cutting down RAM and addressing requirements.

MEDIUM-TERM MASS STORE

Medium-term storage devices are used for temporarily storing blocks of data that are used often enough to require fast random access but are too big to fit into a short-term working store—at least all at once. In microcomputer applications, these devices are often used as long-term storage as well, because microcomputer programs and data are typically short enough to fit into a few hundred thousand bytes of storage.

Devices included in the medium-term mass-store category are non-volatile media such as floppy disks, magnetic-bubble memories, and solid-state disks built from charge-coupled-device technology.

The Floppy Disk

Like the Xerox machine and Wankel engine, the so-called floppy disk is a device that did not initially seem feasible from the standpoint of practicality. A flexible, paper-thin disk spinning at 360 rpm while still inside its "record jacket" doesn't seem like it could possibly be a reliable high-density storage device; but through engineering development by IBM and other firms, this product became not only practical, but quite competitive with other storage media.

Figure 3-11 illustrates a typical drive with a floppy disk inserted into the drive mechanism. The floppy disk spins in its jacket at 360 rpm with the disk

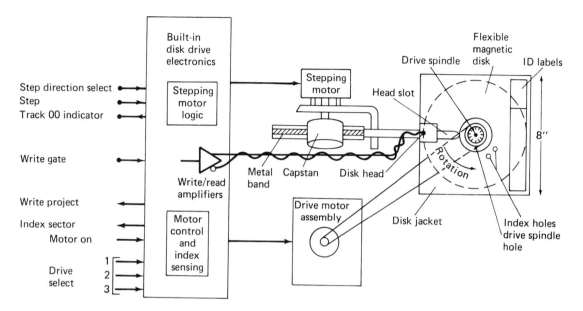

Figure 3-11   Details of a floppy disk drive.

drive's read and write heads contacting the disk through a long narrow slot in the jacket.

The floppy disk contains a number of concentric tracks (77 tracks for a full-size floppy and 35 tracks for a minifloppy) that are accessed by radially moving the read–write heads onto the proper track using a stepping motor or magnetic "voice coil" linear motor. The process of mechanically moving the heads is called *seeking*.

The disk drive has two indications that it is on the proper track. Because stepping motors are used to move the heads, the step movements are counted and the step count indicates the proper track. Secondly, a track identifier code is written at the beginning of the first sector on any given track.

A floppy disk's tracks are each divided into 10 to 26 pie-wedge sectors. Small blocks of data (typically 128 bytes by 8 bits) are stored serially on each sector along with a few bytes of preamble data and empty data gaps to keep sectors well isolated from one another.

Sectors are assigned in two ways, depending on the mechanics of the disk drive. *Hard-sectored disks* have coding holes at the beginning of every sector on the disk; photoelectric sensors recognize the holes and thus the beginnings of sectors. *Soft-sectored disks* have only one coding hole, which marks the beginning of the first sector; it is up to the read head and system software to determine which sector is currently being passed as the disk spins.

The advantage of a hard-sectored disk is reliability. Since the disk drive doesn't have to continuously read track data to "know" its location, the error rates are reduced significantly.

As Fig. 3-11 illustrates, the drive control circuitry for a floppy disk is not as complicated as some people make it out to be. A few simple lines such as *drive select* and *motor on* are self-explanatory. This leaves the head-moving (stepping) controls; direction select, step, track 00 indicator; the read and write data lines; and the write enable or write gate control. A few additional indicators such as *index sector* and *write protect* are also available.

Floppy disk interfaces can range in complexity from a few simple microprocessor-driven latches (which monitor the drive status and submit the proper controls) to a completely automated controller that takes a block transfer command from the microprocessor and performs all the sequencing involved in reading the proper tracks and sectors.

Currently available disk controllers have many advanced features that reduce the disk-controlling software requirements, but most of these are just fancy extras; the basics of the disk drive control are very simple.

One function that is typically done by the disk controller (but which can be done by microprocessor software just as easily) is error detection and correction. Data write-checking is performed by reading the written data the next time it comes around after the write is performed. If it is incorrectly written, the disk drive will try to write it again. After a preset number of tries (usually about 10), the disk drive will give up and declare a write error. This usually indicates a faulty disk or a dirty disk head.

Read errors are constantly being monitored using a checksum-type error code. If a sector's checksum is wrong after a block read, the disk will again try to read it correctly. If it succeeds, the disk is said to have recovered from a *soft error*. If after 10 tries the data is still unreadable, a *hard error* is declared, and the data is assumed to be lost.

Under rare circumstances a *seek error* may occur. In this case, the stepping motor or voice-coil movement has inadvertently moved the head to the wrong disk track. The fact that it is on the wrong track is detected by reading the track identifier at the beginning of the track. Recovering from a seek error involves setting the heads back to the first track (track 00) and stepping to the proper track.

A few interface chips that perform disk control and error checking are currently available, and their use is described in the interface components section of this text.

Floppy disks come in two general sizes. Full floppies (203mm in diameter) have the following characteristics:

- *Disk capacity:* 250K × 8 (single density)
- *Data transfer rate:* 30K bytes per second
- *Number of tracks:* 80
- *Rotational speed:* 360 rpm

The smaller minifloppies usually found in inexpensive microcomputers generally have the following characteristics:

- *Disk capacity:* 110K × 8 (single density)
  220K × 8 (double density)
- *Data transfer rate:* 15K bytes per second
- *Number of tracks:* 35
- *Rotational speed:* 300 rpm

In summation, minifloppies have about half the performance of full-size floppies and cost much less. As to the question of whether to buy two minifloppies or one full-sized floppy disk for a large-capacity micro, it is generally wiser to opt for two minifloppies. It is always a good idea to have two of any magnetic storage device. With only one, you can't easily copy files onto other diskettes. This capability is almost essential in a well balanced system.

Magnetic Bubble Memory

In its early development stages, the floppy-disk seemed to be far-fetched and infeasible; but compared to the magnetic bubble memory, the floppy disk in its infancy looked like a sure thing. Bubble memories are magnetic devices that store data as magnetically oriented domains in a sheet of magnetic material; but unlike most magnetic media, such as disk or tape, the magnetic material stays stationary and magnetic domains or bubbles move around within the magnetic material under the influence of a rotating magnetic field. By forming a long loop of magnetic bubbles using a bubble generator/eater and a magnetic field, a large "shift register" memory is set up.

Bubble memories combine some of the best features of both magnetic and semiconductor memory storage. They are large-capacity nonvolatile storage devices like disk or tape, and the area in which the actual data is being stored requires no power to hold the data. At the same time, a bubble memory can fit into the space of a dual-inline package and be mounted directly on the CPU or memory card of a microcomputer.

The Texas Instruments TBM0103 module is an example of a commercially available bubble memory. This 92,304-bit (not a power of 2) module comes in a 14-pin dual-inline package that includes two built-in magnetic coils, a gadolinium–gallium–garnet magnetic substrate material, and special shields to protect the device from stray external magnetic fields. A data transfer rate of up to 100 kilobits per second is possible with this device, but random access is *not* possible, since it is in essence a large shift register. Table 3-2 gives some specifications of the TBM0103.

Table 3-2   TBM 0103 Bubble Memory Characteristics

Useful capacity (bits)	92,304 bits
Register organization	641 × 144
Drive field rate (maximum)	100 kHz
Input/output data rate (maximum)	50 kb/s
Minor-loop data rate (maximum)	100 kb/s
Average access time (first bit)	4.0 ms
Average cycle time (144-bit block)	12.8 ms
Power (100% duty cycle)	0.6 W
Maximum operating tempurature range	0 to 70 °C
Nonvolatile storage temperature range	−40 to 85 °C
Size	2.5 × 2.6 × 10.1 mm
Pin count	14
Pin spacing	2.54 mm
Pin centers	27.94 mm
Weight	20 g
Maximum permissible external magnetic field in any direction	40 oersteds

The Charge-Coupled Device

The charge-coupled device falls into the same medium-term storage class as the bubble memory because it too is a serial shift register. Charge-coupled devices store data as charges on a row of either T-shaped or chevron-shaped charge storage cells. By applying the proper voltage levels to these cells, charges can be moved around; a circulating shift register is thus formed.

Charge-coupled devices are unlike bubbles in that they are volatile in character. They are also much faster than bubble memories, because they move charges rather than magnetic domains; but CCDs don't pack the same density of storage into a given area, because the actual storage structures (the special shapes) must be fabricated. To make memory access time quicker, many short shift registers and decoding logic are often incorporated into a CCD chip. If sixteen 4096-bit shift registers are used instead of one long 65,536-bit shift register, the maximum access time or latency to read any given bit is reduced by a factor of 16. The overall throughput is also increased by a factor of 16.

A good example of a CCD having precisely the configuration just described is the Fairchild F464 65,536 × 1 dynamic serial memory. This device has 16 randomly accessible shift registers that are multiplexed down to a single data input and data output bit. As Fig. 3-12 shows, the rows are selected by the four address lines (A0–A3). External logic is required to clock data through the shift register using the four clock phases (1, 2, T1, and T2), and the user must keep track of where he is in the shift register.

The F464's performance characteristics are typical of what can be expected of modern CCDs. Data can be clocked through at a data rate of 1 to 5 MHz.

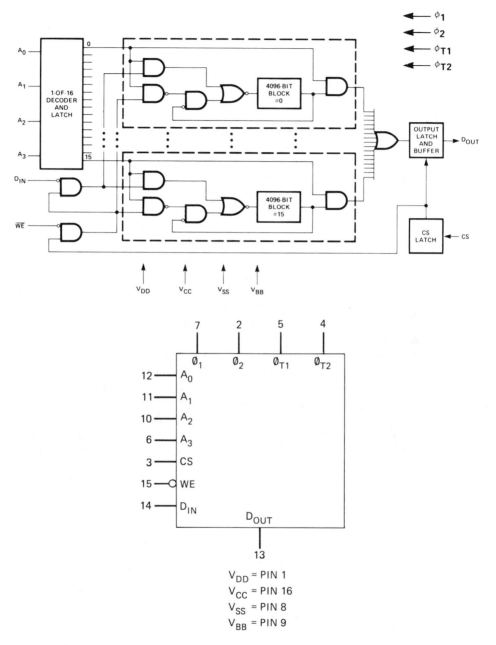

Figure 3-12 The Fairchild F464 65K-bit charge-coupled device. (Courtesy Fairchild Camera and Instrument Corporation, Mountain View, Calif.)

Clocking can be halted for up to 15 microseconds once each interval of 64 or more clock cycles. This half capability is useful for letting logic perform address computations or as a timing margin for other devices.

One of the best applications of the CCD in a microcomputer system is in the implementation of a solid-state disk for medium-term volatile storage. Using just 16 of the F464s, for example, a 131-kilobyte shift register memory with a data transfer rate of 5 MHz could be set up. This solid-state disk could be loaded from an inexpensive tape drive at the beginning of the day and provide minifloppy disk storage functions all day long without any of the wear or noise problems associated with a mechanical device. The file access time would of course be almost instantaneous with the 5 MHz data transfer rate.

LONG-TERM MASS STORE

Long-term storage devices reside at the lowest levels of memory hierarchies and are capable of storing vast amounts of data in a somewhat permanent, nonvolatile form at a very low cost. Access speed and random-access capabilities are of secondary importance for long-term storage devices; memory storage size is the primary goal.

Since the early days of computers, magnetic media have dominated the long-term storage field, followed by paper media. Magnetic tape units and disks are two currently popular magnetic media, but at one time magnetic drum memories were an important part of most computer systems. Paper tape and the familiar "IBM card" are two popular paper media.

In regard to long-term storage for microcomputers, long- and medium-term storage devices are usually one and the same. This situation is brought about by two factors: Microcomputers are slow enough that a tall memory hierarchy (a many-leveled hierarchy with ever-increasing storage device speed) is not needed to get the most out of the microcomputer's microprocessor. Secondly, microcomputers are not typically put to use in extremely large data-base or program applications.

The three most common forms of long-term storage in microcomputer systems are floppy disks, magnetic tape (usually cassette), and paper tape. Floppy disks, which were discussed in the medium-term storage section, are currently dominating the field, while the more cumbersome cassette and paper tape are being phased out. Floppy disks have the advantages of high data transfer rate, convenient storage form (thin, square packet), and semirandom-access capability.

This section discusses the basic principles of magnetic recordings and shows how they are used in a few microcomputer long-term storage devices. Paper tape is also covered.

Magnetic Data Recording

Magnetic materials exhibit many characteristics that are desirable in a memory cell. They can be magnetized in two or more directions to represent ones or zeros; they will hold a magnetic state until changed, thus exhibiting a natural memory characteristic; and they are plentiful and cheap.

Disks, drums, tape, and floppy disks basically use the same magnetic recording principles. A magnetic oxide containing magnetic dipoles is deposited in a thin layer on a plastic or metal surface. The resulting magnetic tape, disk, or drum is then drawn past magnetic heads (electromagnets with a very sharply aimed magnetic field), aligning the dipoles in one direction or the other. This process is defined as recording.

The process known as data retrieving involves passing the recorded tape or disk surface past another electromagnetic or Hall-effect (a semiconductor that is sensitive to magnetic field changes) head. The aligned dipoles generate a current corresponding to the recorded data.

Magnetic Properties. The idea of a magnetic dipole being aligned in one direction or another to represent a 1 or a 0 is somewhat simplistic. There are hundreds of thousands of magnetic dipoles for every few centimeters of magnetic tape, and many sorts of dipoles are used in a magnetic coating formulation. The dipoles tend to align to a greater extent as the magnetic field strength increases. When the magnetic field gets so strong that the dipoles are well aligned, the tape reaches saturation. A tape in saturation is analogous to an amplifier in the same state.

For music and voice recording, a linear, nonsaturating tape response is very desirable. By recording below the saturation level of the tape, analog waveforms can be recorded. Digital data recording, however, is a different story. Data can be more effectively recorded by quickly driving the tape into saturation using a strong magnetic field.

Saturated data recording has a number of advantages over nonsaturated recording. It is a faster recording method because the magnetic dipoles are aligned extremely quickly using powerful magnetic fields. Saturated recordings are also less prone to noise because all the tape's amplitude response has been "used up" in recording the saturated data.

Certain tape formulations are better suited to saturated data recording than others, and these are used on disks, drums, and data cassettes. Nonsaturating tapes such as audio recording tapes are not well-suited to saturated recording equipment, just as saturating tapes are poor audio tapes. The fact that a tape is a computer data tape doesn't mean that it is an extremely high quality tape; it just means it is different, and probably of the saturating variety.

Magnetic tape and disk coatings must be very uniform to avoid dropouts in the data recording. Dropping out a few cycles of a musical passage on an audio tape would hardly be noticeable, but dropping a few bits on a data tape could ruin a whole program or data base. Magnetic coating uniformity is therefore of prime importance on magnetic tapes and disks.

Recording Methods.   As a tape or disk is moved past a magnetic head, logic levels (representing the 1s and 0s) can be recorded one after the other in a serial manner. Upon retrieving the bits off the tape or disk, however, a lot more information than a rapidly changing serial stream of 1s and 0s is needed to make sense out of the data recording. Most importantly, the points at which each bit starts and stops must be determined. The difference between three 1s in a row and one or two 1s must be distinguished. Secondly, since most computers deal with words and bytes, byte boundaries must be distinguishable. Finally, electromagnetic read heads only generate current at the state-transition boundaries where the dipole alignment changes. Logic levels must be determined from these changes.

The solutions to the above-mentioned problems lie in data formats (Fig. 3-13).

Nonreturn-to-zero (NRZ) recording is a logical extension of the simple positive and negative saturation representation of logic states just discussed. The only differences are that (1) a clock track is recorded next to the data on the tape to help determine where bits start and stop, and (2) changes from positive to negative saturation are used to determine the recorded signal, because electromagnetic record heads can only sense tape saturation or flux changes and not levels.

Recording in the NRZ format is simple; data is sent directly to the record head with a 1 representing negative tape saturation and a 0 representing positive tape saturation, as shown in Fig. 3-14.

Retrieving NRZ data is a matter of using a flip-flop to toggle between 1 and 0 every time a saturation direction change is detected. This flip-flop essentially synthesizes the input data that was originally recorded. The clock track is used to clock the data into an input register at the appropriate times.

The problem with NRZ recording is its error propagation characteristic. Because flux changes (rather than absolute levels) are used to determine the original recorded data, reliable reading is dependent on the toggling flip-flop's ability to track the data perfectly and not miss a single saturation transition. If the flip-flop happens to miss a flux change (perhaps caused by a tape dropout), the flip-flop will be set in the wrong direction for that particular bit. Not only will that bit be affected, however; all the following bits will be read "upside down" since the flip-flop is out of phase with the recorded data.

Nonreturn-to-zero inverted (NRZI) recording solves the error propagation problem and is therefore more commonly used in commercial tape equipment. Instead of allowing saturation directions to change from positive to negative on

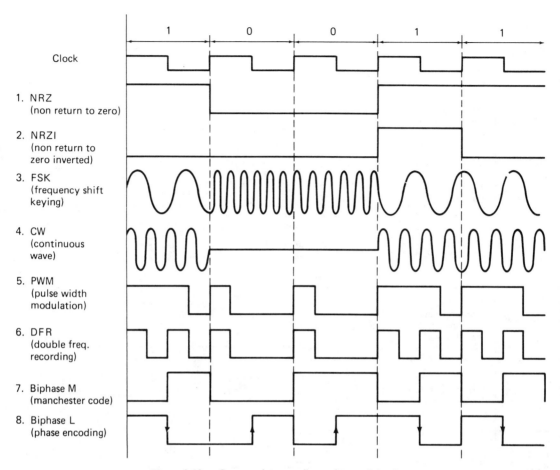

Figure 3-13   Common data recording and transmitting formats.

all 0-to-1 transitions and back again on 1-to-0, the saturation is simply allowed to change, whether it be from negative to positive or vice versa, whenever input data of one is encountered. Zero data causes no saturation change.

Retrieving the data is a matter of determining if a saturation change has occurred. If it has, the data is 1; if not, it is 0. If a saturation change happens to be missed by the read head, a 1 will be misread as a 0, but subsequent data will still be read correctly, since a saturation change still equals 1 and no change still equals 0.

As with NRZ, a separate clock track must be recorded beside the data track on the tape. When a separate clock track is available to tell where bits stop and start, almost any distinguishable 1- and 0-representing signal can be used as the data track.

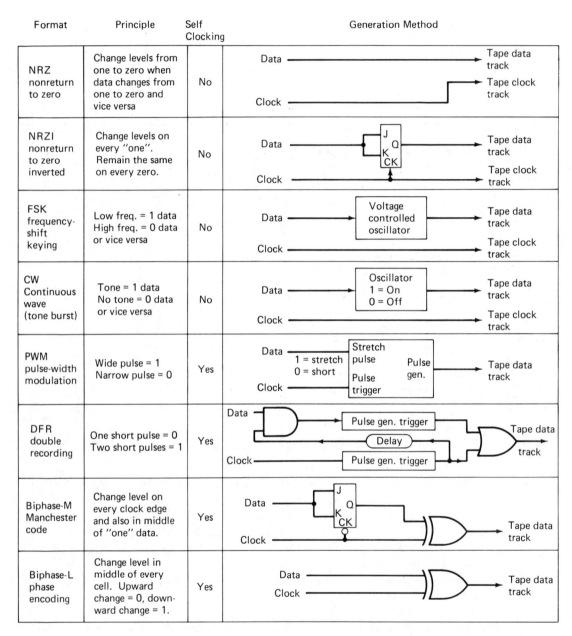

Format	Principle	Self Clocking	Generation Method
NRZ nonreturn to zero	Change levels from one to zero when data changes from one to zero and vice versa	No	Data → Tape data track; Clock → Tape clock track
NRZI nonreturn to zero inverted	Change levels on every "one". Remain the same on every zero.	No	Data → J K CK Q → Tape data track; Clock → Tape clock track
FSK frequency-shift keying	Low freq. = 1 data High freq. = 0 data or vice versa	No	Data → Voltage controlled oscillator → Tape data track; Clock → Tape clock track
CW Continuous wave (tone burst)	Tone = 1 data No tone = 0 data or vice versa	No	Data → Oscillator 1 = On 0 = Off → Tape data track; Clock → Tape clock track
PWM pulse-width modulation	Wide pulse = 1 Narrow pulse = 0	Yes	Data → 1 = stretch 0 = short; Stretch pulse / Pulse trigger → Pulse gen. → Tape data track; Clock →
DFR double recording	One short pulse = 0 Two short pulses = 1	Yes	Data → Pulse gen. trigger / Delay / Clock → Pulse gen. trigger → Tape data track
Biphase-M Manchester code	Change level on every clock edge and also in middle of "one" data.	Yes	Data → J K CK Q → Tape data track; Clock →
Biphase-L phase encoding	Change level in middle of every cell. Upward change = 0, downward change = 1.	Yes	Data → / Clock → Tape data track

Figure 3-14 Tape and communications format generation.

134

Frequency-shift keyed (FSK) recording is a case in point. Using this method, a high-frequency sine wave represents a 1, while a low-frequency sine wave represents 0.

Continuous-wave (CW) recording uses a tone burst to generate a 1 and no tone burst to represent a 0.

Both FSK and CW are seldom used in modern magnetic data recording applications, and both are nonsaturated recording methods; but FSK is still the most commonly used data communication format for remote computer terminals relying on modems.

So far, all the recording methods discussed require two recorded tracks — one for data and one for clocking. Methods that require clock tracks are known as clocked data formats. Their disadvantages include the need for a two-track recorder, their sensitivity to tape skew between the two tracks, and their sparse data packing.

It's true that games can be played to eliminate the need for a separate clock track by going to asynchronous timing methods. A slower-speed clock can also be recorded and multiplied into an in-phase normal-frequency clock using a phase-locked loop, but a more realistic approach to the problem is the use of a self-clocking recording method. Self-clocking recording methods produce a serial stream of 1s and 0s on a tape in such a way that both clock and data can be derived from the single serial stream.

Pulse-width modulation (PWM) recording is a good example of a self-clocking format. Notice in Figure 3-13 that the waveform has a rising edge at the beginning of every bit boundary. By triggering a "pulse-width watching" circuit on the rising edges or by simply examining the waveform in the middle of the third quarter of the waveform, a 1 or 0 can be accurately detected. Basically, a short pulse equals a 0 and a long pulse equals a 1.

Double-frequency recording (DFR) is similar to PWM except that two quick pulses represent a 1 instead of one long pulse. Many floppy disk drives use this recording method. The DFR waveform is identical to the PWM except that the second quarter of the waveform on each cycle is always 0.

It is fairly easy to generate PWM and DFR, because a variable-pulse-width generator is all that is required. The two most common types of self-clocking recording schemes, however, are even easier to generate waveforms for, but the waveforms are quite cryptic and hard to follow in the timing diagram (although the hardware has no problem keeping track of the data).

Biphase-M encoding, or *Manchester code,* is a self-clocking scheme that changes from 0 to 1 or 1 to 0 on every bit boundary, but an additional change only occurs in the middle of bits representing 1. This is basically a form of frequency modulation using only single cycles of each frequency.

Biphase-L encoding is similar to biphase-M; but instead of a transition occurring on the edge of every clock pulse, it always occurs in the middle of every clock pulse. The direction of the transition in the middle of the bit determines whether it is a 1 or 0.

Biphase-L's advantage is that it is slightly easier to generate than Manchester code, but it has the disadvantage of being susceptible to phase inversion. If the playback tape deck has its magnetic head polarity-reversed from the recording deck, or if the playback deck has an extra inverting amplifier stage, the data will be read "upside down."

Figure 3-14 illustrates how biphase is generated. The generation of biphase seems to be a difficult task to accomplish, until you realize the trick: in this case, an exclusive-OR gate.

Microcomputer Magnetic Recording Devices.   Floppy disks are becoming the dominant magnetic recording device in the microcomputer field. Floppy disks typically use saturated recording techniques and NRZI or DFR methods.

Before the widespread use of floppy disks, cassettes were very popular as a data storage medium. Professional companies developed cassette decks that record in NRZ, PWM, and biphase using saturating recording methods.

A number of popular cassette and tape recording methods were introduced by microcomputer hobbyists as well. Hobbyist magnetic cassette recording usually consists of biphase-L recorded data on nonsaturating tape such as audio cassettes (the popular Tarbell cassette format falls into this category), and a self-clocking form of FSK on nonsaturating tape (commonly known as the Kansas City Standard).

The saturated cassette formats offer higher performance than the nonsaturating audio tape formats, but, at this point, upgrading to a floppy disk is a wiser choice for most hobbyists than upgrading to saturated cassette recordings.

Using Magnetic Tape in a Micro System.   While a hobbyist's or small businessman's single-track, low-speed, microcomputer-controlled cassette recorder hardly seems comparable to the multimegabit-rate 9-track high-density "mag tape drives" used in large business and scientific computers, many problems and their solutions are shared by both devices.

The first problem is that of accurately locating and reading the desired byte of data. Unlike random-access memory, tape must be sequentially read. Further, it is not possible to start and stop the magnetic tape drive fast enough or accurately enough to permit reading just one byte at a time. With a tape "density" of 32 bits per millimeter (800 bits per inch), for example, each bit occupies only 31.25 micrometers (microns).

The solutions to the data identifying and reading problems lie in "file management." Information is written onto the magnetic tape in "records" or "blocks" that usually consist of a few hundred bytes of data. Between the records, blank spots or *interrecord gaps* are left to allow the tape drive to bring the tape up to speed before reading the tape and to stop it after reading the single record. The few hundred bytes of data read from the record are stored in a "tape read buffer" area in memory and the program is free to use the bytes one by one. Finally, when the buffer is empty, the tape is restarted and another record is read, filling the tape read buffer again.

The simplest form of program tape storage is the storing of a whole program in one large record. Most microcomputer tape systems designed for use with manual motor control recorders use this method. A more advanced way to store programs and data is in a series of equal-sized records. A series of records is usually called a *file* and is ended with an *end-of-file* mark on the tape. Figure 3-15 illustrates the typical file structure used on most advanced microcomputer tape units. Figure 3-16 shows a common single-record tape format.

The complexity of a cassette tape interface is dependent on the number of features incorporated. Read and write circuitry is essential in any tape interface. With just read and write circuitry, it is possible to dump and load memory by manually turning the cassette recorder on and off at the beginnings and ends of records. Multiple-record files are not practical with manual motor control systems.

Motor start and stop control is an option that essentially comes for free in most cassette recorders, and many inexpensive cassette interface units take advantage of this feature. A computer-controlled magnetic reed switch is typically used to start and stop the tape.

Simple motor start–stop control is a vast improvement over manual control because it offers a crude file management capability. Blocks of data can be read sequentially in a start-and-stop manner, allowing the processor to perform processing on single blocks of data. Two cassette recorders and a cassette interface with motor control make up a single file management system. One cassette is designated as the reading or input unit and the other is the write or output device. Blocks of data or pages of text can be read in through the read cassette, modified or added to by the user, and written out in standard file format on the output cassette.

Assembler programs also benefit from motor control. Assembling a source file of a program takes a relatively long time. Storing a whole source file in memory is not possible with large programs due to the limits in memory size, and taking in data from a large single record without motor control is not possible because there is not enough time to assemble the program between the bytes on the tape. With motor control, the computer can have tape input on demand by using a read buffer and multiple-record file system.

The next step up from motor start–stop control is full motor control. Professional cassette decks usually feature fast forward and rewind as well as motor start and stop control. These features allow for hands-off operation of the cassette unit, which is very convenient.

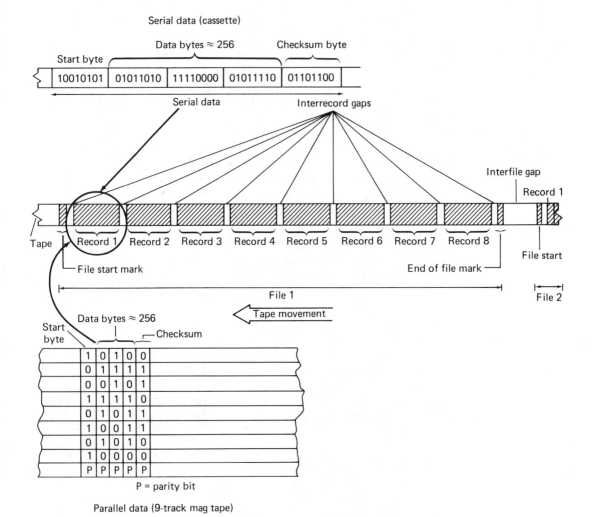

Figure 3-15   Tape file structure for single- and multiple-track tape.

Another feature often found on professional cassette decks is the ability to fast-forward or rewind the tape and search for a certain record in the process of rewinding. Because tape rewinds 10–20 times as fast as it reads or writes, it is not possible to use identifying words written at normal read and write speeds to find a file. Instead, special series of code words—which the cassette electronics can read if passed over at high speeds—are written at the beginning of each record. It is easy to find the desired file using these high-speed-readable file markers.

Typical data transfer rates for magnetic cassette tapes used in microcomputer systems range from 300 to 2400 baud, or 30 to 240 bytes per second, using

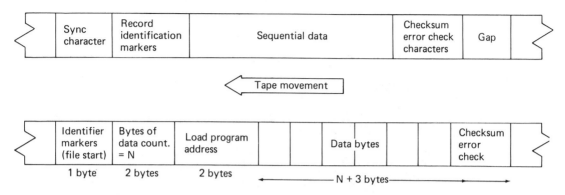

Figure 3-16 Typical direct memory load tape formats. (a) Synchronous record format. (b) Direct memory load format (often used to load programs in microcomputer systems.)

standard audio cassettes at a 1⅞ inch-per-second (4.7625 cm/s) speed, and up to 32,000 bits per second or 3200 bytes per second using 1600 bits per inch (630 bits/cm) saturating data tape at 20 ips (50.8 cm/s). These transfer rates are relatively slow, so serial interfaces are commonly used with cassette tape units.

Paper Media

The earliest forms of computer data storage were paper cards and tapes. Even before the development of the electronic computer, an inventor named Babbage envisioned using gears, mechanical counters, and punched cards to form a "difference engine" or mechanical computer. Difference engines were not successful due to friction problems, but paper media have had very large success in the computer field and remain popular to this day.

Paper media have gained wide support in the microcomputer field because many inexpensive devices are available to handle them and because they have some very desirable characteristics. Paper tape, for example, is cheap, rugged, very reliable, and insensitive to magnetic fields.

The most common paper medium in the microcomputer field is punched paper tape. Not only is it used extensively for long-term data storage; it is used as a program exchange medium as well. The widespread use of paper tape can be directly attributed to the ASR-33 Teletype unit. This teleprinter consists of a keyboard, a 10-character-per-second printer, and a paper tape reader–punch. Many microcomputer users found that this unit met their hard-copy as well as long-term storage needs for a very low price.

Paper tape has characteristics similar in some respects to magnetic tape. It is a serial storage medium and can only be read in one direction. Paper tape is very slow, with read rates ranging from 10 to a few thousand characters per second.

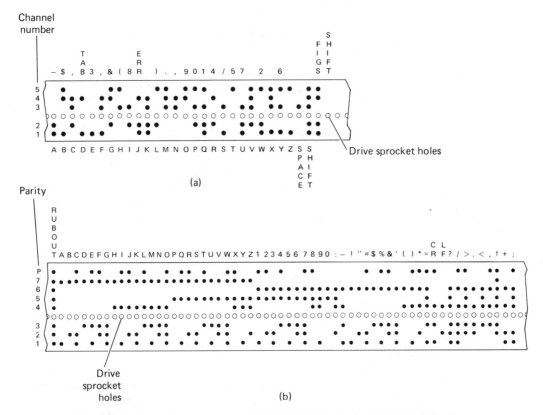

Figure 3-17   Paper tape formats. (a) 5-level code (29-code). (b) ASR-33 8-level code.

One very important difference between paper tape and magnetic tape is paper tape's character-on-demand capability. Magnetic tape requires multibyte records because individual bytes cannot be accurately or selectively read. Because paper tape readers usually pull the paper tape across the reader head with a ratcheting action, it is possible to read just one byte. Due to this capability, file management methods are not used in systems based on paper tape.

Paper tape is a byte-oriented medium. The most common kind of paper tape is the 8-level kind that is compatible with the ASR-33 Teletype's paper tape reader and punch. *Level* refers to the number of bits of data represented in each data byte on the tape. The format for 5-level paper tape (which was popular on earlier non-ASCII teleprinters) is a hole string with five parallel hole positions across it; 8-level tapes have eight parallel hole positions. Figure 3-17 illustrates these two paper tape formats.

Paper tape punching is always done with some sort of mechanical die, but there are three distinct approaches to paper tape reading: mechanical, electro-mechanical, and optical.

Mechanical paper tape reading is the crudest of the three, but it is very reliable. ''Feelers'' are poked up through the holes in the tape to read each byte. The feelers thereby sense which holes are punched, mechanically register the holes, and read the byte. The principal drawbacks of mechanical tape reading is the speed limitation and device complexity.

Electromechanical tape reading is a simpler tape reading method that relies on metal contacts or brushes to conduct through the paper tape holes. Again, tape speed is limited due to the mechanical nature of the making and breaking contacts.

Finally, the most popular method of reading paper tape on modern readers is the optical method. Light shines through the holes as the tape passes by the optical read head. Reading speed on an optical reader is limited strictly by how fast the paper tape can be pulled through the reading mechanism.

Paper tape has developed around the mechanical reader, and some of the characteristics of the paper tape itself hurt the electromechanical and optical tape reading methods.

The most common type of paper tape comes on a large roll, is oiled to reduce mechanical punch friction, and has a dull yellow translucence. While this tape works well on the mechanical teletypewriter, it plays havoc with other types of readers. Electromechanical readers are affected by the oil, which fouls the electrical contacts; and on optical readers, light often is registered through the oiled translucent tape where no holes have been punched. Nonoiled, black or gray paper tape has therefore become very popular for high-speed electromechanical and optical readers.

Because paper tape is a byte-oriented medium, most paper tape readers and punches, with the exception of the ASR-33 Teletype, are driven through parallel interfaces. An 8-bit parallel interface is enough to send the full ASCII character set to a reader or punch. Eight bits are sufficient for alphanumeric data because the ASCII character set includes four control characters that are set aside to control a paper tape reader and paper tape punch. These characters are DC1, DC2, DC3, and DC4 (DC stands for device control), which have hexadecimal values of 11, 12, 13, and 14 and the control codes of *control-Q, -R -S,* and *-T* (reader on, punch on, reader off, and punch off).

If an application requires that a full complement of 8-bit codes be punched or read, the device control codes that turn the reader and punch on and off cannot be used. Whenever these characters are punched or read, the reader or punch stops or starts. In applications requiring complete character-set punching capabilities, a separate 8-bit data and 8-bit control port are incorporated in the device's interface.

Much software is written around the four control characters. Therefore, many microcomputer cassette interfaces as well as paper tape interfaces use the control characters to start and stop the reading and recording devices. This software then becomes useful with both paper tape and cassette.

SELECTING MEMORY
FOR A MICROCOMPUTER SYSTEM

Once short-, medium-, and long-term storage devices and their interfaces are understood, individually interfacing any one of them to a microcomputer system becomes a fairly straightforward task. Deciding which memory units to use, however, isn't quite as easy.

Evaluating a system's memory requirements is a good place to start. A simple microcomputer-based controller usually requires permanent storage for a control program and a small amount of random-access memory for temporary working storage. In simple cases like these, the requirements make the memory choices quite easy.

In the initial design of a microcomputer-based controller, it is wise to allocate about twice as much memory (PROM and RAM) as initial memory estimates call for. Controllers typically take on more tasks as they proceed through the design process, so expandability can be quite important.

The specific PROMs, ROMs, and RAMs should be selected on the bases of price, power, performance, and microprocessor compatibility. Memory devices from the microprocessor's logic family simplify design complexity and eliminate the need for level translator circuits. Memory devices and a microprocessor from the same device family are usually well matched in terms of speed also. NMOS microprocessors, for example, have clock rates ranging from 1 to 4 MHz, while NMOS memory cycle times range from about 0.25 to 1 microsecond (corresponding to a 1 to 4 MHz clock rate). The advantages of individual PROMs and RAMs should be weighed as described in the short-term memory section.

For processing-oriented microcomputer applications, the memory decisions get tougher. Not only does short-term memory have to be considered, but a medium- or long-term storage device must be selected.

First, enough RAM to run all the desired programs must be provided. Text editor programs typically use from 2K to 5K of memory, assemblers 4K to 12K, and BASIC interpreters and compilers 2K to 16K. With today's low memory cost, a good starting point for RAM is 32K. This much RAM allows enough working storage for the above-mentioned programs plus some data and system utility programs.

Programs and data can be stored on cassette or floppy disk, but before deciding on an expensive dual or quad cassette system or dual floppy disks, it is wise to consider the large memory approach. Memory is quite inexpensive compared to floppy disks and cassette drives, and *can reduce or eliminate the need for long-term storage devices if enough of it is used.*

If a microcomputer's prime purpose is to run user-interactive BASIC and assembly language support software (text editors and assemblers), a system consisting of 24K of PROM for BASIC, editor, and assembler programs, and 32K–48K of RAM may be adequate. Not only will a system like this cost less than a floppy disk system, it will perform more reliably and have quicker program access and response time as well. A single, manually operated cassette deck for storing user programs and data may be desirable in a system like this as well.

If a floppy disk or cassette system is chosen over the memory approach, more memory should be allowed to contain the disk operating or cassette control software or "operating system." Putting this software in PROM is nearly essential, especially on a microprocessor that has no front-panel data entry method, because upon power-up the first programs to be run will usually come off the disk or cassette. An alternative to putting the whole operating system in PROM is to put a small initial loader or *bootstrap loader* in PROM and have that initialize the operating system by doing an *initial program load* (IPL).

Two or more of the same magnetic long-term storage devices have many advantages over just one. The advantages include file copying capability, the ability to sequentially read one tape while writing onto another (if cassettes were chosen), and increased storage.

If cassettes are chosen, motor control is imperative for any serious application that involves more than just dumping or loading programs manually at the beginning and end of a session with the computer. Some cassettes with motor control offer nearly the flexibility, random-access capability, and hands-off operational characteristics of floppy disks; but the latency time (file access time) is always longer.

One factor to consider before buying a floppy disk is the amount of data that can be stored. Minifloppy drives of the single-density type can store only about 100K bytes of data, which is barely enough for a couple of large programs and data bases. Working with minifloppies can become a cumbersome hands-on operation (constantly removing and inserting disks) if you require large storage capacities. A full-size floppy disk or one of the high-performance, double-sided, dual-density minifloppies may be more appropriate for your application.

4 Microcomputer Input and Output Methods

New microprocessors, memory devices, interface chips, and other exotic microcomputer components enter the market every year, and it is popular to talk about these fad items. Magazine article after magazine article and even whole books are devoted to the popular devices.

Two important areas of microcomputer systems that are usually overlooked are the control structure of microprocessors and the input and output methods used to get data in and out of the closed microcomputer–memory system. A new microprocessor, such as the Intel 8086, is usually described as a revolutionary processor with so many index registers, so many data registers, and a "pipelined" architecture. Little, if anything, is ever said about a microprocessor's microprogrammed control unit, sequential control point instruction-execution logic, or the internal workings of the priority arbitration logic. Most manufacturers' and authors' block diagrams of microprocessors, in fact, pass off the most sophisticated part of the processor—the timing and control unit—as a simple box with the words "timing and control logic" written inside.

Two factors contribute to this situation: First, a microprocessor's efficiency and overall performance are greatly affected by the control logic, and most manufacturers prefer to keep their unique designs proprietary. Dull subject matter is the second reason for the scarcity of control information. Microcomputer users are more interested in the available registers and the instruction sets of a processor than in the way a processor internally carries out an instruction. Control logic is somewhat invisible to a computer programmer.

The dull subject matter argument also applies to I/O methods. It is much more interesting to read about a microprocessor's potential than about all the little details that allow it to live up to that potential. This subject matter can become *very* interesting, however, when you try to use a microprocessor in an actual application.

A microprocessor's control logic and its I/O protocols play the largest role in a microcomputer's communication with the outside world, and this chapter is devoted to digging into the basics of computer I/O methods. A few basic concepts concerning the low-level logic elements commonly used in I/O are described, followed by explanations of various I/O schemes, from simple to the most complex.

BASICS OF LOW-LEVEL I/O COMPONENTS

It is important to precisely define the functions of various common logic elements before discussing how these elements are used to transfer data in I/O systems. Flip-flops, registers, latches, and memory cells, for example, are all capable of storing bits of information; but the distinctions between these devices are very important, because data I/O is essentially the process of capturing and transferring data to and from these devices.

The Edge-Triggered Register

Data transfers rely on the ability to "catch" a byte of data in a temporary data storage unit at a precise instant in time. If the unit sending the byte is a microprocessor and the temporary data storage register is located in a peripheral device, the act of catching the byte of data would amount to a microprocessor-to-peripheral output cycle. One such data-capturing device is the edge-triggered register.

Figure 4-1 presents the standard notation used to depict a register. A register's input and output signals are well standardized in notation. The D input to the register is the data input, CK is the clock input, and Q and $\overline{Q}$ (commonly called Q-bar) are the data output and inverted data output.

Data at the D input is transferred to the Q output on the positive-going edge of the clock input's signal. The data that is transferred at the positive-going edge of the clock pulse is stored or captured at the Q output until the next positive-going clock signal occurs (when new data at the D input replaces it). The important concept here is that the data is only "looked at" by the register's input during the very short time in which the clock rises from logic 0 to logic 1. In other words, *data need only be "valid" on the rising edge*.

In reality, the data at the data input must be valid a slight bit before the rising edge (called the data *setup* time) and a slight bit after the clock's rising edge (called the data *hold* time) to allow the register's circuitry to respond to the data properly.

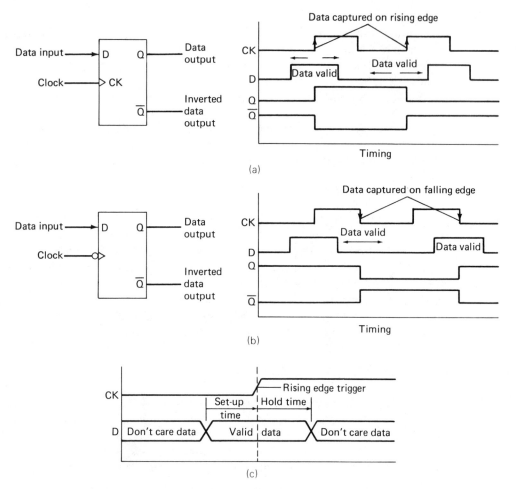

Figure 4-1   Edge-triggered register characteristics. (a) Rising-edge-triggered register.
(b) Falling-edge-triggered register. (c) Setup and hold times.

Rising- and falling-edge-triggered registers are available. Falling-edge-triggered registers capture data on the falling edge of the clock pulse and are really just rising-edge-triggered registers with inverted clock inputs.

To describe the capturing of data in a register, we use the word *clocked*. When data is clocked into a register, it is assumed to be captured on the rising edge of the clock cycle.

The safest way to use a register to capture data is to allow as much setup and hold time as possible on the D input. The input data should be valid for a safe amount of time on both sides of the clock's rising edge. A good way to make sure this criterion is met is to allow data to be presented and removed from the data input at the trailing edge of the clock, and to clock data into the register on the rising edge. As Fig. 4-1 illustrates, valid data is symmetrically sandwiched around the clock pulse, thus allowing very wide setup and hold time margins.

A register's output takes a certain length of time to change to the new input data following the clock's leading edge. This delay is known as the *clock-to-Q* propagation delay. This lag in register output must be considered when using registers.

The Bistable Latch

A latch is capable of storing a single bit of data; but unlike the register, it is not a clock edge that directly causes data to appear on the latch's outputs.

Figure 4-2 illustrates a latch and its timing. A latch has a data input (D), data output and inverted output (Q and $\overline{Q}$), and an enable input (E or sometimes G). A latch is "transparent" in that it allows data to freely pass from the D input to the Q output when the enable is high; but it immediately freezes whatever was at the data input when the enable line is dropped to a logic 0.

At first glance this may seem like a falling-edge-triggered register because data is captured on the falling edge, but it has the transparent property not available on the register when the clock is high.

In some applications the transparent feature of the latch is actually used, but in most cases designers treat latches as registers that capture data on the falling clock edge. The danger in using a latch in this way is that for the whole time the clock is high, whatever data is on the data input is allowed to slip through the latch and appear at the output. This problem is solved by narrowing the positive clock portion down to a narrow pulse. Data can be thought of as being captured by the pulse when this sort of arrangement is used. Capturing data in this manner is referred to as "strobing" data into a latch.

Unless erratic output is acceptable during the time the strobe pulse is high, data must be valid during the whole strobe time and even a little before and after the pulse (setup and hold times again).

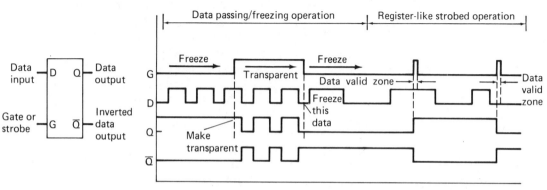

Figure 4-2   Bistable latch characteristics.

If a narrow pulse is generated by counters or if a multiphase clock with narrow pulses is available, the latched I/O method is a reasonable alternative because latches are cheaper and draw less power than registers; but all too often, bad design practice is used to generate the required narrow pulse. An edge-triggered monostable multivibrator (one-shot) is often misused in this application, and system timing becomes dependent on the one-shot's timing components as well as the processor's master clock crystal. Because one-shots are susceptible to electrical noise, a noise burst entering the device containing the one-shot-driven latches could cause false data to be strobed into the latches. It is wise to avoid using one-shot-driven latches.

The Multiplexer

Whether you are inputting, outputting, or processing data, it must be channeled between various processing elements and I/O devices. The logic element used to steer data is the *multiplexer*.

Figure 4-3 illustrates a multiplexer and its equivalent gate-constructed logic. Basically, A data is passed to Y if the select line is low, and B data is passed to Y if the select line is high.

A multiplexer or a series of multiplexers connected in a treelike fashion can be used to select between many data inputs, but more often than not, *virtual multiplexers* are used in I/O systems. A tristate data bus that can only be driven by one tristate buffer at a time is an example of a virtual multiplexer. The buffer driving the bus acts as the selected input on a real multiplexer, and multiplexing action takes place even though there is no actual multiplexer part.

The Decoder

A decoder is a gating network that takes a few input bits (usually three or four in the case of single-chip MSI decoders) and generates a unique output for each 3-bit input combination of 1s and 0s (Figure 4-3 illustrates a decoder).

Decoders come in two distinct types: those that raise only one output at a time to logic 1 for each input code, and those that lower only one output to logic 0 for each input code. In TTL, the AND gate is the dominant building block, and the one-line-lowered type is the most common. The NOR-gate-dominated ECL uses the one-line-high approach in most cases due to ECL's *wired*-OR capabilities.

Decoders play an important role in interfaces in the capacity of device selectors. Because only one output line on the decoder goes high for each input code, device selection codes can be fed to decoders and the individual outputs can electrically enable the specified device.

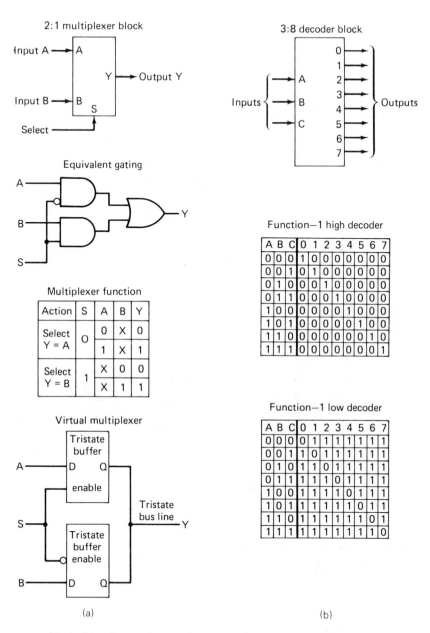

2:1 multiplexer block

Input A → A

Y → Output Y

Input B → B

S

Select

Equivalent gating

A

B

S

Y

Multiplexer function

Action	S	A	B	Y
Select Y = A	0	0	X	0
		1	X	1
Select Y = B	1	X	0	0
		X	1	1

Virtual multiplexer

Tristate buffer

A — D Q

enable

Tristate bus line

Y

S

Tristate buffer enable

B — D Q

(a)

3:8 decoder block

Inputs { → A, → B, → C }

0 1 2 3 4 5 6 7

} Outputs

Function−1 high decoder

A	B	C	0	1	2	3	4	5	6	7
0	0	0	1	0	0	0	0	0	0	0
0	0	1	0	1	0	0	0	0	0	0
0	1	0	0	0	1	0	0	0	0	0
0	1	1	0	0	0	1	0	0	0	0
1	0	0	0	0	0	0	1	0	0	0
1	0	1	0	0	0	0	0	1	0	0
1	1	0	0	0	0	0	0	0	1	0
1	1	1	0	0	0	0	0	0	0	1

Function−1 low decoder

A	B	C	0	1	2	3	4	5	6	7
0	0	0	0	1	1	1	1	1	1	1
0	0	1	1	0	1	1	1	1	1	1
0	1	0	1	1	0	1	1	1	1	1
0	1	1	1	1	1	0	1	1	1	1
1	0	0	1	1	1	1	0	1	1	1
1	0	1	1	1	1	1	1	0	1	1
1	1	0	1	1	1	1	1	1	0	1
1	1	1	1	1	1	1	1	1	1	0

(b)

Figure 4-3 Data engineering elements. (a) The multiplexer. (b) The decoder.

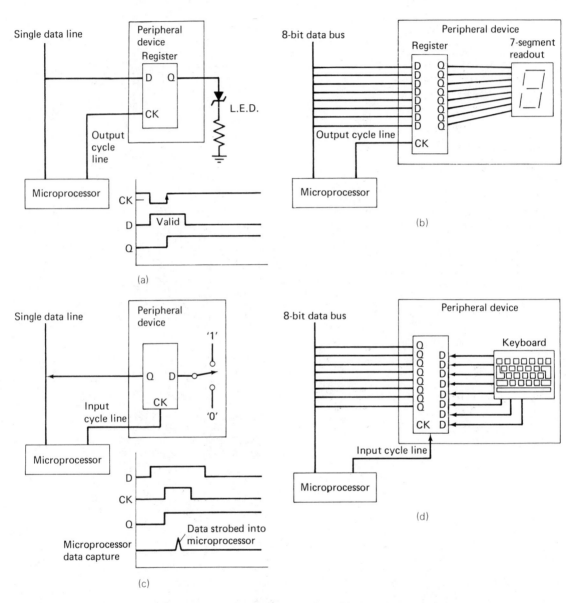

Figure 4-4   Simple output and input data transfers. (a) Single-bit output transfer. (b) Parallel output transfer. (c) Single-bit input transfer. (d) Parallel input transfer.

BASICS OF DATA TRANSFER

The true definition of an input or output operation is the act of selectively transferring data to or from a selected peripheral device. A good place to start in the explanation of how I/O cycles are typically implemented is to take the simple case of sending a single bit of data to a peripheral.

Figure 4-4 illustrates a single-bit data transfer. The output device consists of a rising-edge-triggered register and an LED (light-emitting diode) to indicate the state of the register. Referring to the timing diagram, the microprocessor presents valid data and an output cycle clock line to the register. The microprocessor's control unit raises the output cycle clock line to a logic 1 level at the midpoint of the data-valid interval on the data line, at which time the data is transferred from the microprocessor to the output device's register. A simple one-bit output cycle is thus performed. The LED acts as the peripheral output device in this case.

Most microprocessors have output cycles that are just embellishments of this simple scheme. The data on the line usually reflects a bit in the accumulator while the output cycle clock is generated by an output instruction.

Figure 4-4(b) shows the logical extension of the single-bit data transfer: the *parallel* data transfer. In this case, eight bits of data are sent to the output device, which clocks the data into an 8-bit register where it is used to drive a 7-segment readout instead of a simple LED. Again, the timing diagram of Figure 4-4(a) applies.

Figure 4-4(c) depicts a single-bit input cycle. In this case, the input clock signal issued by the microprocessor is used to sample the data at the input register's D input. A short time after the rising edge of the input clock, the data becomes stable at the register's output and is sampled by the microprocessor. Again, the microprocessor's control unit provides all the proper timing signals for the data transfer and usually transfers the valid data on the line to one of the microprocessor's registers where it can be accessed by the user's program.

Extending this data input principle to 8 bits yields the keyboard input transfer logic of Figure 4-4(d). An 8-bit key code is generated by pressing a key on the keyboard. The microprocessor proceeds to examine the 8-bit code by clocking it into the register and sending it to the microprocessor's accumulator or one of its registers.

What has been described so far is fine as long as there is only one I/O device or peripheral on the microprocessor bus. If two or more devices are used, the question of which is supposed to receive the data is raised. This issue is resolved with *selection logic.*

Figure 4-5(a) illustrates three output devices driven by the same data and control lines. The microprocessor specifies for which device the output is destined by supplying a device code. The decoder in the peripheral devices either enables or disables data transfers to a particular device, depending on the device code.

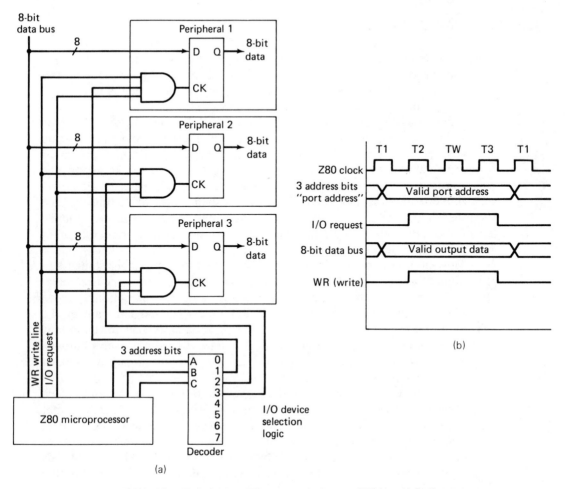

Figure 4-5 The selection of three output devices on a Z80 bus. (a) Logic. (b) Output timing.

Most microprocessor I/O schemes use a few of the address bits as the device code bits. Because a memory cannot be accessed while an I/O cycle is being performed (due to I/O data tying up the data bus), there is no sense in adding additional lines for I/O device code selection.

From the standpoint of microcomputer software, the I/O device code that appears on the address lines is specified in the input or output instruction. An *OUT 5* instruction on an 8080, for example, puts the value 5 on the address lines and the contents of the accumulator on the data lines.

The Zilog Z80's input and output cycles are good illustrative examples of the I/O principles just described. Figure 4-5(b) illustrates the Z80 output cycle. Notice that instead of one output clock line, there are two lines that must be combined (ANDed) to create an output clock line: the IORQ (I/O request) line and the WR (write) line. Notice that the port address or *device selection code* that appears on the 8 least significant bits of the address lines becomes valid *before* the output clock lines are activated. This timing margin is provided to allow the device selection decoders to stabilize and properly select the output device before outputting data to it.

THE I/O DIRECTION STANDARD

When working with simple systems, the terms input and output are quite clear. The simple data transfer examples just presented require no detailed explanation of which devices perform the input and output functions. In complex systems, however, the terms input and output must be explicitly defined to avoid any confusion about which direction data is flowing. When an output transfer between an intelligent graphics terminal and a central processing unit takes place, is the data output from the processor to the terminal or vice versa?

A standard convention was adopted to handle such terminology conflicts. Data transfers are always spoken of with relation to the central processing unit of a computer system. Keyboards, digitizers, light pens, card readers, and paper tape readers are input devices, while graphics displays, line printers, paper tape punches, and the recording sections of cassette interfaces are output devices. An output transfer between a graphics terminal and a CPU means that data flows from the CPU to the graphics terminal.

SERIAL I/O

Presenting a full byte of data to an output register and supplying an input clock to clock the data is a fast and simple way of sending data to a peripheral device. It is not always practical, however, to have eight or more data lines plus a clock line extending out to all the peripherals in a system. In these situations it is advantageous to replace parallel data transfer with serial data transmission.

Serial data transmission is the process of breaking bytes of data down into single bits and shipping them out to the peripheral devices one at a time.

Some problems arise in the implementation of serial communication. First, an effective method of converting parallel to serial data is needed. A microprocessor under software control or a "broadside-loadable shift register" can easily perform this task. A string of eight edge-triggered registers are loaded with the 8-bit byte on the first clock pulse of the serial transmission operation, and the bits are sequentially moved through the register string at the rate of one bit per clock pulse. The bits that "fall off the end" of the register string make up the serial output.

In a similar manner, bits coming into the receiving end are serially shifted into a shift register until 8 bits are accumulated. This full byte of data can then be used by the peripheral device.

As Fig. 4-6 illustrates, an input line, output line, and a clock line are all that is needed for bidirectional serial communication between two devices. If the two devices are in separate cabinets and run on different power supplies, a common or ground line between the devices must also be provided.

Synchronous Communications

With parallel communication it is clear that the rising edge of the clock indicates the transfer of a whole byte, but in serial communication the rising edge of the clock indicates the transfer of a single bit, and a scheme to determine which bit of the byte was transferred is needed. One common approach to this problem is to initially synchronize the transmit and receive shift registers and from that point on assume that the transmit circuitry and receive circuitry, by simultaneously counting to 8 (in the 8-bit shift register case), will keep track of

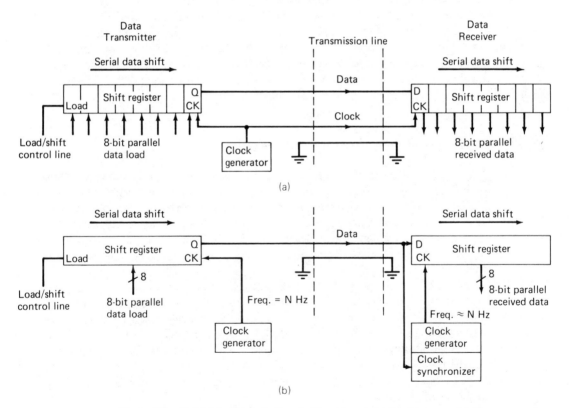

Figure 4-6   Serial data communication clocking schemes. (a) Synchronous serial data transmission. (b) Asynchronous serial data transmission.

the byte boundaries in the bit stream. This type of serial transfer is called synchronous communication.

The practicality of synchronous communication depends on the transmitter's and receiver's ability to stay synchronized after initialization. If the receiver for some reason gets just one bit off (perhaps through the introduction of a noise spike in the clock line), all the following bytes will be received incorrectly. The transmit and receive shift registers must be run off the same clock in synchronous communication modes.

Initialization of the transmit and receive registers is usually accomplished through a character matching process. When a synchronous serial transfer begins, the receiver is put into a bit-stream "watching" mode. The first character sent by the transmit register, known as a match character, consists of a predefined bit pattern known to the receiver. The receiver recognizes the match character on the clock cycle that it is fully shifted into the shift register and starts counting out 8-bit bytes from this point on.

Synchronous serial data transmission requires a clock signal in addition to the input and output data transfer lines.

Asynchronous Communications

A common form of data transmission that eliminates the need for a synchronizing clock is asynchronous communication. Asynchronous serial communication relies on the fact that two clocks of approximately the same frequency stay fairly well synchronized over a short period of time.

An asynchronous data transmitter sends out an initial timing bit called a start bit, followed by eight bits of serial data and one or two "stop bits." The asynchronous receiver syncs up its clock (of approximately the transmitter frequency) upon receipt of the start bit and clocks in 8 bits of data using the just-synchronized receiver clock as a guide. By the time the eighth bit is reached, the receive clock is slightly skewed from where the transmit clock would be if it had been used, but the skew is not great enough to affect the proper capture of the short 8-bit serial stream.

The stop bits at the end of the serial data stream are usually used by the receiving equipment to determine if the clock is too skewed to provide accurate read data. If it is, a "bit-misalignment" or *framing* error is declared. Figure 4-6(b) illustrates the asynchronous communication method.

Serial communication requires much more control circuitry than parallel communication. In addition to the standard parallel interfacing to the microprocessor bus, we must use serial-to-parallel conversion, clock synchronizing, and bit-counting logic. The common use of serial communication has therefore resulted in single-device serial communication chips to handle the complex interface and conversion task. Among these chips are UART (universal asynchronous receiver/transmitter), USRT (universal synchronous receiver/ transmitter), and ACIA (asynchronous communication interface adapter) devices, all of which we discuss in detail in the interface components section.

OPEN- AND CLOSED-LOOP COMMUNICATION

When you send a byte of data to a peripheral device, it is good to know if that byte ever reached its destination. The simple parallel and serial I/O schemes just presented do not have any provisions that allow for checking. Data is sent from the processor to the peripheral and it is assumed that the data correctly reached its destination. This sort of I/O is referred to as open-loop.

There are a number of ways to send data-received status information back to the sending device. After a word has been received it can be sent back to the sending device or *echoed,* thereby "closing the loop." This method is very common in computer-to-terminal communication. In most cases, the data entered through a computer terminal's keyboard is sent to the processor, checked, and sent back to the terminal's display screen or printing mechanism.

Closed-loop operation is provided on the microprocessor bus level with a method almost universally known as *handshaking.* With this method, individual status signals are sent back to the processor acknowledging that the word has been received properly. Handshaking logic adds considerable complexity to a microprocessor's bus, but it also adds reliability and flexibility. Reliability is improved because the processor can determine when data hasn't been received and take corrective action. Versatility is increased because the returned status information can be used to perform powerful timing functions in addition to closing the communication loop. Asynchronous memory operation is one example.

In the discussion of memory interfacing (Chapter 3) it was assumed that the memory address signals, read and write control lines, and data inputs were strictly under the control of the microprocessor. The microprocessor would submit an address and read in the memory's data 250 ns later, for example. With handshaking, a memory can have internal circuitry to tell the processor when its data is valid on a read cycle or when it is finished with bus data on a write cycle. Not only does the processor have an indication that the data was sent or received properly, but it knows the precise instant to terminate the data transfer and move on to the next memory access. If memory access and I/O handshaking are incorporated in a microcomputer system, memory devices (RAMs, PROMs, and CCDs) and peripherals with widely differing speed ranges can be used effectively on the same bus without the addition of any speed matching circuitry.

Handshaking is used extensively on DEC's LSI-11 microcomputer. The data output (DATO) cycle shown in Fig. 4-7 illustrates the sequence.

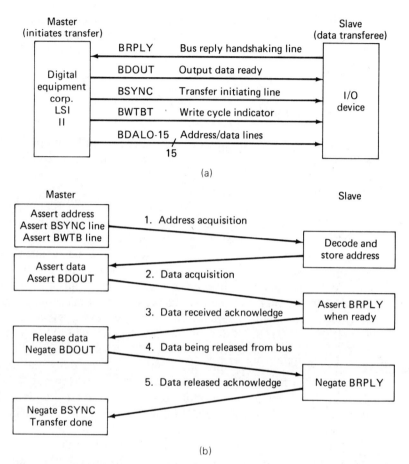

Figure 4-7   Microcomputer I/O and memory handshaking. (a) Logic signals involved in a data output (DATO) cycle on the LSI 11. (b) Sequence of events in a DATO cycle.

One feature that must be incorporated in any handshaking system is a timeout mechanism. When a processor depends on a returned handshaking signal to resume operation, there must be some provision for error recovery if that signal doesn't come back. The LSI-11 handles this situation by trapping (diverting program execution) to a device timeout routine if the accessed memory or device doesn't respond with a returned handshaking signal within 2 ms.

COMMON MICROCOMPUTER I/O METHODS

Every microcomputer has its own way of applying data transfer principles. The specifics of a microprocessor's I/O system as well as the general data transfer concepts must be well understood before successful designs and interfaces can be built. This section deals with the more specific areas of input and output.

With the exception of a few exotic microprocessors, the majority of microprocessors either use data channel or memory-mapped I/O. Most have some sort of interrupt capability and many are capable of direct memory access (DMA).

The Data Channel

In the early days of computers, when circuit and logic optimization were not well understood, computers were thought of as machines consisting of a processor, a memory, and an I/O unit. The memory interfaced with the processor through one interface and to the peripherals through a different interface. Separate processor instructions were set aside for memory reference and I/O operations. This kind of an I/O scheme is called *data channel input/output*.

Microprocessors must have optimized I/O schemes in order to fit a whole computer into a 40-pin integrated circuit, and pure data channels are not used in microprocessors due to I/O pin constraints. The distinct instruction characteristics of I/O channels, however, is carried over from older designs. The 8080 and Z80 are examples of the I/O channel-oriented microprocessors.

Instead of having a separate I/O bus and device selection bus (common in data channel I/O), the Z80 uses the data bus as the I/O bus and the eight least significant bits of the address bus as the device selection lines. I/O devices therefore reside on the same bus as memory. The thing that distinguishes the I/O interfaces from memory is the microprocessor-generated *I/O request* line (IORQ). If this line is *low,* it indicates that the data and address bus are acting as a data channel; if it is *high,* it indicates a memory reference. Figure 4-5(b) illustrates the I/O channel's timing.

The Z80 has a whole set of I/O-oriented instructions that turn the data and address bus into an I/O channel upon execution. The basic input instruction is *IN A,* where *A* represents the device selection or *port address.* (The term *I/O port* is commonly used to describe an interface on an I/O channel.) Because the value of *A* can be 8 bits long, 256 read ports and 256 write ports are available on the data channel. This number of I/O ports is sufficient for nearly every microprocessor application and is convenient because the port number can be stored in a single 8-bit byte of memory. Because there are 16 address lines, and only the 8 least significant lines are used in an I/O cycle, there are 8 lines left over for other functions. The 8080 simply repeats the 8-bit port address on the most significant bits, which serves no useful purpose. The Z80, on the other hand, makes good use of these bits by displaying the contents of the accumulator on these lines. During output instructions, a register can be output to the data lines and the accumulator to the high address lines, allowing a 16-bit transfer. On input cycles, the accumulator can be read by the peripheral interface, resulting in a simultaneous input/output cycle.

Memory-Mapped I/O

As computer science advanced, hardware optimization and simple-to-use instruction sets became sought-after features in computer systems. Processor hardware was optimized and instruction sets were simplified by approaching the I/O and memory interface processor logic simultaneously rather than independently. By treating every device's data transfer register as a location in memory and assigning it its own address, no separate output channel hardware or dedicated I/O instructions are needed. The PDP-11 was a big step forward in small computer design when it was introduced in the late 1960s, and totally memory-mapped I/O was one of its main selling points.

A memory-mapped I/O interface is nearly identical to a memory interface, but instead of using RAMs or ROMs, input and output registers are incorporated. Like a memory interface, the peripheral interface must contain a complete 16-bit (for microprocessors with 16-bit address lines) address recognizer, and any buffers and handshaking logic associated with the microprocessor bus.

Memory-mapped I/O lends itself to program organization. A certain section of a processor's memory addressing space (usually a 4K or 8K block) is allocated for I/O devices. These locations in memory are referred to as device registers (as opposed to ports for data channels). In programs, data is transferred to and from these locations just as data is transferred to and from memory. If a processor has direct memory-to-memory transfer capabilities, such as the LSI-11, data can even be transferred between devices with single memory-to-memory *move* instructions.

The 6800 and 6502 microprocessors are two examples of memory-mapped I/O machines. In both cases, no I/O instructions are available.

I/O Transfer Type Advantages

Like every drastic logic difference in microprocessors, data channel versus memory-mapped I/O data transfers are cause for hours of debate on which is superior. Both sides have their advocates and opponents.

The data-channel advocates argue that interfaces on a data channel require less hardware because a short port address instead of a full memory address is used to select the device. This argument is true for most memory-mapped I/O systems; but Digital Equipment Corporation, realizing the problem, has its LSI-11 generate a separate signal indicating that the top 8K of memory is being accessed. This signal can be used by I/O devices instead of the top 8 bits of address to distinguish the I/O area of memory.

Another argument against memory-mapped I/O is that it clutters the memory. This argument is not valid because the I/O devices are usually grouped in one confined area of memory, and the useful space taken from the processor's memory size is usually so small that it doesn't make any difference. The large addressing space of the memory-mapped I/O has one advantage in special applications. Occasionally in large control or data communication systems, more than 256 output or input devices are needed. With memory-mapped I/O, thousands of peripherals can be accommodated.

The arguments about the advantages of the two I/O methods go on and on, but it is interesting to note that most modern microprocessors are using memory-mapped I/O methods.

I/O TRANSFER INITIATION

We have been assuming that the microprocessor knows which peripheral it wants to send data to and at what time to send it. But in real life it isn't that simple. Peripheral devices can only accept data at a certain rate, and new data may be input at any time. Two methods of determining when to start a data transfer are in common use: the examination of device status under program control or *polling,* and peripheral-initiated program interruption or *interrupt driven I/O.* Let's look at these two methods.

Polling

Submitting only 8 bits of data to a processor and expecting the processor to input the data properly is somewhat analogous to telling a moving company to pick up some goods but not mentioning when or where to pick them up. More information must be submitted to the processor. One of the most common and simplest ways to convey enough information is to have a separate input register built into the interface, which the processor can use to obtain status information about new data submitted to the interface.

The keyboard interface shown in Fig. 4-4(d) is a good example of a processor in need of more information. It is true that the processor can repeatedly read the keyboard's register, but there is no way to tell when a new key has been pressed or if a key has been pressed twice in a row. A separate register with one bit representing *keypress* (logic 1 if the key is pressed, logic 0 if it is released) can improve this situation. The updated keyboard interface is shown in Fig. 4-8.

By getting into a programmed loop that repeatedly examines or polls the status register waiting for the key to be pressed, the microprocessor can be made to jump to a keyboard-data-examining instruction immediately after the key is pressed, thereby reading the new data. The microprocessor can then jump to a routine that waits for the key to be released, and again resume its keypress loop waiting for the next character.

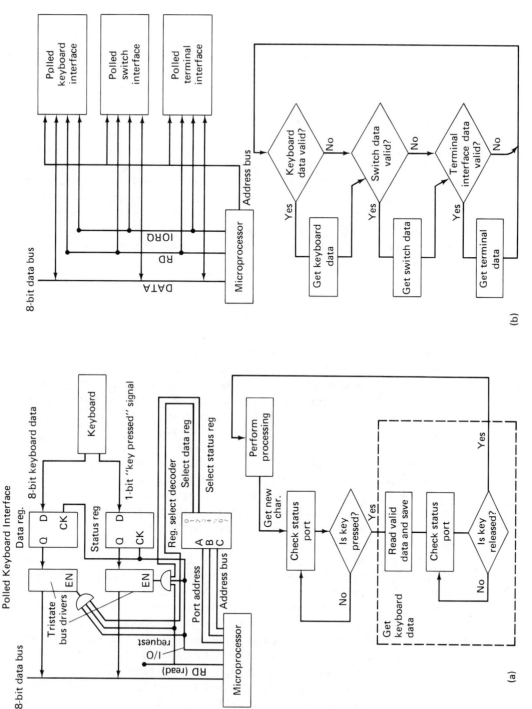

Figure 4-8 Polling-initiated data transfers. (a) A polled keyboard data transfer. (b) Three simultaneously polled peripherals.

161

There is no reason to limit the polling loop to one peripheral. Figure 4-8(b) illustrates a keyboard, switch, and terminal all being polled by a software polling loop. When the data of any device becomes valid, the processor jumps to a quick-executing data input or output routine and returns to the polling loop. The chance of missing data in the short period of time that the data for another device is being input is very small because the data service routine executes so quickly and the peripherals are so slow by comparison.

The major advantage to polled I/O initialization is its hardware simplicity. The major disadvantage is the amount of processing time it takes. Constantly watching the device status flags is time-consuming, and leaving the polling loop for even a short period to perform some other processing may cause data to be missed. The amount of time spent in polling loops may be reduced by having the status bits for many devices packed into a single status word with either one bit representing each device or a code indicating which port is requesting an I/O cycle; but the need for continuous polling remains.

Interrupt-Driven I/O

Because it is the action of a peripheral (the receipt of a new character, for example) that marks the beginning of a data transfer, it seems more reasonable to have the peripheral device "tell" the processor when it is ready with new data than to have the processor continuously ask if anything new has come in yet. This is precisely the idea behind interrupt-driven I/O: when a peripheral device has data to transfer, it lets the processor know.

An interrupt system must be incorporated in the control structure of a microprocessor if this I/O initialization method is used. An interrupt typically causes a program (usually normal data processing) to suddenly halt, and diverts execution to a separate program which inputs or outputs the new data. This form of operation is inconsistent with the idea that programs flow nicely in exactly the sequence you specify, and a change in the basic control rules of the processor are required.

The simplest form is the *single-line* interrupt system. In this system, an interface on the microprocessor bus simply puts a logic 1 on the interrupt line that leads to the processor's control logic. At the end of the currently executing instruction, the program will be diverted to a fixed interrupt address. A program located at this address then inputs data or "services the interrupt."

With the simple one-line interrupt system, it is also possible to have many devices issuing interrupts; but when execution is diverted to the fixed interrupt address, a polling routine must be used for a peripheral to place its service program's start address on the address or data bus when the device interrupts, the processor can take this address and vector execution to the proper service routine.

This sort of interrupt system works well with many peripherals but involves greater interface complexity than the simple scheme of using multiple interrupt lines. Address-generating circuitry and more complex timing circuitry are needed on each interrupt-driven interface.

Interrupt Priorities

In interrupt systems in which many devices can make interrupt requests, eventually two or more interrupts will occur at precisely the same time. In this case, priority arbitration logic must decide which request is more important.

A *daisy-chain* priority system is one of the methods available for deciding priority. With this method, all the devices issuing interrupts activate a single interrupt line leading to the processor, as illustrated in Fig. 4-9. The processor, at this point, realizes that an interrupt is requested and starts to process the interrupt after completing execution of the instruction in progress. The processor begins the interrupt sequence by issuing an *interrupt grant* signal that is sent to the first device in the daisy-chained peripheral string. If this device caused the interrupt, it prevents the grant signal from being passed on to the next device in the string and performs interrupt action by putting its interrupt service address on the bus.

With this method, the first device in the string naturally has the highest interrupt priority, because it will be the one to take the grant signal first if multiple interrupts are issued by different devices.

A second priority-arbitration scheme involves multilevel priority lines. Discrete hardware or an LSI chip called a priority interrupt controller works with the microprocessor to form many (usually 8) interrupt lines. Each line represents an interrupt level. Interrupt lines with low-level numbers have higher priority than interrupt lines with high-level numbers. Interrupt level zero is usually the interrupt level that gets serviced first. By simply placing devices on different interrupt levels, a priority interrupt servicing order is established. Figure 4-9(b) shows a multilevel interrupt system.

Assigning priorities to peripherals takes careful thought. Usually, fast devices that cannot wait with their data are assigned the highest priorities. A disk, for example, has a relatively fast data flow rate (for a peripheral, that is), and should be assigned a high priority. If a disk is assigned a low priority, there is a chance that a byte of data could be missed when the processor is processing interrupts issued by slow teletypewriters that could wait to be serviced.

Special consideration must be given to the console terminal in an interrupt system, however. Even though it is a slow peripheral, the computer operator should be able to interrupt any process and take control of the computer. Priority level zero is therefore often assigned to the console terminal.

Two methods are used to start a particular peripheral's interrupt transfer in multilevel schemes. In sophisticated large systems such as the PDP-11, grant

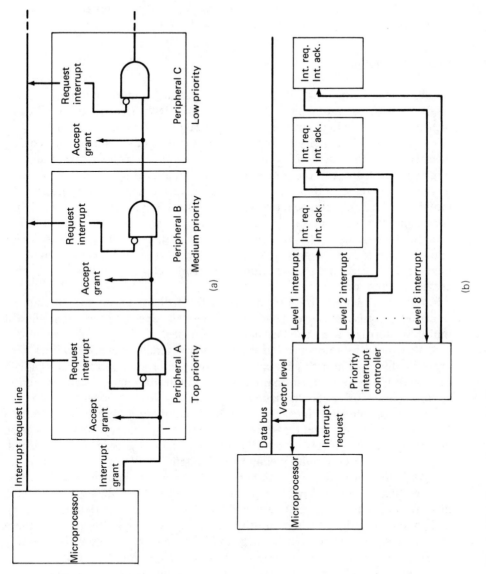

Figure 4-9 Common interrupt handling systems. (a) Daisy-chained interrupt system. (b) Vectored priority interrupt system.

signals at various levels corresponding to the interrupt lines at those levels are sent to the interrupting peripheral. It is then up to the peripheral to generate the branch address. Many microcomputers use a simpler and somewhat more hardware-efficient system, however. The logic performing the priority arbitration generates a vector address that reflects which interrupt level is requested. This method eliminates the need for vector address generating logic on each peripheral interface.

One advantage the peripheral-generated address priority system has over the priority logic-generated address system is the number of devices it can effectively handle. Daisy-chain priority on each of the interrupt levels is possible with the former but not with the latter.

Interrupt Masks

Interrupts can take over program execution in the middle of almost any program. In some cases, such as real-time control or within a timing loop, program interruption ruins the results of the processing. In most interrupt systems a software-controlled switch is provided to turn the interrupt system on and off. On a machine with only a simple single-level interrupt system, simple "interrupt on" and "interrupt off" instructions are provided. In more complex multilevel interrupt systems, interrupt mask words are used.

In a multilevel interrupt system, a mask word sent to the mask register allows only the interrupt levels whose bit in the mask word is set to 1 to cause interrupts. Bits in the mask word are usually assigned so bit 0 enables interrupt level zero, bit 1 enables level one, and so on. The fact that there are usually 8 interrupt levels on popular interrupt controller chips is due to the 8-bit interrupt mask's correspondence to a standard byte.

Allowing a computer system's interrupt system to be masked out totally under software control is unwise. If a program error causes an infinite loop in the software to occur when the whole interrupt system is masked, there is no way for even the highest priority device (usually the console terminal and computer operator) to regain control of the system. Many microprocessors therefore include a separate line on the microprocessor called the nonmasked interrupt line. There is no way to turn this interrupt line off under software control, and if a program accidentally gets into a "fatal loop," the operator can pull the system out of it with his console terminal, which uses this line.

Interrupt Processing

Once an interrupt is accepted and program execution is diverted to the service routine, steps must be taken to insure that the interrupted program can be safely resumed later. First, the location where processing was interrupted in the program must be saved so a return to that point can be made. The logic in

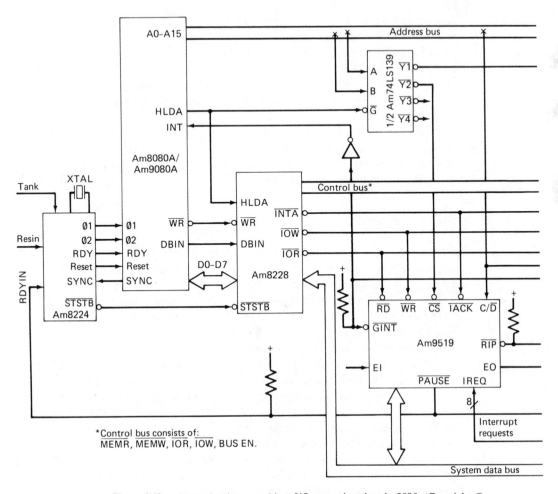

Figure 4-10   A complete interrupt-driven I/O system based on the 8080. (Copyright ©
1977 Advanced Micro Devices, Inc. Reproduced with permission of copyright owner.)

the microprocessor's control unit usually performs this function automatically
when an interrupt occurs. The saved "reentry address" is usually saved on the
top of the microprocessor's stack. The saving of other registers and machine
status information is sometimes performed by the hardware itself, but it is often
left up to the programmer to perform in the service routine software.

A quick way to tell exactly what is automatically saved on the stack when
an interrupt is initiated is to look at the operation of the return-from-interrupt
instruction, which should be executed at the end of every interrupt service
routine. As an example, let's look at the 6800's return-from-interrupt (RTI)
instruction.

The 6800's RTI is a series of seven stack pops. The condition code register
and then the two accumulators are popped off the stack, restoring them to their

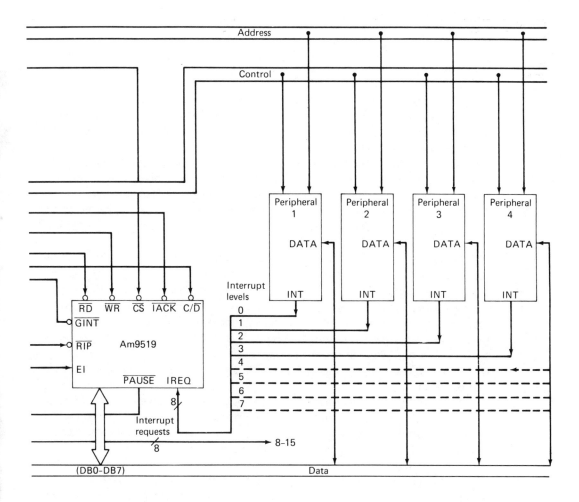

time-of-interrupt values. The index register is popped, and finally the program counter data is popped off the stack. The program counter value is the restart address of the interrupted program, so the program execution is effectively diverted back to the original program.

One hardware-initiated event that takes place when an interrupt is accepted is the setting of the interrupt mask. If more than one interrupt was issued at one time and the interrupt mask bits were not set, the processor would immediately be interrupted again when it entered the service routine. This would keep happening until the final interrupt (usually at the lowest priority level) was serviced. Low-priority devices would therefore be serviced first in a strange nested-interrupt manner. Figure 4-10 puts all the ideas about interrupts together into an operating interrupt system.

Interrupt Software Consequences

Software running in an interrupt environment can be fairly standard if masks are properly set within timing loops and the interrupt routines are independent of main program software; but as soon as interrupt routines and the main program start sharing utility routines, some very strange events can occur.

A multiply subroutine is a fairly often-used utility subroutine in many programs, and a user may be tempted to call the same multiply subroutine from an interrupt program and the main program. The danger here lies in the way data is stored in the multiply subroutine's intermediate calculations. If data is stored in absolute-addressed memory locations, a multiply routine may give wrong results if interrupted in the middle of a calculation. The multiply subroutine may have been used in the interrupt routine, thereby destroying the partial results stored in the absolute memory locations. The program was "reentered" and produced a bad result.

There are three solutions to the reentrancy problem. First, the use of the same multiply subroutine in interrupts can be avoided, and another separate multiply subroutine can be used; but this is a memory-wasteful solution, because two copies of the same program are needed. The multiply routine can set interrupt masks at the start of the subroutine and remove them at the end, prohibiting any interrupts while the multiply is in progress. This is a fairly good solution if long delays in interrupt response time are acceptable. A more eloquent solution to the problem, however, is the use of a *reentrant* multiply subroutine.

A subroutine is said to be reentrant if it can be interrupted at any time and be called again without affecting the interrupted calculation. Reentrancy is typically written into a program by limiting data storage to registers that are saved when interrupted, and to the stack that also isn't affected.

The problem with reentrant code is that it tends to be slow-executing, especially on a memory-oriented machine that relies heavily on time-consuming stack operations. For high-performance applications, it is wise to trade off interrupt response time or memory size for speed and go with one of the first two reentrancy solutions.

Interrupt-oriented programs should be carefully checked for possible reentrancy problems before they are run. Interrupt-generated errors are the hardest kind to find because interrupts act differently on every run of the program.

DIRECT MEMORY ACCESS

It's often said that the quickest way to get a job done is to do it yourself. Instead of going to the bother of asking someone to do the job, explaining how to do it, and waiting for it to be finished, you can do it yourself and it's done. This is precisely the idea behind direct memory access (DMA). Some peripherals with high transfer rates and lots of data to transmit really can't wait around for the processor to take their data and place it in memory; so their interfaces are designed to go off on their own, take control of the microcomputer bus, and directly place data in and take data out of memory with no processor involvement. Direct memory access provides the highest possible memory transfer rates and reduces processor I/O processing time.

The DMA concept is quite simple, but some hardware ingenuity is required to implement it. The main problem is that the processor is in control of the microcomputer bus, and bus control must temporarily be diverted to the DMA peripheral. Microprocessors are usually designed with some sort of DMA provisions in their control units that allow them to be electrically removed from the bus during a DMA cycle. The following paragraphs describe a few DMA methods using these features.

Processor-Halt DMA

Probably the crudest way to take control of the processor bus for a DMA cycle is to shut down the microprocessor and electrically remove it from the bus by *floating* its tristate address, data, and control lines. This is the most commonly used method of performing DMA in microcomputer systems.

The Z80 is a good example of a device that is designed to use processor-halt DMA. A bus request line (BUSRQ) is available to DMA devices. Raising this line causes the processor to "get off the bus" and go into an idle state as soon as it has completed execution of its current instruction. When the Z80 is finally off the bus, the bus acknowledge (BUSAK) signal is sent back to all the peripherals to indicate that the bus is free for DMA use. While DMA is being performed, the processor is internally performing NOPs (no-operation instructions) to keep the dynamic registers in the processor refreshed.

The interface complexity of the DMA peripheral interface is quite high due to the logic needed to take control of the bus and generate processor-like signals. A DMA interface typically consists of a transfer address register (which indicates the memory address to transfer data to or from) and a transfer length register (that indicates how many bytes of data are to be transferred). The transfer address register typically counts as bytes are transferred, thereby placing data in sequentially increasing memory addresses. The transfer length register counts down by one for each byte transferred. When the transfer length count is decremented to zero, the transfer is complete and bus control is returned to the processor.

The transfer address and transfer length registers are usually loaded by the processor, so a DMA device isn't totally on its own. The microprocessor initiates all transfers.

Simple processor-halt DMA works on a principle known as *cycle stealing:* clock cycles that the processor could have used to do useful work are "stolen" by the DMA device for its own purposes. Other DMA methods that require no cycle stealing do exist, but they are not often incorporated in microcomputer DMA interfaces due to their complexity.

Interleaved DMA

Interleaved DMA is the process of taking control of the system bus when the processor is not using it. Because the bus is not going to be used by the processor, no time is wasted in the DMA transfer.

The Intel 8086 allows this sort of DMA. By making optimal use of the bus accesses employing its 6-byte instruction queue, the processor can run for a few cycles and not miss a single clock cycle if a DMA access is initiated. The 8086's philosophy is essentially this: The bus is free at any time as long as you don't use it for too many clock cycles in a row (the instruction queue must eventually receive its data).

DMA Interface Components

Because DMA is a fairly tough function to implement with discrete logic, LSI DMA chips have been introduced. These chips usually contain transfer address and length counters for one or more DMA devices. The cost of DMA chips is usually high compared to other I/O chips, because (1) DMA is not used as often as simpler interfaces and (2) production quantity of the parts isn't nearly as great. Figure 4-11 illustrates a typical DMA interface and an LSI chip that performs the same function. These chips are discussed further in the interface device section.

DATA COMMUNICATION BUSES

The signals coming out of and going into a microprocessor chip are adequate to communicate with any peripheral or memory device controlled by the microprocessor, but the signals rarely are sent directly to interfaces and memory. Instead, additional logic is used to form a standardized communication bus or the microcomputer bus to which memory and peripherals may be interfaced. The LSI-11 Q-bus, IEEE 488 bus and S-100 bus are all examples of microcomputer buses.

Microcomputer buses offer many advantages over haphazard connection of microcomputer interfaces. The advantages include modularity, standardization, high fan-out, and circuit protection. These characteristics will be examined more closely, but first let's be sure we agree on what a microcomputer bus is.

A microcomputer bus is a set of address, data, control and power lines arranged in a standardized manner and operating under a strict set of data communication rules. Physically, a bus is typically a row of standardized parallel connectors, with each pin on every connector assigned a specific signal. The

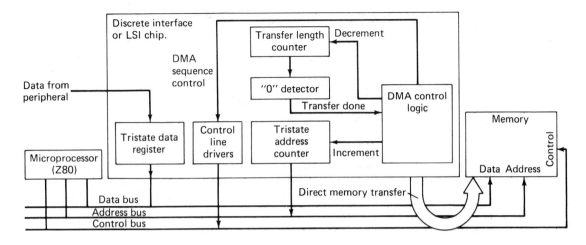

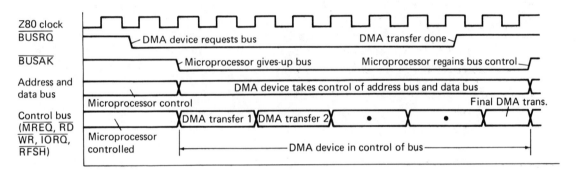

Figure 4-11   A typical microprocessor DMA cycle.

standards for the most common microcomputer bus are presented in Chapter 7, but a typical bus has approximately the complements described in the following paragraphs.

Power Lines

Every interface circuit on a bus needs power to drive its interface logic (and sometimes to drive the peripherals themselves). Microcomputer buses, therefore, usually have a few different power lines of different voltages. A prerequisite for a reliable computer system is a good solid ground for all circuits in the system. A few pins on the bus connectors are dedicated to system grounds. Heavy wire (or a wide printed circuit path if the bus is built on a circuit board) is used for the ground line. On sophisticated microcomputer buses, individual power-ground and signal-ground lines are provided. (The *design practices* section of Chapter 6 details the advantages of the dual ground system.)

The microprocessor, memories, and other components in a microcomputer system use a wide range of voltages for operation. Four power forms are usually provided on a microcomputer bus: +5 volts for TTL and MOS logic; +12 volts for MOS drivers, interfaces, and RAMs; −5 volts for EIA communication drivers and other interface components; and −12 volts for MOS substrate voltages. The +5 volt supply usually has the highest current capabilities.

Two approaches are taken in distributing power on the bus. In one, an external, regulated power supply places a voltage of precisely the proper level on the power lines. Power can then be taken directly from the microcomputer bus and used to power interface circuitry. In the other approach, onboard voltage regulators are used. Unregulated power, a few volts above the desired voltage level, is placed on the bus. The individual cards that plug into the bus must contain their own regulators. An unregulated 8-volt line would be regulated down to a 5-volt level by the circuit boards requiring this voltage level for operation.

The onboard-regulator approach has the advantage that if any one regulator breaks down, only the circuitry on that card will be damaged. Undesirable heat emitted by the onboard voltage regulator is the greatest drawback to this scheme.

Data Lines

Most microprocessors have bidirectional data buses that permit transfer of data to and from memory and peripheral devices. They are bidirectional in order to save I/O pins on the IC package.

A few microcomputer buses abandon the bidirectional approach in favor of individual input and output buses. Separate buses are rather inefficient and wasteful of bus pins if both buses cannot be used at once—and in most microcomputers using this approach, they cannot. The S-100 bus falls into this category. Because most microprocessors use a bidirectional bus, it takes a lot of circuitry to split the bus into separate input and output lines.

Address Lines

Address lines from the microprocessor are usually sent to high-current drivers that drive address lines on the microcomputer bus. The drivers supply sufficient current to drive many interfaces.

Both the data- and address-line drivers of a computer are of the tristate type. During DMA operations, these bus lines can be floated as they are on the microprocessor.

Control Lines

The control lines on the microcomputer bus are dependent on the processor driving the bus. There are a few basic control lines of which most buses have variations.

Clock Lines. These are generated by the processor card and received by the interfaces to use as a master timing reference. On processors having multiphase clocks, such as the 6800, more than one clock line exists on the bus. Occasionally the processor card will also break the master clock frequency down into standard interface communication rates and send these signals to interfaces over the bus. This saves a lot of duplicated clock generation circuitry on the interface cards.

Memory Control Lines. To indicate the processor's requests for memory access and whether a read or write cycle is needed, memory control lines are used on most buses. In systems using I/O channels, a line indicating an I/O channel reference is incorporated.

Initialize Line. To simultaneously reset all peripherals, an initialize line is usually generated by the processor card, power supply, or front panel circuitry.

Interrupt Lines. Any bus that supports interrupt-driven operation uses interrupt lines. In many cases, multiple interrupt lines indicating priority level or nonmasked interrupt requests are used. Interrupt handshaking logic and grant lines are also used.

Halt and Wait Lines. To half processor operation during long memory reference cycles or under front panel control, *halt* lines and *wait* lines are often available.

DMA Status Lines. These provide DMA devices with an indication that the processor is off the bus and free for use.

Bus Compatibility

It is very important that a microcomputer bus be well defined. Many manufacturers build products to operate on popular microcomputer buses; if a formal definition of the bus signals isn't available, they do their best to build something that works. A compatibility problem arises when trying to operate that device with another device designed to different bus interpretations. The popular S-100 bus is plagued by this problem. Very well defined buses such as the LSI-11 bus and the IEEE bus, however, have no compatibility problems.

A microcomputer bus tends to protect easily damaged components from overload conditions. Properly designed interfaces and processor cards have buffers on all lines leading to the bus. Buffers are very rugged and are much less susceptible to damage than lines coming directly out of LSI parts. Buffers are also less noise-susceptible, which results in more reliable operation.

Bus Terminations

Bus lines are limited in length, and the physical distance is typically cited in the bus specification. A bus length of half a meter or so is usually the limit on an unterminated bus. A bus is a transmission line and is subject to the same kind of signal propagation and reflection problems, which are more critical with increased line lengths.

A signal propagates along a line until it reaches the terminal point. If the signal is absorbed entirely at the terminus (the ideal situation), there is a good impedance match between the resistive characteristic of the line and that of the terminal. However, if there is any discrepancy between the impedance of the line and that of the terminal point, the propagated signal will not be entirely absorbed; a portion of the signal will be reflected back down the line in the direction from which it came. These reflected signals are the ones that can cause severe problems, because they can mix with other intended signals in various ways to "confuse" the devices that are interfaced to the line.

Because signals are propagated at a speed that is a sizable percentage of the speed of light, it is easy to see why short bus lengths offer a minimum of difficulty—and why long line lengths create substantial problems. If the line is short enough, the delay between application of a pulse to a line and arrival of that pulse at the destination end of the line is negligible. But when the line is long, the delay—particularly in high-speed systems—can be significant; and when a reflection takes place because of a terminal impedance mismatch, unwanted signals can be propagating along the line while new signals are being output to that bus.

The object of bus terminators is to match the impedance of the bus at its end instead of letting it end with no connection. Resistors are typically used to match the impedance.

LONG DISTANCE DATA COMMUNICATIONS

Data sent from a microcomputer interface card on a bus to a terminal may have to travel as much as 10 meters to reach the terminal. Even longer links are necessary between sensors and other processors in distant locations in an installation. Asynchronous serial data communication is the most common form of general-purpose long-distance links, with synchronous serial communication being more popular for high-performance applications.

Data communication links can be unidirectional or bidirectional. If a device is strictly an input device or strictly an output, data only needs to be sent in one direction. In either case, a serial signal line is all that is required to complete the communication link.

Devices that can operate as either input or output devices require bidirectional communication. There are two possible ways to accommodate such devices. A single line can be provided as a shared communication line. Data can be sent down the line in either direction—but only in one direction at once. This mode of operation is called *half-duplex*.

If simultaneous bidirectional data communication is required, two lines can be sent from the processor to the peripheral. One line would be permanently assigned to input while the other would be an output line. This mode of operation is called *full-duplex*. Figure 4-12 illustrates unidirectional, half-duplex, and full-duplex communication.

Long data communication lines are susceptible to signal losses as a result of noise, cable resistance, and capacitance. Normal low-current logic signals (TTL or CMOS) are not adequate for long-distance communication lines.

Special long-distance serial interface I/O standards have been adopted to provide a universal way of communicating with terminals and other peripherals. Connector pin assignments as well as electrical characteristics are defined. The Electronic Industries Association's RS-232C standard, Teletype's current-loop standards, and various other standards have become quite popular. These provide for large current levels and voltage magnitudes to minimize the losses of long lines. The standards also limit operation to fairly low frequencies in order to minimize capacitive losses (which increase with frequency) and keep reliability high.

Medium-length data transfer lines need not be driven with special drivers if proper impedance matching methods are used. A standard ECL gate, for instance, can successfully drive a 15-meter line at 70 MHz if its differential outputs are connected to an impedance-matched twisted-pair line (two wires twisted together to form a balanced transmission line). Figure 4-13 illustrates this combination.

ERROR DETECTION AND CORRECTION

A byte of data flowing through a microcomputer system has many opportunities to have an error introduced. A single part failure or noise spike in any one of the communication lines can cause a 1 to come out as a 0 or a 0 to become a 1. Because computers depend on 100% reliable data for correct operation, a

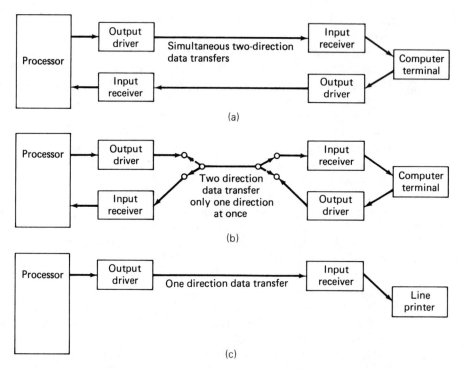

Figure 4-12 Data communication line formats. (a) Full-duplex communication. (b) Half-duplex communication. (c) Unidirectional communication.

whole branch of computer science has developed around detecting and correcting data-transmission errors. Most large computer systems have error correction circuitry within the CPU, memory systems, and I/O interfaces. The I/O channels cause the greatest number of errors. Because I/O lines typically run outside the computer through mechanical connections and noisy environments, they are much more exposed to data-destroying conditions. Microcomputer systems typically use error detection on I/O channels. Error detection on microcomputer memory modules is just starting to appear.

Error handling methods can be grouped into two classifications: (1) those methods that detect an error and warn the processor that an error was encountered, and (2) those methods that detect the error and proceed to correct it. Error correction is much harder to implement than error detection and is therefore used less often.

Parity

The most common form of error detection used in microcomputers is byte parity. Parity is used between peripheral devices and the microcomputer to detect errors on long, error-prone data transmission lines.

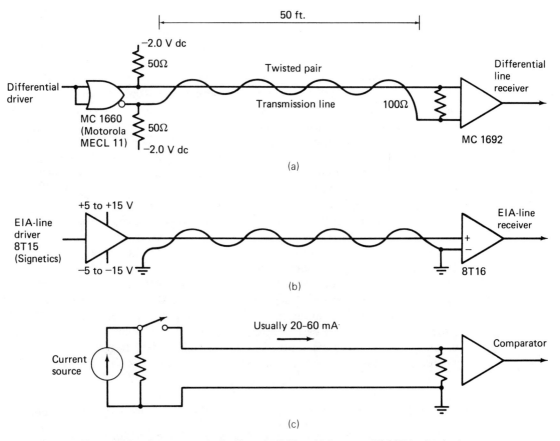

Figure 4-13   Data communication lines. (a) ECL — hi-frequency (70 MHz) twisted pair
differential communication line. (b) EIA — low-frequency (20 kHz) communication line.
(c) Current-loop communication line.

With a parity system, every word sent over a data transmission bus has
either an odd or even number of 1s. Whether a given word has an odd or even
number depends on what value or character is being sent. In odd-parity generation schemes, an extra bit (the parity bit) is added to a word. This bit is used to
insure that each byte, including the parity bit, has an odd number of 1s in it. On
bytes with an even number of data bits set to 1, the parity bit is set to make the
total number of 1s odd. When the data word and its parity bit are received,
parity checking circuitry determines if the number of 1s in the word is odd. If
any one of the bits changes value in the data transmission, perhaps due to a
noise pulse, the number of 1-valued bits will be even and the error will be
detected immediately.

Parity error checking is a single-error detecting scheme. If one bit of data in
a word changes, an error will be detected due to the change in the odd-bit
characteristic. If *two* bits change values, however, the number of 1s will be

changed back into an odd number by the second bit failing. The word will again have an odd number of 1s and the error will go undetected.

There are actually two types of parity. *Odd* parity, which was just described, means that every byte will always contain an *odd* number of 1s. With *even* parity, every byte always contains an *even* number of 1s. Odd parity is most commonly used because the presence of a word can be detected by checking to see if any bits in the word are one. A word with all zeros is an error condition in odd-parity transmissions.

The price paid for parity checking in an interface is twofold: a slower transmission rate, because an extra bit of data must be sent for every word, and additional parity-checking hardware. Parity generation and checking hardware is relatively simple, however.

A tree of exclusive-OR gates determines if the number of 1s in a word is even and sets the parity bit to 1 (for an odd parity system) if it is. The parity checking hardware uses an exclusive-OR tree to determine if the number of 1s, including the parity, is odd. If it isn't, a parity error is flagged. Figure 4-14 illustrates a parity generator and checker.

Parity is a very common feature on serial interfaces, so most LSI data communication chips include parity-checking hardware. The Motorola 6850 ACIA (asynchronous communication interface adapter), for example, can be programmed under software control to check for even, odd, or no parity at all. A bit is set in the peripheral's status word if a data transmission error is detected.

Checksum

In many applications, the extra bit of data added to each word using the parity-error detection scheme is too wasteful to be desirable. In data storage, for example, an error detection method is desirable, but storing one extra bit for every eight means a 12.5% loss of data-storage capacity. For this reason, a less storage-intensive error checking method is used on most disks and tape drivers. The method is called checksum of *cyclic redundancy checking* (CRC).

Checksum error detection spots errors in blocks of many bytes instead of in individual bytes as parity does. This is accomplished by taking all the bytes in the block of data into consideration and adding one byte to the end of the block that reflects a characteristic about the whole block. One characteristic that could be used is the sum of all the bytes in the block. If an error occurred in any one of the bytes in the block, surely the sum of all the bytes would change as well. The problem with this method is the sum grows so large that it overflows a single byte of data. The solution is to let the sum byte overflow. The bottom 8 bits of the sum in an 8-bit checksum scheme are adequate to indicate any errors that may have occurred.

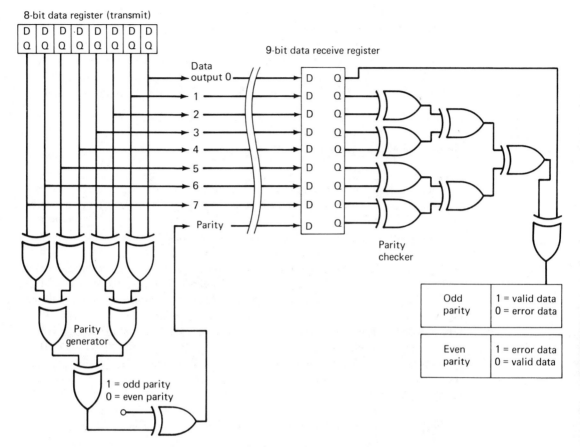

Figure 4-14 Parity generation and checking.

Typically, in a checksum scheme, all the bytes in a block of data are added together without regard to overflow (thus the term cyclic redundancy). The resulting byte is complemented and written at the end of the block. The complemented word simplifies error checking. Upon block readback, all the bytes in the block are added together. The addition of the final byte essentially adds the sum of all the bytes to its complement and turns the result into zero. A valid block can be detected by simply checking for a zero sum.

One common misconception about parity, checksum, and error detecting and correcting codes, in general, is that the extra bits of bytes added to a byte or block of data must be transmitted correctly to perform the error checking task. This is not true, because the check byte or bit is usually treated identically or nearly identically to any other element in the byte or block. An erroneous check bit or byte will be detectable just as an erroneous data byte or bit will.

Once an error is detected, there are several courses of action that can be taken. The data transfer can be aborted, or a signal can be sent back to the transmitting device to indicate that a byte was in error and the block or byte should be set again. Errors in tape and disk reading are usually handled by the second method. If the tape or disk is read about 10 times and the error is still present, a nonrecoverable error is declared and the data transfer is aborted.

Error-Correcting Codes

The need for retransmitting a byte if an error is encountered can be totally eliminated by adding parity-type digits to a byte in a way that lets you correct as well as detect bad bytes. The key to such error-correcting schemes is multiple representations of the same value. If a 4-bit value of 0001 represents a one, a single-bit change in that byte must also be interpreted as a one. The values 0000, 0011, 0101, and 1001 must therefore also be equivalent to one. Many coding schemes have been set up to perform error checking using this principle.

The most common error-correcting code is the *Hamming Code*. This coding scheme relies on parity bits interspersed with data bits in a data word. By combining the data and parity bits according to a strict set of parity equations, a small byte that contains a value that actually points to the bit in error is generated. Figure 4-15 illustrates a simple Hamming Code. The M bits represent memory bits; the P bits are parity bits. The derivation of the parity bits from the data bits is shown.

An error can be detected and corrected if any bit is changed in any value. If the value 7 is transmitted (0 0001 111 binary) but the bit in the third position is accidentally changed to one (0 0011 111 binary), the reconstruction equations shown in Fig. 4-15 can be used to reconstruct the word as illustrated in the figure.

Error-correcting codes are very bit-wasteful, but large memories of the future may rely on error-correcting circuitry to be reliable. If building a multimegabit memory on one chip nearly always results in one or two bad cells, error-correction logic within the chip could be used to mask out the one-in-a-million errors. This method could cause some inefficiency, but a buildable RAM of a million bits (error corrected) is far more desirable than an unbuildable 4-megabit non-error corrected unit.

The hardware used to generate and check error-correcting Hamming Codes is quite complex and essentially implements the error-correction equation of Fig. 4-15.

Hamming and other error-correcting codes offer an additional bonus. They can detect errors of two or more bits, although they can only correct one-bit errors.

	Position						
	1	2	3	4	5	6	7
Value	p_1	p_2	m_1	p_3	m_2	m_3	m_4
0	0	0	0	0	0	0	0
1	1	1	0	1	0	0	1
2	0	1	0	1	0	1	0
3	1	0	0	0	0	1	1
4	1	0	0	1	1	0	0
5	0	1	0	0	1	0	1
6	1	1	0	0	1	1	0
7	0	0	0	1	1	1	1
8	1	1	1	0	0	0	0
9	0	0	1	1	0	0	1

m = data bit
p = parity bit

(a)

Value = m_4, m_3, m_2, m_1 (binary) (5 = 0101 for example)

$p_1 = \overline{m_1 \oplus m_2 \oplus m_4}$

$p_2 = \overline{m_1 \oplus m_3 \oplus m_4}$

$p_3 = \overline{m_2 \oplus m_3 \oplus m_4}$

(b)

$C_3 = p_1 \oplus m_1 \oplus m_2 \oplus m_4$

$C_2 = p_2 \oplus m_1 \oplus m_3 \oplus m_4$

$C_1 = p_3 \oplus m_2 \oplus m_3 \oplus m_4$

C_1, C_2, C_3 binary = binary value
pointing to *position* of error.

(c)

	1	2	3	4	5	6	7
Good value 7 =	0	0	0	1	1	1	1
Transmission error value =	0	0	1	1	1	1	1

Using above equations: $C_1 = 0$ $C_2 = 1$ $C_3 = 1$
Error position = 011 = position 3.
Changing position 3 from 1 to 0 yields:
        0001111, the corrected value.

(d)

Figure 4-15   Hamming error correction. (a) Hamming representation of digits 0-9. (b) Hamming generation rules. (c) Hamming error correction location rules. (d) An error correcting example.

CHAPTER

5 Interface Components and Their Characteristics

Before attempting to design microcomputer interfaces and systems, it is wise to get familiar with the interface components available to the microcomputer designer. What could be more disheartening than spending a week designing a special interface circuit only to find that a one-chip interface component could have performed the task?

There are two general levels on which interface parts should be known: the *functional* level and the *electrical* level. In the past, simple devices such as transistors and resistors were well understood on both levels by most designers mainly because the functions of these devices were directly related to their electrical characteristics. A resistor, for example, could be selected to perform a variety of functions, its value being determined by a simple application of Ohm's law.

In regard to microprocessors and interface parts, however, the functional or logical aspects tend to eclipse the electrical characteristics. Thinking only on the logical level can lead to trouble when designing a system. Unless logic thresholds, noise margins, fan-outs, and propagation delays are taken into account, a logically correct circuit simply will not work. Basically, an interface component will not perform its logical function unless it is run within its electrical limits.

When a 1 or 0 is sent from a microprocessor to an interface part, there are actually three events that take place. A driver circuit within the microprocessor generates a voltage or current level that corresponds to the logic level of 1 or 0.

The resulting current travels down a conductive path that is commonly called a bus line, and the current or resulting voltage is sensed by a receiver in the interface part, which in turn generates a usable onchip voltage corresponding to 0 or 1.

DRIVER CIRCUITS

Driver and receiver circuitry is used on all input and output lines on flip-flops, latches, registers, and even large PIAs, ACIAs, and microprocessors. Designing a reliably running system is simply a matter of properly matching the receivers to the drivers and making sure the interconnecting lines transfer the signals without too much loss or noise pickup. We will look at transmission line layout in Chapter 6. In this chapter we examine drivers and receivers.

TTL Drivers

A driver is an output device capable of generating a standardized voltage or current that other parts can use. A driver consists of one or more transistors that switch voltage levels or apply current to represent logic values. The driver is characterized by its high and low (voltage) output levels, the number of receivers it is capable of driving (its *fan-out*), and its switching speed. Other factors such as rise time and noise threshold are also important, especially in high-speed Schottky TTL and ECL designs.

TTL Open-Collector Driver. Figure 5-1 illustrates five common driver circuits. Perhaps the simplest is the TTL open-collector output stage shown in Fig. 5-1(a). In this circuit the transistor, identified as Q2, is switched on and off by the applied logic signal and the associated one-transistor input buffer (Q1). The output transistor, Q2, goes into saturation to represent a logic 0. In this state, the driver output is in a low-impedance mode at about 300 mV (the emitter–collector saturation voltage of Q2). Current flows through the external pullup resistor, Rx. The output transistor is turned off to represent a logic 1. In this mode, Q2 is a high-impedance state, causing very little current (only the transistor's leakage current) to flow down the Rx resistor. The driver output is thus at a nearly 5 V level, which represents 1.

The open-collector driver's primary disadvantage is its variable impedance. Logic 1 is a high impedance and logic 0 is a low impedance. The transistor can turn on very quickly, thereby generating a very fast high- to low-voltage (1 to 0) transition; but when the transistor is turned off, a very slow voltage rise to 5 V occurs as the stored charge is bled off the driver transistor. Overall slow system operation is the result.

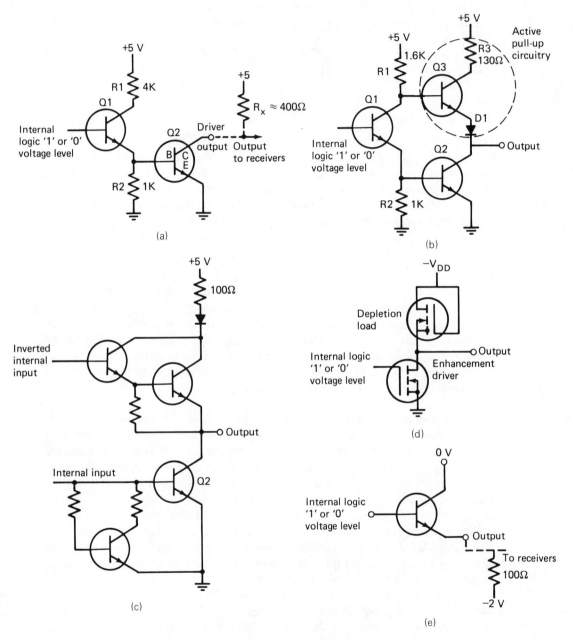

Figure 5-1 Typical driver circuits. (a) TTL open-collector. (b) TTL totem pole. (c) TTL tristate. (d) MOS. (e) ECL.

The stage's high-impedance logic 1 state can be used to advantage, however. The outputs of many open-collector drivers can be connected together to perform a wired-AND function. Only when all the drivers are in their high-impedance state will the output rise to 5 V. The open-collector driver therefore makes a good bus driver when many drivers are connected to a common line. Many minicomputers and microcomputers (notably the PDP-11) use open-collector bus drivers.

TTL Totem-Pole Driver. The variable impedance problem associated with the open-collector driver is solved in the totem-pole driver shown in Fig. 5-1(b). The external pullup resistor is replaced by an internal pullup transistor, diode, and low-impedance (130-ohm) resistor. Instead of letting the voltage slowly drift up to 5 V through the low-impedance pullup resistor, the active pullup circuitry (Q3) is turned on, causing a rapid transition. The totem-pole output results in faster overall system operation due to faster rise times.

Although the totem-pole structure eliminates the disadvantages of the high-impedance logic 1 state, it also eliminates the wired-AND driving capability. If two totem-pole outputs representing 0 and 1 are connected together, current will flow through R3, Q3, and D1 of the logic 1 driver and through Q2 of the logic 0 driver. An undefined logic value will result as the two drivers "fight" each other. Most TTL totem-pole outputs are protected from transistor breakdown resulting from the high current flowing through the low-impedance Q3 stage, but eventually thermal destruction of the top half of the driver totem pole can occur, especially if more than one driver on an interface chip is short-circuited. If is good to know that two connected totem-pole outputs will not cause chip destruction (wiring errors and solder bridges do sometimes occur on interface cards), but connected totem-pole outputs should never be *designed* into a system.

TTL Tristate Driver. The advantages of the totem-pole driver are combined with the ability to put a driver into a high-impedance state in the tristate driver shown in Fig. 5-1(c). A tristate driver's states are 1, 0, and *float* (or high-impedance). An external enable line allows the driver to be manually put into the float state. Most microcomputers use tristate drivers for speed reasons.

TTL Driver Characteristics. The important factors to watch for in TTL or TTL-level drivers are high- and low-voltage (and current) driving capabilities, driving impedance, switching speed, and noise-generation characteristics. These vary greatly depending on the TTL family. Standard TTL gates such as the 7400 (totem-pole output), 7401 (open-collector), and 74125 (tristate) typically have logic 0 current-sinking capabilities of about 16 mA. In TTL, it is the current-sinking capability of a driver that will be the first parameter to be exceeded if too many receivers are being driven. A typical TTL receiver sources about 1.6 mA, so about 10 TTL receivers can be driven by a standard

TTL driver. Special high-power buffer gates are capable of sinking much more current.

Voltage levels for TTL are 0 to 0.8 V for logic 0 and 2 to 5 V for logic 1. Drivers have no trouble supplying voltages within these ranges as long as the fan-out restrictions are observed.

When driving long data transmission lines, high-power impedance-matched drivers such as the 74128 50-ohm line driver must be used. The output stage on these drivers is similar to the totem pole of Fig. 5-1 (b) with R3 being 30 ohms instead of 130 ohms.

High-speed, Schottky, low-power, and low-power Schottky TTL drivers have different characteristics. Schottky current and power levels are slightly greater than standard TTL, while low-power and low-power Schottky drivers use much less current.

TTL output drivers generate power line noise. Open-collector drivers draw substantial current only in the logic 1 state. Transitions from 0 to 1 therefore cause current demand changes that contribute to noise. In theory, totem-pole and tristate drivers reduce this problem, because only low-impedance states are switched between, but in practice these output drivers generate even worse noise than open-collector drivers. The noise is the result of both totem-pole driver transistors being on momentarily while switching from 0 to 1 or 1 to 0. These conditions allow large currents to flow through both transistors, generating huge current spikes. Decoupling capacitors are used to reduce the noise. We will discuss these in Chapter 6.

MOS Drivers

MOS and CMOS systems draw much less power and work with much lower currents than TTL systems (when run at low frequencies) and their drivers use much less current. In principle, however, the MOS driver is very much like the TTL totem-pole driver. Instead of using bipolar (NPN in most cases) transistors, MOS transistors are used, as in Fig. 5-1(d). Because MOS transistors are more like variable resistors than switches, no current-limiting resistor is needed as in the totem pole. Instead, the internal resistance of the MOS transistor is used to limit current.

The most important characteristic to watch for when using MOS drivers is drive-current capability. Most microprocessors use MOS drivers to generate TTL-compatible outputs, but due to the low-power characteristic of MOS devices, these outputs are usually only capable of driving one or two normal TTL loads.

The current driving capability of a MOS driver is usually specified in a different way than that of a TTL driver. The MOS driver acts like a resistor. This means that the more current that is sunk through the driver, the higher (from 0 V) or lower (from 5 V) the output will go. The output reaches its limit when logic levels at the output are no longer distinguishable (1.1 V as zero, for example). MOS drivers are therefore specified by stating how much current they can sink at a given voltage. The Zilog Z80's output low voltage, for instance, is rated at 1.8 mA at 400 mV. This is enough to safely drive one TTL load or a few low-power-Schottky loads.

The MOS driver can drive many MOS receivers, and MOS input capacitance is the limiting factor when doing so. This is discussed in the receiver section.

Pushing the MOS driver past its limits is a bad design practice. The Z80 mentioned above, for example, could probably drive two TTL loads (about 2 mA, typically) but the 0 logic-level voltage would climb above 400 mV and possibly to 700 or 800 mV. This voltage level is right at the borderline of the TTL's zero-recognition voltage, and the slightest bit of noise on the data line could push it over, causing bad data to be sent. The danger here lies in the fact that the system will operate, but unreliably. A failure may not occur until the final product leaves the lab and goes into a noisy environment.

Matching drivers and receivers of different logic families (and even the same logic family) requires examination of noise margins. Figure 5-2 illustrates the noise margins of several logic families. The shaded areas represent voltage levels at which 0s and 1s will be correctly recognized. It is preferable to drive a logic level well into the shaded areas, as the remainder of the shaded area acts as a noise margin. The MOS driver driving a 1 mA load, for example, generates a logic 0 level of about 200 mV. Because anything up to 800 mV is considered as an acceptable signal by the receiver, there is 600 mV to spare—or a 600 mV noise margin. A 500 mV noise spike could come along and not even affect the receiver.

ECL Drivers

Emitter-coupled logic is a current-oriented logic as opposed to TTL, which is voltage-oriented. Voltage and current are indeed related to one another in any form of logic, but ECL is more easily thought of in terms of current. The reason ECL is such a high-speed logic is that it is nonsaturating. TTL turns transistors on and off by saturating them, while ECL channels currents using transistors that operate in their active regions. Because saturation charge is not built up on the transistors, it never has to be drained. Schottky TTL attempts to accomplish the same thing by using Schottky clamping diodes to keep the transistors out of saturation. In this sense, ECL is more like an analog than a digital logic. Many high-speed ECL parts can, in fact, be used as analog devices. The analog nature of ECL must be considered when working with drivers and receivers. Good dc amplifier coupling practices must be adhered to.

The ECL driver shown in Fig. 5-1(e) is similar to the TTL open-collector driver in that the output is driven by a single transistor and is terminated by a

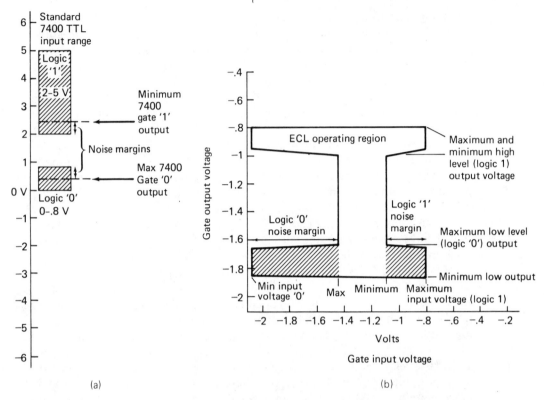

Figure 5-2   Logic thresholds of TTL and ECL logic families. (a) TTL thresholds. (b) ECL's operating region, commonly known as the "Lazy H."

resistor. The big difference, of course, is that the ECL output is coupled to the transistor's emitter rather than its collector. Unlike the open-collector driver, the ECL driver's output transistor is never turned completely on (saturated) or off (cut off). When the transistor is in its lowest impedance or *on* state, a logic 1 is represented. ECL's logic 1 voltage is -850 mV. When the transistor is in its high-impedance state, the output is pulled to a logic 0 value of approximately -1.8 V. The high-impedance state is not as high an impedance as the open-collector output, however, because the transistor remains turned on the slightest bit to keep it out of cutoff.

The ECL driver has all the advantages of the open-collector, TTL totem-pole, and tristate drivers. Outputs from multiple ECL drivers can be connected together to form a wired-OR. A bus can therefore be built with ECL drivers. Because there are no saturating driver transistors, the open-collector desaturation problem is avoided and a noisy (current-spike generating) totem pole is not necessary to increase the speed.

The biggest problems in working with ECL drivers are noise reduction due to the high frequencies involved, and threshold matching. While it is true that

ECL is a current-mode logic, it relies on voltage changes to generate the current changes. ECL has only a 1 V logic swing with appropriately small noise margins (see Fig. 5-2). To make matters worse, the logic level thresholds of ECL parts drift with temperature. Unless the ECL family being used is temperature-compensated, a hot driver may not be able to send data to a cold receiver due to threshold differences. A solution to this problem is the differential driver and receiver. ECL drivers usually have true and complementary outputs, because this feature comes nearly without cost in the design of ECL parts. By sending the true and complementary outputs to a special differential receiver (a differential amplifier or comparator), the threshold shift due to temperature can be rejected by the common-mode rejection inherent in differential amplifiers.

One note of caution about using the wired-OR capability of ECL drivers: Because a driver's output transistor is never completely off, it leaks current in the high-impedance state. If many drivers are combined in a wired-OR arrangement, the sum of their leakage currents can pull the output voltage out of the logic 0 state. With every additional driver wired to an output, a slight loss in noise margin is incurred. So the wired-OR configuration does have its penalty.

RECEIVER CIRCUITS

A receiver is an input device capable of converting a signal from a driver into a signal that is usable within the chip with which it is associated. Figure 5-3 shows a few common input circuits—the standard TTL, the low-power Schottky TTL, a noncomplementary MOS circuit, and an input circuit from the emitter-coupled logic (ECL) family.

Internal voltage levels and current requirements vary widely from chip to chip, and it is the receiver's job to match the internal requirements to the signals arriving at the chip's input pins. A receiver's input characteristics are designed to meet the input specifications of a given logic family, thus making the receiver an easy-to-use building block. Many "TTL-compatible" RAMs and peripheral chips are in fact ECL, MOS, or even I²L internally; but the designer need not concern himself with level matching, thanks to the built-in receivers.

TTL Receivers

The important receiver characteristics to consider when inter-connecting TTL circuits are input current level, input voltage level, and circuit immunity to environmental noise. These considerations apply to standard TTL as well as special TTL circuits such as high-speed and low-power Schottky types, although the susceptibility to excesses varies according to the characteristics of any given TTL family member.

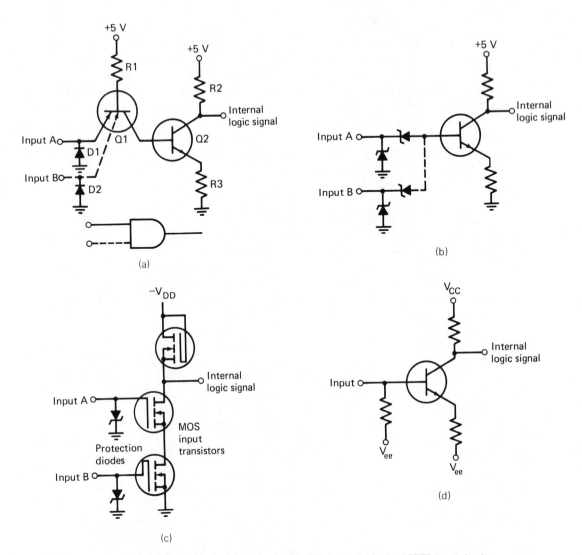

Figure 5-3   Typical receiver circuits. (a) TTL input circuit. (b) LSTTL input circuit.
(c) MOS input (AND gate) circuit. (d) ECL input circuit.

Unit Loads.   Each gate of a given logic subfamily (TTL is a family, the variations are subfamilies) is considered a *unit load*. Because drivers are capable of driving only a finite number of such unit loads, it is essential to keep the number of receiver unit loads to no more than the maximum that can be driven by the associated driver. A driver, for example, with a rated fan-out of 10 may be used to drive a maximum of 10 unit loads. But each unit load must be of the same logic subfamily as the driver, or the fan-out specification becomes meaningless. As long as the unit-load restrictions are observed, the logic circuit arrangements should be well within the design limits of the component elements.

Mixed Logic Families. If devices of mixed logic families are used, the unit-load specifications cannot be used with any reliability. The input currents and voltage requirements and capabilities of the drivers and receivers must be compared to determine compatibility. Figure 5-4 illustrates the comparison process. In this example, a low-power Schottky TTL (LSTTL) driver is driving two standard TTL receivers. First, the threshold voltages of the two logic families are compared (tests 1 and 2). For a logic 1, the receivers need at least 2 V; the driver supplies 2.5 V, leaving a 500 mV noise margin. On the logic 0 side, the receiver will tolerate no higher than 800 mV as a logic 0. The driver puts out 500 mV maximum as a logic 0, so logic 0 leaves a 300 mV noise margin.

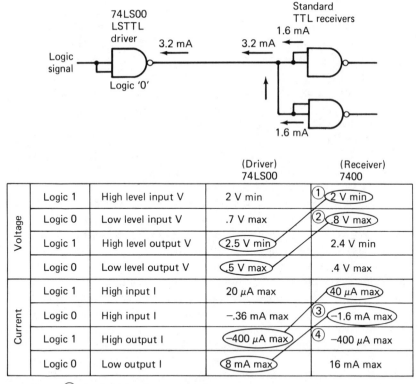

			(Driver) 74LS00	(Receiver) 7400
Voltage	Logic 1	High level input V	2 V min	① 2 V min
	Logic 0	Low level input V	.7 V max	② .8 V max
	Logic 1	High level output V	2.5 V min	2.4 V min
	Logic 0	Low level output V	.5 V max	.4 V max
Current	Logic 1	High input I	20 µA max	40 µA max
	Logic 0	High input I	−.36 mA max	③ −1.6 mA max
	Logic 1	High output I	−400 µA max	④ −400 µA max
	Logic 0	Low output I	8 mA max	16 mA max

Tests: ① Logic high voltage comparison
② Logic low voltage comparison
③ High current test
④ Low current test

Figure 5-4   Interfacing mixed logic families.

Because both logic families are TTL, voltage thresholds cause no problem and are in fact nearly identical for standard and LSTTL parts.

Drive Current Considerations.   Next, the driver and the sum of the receiver's currents must be checked to insure that the driver can indeed supply enough drive current. Because two TTL receivers are connected, the sum of two input currents must be matched against the single driver's total current capability. As Fig. 5-4 shows, -3.2 mA is required to drive to logic 0. The driver can supply 8 mA, so there is no problem. Likewise, with the sum of the logic 1 currents, -400μ A can easily handle the 80μ A high current.

From these specifications it is obvious that the first area in which trouble will occur if more recievers are driven is the low output current level. Five standard TTL loads will push the LSTTL driver to its 8 mA limit. As stated in the driver section, it is typically the low-level output current of the driver that is the limiting factor in TTL.

In cases in which AND gates are used as receivers (see Fig. 5-4), it is a common practice to connect the two or more inputs together if the AND function is not desired. Because the two or more inputs are connected to the emitters of the same transistor, this receiver acts as a single load—1.6 mA in the TTL case. (This rule doesn't apply to LSTTL, however; because individual diodes are used for each input, tied-together inputs act as multiple loads.)

Floating Inputs.   On the logical function level, an input that is not connected to anything is at an undefined logic level. On the electrical level, however, open TTL inputs float to a logic 1 level, and ECL inputs float to 0. As Fig. 5-3(a) illustrates, if nothing is connected to the A and B inputs, current flows through R1 and turns the Q2 transistor on.

Although the floating-input feature can be used in system design, it is better to connect any open inputs to a solid logic 1 (or 0) level if they are not being used. Because open inputs on some TTL circuits are susceptible to noise, reliability problems can result.

The best way to set an input to a 1 or 0 is to tie it to +5 V or ground. Many designers prefer to tie to +5 V through a mild pullup resistor, thereby reducing current flow through the input transistor caused by power-line transients exceeding maximum input voltages. One 1000-ohm resistor can be used to tie up to 10 inputs to a logic 1 level and should be used for all inputs with input breakdown voltages of less than 7 volts.

Standard TTL Input Circuit.   In the standard TTL input circuit (Fig. 5-3(a)), an input signal is taken through the input transistor's emitter electrode (Q1). The resulting high or low voltage value—depending on a 0 or a 1 input value—is used to turn on (or off) the internal logic-level generating transistor (Q2), thereby creating the logic signals for internal operation.

Two points should particularly be noted about this design: (1) the input portion of the stage often has multiple emitters, and (2) clamping diodes are used on the emitters. The incorporation of multiple emitters constitutes an AND gate; Q2 cannot be turned on until all the emitters are at a high voltage level. The shunting emitter diodes provide the necessary forward voltage drop during negative excursions of the input signal and create a clamping effect that prevents ringing or oscillations after gating.

Low-Power Schottky TTL Input Circuit. Low-power Schottky TTL inputs differ from standard TTL circuitry. Instead of using multiemitter transistors as the input element, hot-carrier (Schottky) diodes are used [Fig. 5-3(b)] , with the result that less current is needed to operate the gate. While a standard TTL gate requires about 1.6 mA in the logic 0 state, the low-power Schottky input requires but 0.36 mA. As with the other input circuits, clamping diodes are used to prevent ringing and to stabilize the circuit upon receipt of the gating signal.

Tristate TTL Receivers. A common feature found on interface components designed for microprocessor-bus use is the ability to "turn a receiver off" or put it into a high-impedance state. At first this may not seem to make much sense, because you cannot use wired-AND inputs anyway. The real reason behind this feature is bus loading reduction. Many more receivers can be put on a microcomputer's address and data bus if most of the receiver inputs are in a high-impedance state most of the time. A high-impedance input draws an order of magnitude less current than an active input.

Schmitt-Trigger Input. Standard TTL inputs are fine as long as clean waveforms with quickly rising edges are available. However, in the real world, conditions are not always ideal; noisy or slowly rising waveforms can cause noise generation problems with standard inputs. The problem lies in the area in which the waveform crosses the receiver's switching threshold. Because this is the point at which the receiver switches between 1 and 0, a slowly rising waveform that stays at this level for any length of time will cause rapid toggling between 1 and 0, especially if there is noise on the line—as Fig. 5-5 illustrates.

A circuit that solves this problem is the Schmitt trigger. This circuit actually varies the switching threshold depending on whether the receiver is in a 1 or 0 condition. The instant a rising waveform crosses the threshold from 0 to 1, the Schmitt trigger drops the threshold to a lower value so small excursions around the original threshold point have no effect on the output waveform.

On the falling waveform, the Schmitt trigger does just the opposite; it raises the threshold as soon as a 1-to-0 transition occurs. The variable threshold effect is called hysteresis. A typical Schmitt trigger (the 74S132) has a 0-to-1 threshold of 1.77 V and a 1-to-0 threshold of 1.22 V. A 550 mV hysteresis is the result.

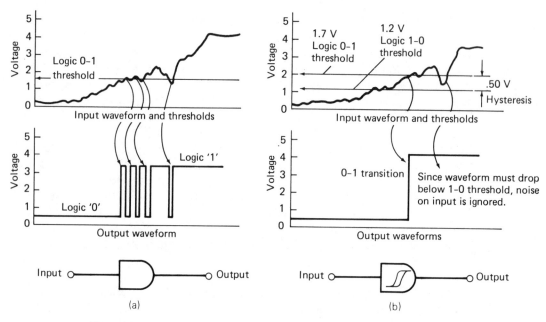

Figure 5-5   Transfer characteristics of standard versus Schmitt trigger gates. (a) Standard gate. (b) Schmitt trigger gate.

Schmitt triggers are used extensively for inputs that do not change very quickly, such as inputs from slow logic and analog devices. Schmitt triggers also find use in converting slow rise times to fast rise times and in microcomputer bus receivers in which ringing can be a problem.

MOS Receivers

Figure 5-3(c) illustrates a typical MOS input circuit. The main feature is its MOS input transistor. Input operation is quite simple. Voltage levels are detected by the MOS input transistor, causing it to act as a variable resistor. This variable resistance is used to switch between logic levels.

Loading.   MOS input circuits are characterized by their extremely high input impedance. MOS transistors are charge-oriented devices and only draw current when they are changing their resistance (current is induced by the buildup of charge). The more often the input logic state is changed, the more power the input circuit will consume. Due to this charge-transfer characteristic, MOS inputs are treated as capacitive loads. The number of unit loads a driver can handle is limited by either how fast the capacitive inputs can be switched or the instantaneous current required to switch all inputs. When designing with MOS receivers, it is necessary to compare input capacitance as well as voltages.

This fact is illustrated in the specifications for the 6800 microprocessor. The number of peripheral chips of the 6800 variety that can be placed on the MOS-driven bus is 8, limited by the 130 pF loading specification of the MOS drivers. Motorola allows 100 pF for data bus driver capacitance and 30 pF for interconnection capacitance.

Operating Voltages.   Because MOS receiver impedances are so high, it is easy to change the voltage on the input pin. A 5 V input signal moves the input to 5 V with practically no current at all. The same thing applies to a 10 kV static charge that you might have on your hand. High impedance makes MOS devices highly susceptible to static electricity damage. In the early days of MOS devices, just touching an open lead with a fingertip would virtually assure a burned-out part, but today's devices are well protected against static charges with zener diodes.

Figure 5-3(c) shows the zener diode on the MOS transistor input. If voltage exceeds the maximum safe voltage, the zener diode provides a low-impedance path to ground to absorb the charge. Most MOS parts are still labeled with caution warnings concerning static discharge, but most new devices are in fact extremely rugged and will only be damaged by the greatest abuse.

ECL Receivers

The ECL receiver shown in Fig. 5-3(d) is simply an NPN transistor that is turned on and off by input current from the emitter-coupled driver. This receiver is basically a one-transistor amplifier that operates in its linear region. Operation within its linear region means that the transistor does not have to be driven completely into saturation to achieve full turn-on; the stage is turned on at virtually the instant the device begins to conduct. Because current goes into the base of the transistor instead of the emitter, very low current is demanded by the input. ECL drivers are capable of driving up to 90 ECL input loads. This figure is somewhat misleading, however. At ECL's high operating speed (20 to 500 MHz), the relatively small capacitances introduced by the inputs and associated transmission lines reduce the drive capability down to 10 or less unit loads. In ECL design, fan-out must be sacrificed for high-speed operation.

INPUT/OUTPUT INTEGRATED CIRCUITS

Now that the basics of data transfer have been covered on the functional and electrical levels, some of the commercial parts available to perform simple and advanced I/O functions will be examined. Because microcomputers are bus-oriented machines, the bus transmitter (buffer or driver) is a good place to begin.

Figure 5-6 illustrates the Signetics 8T96 bus driver. Bus drivers are designed to take low current and two-state outputs from microcomputer components and discrete logic and put them into a high current, standardized tristate (or open-collector) compatible driving format. Bus drivers such as the 8T96 have four characteristics that make them ideal for bus driving applications: high current drive, a low-leakage high-impedance state so many drivers can be placed on one bus, short propagation delay due to the Schottky technology, and the ability to maintain a high impedance during power-up and power-down. The last feature is desirable, because it prevents an intentional or unintentional power-down of a device on the microprocessor bus from tying up the bus.

Bus drivers usually come in 14- and 16-pin packages and have one or more common enables that control 4–6 drivers within the package. These common enable lines are useful for coincident bus control.

Buffers are available in inverting and noninverting versions. It is traditional to have data inverted on a data bus because most old computers use open-collector bus drivers to form a wire-AND inverted bus. With tristate logic, there is no advantage to the inverted bus.

Receivers are also available in 14- and 16-pin quad and hex versions. The 8T380, an example of such a receiver, is shown in Fig. 5-6.

Bus receivers are characterized by their high impedance, which allows many to be put on a bus without undue loading. In many cases, a high-impedance PNP input transistor is used to provide high impedance as well as fast switching.

Bus receivers often contain Schmitt-trigger input circuitry also. This enhances the noise immunity of a computer system and increases overall system reliability.

Transmitters and receivers are often connected to the same line, and special parts that combine transmit and receive functions are useful in these applications. The 8T26 bus transceiver shown in Fig. 5-7 is one such part. Four bus transceivers are provided in a single 16-pin package. The 8T26 has tristate outputs as well as tristate inputs controlled by the driver enable and receiver enable inputs. Like the 8T96 bus driver, the 8T26 goes into a high-impedance state on power-down.

Detailed information about interface components is available in manufacturers' catalogs. Signetics has a very broad line of interface components (their 8T series), as does National Semiconductor. Microprocessor manufacturers such as Motorola, Intel, and Fairchild have nearly identical parts that go by microprocessor series numbers. The Motorola XC6885, for example, is basically an 8T95 driver.

One-Chip Parallel I/O Ports

The one-chip parallel I/O port, which is often called a *peripheral interface adapter* (PIA) or programmable peripheral interface, is a combination of bus transceivers and registers designed to interface peripheral equipment in a paral-

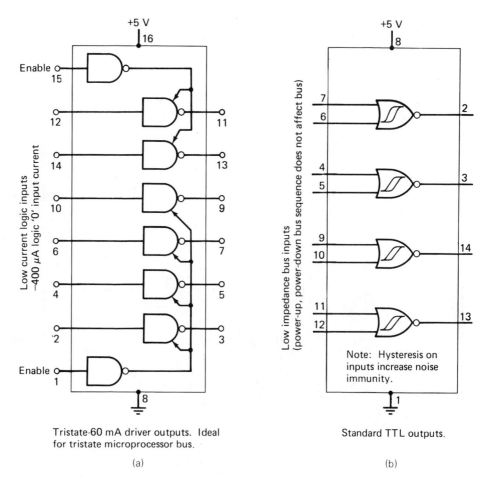

Figure 5-6   One-chip bus drivers and receivers. (a) 8T96 hex bus drivers.
(b) 8T380 quad.

lel manner to external equipment. Two or more parallel input/output channels whose I/O directions are programmable under microprocessor control are usually available.

The 6821 PIA.   A good example of a one-chip I/O port is the 6821 PIA, designed for use with the 6800 microprocessor family (Fig. 5-8). Data and control signals enter the PIA through data bus buffers (transceivers) and are sent to data output or control registers under program control. The PIA provides all necessary bus communication and handshaking. As far as the microcomputer programmer is concerned, the registers appear as memory locations, because they are decoded (using CS1, CS2, and CS0) to respond to certain addresses.

The 6821 has two 8-bit parallel input/output ports called *PA* and *PB*. Data can be sent to or read from the data registers that drive these ports. The PA

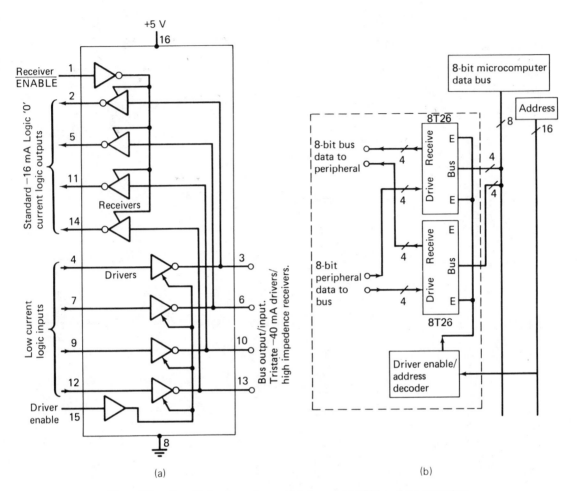

Figure 5-7   One-chip bus transceivers and their uses. (a) 8T26 quad bus transceiver.
(b) Use of bus transceivers.

port can be programmed to act as either an input or output port by setting all 8 bits in the data direction register to 0 or 1, respectively. Because each of the 8 bits in the data direction register corresponds to a line in the PA port, selected lines of the PA port can be programmed to act as individual outputs and inputs.

When the microprocessor or DMA device reads the PIA's PA register, the data on PA's input-programmed lines appears directly on the microprocessor data bus. Data written into the PA register appears on the output-programmed lines as logic 0 and 1 levels. In the input mode, the PA lines will accept anything below 800 mV as a 0 and anything above 2.0 V as a 1. In the output mode, the PA lines will each supply 1.6 mA of sink current or one standard TTL load.

The PB port is similar to the PA port from a functional standpoint. The PB port and its corresponding control and data direction registers respond to different bus addresses, however. The electrical characteristics of the PB lines in

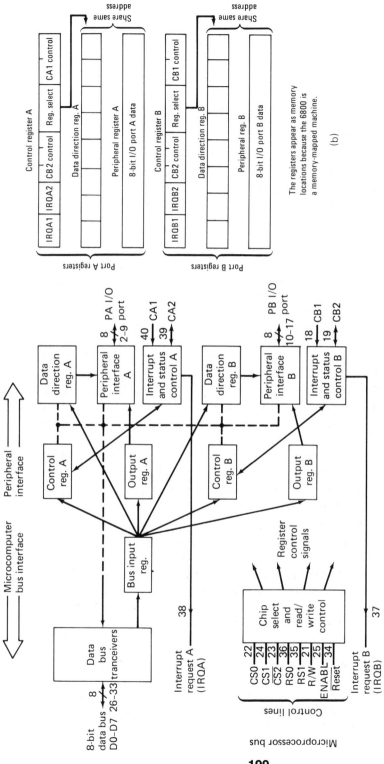

Figure 5-8 The 6821 programmable interface adapter (PIA). (a) Block diagram. (b) Programmer's view of a PIA. (Courtesy Motorola Semiconductor Products, Phoenix, Arizona.)

199

their output mode are quite different from the PA outputs. These lines have the tristate character and enter their float state when programmed as inputs. In addition, these lines are capable of supplying up to 1 mA of current at 1.5 V to a transistor. It is obvious that Motorola had high-power control switching applications in mind when this feature was incorporated.

In addition to the two 8-bit-wide PA and PB ports, the 6821 has two discrete programmable I/O lines (CA2 and CB2) and two discrete input-only lines (CA1 and CB1). These lines are under direct control of bits in the control register. The CA1 and CB1 lines can be programmed to cause interrupts on the rising edge or falling edge of data at the CA inputs. The CA2 and CB2 lines can be programmed to act as interrupt lines or output lines. These discrete output lines are ideal for use in which the PA port is an 8-bit output port and PB is an 8-bit input port from a peripheral. Peripheral motor control, handshaking control, or some other discrete function can be controlled by CA and CB.

Because the PIAs are programmable devices, the first thing you must do in a program is initialize the PIA in the microcomputer system. This involves setting all the data direction registers to their proper values. When a PIA is reset during power-up, all the programmable I/O lines are activated as inputs and must be programmed to be outputs if desired.

The 8255 PPI.   The 8080 family of microprocessors has a part that is similar to the PIA called the programmable peripheral interface or PPI (Fig. 5-9). Like the 6821, the 8255 has dual 8-bit PA and PB ports, but the remaining I/O lines are slightly different. Two groups of four control lines corresponding to the PA and PB I/O ports can operate in three modes:

1.   Each group of 12 lines (PA and its 4 control lines) can be programmed to act as an output or input.

2.   A group of 12 lines can act as 8 data lines, 3 handshaking lines, and 1 interrupt line.

3.   A group of 8 lines can act as a bidirectional bus with 5 lines (one borrowed from the other port) acting as handshaking.

The output characteristics of the PA and PB lines are similar to the outputs of the PB section of the 6821. The outputs can source 1 mA to 1.5 V. Intel suggests that these lines can be connected to darlington transistors to directly drive printers and high-voltage displays.

Serial Interface Chips

The process of sending serial data to and from peripherals is so common that a wide assortment of one-chip serial-to-parallel and parallel-to-serial converter/controllers has been developed. These chips go by different names, depending

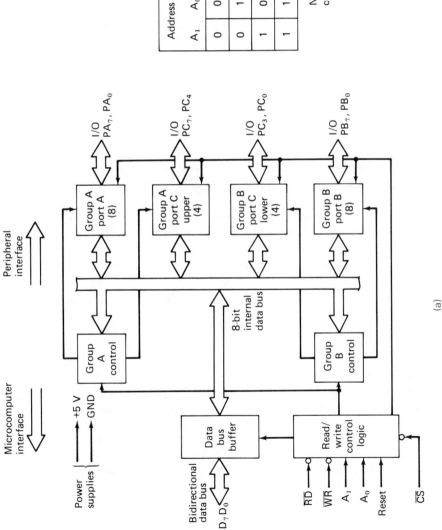

Address		Action	
A_1	A_0	Read	Write
0	0	Port A → data bus	Data bus → port A
0	1	Port B → data bus	Data bus → port B
1	0	Port C → data bus	Data bus → port C
1	1	No action	Data bus → control

Note: The word written into the control word determines I/O mode.

(b)

(a)

Figure 5-9 The 8255 programmable peripheral interface (PPI). (a) Block diagram. (b) Programmer control commands. (Reprinted by permission of Intel Corporation, Copyright 1977.)

on what kind of serial communication they handle. The UART, ACIA, and USRT are but a few of these chips.

The UART. One of the first MOS LSI chips to gain popularity (prior to the microprocessor in fact) was the universal asynchronous receiver/transmitter, or UART. This chip is used widely in data terminals and on large computer interface cards to provide bidirectional full-duplex asynchronous data communications.

For ease of understanding, a UART can be split into two completely separate sections: transmit and receive. Figure 5-10(b) illustrates this functional breakdown. The transmit section consists of a transmit data shift register (to shift data out at the transmit clock rate) and a holding register (to hold new data until the shift register has emptied its previous data). Data is automatically loaded into the shift register when it is empty. A number of status lines are presented to the user by the transmit section. Lines indicating an empty transmit register (TRE) and empty transmit holding register (HTRE) indicate when new data can be submitted to the UART.

The user must program the parity and number of start and stop bits to be transmitted. In the case of the UART, the term "programmed" has a different meaning than in the PIA.

Separate inputs on the UART's 40-pin package are set aside for these functions. These pins can be connected to an external control register or simply hard-wired to logic 1 or 0 values. The hard-wiring feature is nice because initialization programming is not required.

The UART's receiver section is basically a transmit section in reverse. Data is shifted into the input shift register at the receive clock rate. When a full word has been received it is sent to the receive holding register and can be read by the user. The UART checks parity, overrun and data framing, and indicates errors on discrete outputs.

UARTs certainly replace a large number of registers and timing circuitry in an interface and are especially useful in nonmicroprocessor interfaces (such as a data-terminal interface) in which program-controlled initialization is not possible. UARTs offer a great deal of interface capability for just a few dollars.

The ACIA. A UART can be connected directly to a microprocessor bus for serial data communication by connecting the inputs to the transmit holding register and the tristate outputs of the receive holding register to the microprocessor's data bus. A small amount of decoding circuitry would, of course, be necessary to make the UART respond to the proper address and control signals of the microprocessor. There is an even easier way of implementing serial communication, however. A part called an *asynchronous communication interface adapter* or ACIA performs the task of the UART and incorporates all the necessary handshaking and control signals required to interface it to a microprocessor.

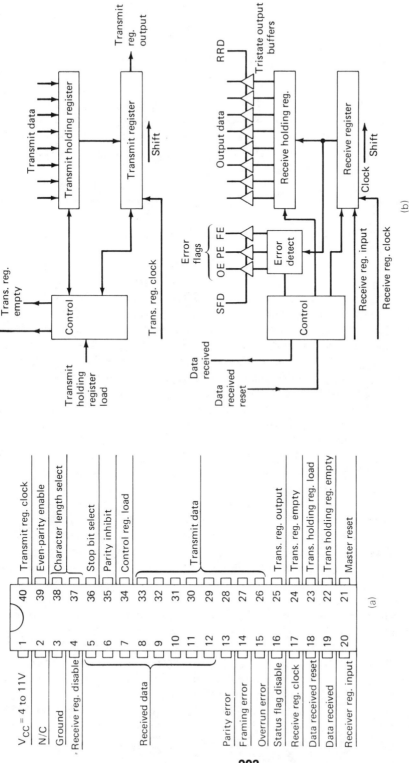

Figure 5-10 The IM6402A universal asynchronous receiver-transmitter (UART). (a) IM6402 UART. (b) Functional diagram.

203

The 6850 is a good example of a popular ACIA. The ACIA's structure (shown in Fig. 5-11) closely resembles that of the UART of Fig. 5-10. The transmit data register and transmit shift register correspond to the transmit holding register and transmit register of the UART. Because both transmit and receive data are sent to the data bus lines (D0–D7) through the DATA bus buffers, there is no need for separate receive and transmit output pins. Many of the discrete status lines such as the *parity error, framing error,* and *transmit data register ready* signals are interrogated by the microprocessor through the data bus, thereby saving more I/O pins.

Unlike the UART, individual hard-wirable programming pins for parity and number of stop bits are not available on the ACIA and must be loaded into the *control* register through the data bus. This feature also saves I/O pins but necessitates program-controlled initialization when the microcomputer system is initially turned on.

The I/O pin reductions caused by combined receive, transmit, control, and status lines—plus the savings in power pins (the 6850 requires only one 5 V power supply as opposed to the UART's three)—allow the ACIA to be built into a 24-pin package with 4 pins to spare. These pins are used for data communication lines associated with terminals and modems. Request to send, clear to send, data carrier detect, and interrupt request lines are provided.

Figure 5-11(b) shows what an ACIA looks like from the programmer's point of view. On a 6800-based processor, the ACIA looks like four registers located at two addresses in memory. The transmit data register and the receive data register share the same address (one is read and the other write), as do the status and control registers. Data transmission is accomplished by reading the status register (under polled or interrupt control) to determine if the transmit holding register is empty. If the first bit is set to 1, data is written into the transmit data register and the microprocessor can resume its original program while the ACIA serially shifts the data out. If the bit is not set, however, a data transfer is still in progress and the program must wait by looping or executing another program.

A receive sequence is similar to the transmit sequence, except that the "receive data register full" status bit is checked and data is read from the receive data register if set. The framing error, receiver overrun, and parity error bits of the status register can also be checked by the program if error checking is important to the programmer.

Initialization of the ACIA involves writing a reset word and a program word into the ACIA control register. Upon power-up, the ACIA goes into a bus protection mode automatically and must be reset by sending a reset word to the control register with bits D0 and D1 set to logic 1. The program word, which determines the transmit and receive clock divide rate, the number of stop bits, and even or odd parity, must then be set.

Other ACIAs include the TMS 9902 for the TI 9900 series, the 8251 for the 8080 series, and the TR1953 for the 16-bit Western Digital MCP-1600/WD-16 series microprocessors.

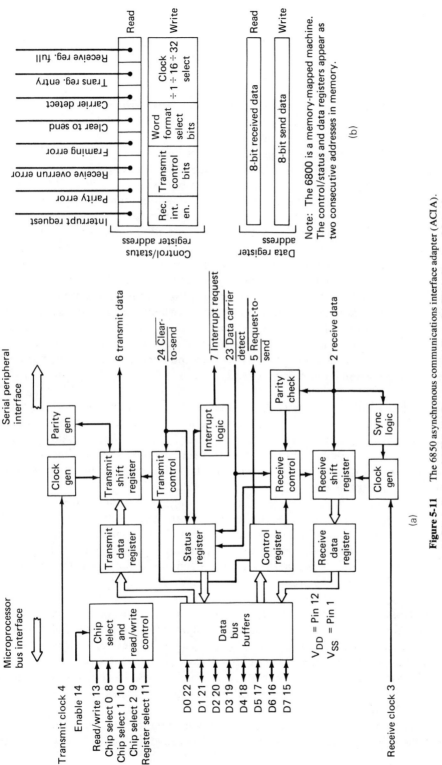

Figure 5-11 The 6850 asynchronous communications interface adapter (ACIA). (a) Block diagram of ACIA. (b) Programmer's view of ACIA. (Courtesy Motorola Semiconductor Products, Phoenix, Arizona.)

Synchronous Devices.   Synchronous data communication is desirable in high-performance data links, and chips that handle the synchronous serial communication function are available. The first of these chips were the synchronous receiver and synchronous transmitter chips. Later, these two functions were combined into *universal synchronous receiver/transmitter* or USRT chips. Finally, microprocessor-bus-oriented versions, called *synchronous serial data adapters* (SSDAs), were developed.

The 6852, an example of such a chip, is illustrated in Fig. 5-12. Because synchronous communication does not require start-bit sensing, it would seem that the SSDA would be much simpler than the asynchronous ACIA. This is not true, however, due to the need to keep data continuously synchronized. When data transmission begins, the receiver must "watch" for a match character that signals the start of a data stream. The SSDA contains a *sync* code register and a *comparator* to perform this function. Because a break in the serial stream of data causes desynchronization, the SSDA's transmit section must generate *fill* characters (dummy characters that do not contain data) to keep the data stream in sync when the microprocessor has no new data to send.

Because SSDAs are meant for applications where high data rates are necessary, a few features that help keep a constant stream of valid data flowing are incorporated. Three-level FIFO (first-in–first-out) registers are used to stack transmit and receive data. The FIFOs give the microprocessor much greater leeway in data send and receive timing.

One-Chip Modems.   Serial data transmissions over telephone lines to time-sharing computers became popular before it was feasible for an individual to have his own personal microcomputer. Today, time-sharing remains popular due to the large storage capacities and software resources of large mainframes; but the arrival of the microprocessor has had an impact on this area of computer technology as well.

Intelligent terminals with built-in computing power that allow simple functions to be performed in offline modes are now popular. Networks of terminals, each with its own processing resources, are in the experimental stages and go by the name of *distributed processing*. At any rate, the advent of the microprocessor has increased the need for low-speed serial data transmission over voice-grade telephone lines.

As might be expected, single chips that replace many discrete circuits are now available to provide the *modulation/demodulation* or *modem* function needed for this communication. Modem chips differ from the serial interface chips described so far in that they digitally synthesize and decode analog waveforms that are transmitted on telephone lines.

Transmission over a voice-grade telephone link is accomplished using asynchronous data transmission with two pitches of tones representing the 0 and the 1 state (FSK data transmission).

Figure 5-13(a) shows a terminal communicating to a large computer over a telephone link. The user terminal of the link is called the *originate* end, because

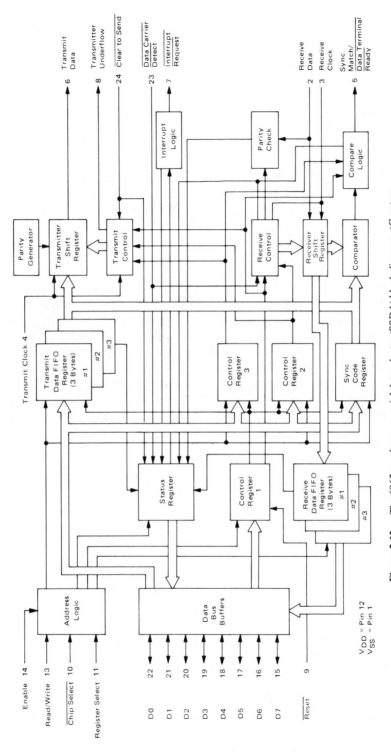

Figure 5-12 The 6862 synchronous serial data adapter (SSDA) block diagram. (Courtesy Motorola Semiconductor Products, Phoenix, Arizona.)

207

the person at the terminal originates the communication by calling the computer. The computer's end of the link is the *answer* end.

Data can be sent bidirectionally in a full-duplex mode because two sets of communication frequencies are used. The originate frequencies are 1070 Hz for a space (0) and 1270 Hz for a mark (1). The answer modem has filters to receive and decode these two audio frequencies. The answer modem's transmit frequencies are 2025 Hz for a space and 2225 for a mark. Data transmission rates of up to 600 bits per second are possible using these modulation frequencies, but 300 bps telephone-terminal communication is most often used for reliability and because of the limitations of the terminal printer.

Figure 5-13(b) depicts the MC6860 digital modem chip. The chip does not perform the necessary serial-to-parallel conversion for use with a microprocessor bus, so an ACIA must be used for this purpose. The 6860 is designed to operate in either originate or answer modes, making it usable on both the terminal and computer ends of a system. Additional control functions are also provided. An input for a telephone ring sense signal can be used in conjunction with the "answer phone" output to implement an automatic telephone answering data communication link at the central computer. This is commonly referred to as a dialup system. Internal chip timing allows timing margins of a few seconds for automatic hangup after a loss in the carrier signal (terminal's signal).

Although a sine wave is digitally synthesized and sent to the transmit carrier output, a low-pass filter, duplexer, and data coupler must be used to connect the 6860 to the telephone line. The inductive and capacitive elements needed to meet the telephone system interface standards were just too large to fit on an integrated circuit.

ONE-CHIP CONTROLLERS

Interface chips that handle complex control as well as data functions are available for many of the common microprocessors, and many are designed for use on a stand-alone basis as well. This class of interface device includes cassette controllers, floppy disk controllers, DMA controllers, and CRT controllers. New controller interface chips seem to be introduced when the demand for a specific application becomes large enough.

Floppy Disk Controllers (FDCs)

Floppy disk controllers provide a simple one-chip interface to floppy disk drives, thereby replacing many discrete interface components and reducing overhead support software for disk read, write, head control, and error checking. Floppy disk controllers are now available for the 6800 and 8080 microprocessors as well as in stand-alone versions that can be interfaced to nearly any microprocessor with a couple PIAs.

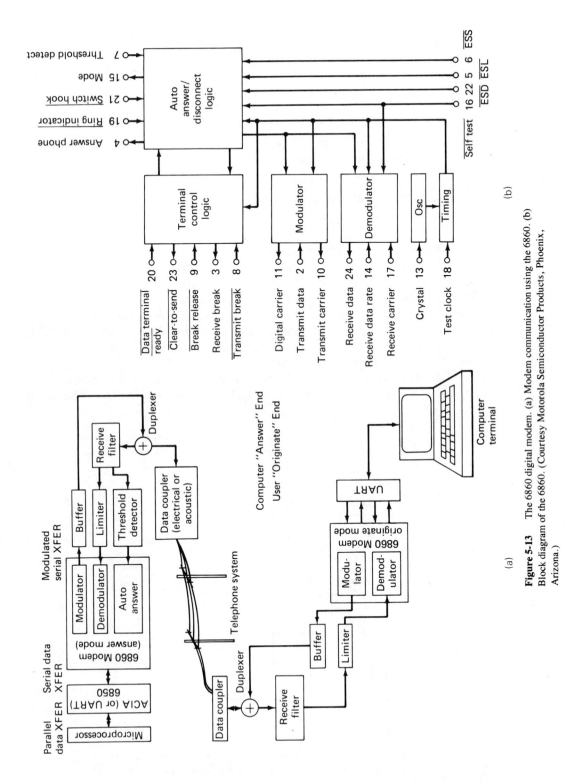

Figure 5-13 The 6860 digital modem. (a) Modem communication using the 6860. (b) Block diagram of the 6860. (Courtesy Motorola Semiconductor Products, Phoenix, Arizona.)

209

One-chip floppy disk controllers generally provide the following functions:

1. Track-to-track head stepping and status checking.
2. Read and write control for single or multiple records.
3. Full-track read and write capability.
4. Soft-sector timing generation.
5. Automatic sector searching.
6. DMA disk data transfer capability.
7. CRC error checking.

The 6843.   This controller is a good example of an FDC designed for use with a particular microprocessor—in this case, the 6800. Fifteen internal registers are built into this 40-pin controller chip. Twelve are programmer accessible, as Fig. 5-14 illustrates, and three are nonaccessible registers that perform serial-to-parallel, parallel-to-serial, and data-clock pattern generation. Floppy disk status (error, interrupt, and capstan) can be monitored by reading the three appropriate registers. By using the three registers, track and sector address can also be monitored while the disk spins.

The setup register is a user-programmable register that is meant to be initialized during power-up along with all the PIAs and ACIAs. The setup

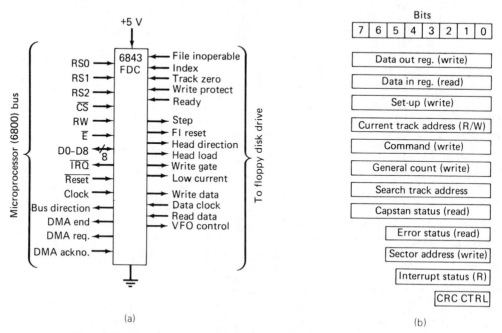

(a)   (b)

Figure 5-14   The 6843 floppy disk controller. (a) Floppy disk control lines. (b) Programmer's view of 6843 registers. (Courtesy Motorola Semiconductor Products, Phoenix, Arizona.)

information includes the seek time and the settling time the FDC will produce. The values used are dependent on the model of disk drive being controlled.

The command register has one bit allocated to specify DMA or PIO disk data transfers, and the remaining bits are set aside for disk control commands. The 6843 has a set of macro commands that perform complex disk operations that would normally require extensive software. These commands include track seeks, single sector reads and writes, CRC reads, multiple-sector reads and writes, and free-format reads and writes. The general count register provides track number and sector count values for the macro commands. The *data in* and *data out* registers are used in PIO transfers to read and write to the disk.

The uPD372. The NEC uPD372 is a floppy disk controller designed to work with the 8080 microprocessor. This FDC is IBM 3740 format-compatible and provides programmable step-pulse and stepping rate, CRC generation, and a programmable data-transfer rate. The 372 can control up to four disks simultaneously.

One-Chip Cassette Controllers

The NEC uPD371 is an interface chip designed to mate directly with the 8080 bus to control two digital cassette transports. The chip performs all the parallel-to-serial conversion as well as the phase-encoded data generation. Like the floppy disk controllers, the 371 performs cyclic-redundancy error checking.

CRT Controllers

The process of putting characters and graphics onto a cathode-ray tube (CRT) screen is really quite simple, but it involves considerable circuitry. Horizontal and vertical counters, character generators, and refresh memory, as well as an interface to the microcomputer or mainframe are needed. To understand the function of the CRT controller, it is first necessary to understand the basics of CRT raster-scan display.

A standard TV monitor—or even the standard home television set, for that matter—"draws" an image on a phosphor-coated screen by sweeping an electron beam across it. When struck by the beam, the phosphor emits light. By modulating the intensity of the beam, a selectively dotted or dashed line is drawn. To form an entire TV picture, a monitor starts its electron beam in the upper left corner of the screen and scans 262 horizontal lines across the screen starting from the top, going down. The beam sweeping is caused by oscillator-controlled electromagnetic or electrostatic deflection.

The 262 lines scanned on the first frame are not quite above one another. There are black (nonscanned) lines between them. The electron beam, therefore, proceeds to rescan the screen, filling in the spaces. This second frame is called the *interlaced* frame.

It is important to remember the following facts about raster scan when working with CRT display generators:

1. Each 262-line frame takes 1/60 second to scan.
2. A full interlaced frame of 525 lines takes 1/30 second and consists of two 262-line frames.
3. The electron beam must move back to the left of the screen when a line is done, and back to the top when a frame is finished. These actions are called horizontal and vertical retrace, respectively.
4. A horizontal line is 64 microseconds wide, of which about 50 show up on the screen (some is lost off the screen and on retrace).
5. Only about 240 lines of the 262 appear on the screen (some are lost off the screen).

A video waveform must be fed into a TV monitor to provide the beam-sweep timing. An NTSC standard for the voltage levels and timing requirements required at the monitor's video input is shown in Fig. 5-15.

An image can be put onto the screen using a device that scans out frames at exactly the same rate as the monitor. This device must use a photodetector to detect and modulate a video signal, which in turn is sent to the monitor. Image orthicons and vidicon tubes are such devices and are commonly used in TV cameras.

Another way of putting an image onto a screen is to use a circuit that scans out frames at exactly the same rate as the monitor and uses a long stream of serial bits read out of a memory to modulate the scanning beam. By simply letting 1 equal a white level and 0 equal a black level (see the waveform standard of Fig. 5-15), any desired black and white (or bilevel) pattern can be put onto the screen. The process just described results in a large grid of points or pixels (picture elements)—commonly called a *raster-scan bit map*.

It is easy to visualize how bits on the screen could be turned on and off to create graphics patterns and alphanumeric symbols, but a few quick arithmetic calculations show that this is a very expensive way to generate an image. First, to generate a 525 vertical (one for each scanned line) by 525 horizontal (to make it a square) bit map requires 275,625 bits of memory. To fit the 525 bits across the $50\mu s$ portion of the $64\mu s$ line requires that bits be accessed at a rate of 95 ns per bit.

Paralleling banks of slow memory, simultaneously reading many bits, and shifting bits out through a high-speed shift register decreases the 95 ns memory access requirement, but the need for a large memory still exists. In graphics systems in which any random pattern can be put onto a screen, users must live with this large memory requirement. In a data-terminal application (which is synonymous with "most applications"), a form of data compression can be used to save on the amount of display memory used.

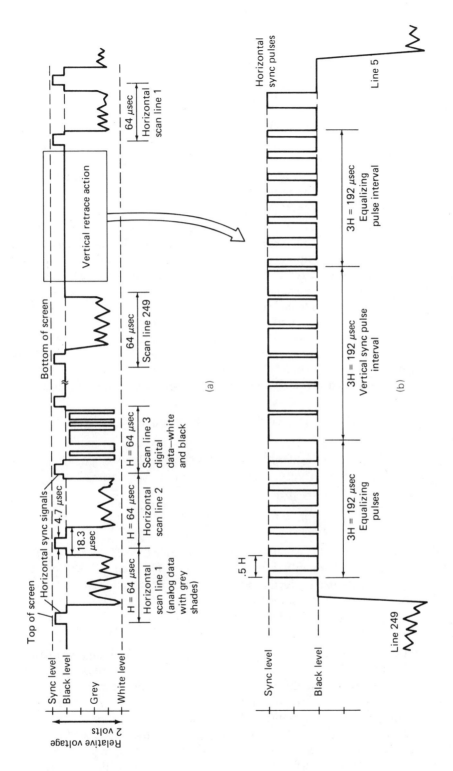

Figure 5-15 Black-and-white standard television timing. (a) 250 visible horizontal line sweep format. (b) Vertical retrace format.

Characters on CRTs are typically constructed on 5×7- or 7×9-bit pieces of the bit map. Each character therefore takes up 35 or 63 bits of the bit map. When you consider that a 1-bit wide space is left on the top and right of each character, these figures increase to 48 and 80 bits. Because 64 characters (or 128 if a full character set is used) are all that are needed for a terminal, a 6- or 7-bit code is all that is needed to specify what is needed to fill the 48 or 80 bits of the bit map. This is about a 10:1 savings over specifying each of the 48 or 80 bits. Something to convert the 6- or 7-bit code to the 48- or 80-bit character is needed within the CRT generator, however. The part that performs this function is a *character generator ROM*.

Putting a typical 80-character-wide by 24-line display on a CRT is a matter of having an $80 \times 24 \times 7$ bit memory (approximately 1920 8-bit bytes) that is accessible to the microcomputer, and a screen display controller. In this case the CRT controller simply reads out a character and sends it to the character generator ROM, which in turn uses a shift register to serially send it out to the screen as the beam moves from left to right. On the horizontal scan, 80 characters must be read in about 50 μs, which works out to one byte every 626 ns. This read rate is easily accomplished. Because each character is more than one scan line high, each character must be repeatedly read for 7 or 9 scan lines before going on to the next row of characters.

The hardware needed to perform the CRT control operations includes:

1. A horizontal character counter to keep track of the character column.
2. A vertical counter to keep track of the scan-line row.
3. A high-speed shift register to shift data onto the screen.
4. A memory for the 1920 characters.
5. A video generator to mix the serially shifted data with sync signals that generate the NTSC waveform of Fig. 5-15.
6. Interface circuits to allow a microcomputer to get into the character memory and modify it when it isn't being used by the scanning process (typically during retrace time or on an interleaved basis, if the memory is fast enough).
7. A character generator ROM.

The AMI68047 is a single-chip CRT controller that contains all of these parts but requires external display memory. A number of desirable additional features are also incorporated. Some of the features include timing and control circuitry; address buffers; an internal 64-character, 5×7-dot, ASCII-encoded alphanumeric character generator; and a color generation system.

In a typical application, a system would consist of the CRT generator chip, a 6800-type microprocessor, a 1K- by 10-bit display memory, an external 3.58 MHz clock for timing, and a few additional interface gates. With such a system, the user can generate normal or inverted characters using the internal character generator ROM. Two "semigraphic" display modes allow the user to display combined alphanumerics and graphics using the 8 bits of the display word to form a small dot matrix rather than sending them to a ROM. These graphic modes can be switched on or off for each display line scanned.

With larger external memories the 68047 can operate in 8 full-graphic modes. A low-resolution 128 × 192 pixel display with 4 colors per element, or a high-resolution 256 × 192 two-color display can be generated. A 6K- by 8-bit memory is required for these modes. Versatile alphanumeric and graphic field capabilities are possible using the 68047, because the device can switch between any of the display modes every 12 lines.

Another interesting feature is the chip's ability to produce a screen border in all the graphic modes. A border makes graphic images look much more impressive and complex.

The 68047 is oriented towards graphics as well as alphanumerics, but most CRT controllers (including the Motorola 6845 and Intel 8275) are designed mainly for character generation within a data terminal. These chips replace the complex graphic control functions with powerful cursor control capabilities (auto-feeding, scrolling, blinking of cursor, and the like). Other valuable features of the 6845 are its programmable character generator and light-pen control registers.

Other Controllers. A number of specialized complex controllers that interface directly to microcomputer buses are available. The 6854 advanced data-link controller (ADLC) provides complex communication formatting to meet *Advanced Data Communication Control Procedures* (ADCCP), high-level data link control (HLDLC), and synchronous data link control (SDLC). Primary and secondary data communications stations can be handled in stand-alone, loop, and polling configurations.

Another specialized microprocessor interface is the 68488 chip. This device is designed to interface the standard IEEE 488 instrument-and-microcomputer bus to the 6800 bus structure. This chip is useful for moving data to and from instrument interfaces designed around the 6800 microprocessor. This chip greatly reduces the amount of discrete circuitry needed to meet the IEEE 488 bus protocol.

MONOLITHIC ARITHMETIC
PROCESSING UNITS

Real-time processing is the act of processing data as it arrives, as opposed to storing it, and processing it at a leisurely pace. Real-time data processing presents a problem for most microprocessors, especially if complex arithmetic operations are involved. Multiplication and division naturally slow most microprocessors, because few have hardware multiply and divide instructions (the new generation of microprocessors is changing this). At least 16 bits of data are used in any serious arithmetic processing, so double-precision mathematics must be performed on 8-bit microprocessors, further hindering processor performance. In many applications involving wide ranges of numbers, floating-point arithmetic must be used, reducing performance even more.

A number of approaches can be taken to solve the computational throughput problem. Multiple microprocessors are one solution, of course, but dividing a software task between many processors is a very difficult task, especially if a compiler or interpreter must write the machine code.

A more reasonable approach to this problem is the use of an external arithmetic processing unit dedicated to performing floating-point or double-precision arithmetic at a very high rate. Such a processor can be built out of discrete components, or one of the new monolithic processing units can be interfaced directly to a microcomputer bus. We will look at two such units.

The AM9511 APU

The AM9511 arithmetic processing unit (APU), built by Advanced Micro Devices, is designed to increase the mathematical capabilities of microcomputers as well as large systems. While the 9511's repertoire of functions resembles that of a powerful scientific calculator, its internal circuitry and performance are a far cry from slow calculator chips. Fixed- and floating-point trigonometric, logarithmic, and power functions, as well as the four basic functions are provided. Figure 5-16 illustrates the 9511.

The APU performs its functions by taking 8-bit bytes of data representing operands and pushing them onto the internal 8×16 operand stack. Operands may be 16- or 32-bit twos' complement binary numbers or floating-point numbers with 24-bit mantissas and 8-bit exponents. Each operand, therefore, takes two or four 8-bit transfers from the microcomputer bus. Function commands are then sent to the command register and the function is performed using the ALU, working registers, and the constant ROM (which contains essential log and trig constants). The result of the function is finally put back on the operand stack and can be retrieved as a 2- or 4-byte answer by the microprocessor through the bus buffers. Alternatively, a DMA controller can interface the 9511 to the bus, allowing arrays of data to be automatically processed. Figure 5-16 shows the command word format and Table 5-1 lists the available commands.

It is interesting to compare the processing throughputs of APUs to the inherent processing power of the latest high-performance microprocessors to see how the APUs fare. A single-precision multiply takes 92 clock cycles or 23 μs with a 4 MHz 9511 and 150 clock cycles of 30μs with a 5 MHz 8086. The 8 MHz 8086, however, only requires 19μs. At any rate, the new microprocessors are similar to the 9511 when it comes to single-precision multiplication and division. The 9511, however, can easily outrun the 8086 on 32-bit floating-point and advanced trig and power functions, because the 8086 would be forced to perform these tasks under software control.

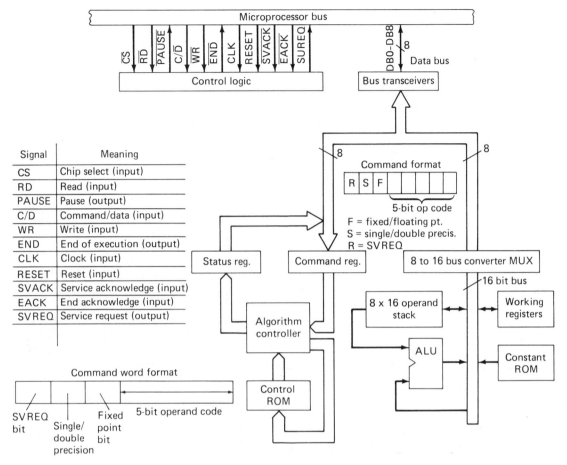

Figure 5-16 The AM 9511 arithmetic processing unit (APU). (Copyright © 1978 Advanced Micro Devices, Inc. Reproduced with permission of copyright owner.)

The TRW MPY-16AJ

A 16- by 16-bit multiply in 23 μs with the 9511 is certainly a vast improvement over the 150 μs needed to perform multiplication on a simple 8-bit microprocessor, but for many forms of processing that require vast amounts of multiplies, such as graphics, image, and signal processing, an even higher multiply rate is necessary. For these applications, high-speed monolithic multipliers such as TRW's MPY-16AJ can be used.

The MPY-16AJ is a 16- by 16-bit one-chip multiplier (Fig. 5-17) that can generate a 32-bit product in 200 ns. The chip comes packaged in a 64-pin DIP with a large integral heatsink; it dissipates 8 W of power. Internally, the multiplication is performed by emitter-follower logic that resembles ECL, but the device is TTL-compatible at the pins.

Table 5-1   The Commands and Timing of the 9511 APU

Command Code								Command Mnemonic	Command Description (1)	Clock Cycles (Max.)
7	6	5	4	3	2	1	0			
Fixed Point Single E Precision										
R	1	1	0	1	1	0	0	SADD	Adds TOS to NOS. Result to NOS. Pop Stack	17
R	1	1	0	1	1	0	1	SSUB	Subtracts TOS from NOS. Result to NOS. Pop Stack	30
R	1	1	0	1	1	1	0	SMUL	Multiplies NOS by TOS. Result to NOS. Pop Stack	92
R	1	1	0	1	1	1	1	SDIV	Divides NOS by TOS. Result to NOS. Pop Stack	92
Fixed Point Double Precision										
R	0	1	0	1	1	0	0	DADD	Adds TOS to NOS. Result to NOS. Pop Stack	21
R	0	1	0	1	1	0	1	DSUB	Subtracts TOS from NOS. Result to NOS. Pop Stack	38
R	0	1	0	1	1	1	0	DMUL	Multiplies NOS by TOS. Result to NOS. Pop Stack	208
R	0	1	0	1	1	1	1	DDIV	Divides NOS by TOS. Result to NOS. Pop Stack	208
Floating Point										
R	0	0	1	0	0	0	0	FADD	Adds TOS to NOS. Result to NOS. Pop Stack	350
R	0	0	1	0	0	0	1	FSUB	Subtracts TOS from NOS. Result to NOS. Pop Stack	352
R	0	0	1	0	0	1	0	FMUL	Multiplies NOS by TOS. Result to NOS. Pop Stack	168
R	0	0	1	0	0	1	1	FDIV	Divides NOS by TOS. Result to NOS. Pop Stack	171
Derived Floating Point Functions (2)										
R	0	0	0	0	0	0	1	SQRT	Square Root of TOS. Result in TOS.	800
R	0	0	0	0	0	1	0	SIN	Sine of TOS. Result in TOS.	4464
R	0	0	0	0	0	1	1	COS	Cosine of TOS. Result in TOS.	4118
R	0	0	0	0	1	0	0	TAN	Tangent of TOS. Result in TOS.	5754
R	0	0	0	0	1	0	1	ASIN	Inverse Sine of TOS. Result in TOS.	7668
R	0	0	0	0	1	1	0	ACOS	Inverse Cosine of TOS. Result in TOS.	7734
R	0	0	0	0	1	1	1	ATAN	Inverse Tangent of TOS. Result in TOS.	6006
R	0	0	0	1	0	0	0	LOG	Common Logarithm (base 10) of TOS. Result in TOS.	4490
R	0	0	0	1	0	0	1	LN	Natural Logarithm (base e) of TOS. Result in TOS.	4478
R	0	0	0	1	0	1	0	EXP	Exponential (e^x) of TOS. Result in TOS.	4616
R	0	0	0	1	0	1	1	PWR	NOS raised to the power in TOS. Result in NOS. Pop Stack.	9292

Data Manipulation Commands (3)

R								Mnemonic	Operation	
R	0	0	0	0	0	0	0	NOP	No Operation.	4
R	0	0	1	1	1	1	1	FIXS	Converts TOS from floating point to single precision fixed point format.	216
R	0	0	1	1	1	0	0	FIXD	Converts TOS from floating point to double precision fixed point format.	346
R	0	0	1	1	0	1	1	FLTS	Converts TOS from single precision fixed point to floating point format.	186
R	0	0	1	1	0	0	0	FLTD	Converts TOS from double percision fixed point to floating point format.	378
R	1	1	0	1	0	0	0	CHSS	Changes sign of single precision fixed point operand on TOS.	26
R	0	1	0	1	0	0	0	CHSD	Changes sign of double precision fixed point operand on TOS.	34
R	0	0	1	1	0	1	1	CHSF	Changes sign of floating point operand on TOS.	16
R	1	1	0	1	0	1	1	PTOS	Push single precision fixed point operand on TOS to NOS.	16
R	0	1	0	1	0	1	1	PTOD	Push double precision fixed point operand on TOS to NOS.	20
R	0	0	1	1	0	1	1	PTOF	Push floating point operand on TOS to NOS.	20
R	1	1	1	0	0	0	0	POPS	Pop single precision fixed point operand from TOS. NOS becomes TOS.	10
R	0	1	1	0	0	0	0	POPD	Pop double precision fixed point operand from TOS. NOS becomes TOS.	12
R	0	0	1	0	0	0	0	POPF	Pop floating point operand from TOS. NOS becomes TOS.	12
R	1	1	1	0	1	0	1	XCHS	Exchange single precision fixed point operands TOS and NOS.	18
R	0	1	1	0	1	0	1	XCHD	Exchange double precision fixed point operands TOS and NOS.	26
R	0	0	1	1	1	0	1	XCHF	Exchange floating point operands TOS and NOS.	26
R	0	0	1	0	1	1	0	PUPI	Push floating point constant "Π" onto TOS. Previous TOS becomes NOS.	16

Note: NOS = Next on Stack
TOS = Top of Stack

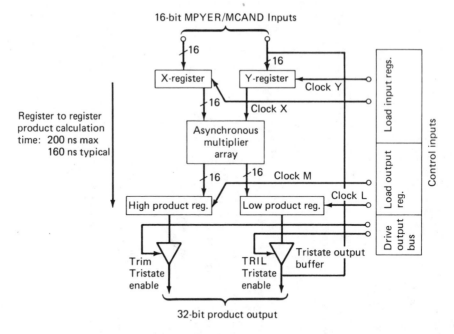

Figure 5-17   The TRW MPY16 AJ 16 × 16 200 ns multiplier.

When interfacing chips such as this to a microprocessor, careful analysis must be done beforehand to determine if the vast multiplying power can successfully be utilized by the microprocessor. Interfacing a 200 ns multiplier to a 1 MHz 6800, for instance, would be overkill, because it takes at least 12 μs just to move two operands to the multiplier under processor control. For faster processors such as the 8086 (8 MHz version), and for bipolar processors built from the TTL 2900 or ECL 10,000 series, the MPY-16AJ makes more sense. Both 8- and 12-bit versions of this 16-bit part are available; these are more appropriate for lower-performance processors.

ANALOG-TO-DIGITAL CONVERTERS

The process of taking analog signals from the real world, preprocessing them, converting them to digital data, and finally bringing the resulting digital data into a computer's memory is called *data acquisition*. In this section we examine the principles and components involved in this process.

Figure 5-18 illustrates an overall picture of a data acquisition system. Voltage levels, current flows, fluid flow, pressure, or some other physical parameter is first converted to an electrical signal by a transducer. If the transducer doesn't already generate enough of a signal for the processing circuitry to work with, an amplifier is used to amplify the voltage level. An active filter removes unwanted high- and low-frequency signal components, and special conditioning

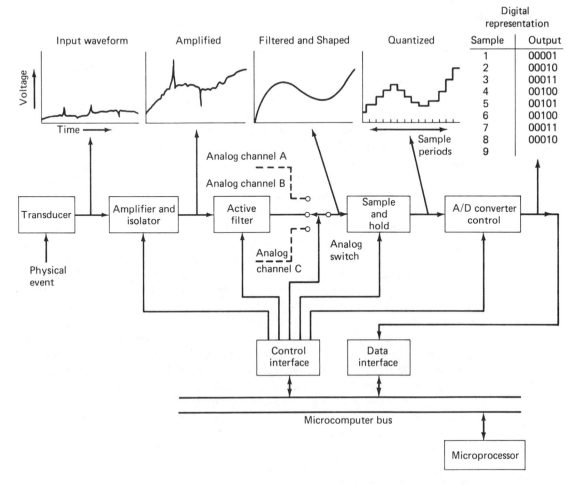

Figure 5-18 A microprocessor-based acquisition system.

circuits are used as necessary for signal compression, multiplying, and squaring. The filtered signal is switched by an analog multiplexer and sent to a sample-and-hold circuit, itself an analog memory of a sort. The multiplexer switches between many analog signal sources, thereby reducing the need for repeated circuitry upstream. The sample-and-hold unit samples the voltage level of the input at a specific instant of time and holds it constant at its output so the analog-to-digital (A/D) conversion circuitry can sample a steady voltage level. The A/D unit converts the stable voltage level to a digital value corresponding to the input voltage. This data can be put through some interface parts (perhaps a PIA) and sent to a microprocessor.

The microprocessor or discrete control circuitry must control the signal acquisition and processing circuits to insure that (1) the proper analog inputs are selected, (2) data is sampled at the proper time, and (3) the data is held long enough for the D/A converter to make a valid conversion.

Quantizing

Quantizing is the process of dividing an analog input signal into a string of equally spaced discrete outputs, each of a constant amplitude. Binary codes can be generated for each of these levels, and the quantized waveform can be stored in a microcomputer memory. The sample-and-hold function performs the equally spaced sampling of an input signal, while the A/D converter performs the binary coding. Figure 5-18 illustrates the input, quantized, and coded waveforms. The quantized waveform differs slightly from the input waveform, because it is constructed as a series of discrete steps. The difference in the waveforms is the quantizing error. The degree of the error is dependent on the sampling resolution and the irregularity of the waveform. The duration of one sampling period is defined as Q, and the quantizing error is defined as the time between samples, as measured from the center of each sampling period. Quantizing error can be reduced by reducing Q through faster sampling.

The rate of sampling is limited to the rate at which samples can be converted to output codes by the A/D converter. The *aperture time* is the time it takes an A/D converter to perform one conversion. The coding error introduced by the A/D is called the *amplitude uncertainty*.

The questions asked most often in regard to choosing a data acquisition system are these: What amplitude resolution should the sampling be? How many bits should the A/D converter generate? How fast should the sampling rate be? One guide often used in determining sampling rate is the theorem that states that an input signal with a highest frequency component of f can be recovered without distortion using a sampling frequency of $2f$. A sampling rate of $2f$ or greater will therefore minimize the likelihood that analog information is being lost in the quantizing process.

Sample-and-Hold Circuitry

Sample-and-hold circuits are designed to accept an input voltage level at a precise instant of time and hold that voltage level at an output until the next sample is taken. A device capable of "remembering" a voltage is needed in such circuitry, and a capacitor has precisely this characteristic.

A crude sample-and-hold circuit can be constructed using a capacitor and a switch, as Fig. 5-19(a) illustrates. When the switch is closed, the capacitor's voltage follows or tracks the input voltage. The moment the switch is opened, the tracking stops and the voltage level of the capacitor remains constant at the last switch-closed value.

A capacitor and a switch cannot be connected directly to analog circuitry because of the capacitor's effect on the driving waveform, so a buffer must be used for isolation. The switch used to turn the sampling on and off must be a very low-leakage, electrically controlled unit such as a field-effect transistor to

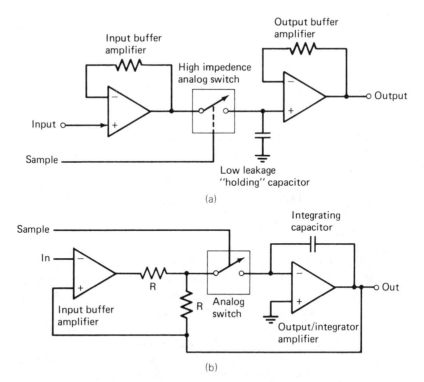

Figure 5-19 Common sample-and-hold circuits. (a) Simple switched capacitance. (b) Accurate operational integrator.

prevent current from leaking from the input buffer to the capacitor when the switch is open.

Figure 5-19(a) depicts a common open-loop, fast sample-and-hold circuit. Figure 5-19(b) illustrates a very accurate and linear circuit that uses an operational integrator (capacitive feedback amplifier) for the hold circuit.

The five most important parameters of a sample-and-hold circuit are:

1. *Acquisition time* (the time between start of sampling and stable output — analogous to digital propagation delay.)

2. *Aperture time* (the time it takes for the sampling switch to fully open).

3. *Aperture uncertainty time* (the variation characteristics of the aperture time).

4. *Decay rate* (the change in output voltage resulting from capacitor discharge per period of time).

5. *Feedthrough* (the amount of input signal that manages to leak through to the output when in the hold mode).

A/D Conversion Circuitry

Converting an analog level to a digital signal is not a trivial process, and many methods of performing conversion are used. The method used is dependent on conversion speed and accuracy requirements.

Servo.   The simplest and cheapest form of converter is the counter or servo type shown in Fig. 5-20(a). A counter controls a D/A converter, which generates a rising voltage staircase as the counter increments from zero. A comparator compares the input waveform to the generated waveform and indicates when a precise match in voltage exists. At that instant, data in the counter can be read to determine the input voltage level. Conversion rates are low with this type of A/D converter due to the counting time needed to reach the desired voltage level.

Dual-Slope Integrator.   The dual-slope integrating A/D converter is illustrated in Fig. 5-20(b). An integrator first integrates the input signal over a constant time. A charge that is proportional to the input voltage builds up on the integrator's capacitor. The second stage of the conversion involves bleeding the charge off the capacitor (by integrating down to a negative reference) and determining how much charge was on the capacitor by how long the capacitor takes to discharge. A counter keeps track of the time, and the converted voltage is the product of the reference voltage and the ratio of discharge-to-charge time. Dual-slope A/Ds are inexpensive and accurate. The accuracy feature makes them very desirable for digital panel meters, where they are used extensively.

Successive Approximation.   The successive-approximation type of A/D converter is commonly used and is noted for its ability to perform fast and accurate conversions. Conversions are performed by a trial-and-error process that starts with the most significant bit (MSB) of the converter's output word. The MSB is first turned on, and a D/A converter generates a voltage corresponding to the output word. If the input voltage is exceeded (as determined by a comparator), the bit is turned off. If it is not exceeded, it is left on. The next most significant bit is then processed in a similar manner. This process continues until the least significant bit of the converter is determined. The successive-approximation A/D essentially "homes in" on the proper answer.

Parallel Conversion.   The parallel A/D converter is the fastest and most expensive of all A/D converters. In principle, its operation is simple. A separate comparator is assigned to every possible voltage step in the converter's resolution. The comparators' references are set with a precision voltage divider network. All the comparators with references below the input voltage level will generate 1s, and all comparators with higher references will generate 0s. A

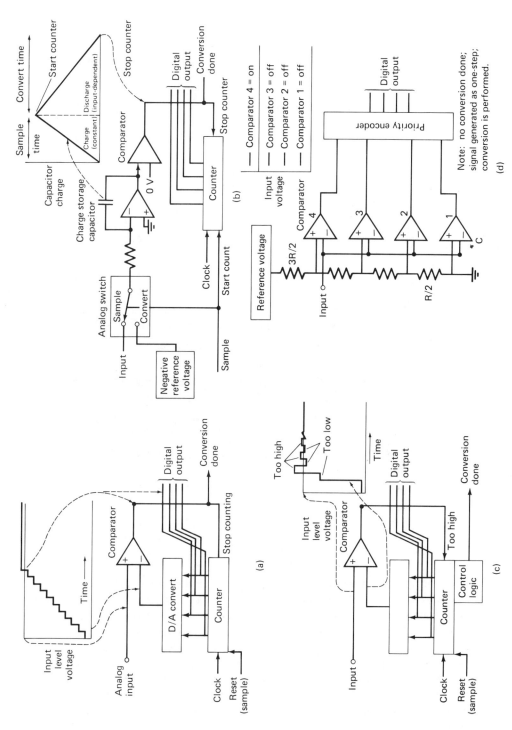

Figure 5-20 Representative analog-to-digital conversion methods. (a) Counter or servo. (b) Dual-slope. (c) Successive-approximation. (d) Parallel.

decoder then decodes the bit values and generates a binary output code. The problem with parallel A/D converters is the number of comparators they require. As a rule, 2^n comparators are needed; a simple 8-bit A/D converter therefore requires 256 comparators.

Selection Criteria.   When choosing an A/D converter, there are a few important parameters to consider:

1. *Range* (the voltage difference between the converter's minimum and maximum input voltage).

2. *Resolution* (the size of the voltage steps). Resolution is expressed as the number of bits in the output code and the percentage of the range covered. A 10-bit A/D is a 0.1% A/D.

3. *Linearity* (the maximum difference between the voltage steps). Ideally, all voltage steps should be precisely the same size.

4. *Monotonicity* (the property of having an increasing output for an increasing input over the converter's entire range).

5. *Missing codes* (the property of a converter skipping a code due to nonlinearity).

6. *Quantizing error* (the maximum voltage error due to the converter's noninfinite resolution).

7. *Relative accuracy* (the full-scale error in output voltage for any two input voltages across the entire range).

8. *Absolute accuracy* (the full-scale error in output voltage for full-scale input voltage).

9. *Offset error* (the value output by the converter when a 0 V input is applied).

DIGITAL-TO-ANALOG CONVERTERS

Converting a digital word to a proportional analog value is a necessary task in counter and parallel types of A/D converters, and is useful for digitally generating analog control signals as well. The D/A converter performs this task. One common device used to turn a word into a voltage is a precision resistor network driven by electronic switches controlled by each bit in the input word. Each bit of the input word contributes a current proportional to its binary weight to a common line. Figure 5-21(a) shows the weighted-current-source D/A converter. A final output amplifier with resistive feedback converts the current to a proportional voltage. This D/A conversion method is fast and accurate.

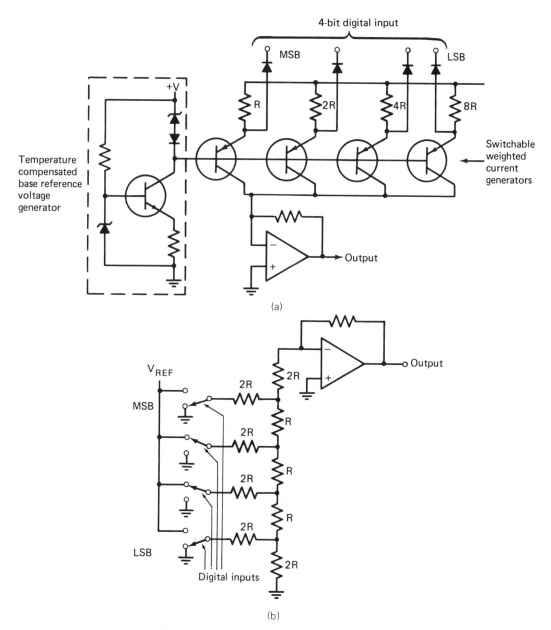

Figure 5-21 Two common digital-to-analog conversion methods. (a) Weighted-current-source D/A. (b) R-2R network D/A.

Another D/A configuration is the $R-2R$ network shown in Fig. 5-21(b). Again, the sum of currents from all the bits in the input word are fed to an amplifier and converted to a voltage. The MSB has a much greater effect on the amplifier because it is closest to it in the resistor ladder, while the LSB has the least effect of all. The values of R for series resistors and $2R$ for shunt resistors provide proper weighting for the binary system.

The following features should be evaluated before purchasing a D/A converter:

1. *Resolution* (the number of bits converted).

2. *Accuracy* (typically measured as percentage error in voltage output).

3. *Settling time* (the time it takes for the digital input to be converted to an analog output with the rated specification characteristics).

4. *Linearity* (the maximum error in the conversion between adjacent input codes)

5. *Output range* (the voltage difference between the maximum and minimum output voltage).

6. *Input coding* (the binary or BCD format of input code).

HIGH-POWER INTERFACE DEVICES

The TTL logic gate (which can sink about 16 mA) has been the largest current handling device discussed so far in this book. Turning on a 220 V, 50 A industrial motor can hardly be handled by this gate—directly, that is. Additional amplifying or high-power switching is needed. There are many approaches to the power switching problem. Solutions range from the antiquated relay to the rapidly dominating VFET.

Buffer–Interface Gates

The next step from the standard 16 mA TTL output gate is the buffer–interface gate. Buffer–interface gates come in the same packages and even pinouts as regular TTL gates such as the 7400, and they can be used in the same way as far as the inputs are concerned. The difference lies in the output driver's characteristics. The voltage- and current-handling capabilities are three times as large in many cases.

The 7438 is an example of an interface gate. This part looks exactly like a 7400 quad NAND gate in function and pinout, but it has an open-collector driver instead of a totem-pole output. The 7438 can sink 48 mA as opposed to the 7400's 16 mA.

Interface gates are useful in applications requiring high logic fan-outs or low-current peripheral drive currents (such as LED drive current). They are often used as drivers for even higher-power switching devices as well.

MOS driver gates fall into the interface gate category also. Many older memory IC designs brought high-capacitance MOS lines directly to the memory I/O pins, and it was up to the external circuitry to drive these fast-rise-time lines. Interface gates such as the Intel 3207A *quad bipolar-to-MOS level shifter and driver* provide MOS drive capability. The 3207A is capable of driving 100 mA of current with a 200 pF capacitive load while maintaining a 45 ns rise time. The 3207A has a totem-pole output that improves the rise characteristics. Gate output swings between 0 and 16 V.

Power Transistors

Discrete transistors designed to handle high current levels can be successfully used as peripheral control devices. By varying the transistor's base current, an amplified collector-to-emitter current can be variably controlled.

When a transistor is used as a switching element, it is usually acting in an amplifying capacity: the output current is the input current multiplied by transistor gain. This means that a transistor must be driven with a fairly heavy drive current if large current outputs and low-gain transistors are used. Figure 5-22(a) shows the simplest form of discrete transistor interface: a gate driving a transistor.

The 2N2222 is a good example of an NPN transistor designed for high-speed, medium-power switching and general-purpose amplifier applications. The 2N2222 can drive up to 800 mA and has a breakdown voltage of 40 V. Up to 1.8 W can be dissipated if the transistor has an appropriate heatsink. At 500 mA and 10 V, the 2N2222 has a static forward-current transfer ratio (amplification) of 30. At least 17 mA of base current from the driving gate is needed to switch 500 mA of load current, making the use of an interface gate desirable.

It is important that the drive current to a switching transistor be high enough. If insufficient drive current is available, the transistor will limit the load current by dropping voltage across the transistor, thereby destroying it. In the normal 2N2222 switching mode, the 1.8 W thermal dissipation is not considered too important because the transistor either has a high voltage with nearly no current across its emitter-collector path when off, or a high current (of 800 mA in this case) and only about 300 mV across the junction when on.

The maximum power dissipation is 240 mW, but during the switching transition the transistor goes through a dangerous "burnout" zone. When the transistor is sinking only half the current while in the middle of its turn-on transition, it drops half the load voltage across the collector–emitter junction. The worst case for the 2N2222 is 40 V at 400 mA, or 16 watts. It is acceptable to

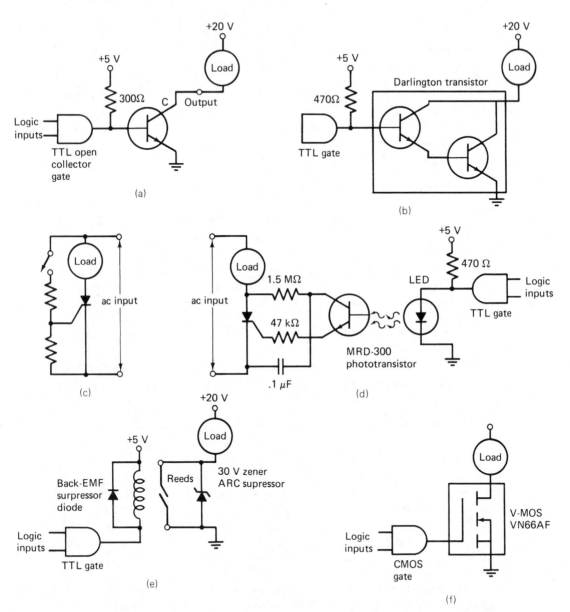

Figure 5-22 Power switching circuits. (a) Simple transistor driver. (b) Darlington driver. (c) SCR driver. (d) Optically isolated SCR. (e) Reed relay. (f) VMOS driver.

swing switching transistors quickly through dangerous zones because it is the thermal effects, which take time to build up, that destroy in these areas; but if too low a current is used to drive the transistor, the transistor could get stuck on one of these zones and burn up.

Darlington Power Devices

There are three solutions to the drive current problems of regular switching transistors: more drive current, more stages of amplification, and higher transistor gains. The darlington power transistor is a device that combines the latter two advantages. The darlington power transistor is really two transistors in one, as Fig. 2-22(b) illustrates. This configuration results in a high input impedance and a very high gain.

The General Electric D40 series of power darlingtons is designed for use in IC interfaces, audio output stages, lamp-driver circuits, and relay substitutions. The D40K1 is an NPN darlington in a TO-202 package (power tab). The collector–emitter potential is rated at 30 V, the power at 10 W, and the minimum gain is 10,000 (at 200 mA). With a gain this high, even a CMOS circuit can control high-power switching: It takes only 20μ A to switch 200 mA!

Thyristors

Silicon controlled rectifiers are solid state devices that act as rectifiers when on and high-impedance circuits when off. They are three-terminal devices, with the anode corresponding to a transistor collector, the cathode to the emitter, and the gate to the base. Unlike transistors, SCRs are not designed to operate in the active region and so cannot be used as linear amplifiers. They are either on or off.

It takes very little current to switch an SCR on. The ratio of load current to drive current (similar to a transistor's gain) is rarely less than 1000. A gate current of 50 mA can switch 50 A or more. The SCR would seem to be the ideal switching element, but it has one important characteristic: once it is on, it will not turn off—even if the gate current is removed. This is due to the internal feedback characteristics of the device. The device will turn off, however, if load current is removed and then reapplied.

Because of this characteristic, SCRs have found wide use in heavy-duty ac switching circuits. Alternating-current waveforms drop to zero every cycle, so turnoff is no problem. Because SCRs can only be on or off, the duty cycle of the ac waveform is typically varied to increase and decrease power going to a load if variable power is required. Figure 5-22(c) illustrates a simple SCR switching circuit. Because SCRs usually control large loads with large voltage swings, it is difficult and dangerous to connect an SCR switching circuit directly to digital logic circuitry. Some form of isolation is necessary. Optical and inductive coupling are often used.

SCRs act as rectifiers when used with ac signals and thus permit only half-cycle current to pass through them. A related device—the triac—is bilateral in character and permits anode–cathode conduction with either polarity.

With triacs, the terms anode and cathode are virtually meaningless because of the bidirectional character of the conducting electrodes; instead, these electrodes are referred to as main terminal 1 and main terminal 2. The triac may be thought of as a pair of SCRs connected in reverse parallel with the gates tied together. A small current of either polarity gates the device on, but removal of gate voltage causes turnoff when used in ac applications. Like SCRs, triacs are used to switch large currents and for phase control of high-current resistive loads.

SCRs and triacs can create a large amount of electrical interference when turning on a load. If the ac voltage is in the middle of either half-cycle of its waveform, a fast-rising current step will result when the SCR is turned on, generating a large amount of electrical interference. Zero-point switching circuits are designed to trigger an SCR or triac when the ac voltage is at the beginning of its cycle so that no large voltage steps result upon turnon. It is wise to use these circuits for noise-reduction purposes when using SCRs. Semiconductor power circuit handbooks, published by SCR makers such as Motorola and RCA, contain these and many other useful power control circuits.

Mechanical Relays

Mechanical relays are used in conventional controls in which low-current toggle switches must control large loads, and there is no reason why they cannot be digitally controlled as well. Over the past few years, many mechanical relays designed to be directly driven by logic circuitry have entered the market.

Reed relays consisting of two magnetic reeds that contact one another when exposed to a magnetic field usually require very little control current. The Electronic Applications Company 1A6AH reed relay, for example, has a coil resistance of 380 ohms and can be driven by a 5 V input voltage. A 13 mA drive current is all that is required to operate it.

Contacts on reed relays can handle anywhere from 500 mA to tens of amperes, depending on the model; but logic-compatible reed relays seldom handle more than an ampere.

The biggest problem reed relays have is contact arcing. Because very minute spring force is used to separate the relay contacts (the torsional forces of the relay reeds), the small amount of arcing associated with a contact closure may be enough to weld the reeds together. A zener diode across the relay contacts as illustrated in Fig. 5-22(e) prevents arcing and avoids this situation.

Conventional switch-and-coil relays are available in miniaturized form for digital circuits. The Teledyne TO-5 relay series is a good example of these miniaturized relays. Like large relays, multiple-pole and latching versions are available.

When interfacing mechanical relays to a microcomputer system, it is important to remember that these devices are mechanical and they take time to respond to an input signal. If a relay has to be on before another event occurs, a waiting loop of some sort must be programmed into the control program to allow for the mechanical contact closure and magnetic field buildup and collapse.

It is necessary to put a diode across the input coil of a relay to absorb the inductive back-emf voltage spike generated by the collapsing magnetic field when the relay is turned off. Unless there is a diode or some other protective circuit to attenuate this voltage spike, a breakdown of the driver transistor or gate can result.

Solid-State Relays

Solid-state relays are designed to be nearly direct, one-package replacements for conventional mechanical relays. To obtain the amplified switching characteristics of a relay, triacs are usually used. Total input/output circuit isolation (another mechanical relay feature) is accomplished by photon coupling— coupling the input to the output circuitry with an LED and phototransistor. Appropriate input circuitry allows a user to turn the relay on by applying the proper input voltage; but unlike the mechanical relay, there is no inductive kickback because no inductive coil is used.

The North American Philips 501 series solid-state relays are tiny modules with two input and two output terminals. Input control voltage is typically 5 V at 7 mA. The outputs can control ac signals of 115 V with currents up to 2 A. Turnon time is 8 ms, and turnoff time is 32 ms (typical). These solid-state relay modules can be soldered directly to a board and require no heatsink, even at full-rated load.

VFET Devices

Field-effect transistors have always offered desirable switching characteristics, and MOS technologies are built around them; but it was not until the mid-1970s that these devices could handle even moderate power levels. With the advent of VMOS (a MOS device employing a V-shaped semiconductor channel), moderate- and even high-power FETs became available. Some of the VMOS' important features include high-frequency operation, low input current, and the ability to be turned off at will (as opposed to the SCR, which stays on).

The primary advantages of VMOS from the interface standpoint is the control current requirements. Because FETs are charge-oriented devices, drive current is only necessary to turn the FET on or off. Normal transistors are current-oriented and require a continuous drive current. VMOS power FETs require *microamperes* of input current (for control) versus milliamperes for standard bipolar transistors. VMOS devices, therefore, offer all the advantages of the transistor and the SCR but few of the disadvantages of either. For this reason, VMOS devices are gaining wide popularity as interface and control elements.

The Siliconix VN84GA is an example of one of the more recent VMOS power FETs. This device can dissipate 80 W at low frequencies and 50 W at 30 MHz. Up to 12.5 A can be controlled. Figure 5-22(f) illustrates a VMOS motor control utilizing the VN66AF, a lower-power VMOS device.

Servoamplifiers

Often an analog drive voltage or current much higher than a D/A converter's output is required to drive a variable-voltage peripheral. None of the switching circuits so far described will perform the task, because more than *on* and *off* conditions are required. The dc amplifier or *servoamplifier* is designed to fill this control circuit gap.

Servoamplifiers are simply linear dc amplifiers that accurately amplify an input voltage. Servoamplifiers are similar to audio amplifiers, and can in fact be used as audio amplifiers, with one exception: There is no capacitive or inductive coupling between amplifier stages.

One-chip operational amplifiers driving high-power single-ended or complementary-output transistor stages are the most common types of servoamplifiers. The VMOS transistor promises to become a desirable output stage component for servoamplifiers as well.

Details concerning servoamplifier design can be found in semiconductor power circuit handbooks and in linear component handbooks published by semiconductor manufacturers. Motorola, RCA, and General Electric are big in the area of industrial control and have wide selections of circuit products.

Analog Switches

Digital waveforms can easily be switched using a multiplexer logic element. The digital multiplexer simply gates the appropriate select and data signals together and generates a digitally "perfect" output corresponding to the input channel. No data bits are lost because this is digital circuitry. Multiplexing analog signals, unfortunately, is not this easy. Noise and distortion can be introduced by the analog switching element, so efforts have been made to produce linear, low-distortion analog switches.

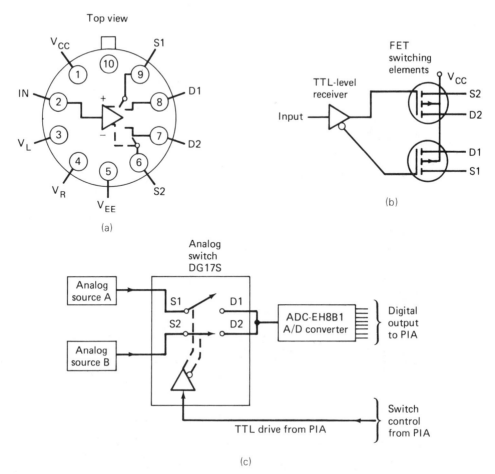

Figure 5-23 Siliconix DG175 analog switch. (a) Package and function. (b) Block diagram. (c) Typical application in A/D input selector.

One of the best analog switches is the mechanical relay. Analog signals from dc to radio frequencies can pass through the contacts of a relay with virtually no noise or distortion. Low switching speeds and mechanical unreliability make relays undesirable in many analog switching applications.

Solid-state analog switches are usually constructed around FET switching elements. The FET makes a good analog switch, because it has a very high impedance when off, and it can act as a very linear resistor when on.

The Siliconix DG175 is an example of an analog switch with a P-channel MOSFET output stage. This analog switch performs a single-pole, double-throw, make-before-break switching function and has TTL-compatible control inputs that eliminate the need for complex MOS level interfacing. Figure 5-23 illustrates the DG175 and lists its characteristics.

TRANSDUCERS

A transducer is officially defined as a device that converts electrical energy to mechanical energy or mechanical to electrical energy. Transducers, with relation to microcomputers, are those devices that allow a system to sense and control events in the real world.

Input Transducers

The final output from all transducers is a voltage or current level. Interfacing a transducer to a microcomputer is simply a matter of amplifying the input signal with a preamplifier and either counting the resulting digital waveform (in the case of the switch) or converting the analog voltage level to a digital form with an A/D converter. It is often necessary to filter and limit the input waveform as well. Commercially available transducers specify exactly what sorts of outputs to expect and usually come with application notes that specify the proper filter components for their use.

Motion-Sensing Transducers. The function of a motion transducer is to convert mechanical motion into an electrical signal, and there are four common means of accomplishing this task.

Electromechanical switches can determine the rate of mechanical motion if set to toggle synchronously with the motion. The breaker points in an automobile's ignition system are a perfect example: A cam causes switch closure once every shaft rotation. An appropriate closure sensing and counter circuit can be used to count the number of switch closures in a given period of time, and the resulting value can be used by the microcomputer.

Magnetic induction can be used in two ways to determine the rate of mechanical motion. A magnet rotating on a shaft causes current pulses to be generated in a coil next to the shaft. The faster the shaft rotation, the higher the pulse rate. These pulses can be counted, just as the switch's closures were counted, or the pulses can be integrated with a capacitor to produce an analog voltage level that is proportional to the shaft rotation rate. In the second case, an A/D converter is necessary to convert the voltage level to a usable digital value.

Magnetic induction coils sense the change in magnetic fields as a magnet moves by. When the motion is very slow, the magnet does not move by the induction coil quickly enough to generate a readable pulse. In such cases, Hall-effect devices are used to sense the magnetic field. Unlike coils that detect changes in field strength, Hall-effect devices are semiconductors that vary their conduction directly with magnetic field strength. Hall-effect devices find application in slow-motion sensors as well as in keyboard switches.

Another method of determining motion is the optical method. A slotted wheel on a rotating shaft can break a light beam that is detected by an optical sensor. This signal can be counted and the rotation rate measured. Two common motion sensors are the rotary encoder and the odometer.

Pressure-Sensing Transducers.   Capacitive sensors are often used to detect pressure. By sandwiching a layer of compressible dielectric material between two metal sheets, a capacitor is formed. Pressure applied to the capacitor moves the plates closer together, thereby changing the capacitance. The variable capacitance can then be fed to a circuit that converts capacitance to a voltage level. The voltage level can be sent to an A/D converter, and finally to a microcomputer.

Piezoelectric materials (materials that generate electricity when compressed) are occasionally used for pressure sensors, especially when a device to detect changes in pressure (versus absolute level) is needed.

Flow-Rate Transducers.   Fluid flow rate can be measured by monitoring a pump or regulating device on a fluid line or by installing a flow-rate transducer directly into a line.

Pumps usually deliver a constant volume of fluid on every stroke (if reciprocating) and on every rotation (if centrifugal). The rate may vary in the case of the centrifugal pump, depending on the viscosity of the fluid; but for one type of fluid, the rate remains relatively constant. By counting the number of pump strokes using a switch or magnetic transducer, or the number of rotations using a rotation transducer, a very accurate flow rate can be established.

An alternative to the indirect pump approach is the inline flow transducer. This device usually consists of a turbine with a built-in magnet contained in a tube that splices into the line. Fluid flow causes the turbine to spin at a flow-proportional rate. An external coil monitors the turbine's rotation.

Smoke Detectors.   There are three methods currently used to detect smoke: resistance changes in gas sensors, current changes due to smoke slowing the travel of alpha particles in an ionization chamber, and optical smoke sensing methods. Single components that perform these functions are available. The MCC 158 is an example of a commercial smoke sensor. The device is built around a gallium-arsenide infra-red emitter that works with a photodiode and I^2L amplifying circuitry to detect a 2% obstruction of light transmission. The sensor has built-in test and sampling circuitry that operates the sensor in a pulsed mode. The LED is pulsed once every 5 s with a 50 μs pulse. This reduces the chance for false triggering and cuts down on power drain in battery-powered applications.

Output Transducers

Output transducers require either a switched current to actuate a stepping motor or solenoid or a precisely controlled current or voltage to drive a motor or other voltage-dependent device. A simple power-switching circuit that utilizes an SCR, transistor, or VMOS device is all that is required in the switching case. For precise voltage control, a D/A converter and servoamplifier are required.

Solenoids.   A solenoid is a transducer that turns current into linear motion. Solenoids consist of one or more electromagnets that move a metal plunger. The plunger is sometimes returned to its original position after an excursion with a spring or permanent magnet.

The motion created by a solenoid can be used as is, or it can be used to control a switch or hydraulic valve to actuate an even larger mechanical motion.

Stepping Motors.   In many applications, a precisely controllable rotating source is desirable. Stepping motors work well in these applications. A stepping motor consists of a gear-like inner rotor surrounded by three or more gear-like stators, as Fig. 5-24 illustrates. The rotor tends to align itself with the stator, which is actuated with an electromagnet due to magnetic induction. By switching current sequentially between the stator magnets, the rotor can be stepped in a rotary or back-and-forth motion.

Controlling a stepping motor is simply a matter of sending current to the appropriate stator magnets at the proper times.

Servomechanisms.   A servomechanism or *servo* is a device that converts electrical input signals to controllable linear or rotary motion. Servos consist of

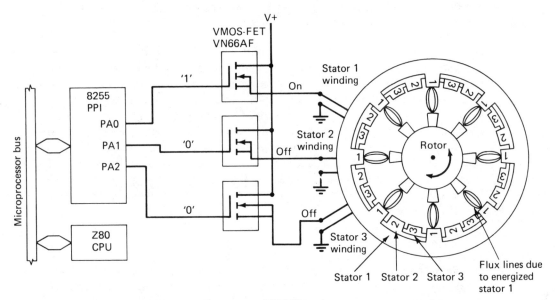

Figure 5-24   Microprocessor/VMOS/stepping-motor system.

an electrically controlled mechanical motion source (a geared motor, a stepping motor, or a solenoid-controlled hydraulic or vacuum piston) and a motion-sensing transducer to "report" movement information to the controlling logic. Precise positioning is thus possible using feedback to judge position.

OPTICAL DISPLAYS AND SENSORS

It used to be that you had a choice between an incandescent or a neon bulb for an indicator and a phototube or cadmium-sulfide cell for an optical sensor. If you could afford the luxury of a digital readout, the neon-filled Nixie tube was the obvious choice. Today, new display devices such as light-emitting diodes and liquid-crystal displays, and new sensors such as photodiodes and photo-transistors are available. Updated versions of the older devices, manufactured by companies trying to keep competitive with the new technologies, are also available and are actually the best choice in many applications.

Light-Emitting Diodes

For status indicators, pilot lamps, and multisegment digital displays, the LEDs are by far the most common device in use today. These solid-state light sources provide good visibility, do not burn out as incandescent lamps do, and require very low current and voltage levels for light generation. One of the LED's major advantages with regard to microcomputer interface components and digital logic in general is its ability to be driven directly by low-voltage and low-curent signals.

The discrete LED comes in many package forms and four major visible colors (red, orange, yellow, and green). Infrared LEDs are also available for use as invisible light sources. To understand the characteristics of the LED it is necessary to look at the physics behind it.

In most light sources, photons are generated by electrons falling to a lower energy state. It was discovered that certain semiconductor materials generate light when the electrons fall from the conduction to the valence energy bands at a diode junction. The physical properties of the semiconductor material determine how large an energy drop exists between bands, thus establishing the color of the LED. Unlike incandescent lamps, in which energy drops of many levels are generated thermally, LEDs only drop their energy at certain levels. Light-emitting diodes, therefore, generate light in very narrow color ranges and can in fact generate coherent (essentially monochromatic) laser light.

Materials that generate photons in the infrared and a portion of the visible light region have been found. Gallium-arsenide phosphide is a good red emitter; gallium-arsenide phosphite on gallium phosphide is a good yellow emitter, and gallium phosphide is a fairly good green emitter. There are no blue or violet

Table 5-2   Typical LED Characteristics

Characteristic	Values			Units
	High-Efficiency Red (Gallium-arsenide phosphide on gallium phosphide)	Yellow (Gallium-arsenide phosphide on gallium phosphide)	Green (Gallium phosphide)	
Axial luminous intensity	11.0 @ 10 mA	11.0 @ 10 mA	11.0 @ 20 mA	Mcd
Peak Wavelength	635	583	565	nm
Speed of response	90	90	200	ns
Forward voltage	2.2	2.2	2.4	V
Reverse breakdown	5.0	5.0	5.0	V

emitters commonly available because semiconductor materials that exhibit an energy transition in the blue range are rare.

Table 5-2 lists the characteristics of a typical LED. The forward voltage drop across the LED ranges from 1.6 to 3 V, depending on the LED's color.

The axial luminous intensities shown in the table reflect a characteristic that is true of all LEDs: green LEDs draw much more power for the same light intensity output than red or yellow devices do. In order to output 11 millicandelas (11 mcd), the green LED requires 20 mA at 2.4 V (48 mW) versus 10 mA at 2.2 V (22 mW) for the red and yellow LEDs.

The speed of response of the LEDs shown is 90 ns for the red and yellow LEDs and 200 ns for the green LED. Because LEDs are semiconductor devices and do not rely on thermal effects to generate light, they can be switched on and off very quickly. This characteristic makes LEDs ideal for light modulation and communication applications. Some LEDs are capable of operating in the hundreds of megahertz (1 to 5 ns range).

Interfacing an LED to a digital system is a trivial matter. A gate capable of providing the LED with its required voltage and current levels can be used. Because an LED is a diode, it will always drop its forward voltage across the diode junction, and it draws as much current as is supplied to it. A current-limiting resistor is therefore required to put a ceiling on this value.

Figure 5-25 illustrates a few common LED driving circuits. In Figure 5-25(b), an LED with a built-in resistor (the Hewlett-Packard 5082) is used, thereby eliminating the need for a separate current-limiting resistor. Advanced LEDs with built-in constant-current sources (actually small integrated circuits) are becoming commonplace. These LEDs will provide a constant light output for any given input voltage as long as it is above a minimum threshold voltage.

Figure 5-25(e) illustrates an ingenious device: the back-to-back red–green LED. This basically consists of red and green LEDs mounted in a common package, connected with opposite polarities. When current flows through the diode in one direction it outputs red. In the other direction it outputs green.

There's only one problem with most red–green LEDs: Because green LEDs are much less efficient than red ones, a much higher current is required for green displays. This makes interfacing difficult.

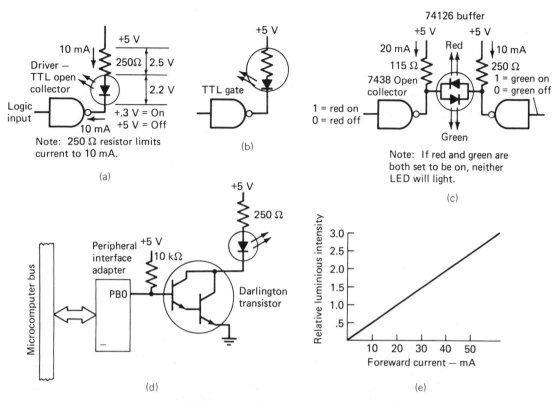

Figure 5-25 LED driving methods and characteristics. (a) Standard LED with TTL driver. (b) LED with built-in resistor and TTL driver. (c) Red/green LED with dual current drive. (d) MOS device driving an LED. (e) Typical LED intensity curve.

If not enough current is available to drive an LED in a given application, a high-power driver can be used. If the drive current is marginal and less light is acceptable, good results can be obtained by simply lowering the drive current. As Figure 5-25(e) illustrates, the output of an LED is very linear with current variations.

LED Arrays

Arrays of LEDs can be used to represent alphanumeric characters. There are many preassembled LED arrays available, ranging from the simple 7-segment types found in calculators and digital clocks to 5 × 7 and higher dot matrix units. Figure 5-26 illustrates two common configurations.

Interfacing LED arrays is, in theory, no different from interfacing a lot of single LEDs. Individual segments can be driven with one gate apiece. Special decoder–driver circuits such as the 7447 TTL IC are designed to take a binary-coded-decimal code and drive appropriate array segments to indicate the input code on the array. For larger displays, such as in a calculator in which 12 to 16 of these decoders would be required to drive all digits, scanned displays are used.

Figure 5-26(d) illustrates a scanned display circuit. Basically, external counting and addressing circuitry select individual LEDs in the LED array and strobe them with a short current pulse if they are to be lit. The scanning circuitry addresses and pulses all array elements many times per second, thereby giving an illusion of a solid multidigit display. Because the LEDs are operating in a pulsed mode, higher input currents are required to give a visible intensity equal to a corresponding nonscanned display.

Incandescent Displays

Filament-lamp technology has advanced in parallel with the development of modern LEDs, and a wide selection of small, low-current, almost logic-level-compatible incandescent lamps and displays are now available. The primary

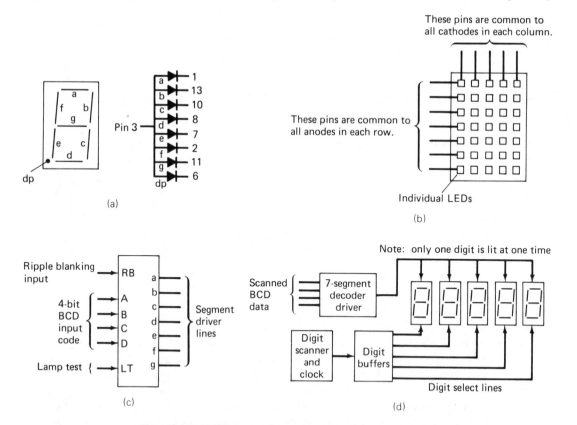

Figure 5-26 LED arrays and array drivers. (a) Common-anode 7-segment.
(b) Alphanumeric 5 × 7 dot matrix. (c) 7448 BCD-to-7-segment decoder/driver IC.
(d) Scanned 7-segment digits.

advantage the incandescent display has over an LED array is its ability to emit light of a wide spectrum—white light. By using color filters, colors that are not available in LEDs can be created. Another advantage of incandescent lamps is their high-intensity capabilities. An inexpensive incandescent lamp can light up a whole room if necessary—something considered impossible for even the largest noncryogenically cooled LED.

An example of an advanced miniature incandescent lamp which is competitive with LEDs is the Chicago Miniature Company's CM22-1-XX-43. This lamp, rated at 3.0 V at a drain of a mere 15 mA, can be driven with a standard TTL gate. Although this lamp does not have a 100-year lifetime (the claim for most LEDs), its rated 10,000-hour life is quite acceptable in most applications.

Like LED arrays, incandescent lamps have also been built into arrays and digits. Incandescent 7-segment displays whose segments consist of single long filaments find wide use in automobile instrumentation in which the red characteristic of the standard LED is not acceptable. These displays are also quite desirable in scanned displays. Due to the incandescent lamp's slow turnoff and turnon response (persistence), flicker problems associated with display scanning are eliminated.

Interfacing an incandescent display or indicator is a simple task, but a few restrictions must be carefully observed. Incandescent lamps are voltage-specified devices, while LEDs are current-specified. When choosing a lamp to be driven by a driver, you must calculate the voltage that will be put across the lamp and make your choice accordingly. Because the current of the lamp will be self-limiting at the specified voltage, no current-limiting resistor is required.

Incandescent lamps are nonlinear devices: They act like resistors of the lamp's rated value once they are turned on; but when they are not lit, they have very low resistance. A resistance change of 10:1 is not uncommon for incandescent lamps. When choosing a driver for a lamp, you must keep this in mind. When the lamp is initially turned on, a current surge of up to an order of magnitude greater than the driving value can be anticipated. Most driver circuits can withstand the initial current surge, because it is long-term thermal effects that limit driving current; but it is wise to look into the lamp and driver characteristics before deciding on a final design.

Liquid-Crystal Displays

Incandescent, LED, and gas-discharge displays fall into the active-device category: they emit light as a function of the electrical energy applied to them. The liquid-crystal display or LCD is a device that we consider passive, because it simply controls light reflection and transmission as a function of supplied voltage. The LCD acts as a light shutter.

Two characteristics make LCDs particularly desirable in certain applications. First, LCDs draw very little power (in the millionths of a watt), because controlling light with a shutter takes much less power than creating light. The LCD cannot be drowned out by high-level ambient light like an LED can.

Because the LCD is a shutter, the more light you shine at it the more it will reflect.

The passive nature of the LCD creates its disadvantages as well as its advantages. Because the LCD emits no light, it cannot be seen in the dark as an LED can. Solutions to this problem are (1) the use of built-in lights in front or in back of the LCD for in-the-dark applications, and (2) use of special fluorescence-activated LCD displays (FLADs), which essentially grab as much ambient light as possible and direct it toward the digits (FLADs still require some light, however).

Liquid-crystal displays are easy to interface to almost any logic family. Because they draw current in the microampere range at potentials of only a few volts, even CMOS circuitry can successfully drive them directly. The only precaution in using LCDs is to stick to the recommended drive voltages for the LCD being used. Too much drive voltage can seriously damage the liquid crystal dyes used in the LCD display panel.

Photocells

One of the oldest, cheapest, and slowest-responding photodetectors is the cadmium sulfide (CdS) photocell. This device is essentially a light-controlled variable resistor that is very sensitive to light in the visible spectrum.

Three advantages of the CdS photocell are its high power-dissipation capability, good sensitivity in the visible light spectrum, and its very low *on* resistance. The CdS cell is ideal for use in light-level sensors, light on–off sensors, and in low-frequency counting applications where a breaking light beam indicates an event.

A CdS cell can be treated as a switch or variable resistor in microcomputer interface applications, because the dark-to-light resistance of a CdS cell can vary from 2 MΩ to 10 Ω. As Fig. 5-27 illustrates, a minimum of components is needed to make a CdS switch and CdS light-level detector.

The PbS (lead sulfide) cell is very similar to the CdS cell, but it is more sensitive to infrared radiation. This cell should be used in applications requiring infrared detection or absorption measurements.

The selenium cell is another form of photocell and is sensitive to radiation toward the blue end of the spectrum.

Photodiodes

In many applications, such as light-beam communication and high-speed tachometry, the slow response times of CdS, PbS, and selenium cells (up to 1 or 2 seconds to turn off) are too slow to be useful. The photodiode is a device that exploits light's effect on reverse-biased semiconductor junctions to produce an

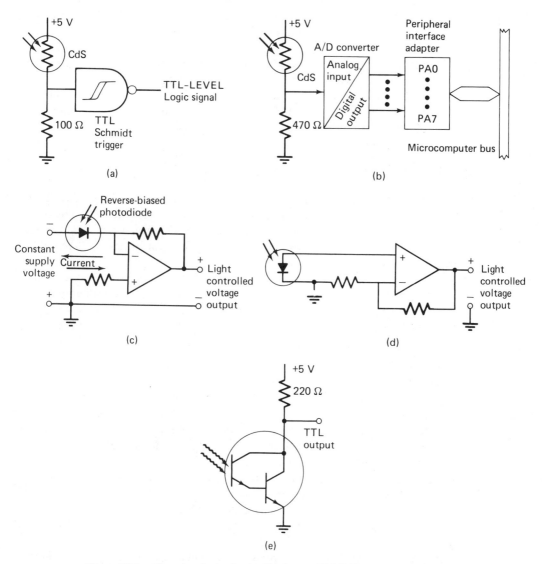

Figure 5-27   Photoelectric circuits. (a) Simple on—off CdS photosensor. (b) Simple microcomputer-based light-level sensor. (c) Photodiode sensor (linear operation). (d) Photodiode sensor (logarithmetic operation). (e) Phototransistor (photodarlington) TTL-level light sensor.

optical sensor with a response time in the nanosecond range. These devices are used in high-speed applications.

A photodiode acts as a variable current source. By reverse-biasing a photodiode with 10 to 40 V, a linearly light-dependent current, which ranges from a few (dark) to a few hundred (light) microamperes, results. This current can be used to control an operational amplifier to generate a usable signal for microcomputer interfacing. Figure 5-27 illustrates two photodiode applications.

It is true that photodiode circuits require more interface components than CdS systems, but the added operational amplifiers can be used to advantage in varying the response characteristics of the overall sensor. The exponential detector "sees" light levels more closely to that of the human eye, which may be useful in some applications.

Phototransistors

High-frequency light response, as well as good current-handling capabilities, can be obtained using a phototransistor. This device is similar to a standard transistor, but instead of having an input lead for the transistor's base, a light window is provided. Light turns the transistor on and off by light-generated current carriers in the transistor junction.

The phototransistor can be used in interface applications in the same way a normal transistor would. Phototransistors can handle many milliamperes of current and therefore require little amplification when used in switching or level-detection circuits. Figure 5-27e illustrates a phototransistor circuit.

Optoisolators

It is often necessary to send signals back and forth between two circuits that must be electrically isolated from one another. Data communications between computers in two adjacent buildings is an example of such a situation. If either building is struck by lightning during a storm, thousands of volts of potential difference can build up between the two buildings. Electrical isolation of the two computers can save their circuitry. High-frequency pulse transformers were once used extensively for these applications, but the advent of LEDs and high-speed photodiodes and phototransistors resulted in an equally reliable, higher performance and lower cost alternative: the optically coupled isolator or *optoisolator*.

An optoisolator is basically an LED aimed at a phototransistor or amplified photodiode encapsulated in a single package. Figure 5-28 shows three common optoisolator configurations. The phototransistor is less expensive than the amplified photodiode isolator, but the photodiode version has a much higher frequency response.

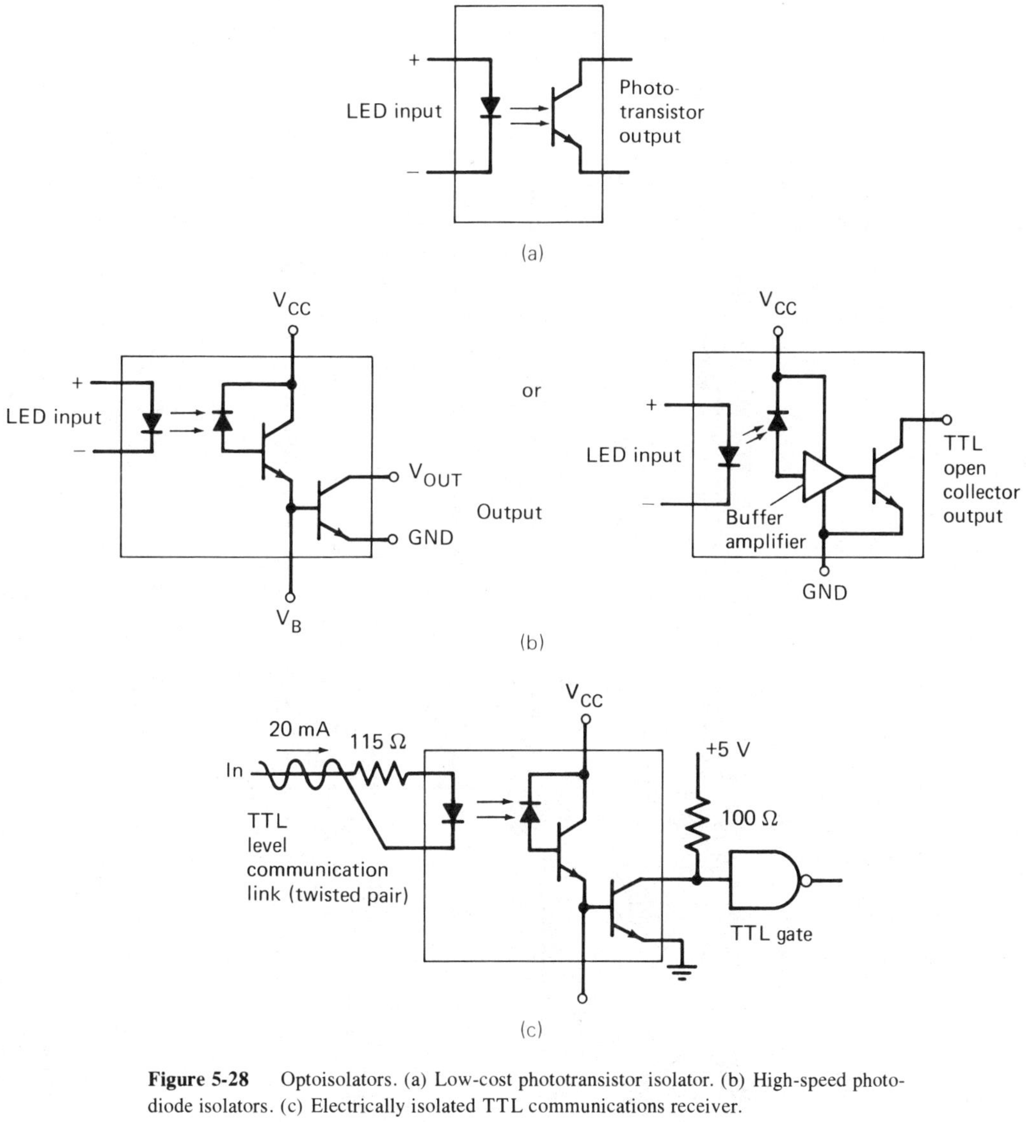

Figure 5-28 Optoisolators. (a) Low-cost phototransistor isolator. (b) High-speed photo-diode isolators. (c) Electrically isolated TTL communications receiver.

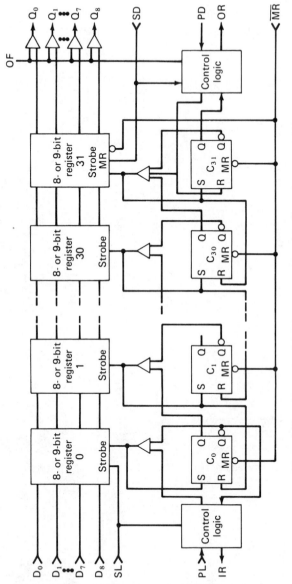

Figure 5-29 The Am2812 FIFO memory. (Copyright © 1976 Advanced Micro Devices, Inc. Reproduced with permission of copyright owner.)

Inputs and outputs on optoisolators are often matched to standards to provide easy interfacing. The LED end often has appropriate built-in current-limiting resistors to meet the EIA RS-232C standard for line receivers, and standard 16 mA current sinks (output transistors) are frequently used as outputs. Interfacing to optoisolators is simply a matter of interfacing to whatever the inputs and outputs are set up to look like. If an input is a pure LED with no current-limiting resistor, it must be driven as such. If the output is a TTL driver, it can directly drive a number of TTL gates.

FIRST-IN – FIRST-OUT MEMORIES (FIFOs)

Catching information "on the fly" can often be a problem for a microprocessor-based system. A system may have the processing power to accept data at an overall fast rate, but at times other processing tasks may cause a few words to slip by unread. One solution to this problem is to build a small memory circuit to pile up data as it comes in. With such a memory system the microprocessor can process the data when it gets around to it; as long as the memory never gets filled to capacity, no harm is done.

There are single integrated circuits designed to do precisely what has just been described. First-in–first-out (FIFO) memories are devices that have data input lines (usually 8 or 9) with a control called *push*, plus data output lines with a control called *pop*. Data is "pushed onto the top" of an internal memory when the push line is pulsed; it ripples through the FIFO, "stacking up at the bottom," where it can be conveniently popped off when needed. Pushes and pops can be done completely asynchronously.

The Advanced Micro Devices 2812 is a good example of a FIFO. It consists of 32 ripplethrough memory locations of 8 bits' width plus corresponding control logic. Figure 5-29 illustrates the 2812. A low-to-high transition on the PL line (parallel load) causes the 8-bit input data (D0–D8) to be loaded into the FIFO, while PD (parallel dump) causes it to be popped off. This FIFO also features a serial load and dump capability and a master reset (MR) line. Input ready and output ready lines are provided to help external control logic determine FIFO overflow and out-of-data conditions, and a *half-full flag* line indicates that the FIFO's bottom 15 locations are full. The half-full flag is useful in applications in which control over input and output data is possible. A half-full FIFO provides the best I/O rate matching for varying I/O rate buffering. The half-full flag can also be used to send a "you'd better start unloading this FIFO" signal to the microprocessor. An interrupt line connected to the half-full flag is a possible implementation.

CHAPTER

6 Designing Interface Circuits

After a system has been fairly well specified and all the desired microprocessor components, interface parts, and transducers are well understood, it is time to begin the system design. This is the most critical stage in the system development, for a few errors or a large amount of rule-bending at this point will result in an unreliable piece of digital equipment. This chapter discusses design procedures and outlines desirable design practices. Bad design practices are also presented.

THE MANY-PARTS PROBLEM

A single part functioning by itself or a few parts connected to function as a very simple circuit usually poses no problem as far as "system design" goes. The engineers who designed the parts, especially if the parts are of a universal digital logic family type such as TTL, have done their best to make sure their designs have adequate noise margins, are free of redundancy, are logically optimized, and are in general good designs. Unfortunately, most systems consist of more than a few parts. An average microcomputer can, in fact, consist of many hundreds of parts. At this level of system complexity, the integrated circuit designers at the factory are no longer responsible for overall system operation. It is up to the system designer to make it work and make it work well.

All too many systems these days are thrown together by people who lazily fall back on the inherent reliability and versatility of today's components instead of following good design practices and working out all circuit problems in an optimized way. Thus, poor designs are not restricted to one-of-a-kind, homebrew projects but are propagated throughout the microcomputer industry. The fact of the matter is that you cannot learn good system design by following the circuitry of others, even if the designs are disseminated by "high class" companies and trade journals.

How, then, does one design "good" logic and circuitry? The answer is simple: in exactly the same way hard-working professional engineers do and the way lazy engineers know they are supposed to. You must define your specifications, study the available component options, set up design rules, and strictly follow those rules. You must take the professional approach.

The microprocessor, memory, and components sections of this text have described how to select the proper components to meet your specifications. From the initial design specification process, a system block diagram should have been generated. Before starting to translate the block diagram and components into final schematics you must take the most often neglected step in system design: defining the design rules.

DEFINING DESIGN RULES

Design rules are a series of conventions that are established to account for physical constraints in a system and to make drawings and documentation understandable to all design team members. These rules should be written out, and copies should be given to all members of the design team (if one exists). Design rules also help new design team members to quickly familiarize themselves with the project if they enter late in the program.

You must first define how documentation will be written. Large systems require many drawings. You must specify how signals will be passed from one drawing to another. For simple systems with just a few drawings, a circle can represent a signal that goes to another page. For larger systems in which many drawings are used, a notation indicating to which drawing the signal goes and from which drawing it comes is necessary. Signals that go to a card's edge can be represented by another symbol—perhaps a triangle or, more conventionally, a pointed tab as shown in Fig. 6-1.

It is also a good practice to give all signals and components names. This makes explanations and references in discussions and documentation less confusing. By assigning functional names to system components such as "memory control ROM" or "output selection decoder," it will be easier to relate the detailed schematics to the overall system block diagram. In the case of naming signals, shorter abbreviated names are preferable. An 8-bit data input bus might be given the name DI0 through DI7.

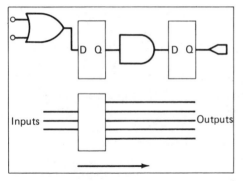

1. Data flow on drawings should be from left to right.

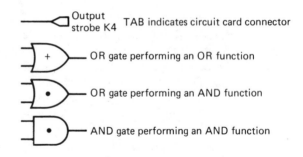

2. Symbols should be specified.

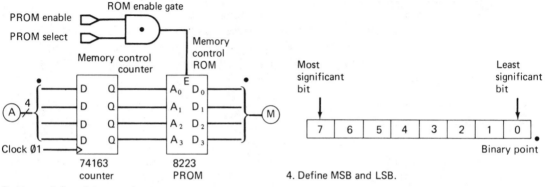

3. Name all parts for easy reference.

4. Define MSB and LSB.

Figure 6-1   Design rule conventions.

The design rules must also state how buses are to be numbered. In many computers the 0 line represents the most significant bit; in others it represents the least significant bit. Problems could arise if the designer of one card numbers his bus from DI0 to DI7 while another numbers his DI7 to DI0.

A convention for representing wide buses on drawings must also be defined. A coded representation with a slash indicating how many lines run down the bus is preferable. In some cases, designers assume that buses should expand the same way they contract. This is acceptable for a single bus with just one start and end point; but if the bus goes to more than one location, an inconsistency exists as Fig. 6-2 shows. By using a dot as a key on bus ends, the ambiguity is resolved.

More extensive documentation rules are appropriate on very large projects. Recommendations concerning drawing sizes, pencil lead hardness (so drawings do not smear), and data flow direction (data on drawings should always flow from left to right, for example) should be specified.

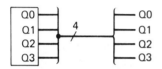

1. Simple compressed bus notation works well in simple cases.

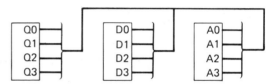

Note: If you straighten-out D to A connections D3 corresponds to A0.

2. Simple bus notation is ambiguous in complex wiring.

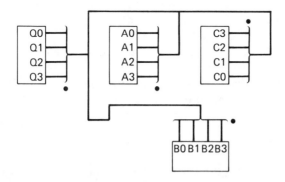

3. Keyed bus notation is always well defined.

Figure 6-2   Bus notation conflicts.

Physical restrictions must also be laid out in the design rules. The logic families being used should be studied and a limit should be put on gate fan-out. Design recommendations are usually given at the beginning or ends of data catalogs and on parts specification sheets. These can be used as a general guide, but be sure to consider all variables. A current fan-out of eight may be specified, but too much capacitance may cause the actual limit to drop to six if high frequencies are used.

Maximum signal-wire lengths should be specified. Long lines can cause ringing and excessive propagation delays in a system. Methods for transmitting signals over long distances through the use of differential drivers should be specified.

Noise reduction methods such as the use of decoupling capacitors (which will be discussed shortly) on TTL logic boards, and termination and line impedances on ECL circuits must be clearly described. The power supply and clock distribution system for the overall system should be defined.

Finally, a more qualitative characteristic must be presented: the philosophy of the design. The general method of moving data around the system must be outlined. Logic design guidelines must be laid out. The next section presents many guidelines that will help improve a system design.

LOGIC DESIGN GUIDELINES

Computer system design can be broken into two categories: theoretical design and practical design. The theoretical aspects are at the highest level of system design and are already fairly well laid out in a microcomputer system. The microprocessor that is chosen determines the overall designs of most microcomputers. Practical design aspects of a microprocessor must be well understood to implement the theoretical design on a logic-level basis.

Theoretical design information for a microcomputer can be obtained from most microprocessor specification booklets. The detailed practical design aspects, however, apply to all microprocessors in general and none in particular and are therefore infrequently covered in microprocessor literature.

Many of these important practical design guidelines are presented here. Additional discussions of these guidelines can be found in logic family catalogs (not concentrating on microprocessors) and in manufacturers' application notes. Advanced Micro Devices, Motorola, and RCA are particularly good sources of practical design information.

Synchronous and Asynchronous Design

There are two ways to build a logic circuit. One way is to have some flip-flops and registers clock in data on the rising edge of a system clock, and other registers preset, reset, or clock as a result of new data generation. This is *asynchronous* design. An example of this type of design is shown in Fig. 6-3. On the rising edge of the system clock, new data enters flip-flop A and causes the Q output to change, thereby clocking flip-flop B and setting flip-flop C.

The second way of building the same circuit is shown in Fig. 6-3(b). Notice that in this circuit all devices are clocked by the master system clock. No clocks are driven by anything other than system clocks, and preset and clear inputs are not used.

There is no logical difference between these two circuits, for they provide the same logic function; and if there were no such thing as propagation delay or noise, both circuits would be equally desirable. This, however, is not the case.

The first thing you can do to greatly improve the reliability of your system design is to write the words "no asynchronous logic permitted" in your design rules. The noise graphs of Fig. 6-3 help explain why synchronous design is superior to asynchronous design. When the system clock's rising edge comes along, many registers and flip-flops change states; these state changes cause data lines throughout the system to change. Due to propagation delays, data changes at slightly different times on data lines, creating system noise. This noise is radiated as radio-frequency energy through the power supply lines and is picked up by other system lines that act as antennas. In the asynchronous case, noise is generated continuously as data ripples through the system and more flip-flops are clocked or preset (generating more noise).

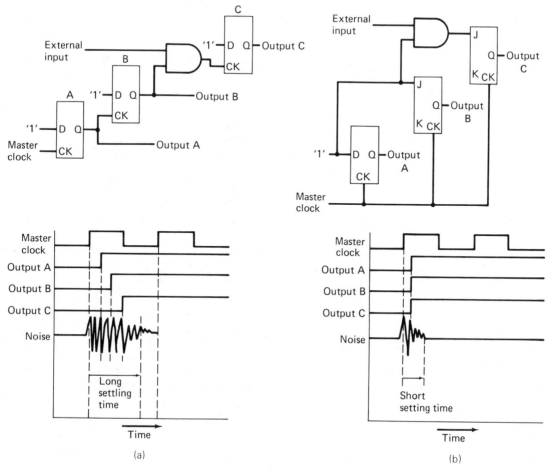

Figure 6-3   Synchronous versus asynchronous logic. (a) Asynchronous logic circuit
and timing diagram. (b) Equivalent synchronous logic circuit and timing diagram.

In the synchronous case, one large noise burst occurs, then things settle
down nicely. Synchronous logic therefore runs faster, because no ripple propagation is used and because the system stabilizes faster. More importantly,
synchronous logic is immune to noise that occurs at times other than at the
rising edge of the system clock. As long as the system clock is well shielded
against crosstalk (which is not hard to accommodate) and the data is stabilized
by the next system clock edge, system noise poses little threat to reliability.

Reliability is low in asynchronous systems because noise-susceptible data
lines are used to drive reset, set, and clock lines. A noise glitch at any time on
any one of these data lines is enough to change the system's state by unintentionally setting or resetting a flip-flop.

Noise from external sources has less of an effect on synchronous circuits as
well. Data is only clocked into registers on rising edges of clocks, so noise must

enter the system at precisely the time of the rising edge of the system clock to have an effect. This leaves only a small window of noise-sensitive time. If this noise window is 5% of a system clock's cycle time, the design is said to be 95% glitch-free. Because noise can affect an asynchronous design at any time through a data-driven clock, preset, or clear input, an asynchronous design is glitch-prone.

Another advantage to synchronous design is that it is much easier to conceptualize the system action on timing diagrams. A synchronous design is more likely to work the first time than an asynchronous one, and if it does not work, it is much easier to troubleshoot.

Finally, synchronous designs are not as easy to design as asynchronous ones. If a flip-flop must be set at the time a convenient data line happens to change, it is much easier to connect the flip-flop's clock or preset line to the data line than carefully reason out a synchronous way to determine the signal one clock pulse ahead of time and clock it in on the system clock edge. In some cases it even requires an extra gate or two, but the extra design effort and small increase in parts are well worthwhile. A synchronous design will return your investment many times over in reliability, ease of debugging, and increased processing speed.

Simplicity in Design

Simplicity is often said to be the ultimate sophistication. This is definitely true in regard to the number of gates and flip-flops required to implement a certain logic function. The less parts a system has, the less chance for failure there is. Two ways of simplifying a system design will now be presented.

Gate Reduction.   Logic gating in a system can usually be simplified from the first-cut design by applying the theories of Boolean algebra. An OR gate feeding an OR gate can be consolidated into one large OR gate, and an AND gate feeding an AND gate can be combined also. Figure 6-4 illustrates some of the most common logical reductions.

In system design, there are a few conflicts that do not arise in theoretical Boolean algebra. The first is package count. It is better to have three packages of 2-input OR gates than four packages of optimal Boolean gating. As long as the combination of gates causes no unacceptable propagation delay, it is wisest to opt for the lowest package count.

Another conflict is having spare gates after a design is completed. If an AND gate and three inverters are available as spares, it is wiser to use them to make an OR gate than to add a new chip to the design.

One of the most powerful Boolean algebra laws for gate reduction, especially when wired-OR connections are allowed, is De Morgans law. This law can help change AND gates to OR gates and vice versa. This law can be related as a

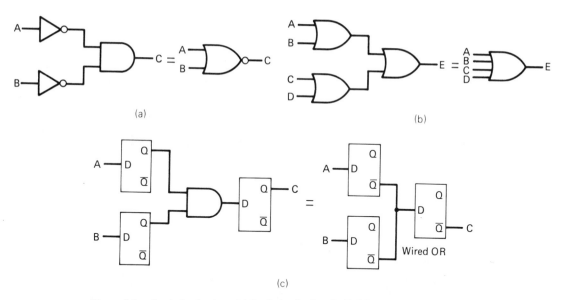

Figure 6-4 Logical reductions. (a) Logical reductions by DeMorgan's law. (b) Consolidated gate reduction. (c) ECL gate reduction using wired-OR approach.

complex Boolean expression, but an easier way to remember it is: change the outputs, change the input, and change the gate (from an AND to OR, or an OR to AND). Because inverting outputs are usually available on flip-flops and registers, this can easily be accomplished in most cases. It can reduce signal propagation time. Figure 6-4(c) shows such an ECL reduction that saves parts as well as increases speed.

When the high speed of gates is not required, large gating networks can be replaced by ROMs and PROMs. By simply feeding all the gating network's input lines to the ROM address and taking the outputs from the ROM data lines, extremely complex gating functions can be implemented. One advantage to this method is that a gating network can be changed by simply reprogramming a PROM instead of tearing apart a circuit board.

It is wise to do a preliminary gate reduction before implementing a ROM gating network, however. It may be that no gates or ROMs are needed. It is also desirable to do a tradeoff study between gates and ROMs. It takes one quarter of a 4-data-line ROM to implement one gating input. If a simple gate that takes one quarter of a package can implement the same function, it is better to use the gate. Gates are simpler, more reliable, and draw less power than ROMs.

State Reduction. Every unnecessary flip-flop and register doubles the number of states a digital device can be put into. The probability of the device going into the wrong state is increased accordingly. By reducing the number of states a machine has, reliability can be increased and parts can be eliminated.

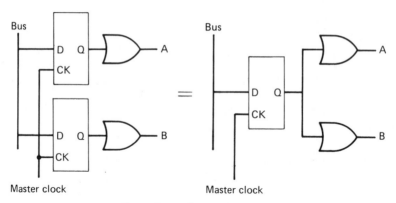

Note: One register is eliminated.

(a)

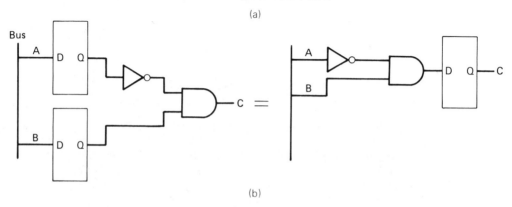

(b)

Figure 6-5   State reductions. (a) Redundant register elimination. (b) Pushing gates in front of registers.

One way to reduce the number of flip-flops and registers in a system is to look for similarities in the output of each register and determine if some other register outputs the same signal under the same conditions. If it does, one of the two registers can be eliminated.

Registers can also be eliminated by "pushing" gating networks to the inputs of a register instead of the outputs, as Fig. 6-5 illustrates.

In some cases registers can be saved by moving the gating to the outputs instead of the inputs. This should also be considered in state reduction.

Finally, it is sometimes possible to create signals, which were formerly created by a register, with a gate fed by two or more other registers. Unless the single-gate delay propagation is too long for a given application, trading a flip-flop or register for a gate is a good move, because complexity remains about the same but the number of states is cut in half.

Synchronous design lends itself to state reduction more readily than asynchronous logic. Replacing a flip-flop in an asynchronous string of flip-flops is likely to upset a timing cycle.

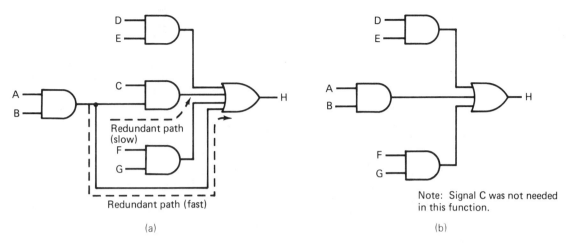

Figure 6-6 Redundant signal paths. (a) Gating network with redundant signal path.
(b) Equivalent, logically reduced gating network; no redundant paths exist.

Redundancy Avoidance

A redundant signal (Fig. 6-6) is one that duplicates the function of one or more combined signals in a gating network. If the redundant signal line were cut, the circuit would logically be the same. At first glance, such a signal seems quite desirable. If the redundant signal happens to break or get stuck at a 1 or 0, the machine would keep on running. If this sort of redundancy is planned, it can be advantageous; but if it happens by accident, it can cause major reliability problems.

Redundant signal paths are often formed unintentionally in large gating networks in which the redundant signal takes a long multigate path to its final destination. If the intended signal (which the redundant signal is backing up) happens to fail, the logic function may keep on working due to the redundant signal, but a much larger propagation delay in the final output caused by the delayed redundant signal is the result.

A computer system that is relying on its redundant signal after a main signal failure may fail in one out of a billion operations due to borderline propagation delay. Finding the fault would be nearly impossible, because all gate outputs downstream from the error as well as upstream would seem normal in most tests.

Large computer companies rely on simulation programs to check their circuits for redundancy. If a redundancy checking program is not available, the only way to check for redundancy is to evaluate a circuit and assure yourself that an error in any line would cause a failure. Gate optimization also tends to eliminate redundant signals from a system.

Using Large-Scale Integration

The reliability of integrated circuits has increased to a point at which system reliability is essentially a function of package count. Reliability, for the first time, is not a function of circuit complexity. In order to increase system reliability, it is advisable to use the largest-scale integration possible, even if it requires a slight increase in overall system complexity.

In some cases the use of LSI may seem wasteful. An example is using a one-chip 8-bit counter when only a 4-bit counter and a single flip-flop are necessary. When compared on the bases of cost, reliability, and circuit-board complexity, however, the LSI usually wins. Just as you would not think of building gates out of discrete transistors to save a few resistors, you should not consider building counters out of flip-flops if LSI is available to perform the task.

Timing Margins and Sampling

When data is transferred from one register to another using a common system clock, successful transfer relies on the fact that data is available for the specified setup and hold times of the register being used. As the timing diagram of Fig. 6-7 illustrates, the hold time on data in register-to-register transfers can be quite low due to the data changing immediately after the clock edge. Registers are designed to work with common clocks in this manner. There are usually no hold time problems as long as parts of the same logic family in close proximity to one another are used. If parts of different logic families are used, or long clock and data paths between cards are encountered, the data to be clocked into a register may indeed change before the clock edge has arrived.

There are many solutions to these types of problems. The most obvious is to add more delay between the output of one register and the input of another. The hard-wired clock signal will surely beat the data propagated through a gate, to the next register for example. This solution is inefficient, however, because it involves additional parts. Another solution is to move the second register's data clock-in time to the middle of the data-valid period of the first register by clocking data into the second register on the falling edge of the clock, as shown in Fig. 6-7(b). The disadvantage to this method is that it could change system timing in an undesirable way due to a 180° phase shift in the output signal.

The simplest way to solve the problem is to run the system clock line in a direction opposite data flow as illustrated in Fig. 6-7(c). There is no possible way for changed data to get to a register before a clock edge because the clock always arrives at the second register before new data is clocked into the first register.

Even if a reversed clock, central timing, or the extra delay method is used to eliminate register-to-register hold-time problems, it is a good idea to check hold times specified for parts, especially if parts of mixed logic families are used.

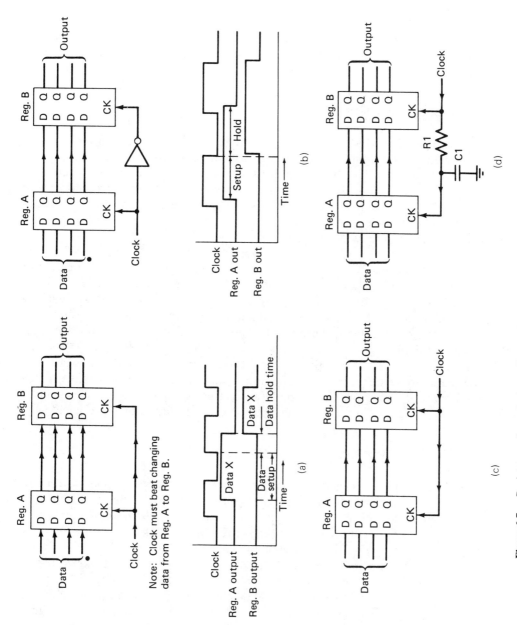

Figure 6-7 Register transfer methods. (a) Simultaneously clocked registers with short data hold time. (b) Out-of-phase clocked registers with equal setup and hold times. (c) Good design practice to ensure that clock reaches Reg. B before Reg. A data changes. (d) Bad design practice that slows clock to Reg. A (should not be used).

261

One practice to be avoided in solving the hold-time problem is the use of a capacitor and resistor to cause some added delay. Figure 6-7(d) illustrates this practice. Logic families have well matched inputs and outputs that allow you to easily build complex circuits. Randomly throwing resistors and capacitors across lines causes impedance mismatches, reduces noise immunity, and adds dangerous noise-generating capabilities to a system.

Replacing Registers with Register Files

Both registers and RAMs have their place in digital design. Registers are well suited for storing single words of data on a temporary basis and can be read and written into simultaneously. Random-access memory is desirable when large blocks of data must be stored on a somewhat less temporary basis. There comes a point in the design of many systems, however, when a bank of registers seems to take up too many packages and the storage requirements are not large enough to fully justify a large RAM.

In these cases it is necessary to look at not only the data storage circuitry, but the control circuitry as well. It usually takes more control circuitry to address, write into, and read data out of a RAM than to simply clock a register. This control circuitry is harder to design and debug and can pose some tricky timing problems if data must be read and written at the same time (a multiport register file can solve this problem). A general rule to follow when deciding to use a multiple register implementation or a highly controlled RAM is: Use the registers if it requires only a few more parts overall (25% is a good figure). Unless the system is a high-volume consumer item with which expense has high priority, or if the circuit module is extremely tight on space, the simpler register scheme will solve the design problem in the fastest, most efficient way.

Interfacing Asynchronous Devices

Data that comes in from devices running on different clocks cannot be directly clocked into a synchronous system. Data transitions from the external device can happen at any time, and if data happens to reach the inputs of a few registers at exactly the same time the synchronized clock does, some registers may correctly receive the data while others may miss it.

Incoming data must be synchronized to a system's master clock before it is sent through the system. This can easily be done with a sampling flip-flop. As the signal enters the system, it should be clocked into a single flip-flop clocked by the system's master clock. With this system there is no chance of the signal being received by some system components and missed by others. If the synchronizer flip-flop misses the signal, the whole system misses it and it will be clocked in on the next pulse.

Commercially available pulse synchronizers such as the 74120 can also be used to "sync up" asynchronous input signals.

The Proper and Improper Use of One-Shots

The monostable multivibrator, or one-shot, is designed to generate controllable-duration pulses when triggered by the rising or falling edge of a trigger clock. In the case of bidirectional one-shots, pulses are generated on both the rising and falling edges of the clock.

One-shots have their place in logic design, but they are probably misused in most designs. There are two main problems with one-shots: they are time-independent of the system clock and tend to set up their own timing reference frames; they tend to trigger by themselves if they encounter even a small amount of noise (they are noise amplifiers).

One-shots should never be used to drive set, clear, or clock inputs of logic devices. Clocking data into a register at the wrong time can result from a falsely triggered one-shot. The practice of not driving clock inputs with anything other than system clocks is consistent with synchronous design practices also.

One-shots should not be used to stretch pulses to meet setup, hold, or standardized times. Because the pulse widths of the one-shots will not change as the system clock varies (due to thermal changes, time drifting, or an intentional system-clock speedup for higher performance), system timing will become faulty at any speed other than the speed the one-shots are tuned for.

In system-timing cases, it is much wiser to produce single pulses with the synchronous "one-pulse" circuit shown in Figure 6-8. This circuit varies appropriately as system clock frequency changes.

There are a few good applications for one-shots. Areas of application include display and interactive interfaces in which an accidental triggering of the one-shot will have no harmful effect on system operation. A one-shot can be used to control the horizontal scan delay on a data terminal character generator, for example, because a false triggering will merely cause a nearly unnoticeable glitch in the image that the viewer sees. The system will operate normally on the next scan line.

Many one-shots have built-in features to help reduce the problem of false triggering, and these features should be used to increase the one-shot's noise immunity. The one-shot illustrated in Fig. 6-8, for example, has two inverted trigger inputs and a master gate that enables the pulse. The AND gate has hysteresis characteristics to increase its noise immunity. This gate can be used to disable the one-shot during noisy periods (the time immediately after the master clock's rising edge) and reduce the chance of false triggering.

PHYSICAL DESIGN GUIDELINES

The design guidelines just presented are surely on a less theoretical level than the architectural concepts of the microcomputer system, but in order to build a good system, it is necessary to go down even one level further — to the

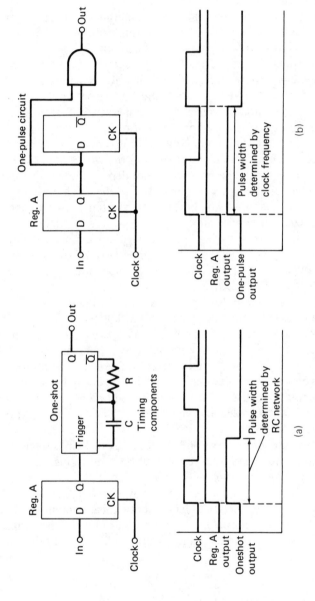

Figure 6-8 Asynchronous and synchronous pulse-generating circuits. (a) One-shot operation (asynchronous). (b) One-pulse circuit and operation (synchronous).

nuts-and-bolts level of computer design. On this level we find topics such as power distribution, transmission line effects, propagation delay analysis, and other nonideal aspects of microcomputers.

Deciphering the Spec Sheet

To supply all the components of a system with their specified values, it is necessary to know what those specified values are. All the data needed to use a device properly can be obtained from the manufacturer's specification sheet. Manufacturers sometimes tend to exaggerate the true capabilities of their parts and cover up the bad features by mentioning them in fine print near the bottom of the sheet. In some cases, disadvantages are turned around to look like advantages. In one case, for example, a large memory manufacturer produced specifications for a 4K RAM and a 16K RAM of similar design. The only difference between the parts was the addition of a chip select line on the 4K version where an address line previously appeared on the 16K part. The 4K RAM spec sheet boasted "chip select line improves design flexibility," while the 16K RAM spec sheet claimed "no chip select line to complicate designs." When reading a spec sheet, you must look beyond the boastful claims and decide what the features and device limitations mean to *your* design.

The propagation delays specified in spec sheets should be used to determine if your designs have large enough timing margins. Propagation delays, often appearing under the title of switching characteristics, are specified in a few ways. Minimum, typical, and maximum times are given, and in some data books these figures will be given at two or three temperatures. The parts received from the manufacturer are only guaranteed to the maximum worst-case propagation time; and if a logic circuit does not work because typical values were used in the design, it is no one's fault but the designer's.

The added propagation delay in a long string of gates with maximum propagation delay versus the same string with typical delay can be substantial (sometimes nearly 2:1).

The same typical–maximum argument applies to current draw and power consumption. The maximum values are the only ones that can be relied on. With power ratings, it is also necessary to consider the external devices needed to make a device work. Typical and even maximum power ratings do not include such items as ECL termination resistors, open-collector pullup resistors, and full driver output on each line. These figures must be considered in addition to the component's rated specifications.

Spec sheets also present temperature data and give operational voltage ranges of their parts. Commercial versions of parts are usually designed to operate between 0 and 70°C. This range can easily be exceeded on a cold winter day or within a warm chassis without proper cooling. In applications destined for outdoor use, such as automotive electronics, military-specification parts must be used. This decision must be made early in the design because the specifications for military parts are sometimes different (usually longer delays) and must be compensated for.

Lack of Statistical Mix

In mass production applications, in an effort to cut costs, it is often thought that typical values (or values somewhere between typical and maximum) are adequate for a large production run. The reasoning is that a probabilistic mix of parts will yield a high percentage (say 90%) of operational units, and the money saved by using less expensive parts will make up the 10% difference many times over. Using this philosophy with semiconductors can have unwanted consequences, unless the manufacturing organization has very close contact with the manufacturer. The major reason for this is the lack of a statistical mix of parts.

Many logic elements, and most microprocessors and memories, come in a number of versions of varying speed. These devices are rarely built especially to be high-performance parts but, rather, are selected from a total yield of parts. The selection process varies from batch to batch, depending on how many parts of which version are needed. If there is currently a surplus of high-speed parts, parts that pass high-speed screening may be marked as slow parts and sold as such. If the supply of high-speed parts is low, all the high-speed parts will be pulled from a batch and sold separately.

In the end, the user who is trying to economize by using low-speed parts may find most of his parts to be typical one day, above average the next, and all at their minimums the third day, depending on how many high-speed parts were pulled from his batch. Figure 6-9 illustrates this situation.

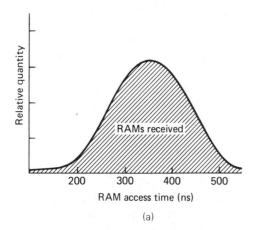
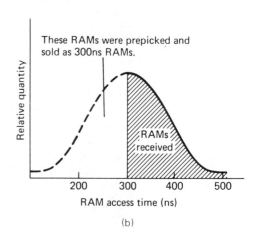

Figure 6-9 The inconsistencies of statistical component calculations. (a) RAMs received from vendor on Week 1. (b) RAMs received from same vendor on Week 2 (production run has been prepicked, upsetting the statistical mix).

Critical-Path Analysis

A system's critical data path is the signal path with the longest propagation delay necessary to proper system operation. This path may be the time it takes a signal to leave a register, go through an ALU, and enter another register; or it may be the time it takes an address to reach RAM and result in a data output. This critical delay path must be determined to insure that the system clock is slow enough to allow proper system operation.

A critical path can be found by tracing all delays through all possible data paths. This method, however, is difficult and time-consuming. The best way to find a critical path is to first look in likely candidate areas. The areas around RAMs and ROMs are usually good candidates. Large arithmetic units and many-leveled gating networks also create critical paths. Direct register-to-register transfers and one- or two-level gating networks can be eliminated from consideration almost immediately. Figure 6-10 illustrates the determination of a critical path.

It is important to use maximum delay values in critical-path analysis.

Power Distribution

Many small integrated circuits drawing a couple of hundred milliamperes apiece can very quickly add up to create current requirements of ten to one hundred amperes. This is particularly true of dense logic such as that found in large memory systems and high-speed–high-power logic designs (ECL designs, for example).

High-current requirements combined with the low-voltage levels at which most logic operates creates power distribution problems. Just a tenth of an ohm resistance in a 10 A, 5 V power-supply line is enough to reduce onchip voltages to 4 V.

Digital parts, by their very nature, turn signals on and off at extremely high frequencies, thereby placing high-frequency current demands on power supply lines. Noise on power supply lines is another one of the most frequent problems in digital systems.

Noise and voltage variation problems in a microcomputer system must be solved using good overall power system design. A high-quality power supply alone is not enough to solve a system's power problems.

The first requirement of a good power distribution system is a solid ground. A system's ground line must sink all the current from all the system's power supplies and is therefore exposed to the highest currents and voltage drops. Because many digital and analog ICs use ground as an absolute voltage reference, it is important to keep it noise-free.

A good grounding system begins at the power supply connections. Low-gage (thick) wires should be used to connect the power supply to the circuit

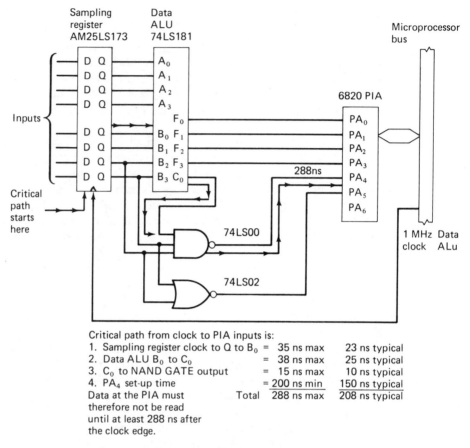

Figure 6-10   Critical path analysis.

board or circuit card cage. Ground lines should be kept short and direct. The connections at which ground enters circuit cards should also be of heavy-duty design. On plug-in circuit cards, it is wise to allocate many pins for ground level, preferably spaced evenly along the connector width.

On circuit cards it is desirable to have a ground plane. This can be either a whole plane of ground metal as a conductor on a multilayer board or a partial plane with conductors and cutaways as necessary on a two- or one-sided board. The idea is to get as much ground conductions to the IC ground pins as possible. A ground plane also helps reduce signal noise and crosstalk between lines separated by it. Figure 6-11 presents good grounding techniques.

In large computer systems it is a common practice to have a power ground and a signal ground. This concept can be used in microcomputers as well to add an extra margin of noise immunity.

Figure 6-12 illustrates a separate power ground and signal ground system. High currents flow through the power ground, and switching noise from high-

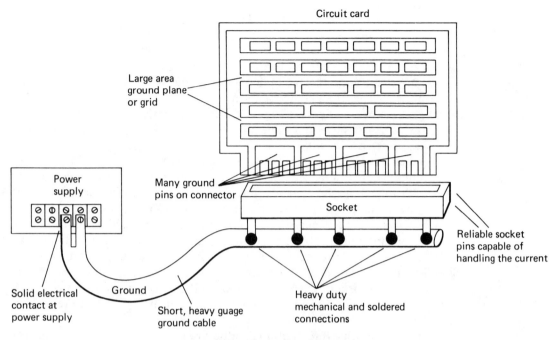

Figure 6-11 Circuit ground practices.

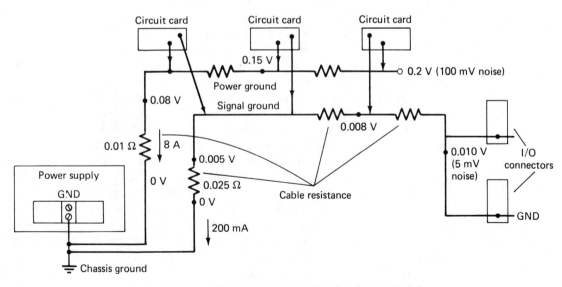

Figure 6-12 The concept of separate signals and power grounds.

frequency current demands is high. Due to the high current flow, ground level is raised to 200 mV and has a 100 mV ripple and noise level. The signal ground, however, is used as a voltage reference instead of a current sink. In this case, only 200 mA of current flows through the signal ground, and ripple is 10 mV. Gates, registers, and other components using the signal ground have 190 mV more noise margin than components using power ground. They are also *exposed* to less noise. Sending signal grounds to peripherals on long, noise-sensitive cables is more desirable than sending power ground because they have less noise to start with.

Sending power forms (+5 V, +12 V, −5.2 V, −15 V, and so on) to circuitry is not quite as critical as sending ground, but the rules of power distribution must still be applied. Heavy power lines, many connector pins for high-current power forms, and power planes for common voltages are desirable.

There are two basic philosophies concerning power regulation: the oncard and the offcard philosophies. Offcard regulation consists of a high-current, precisely voltage-controlled power supply feeding the circuit card or cards directly. The advantages of this method include the need for only one central power regulator circuit, even power application and removal of power to all cards simultaneously, and a reduction of onboard heat that onboard regulators dissipate.

Before monolithic three-terminal voltage regulators became commonplace, offboard regulation was the only available mode. The availability of new IC regulators has allowed the regulation task to be performed on individual cards.

As Fig. 6-13 illustrates, the power forms feeding the cards are unregulated and higher in voltage than required. Onboard regulation therefore simplifies power supply design and entirely removes the regulator from the central supply. It does, however, increase overall system complexity because each card must have a regulator. The primary disadvantage of onboard regulators is the heat they generate and the necessity for associated onboard heatsinks. Onboard regulated cards cannot be packed as closely together in a card cage due to heatsink height.

Cards using onboard regulation tend to be "safer" cards. Onboard regulators have built-in current limiters; an oncard short circuit will cause them to limit at about half an ampere of current. Circuit cards fed directly by a 100 A power supply can literally go up in smoke if a short circuit occurs.

Whether onboard or offboard regulation is used, it is good to put a filter capacitor at the power input of every card as shown in Fig. 6-13. Small (10–100 μF) electrolytic and tantalum capacitors are ideal in this application. Sudden current demands can be supplied by these capacitors, thereby reducing the noise and ohmic power-line drops caused by current spikes.

Very fast current spikes caused by totem-pole driver switching cannot be eliminated by one large capacitor on a circuit card. Current spikes in the hundreds-of-picoseconds range are over before they even have time to propagate through the power and ground plane to the filter capacitor. These high-

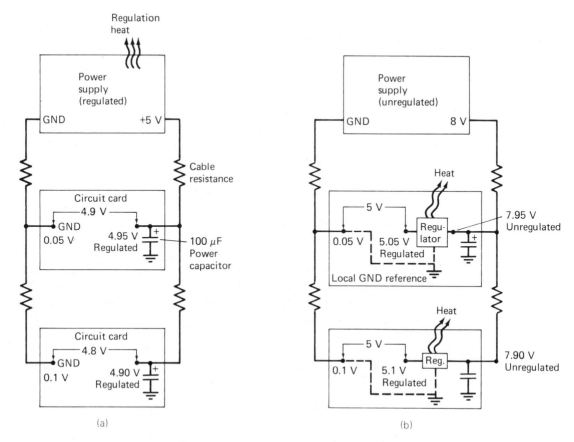

Figure 6-13 (a) Central and (b) onboard voltage regulation.

speed current spikes can be successfully damped on circuit boards using *decoupling* capacitors. Many small capacitors (typically 0.01 to 0.1 μF) should be spread evenly around circuit cards using the general rule of *1 capacitor for every 4 ICs* for standard TTL. Other logic families require different decoupling capacitor spreads, which can be found in manufacturers' applications manuals. ECL designs need few decoupling capacitors because they do not use totempole outputs; CMOS requires few due to its noise immunity and low current draw.

A power supply, like any other device, can fail. Ideally, when a power supply does fail, it will do so in such a way that voltage and current output will drop; but in some cases the voltage will go wildly out of control. It is wise to protect a microcomputer system's logic circuitry against such a catastrophe. Overvoltage protection (OVP) circuits serve this purpose. Figure 6-14 illustrates two OVP circuits. The first circuit is good for low-current power supplies. Simple zener diodes mounted on each card's power-form inputs will limit input voltage to a safe value. A 5.5 V zener for a 5 V supply is a good choice. The zener diode also offers reverse-voltage protection. If a -5 V level is accidentally applied to the circuit instead of $+5$ V, the zener will limit the reverse voltage to -700 mV (one diode drop), saving the logic circuitry.

The zener diode OVP circuit can be used in a second mode. If the power line being protected carries too much current to effectively limit with a zener, a zener diode that is rated far below the power lines current can be chosen to protect the circuit. When voltage surges over the zener's value, the diode will burn out (break down), causing a direct short circuit across the power supply, thereby blowing the fuse. (Needless to say, the line being protected should have a fuse.)

A better OVP circuit is shown in Fig. 6-14(b). The OVP "crowbar" consists of a zener diode that triggers an SCR to short out the power supply. This circuit has the advantage that it is not self-destructive (unlike the zener-breakdown OVP), and it is adjustable. Perfectionists are often tempted to adjust an OVP crowbar to a hair's width above the supply voltage. This practice should be avoided because the slightest bit of power-supply noise is enough to falsely trigger a sensitive crowbar. A rule-of-thumb for crowbar adjustment is 10% of the supply voltage plus 1 V. A 5 V power supply should have a 6.5 V crowbar, a 12 V circuit a 14.2 V crowbar, and so on.

Clock Distribution

The master clock lines are among the most important signals in a microcomputer system. They have very high fan-outs because they drive many registers, flip-flops, and interface components and because their routing is important (it should be opposite the data flow through registers). A synchronous system's reliability is based on the premise that a noise-free, well shielded clock is available.

Clocks should be run as far from data buses as possible, and they should be separated by a strip of ground plane if possible. It is also a good idea to put the

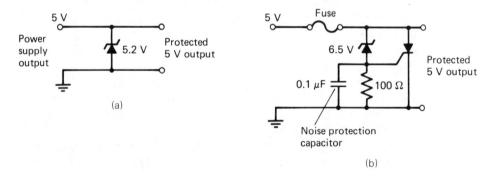

Figure 6-14   Overvoltage protection circuits. (a) Zener-diode voltage limiter. (b) SCR OVP "crowbar" fuse blower.

clock pin on a module connector between two ground pins to reduce crosstalk between pins. In large system applications it is a common practice to send clock signals from module to module using differential drivers and receivers connected with balanced twisted pairs of wire or shielded cable.

Clock line lengths should also be controlled as tightly as possible. Extra cable on the computer's backplane should be added to match the clock's signal propagation distances to all cards. In some cases a clock signal can be strung from module to module, but register data-flow direction must first be determined, then opposed.

Because clock lines typically have high fan-out, high-current buffers should be used to drive them.

Unused Input and Output Pins

In applications in which inputs and outputs that serve no useful purpose are left over after a logic design is complete, it is bad design practice to leave the inputs and outputs free-floating. Floating inputs can act as antennas and cause gates and flip-flops to accidentally preset, clear, or generate noise. Open outputs can cause unbalanced current draws in some logic families.

In TTL, inputs will float to high (logic 1 state if left open). For this reason, most inputs that are unlikely to be used in many applications (such as preset, clear, and enable lines) are inverted. A flip-flop with inverted preset and clear inputs, for example, acts as if the preset and clear lines are turned off when nothing is connected to the input pins. Just to be sure the inputs on unused input pins remain at logic 1 levels, it is a good idea to clamp them to +5 V either directly or through a mild (1000 ohms) pullup resistor. The resistor is a precaution against high current caused by power-line spikes, and one resistor can be used to drive about 10 inputs.

If an open TTL input must have a logic 0 level to make a part operational, the input can be tied directly to ground.

Open-circuit ECL inputs float to a logic 0. Internal input pulldown resistors insure that an open pin will remain below the low threshold level. Open ECL inputs that must be clamped to a logic 1 level can be either tied to the output of a gate generating a logic 1 or tied to ground through a silicon diode. Current must flow through the diode in the forward direction to insure a voltage level of −700 mV at the input.

In large systems it is desirable to terminate unused ECL outputs in order to balance the current draw of gates and flip-flops. Because ECL generates no totem-pole transients when it switches logic states, the only power-supply noise is caused by devices switching from driving a load to not driving a load. Because most ECL gates have complementary as well as true outputs, it is possible to eliminate switching noise by terminating an equal number of inverting and noninverting outputs on gates and flip-flops. This principle is used on all the circuitry in one of the most powerful mainframe computers in existence: the *Cray One* (by Cray Research, Chippewa Falls, Wisconsin). This mainframe runs essentially noise-free due to its balanced ECL design. One note of caution is in order concerning balanced ECL: If MSI and LSI ECL parts are used, there are most likely unbalanced gates inside packages. It is impossible to terminate these gates, so balanced design is not possible using these parts.

MOS inputs should always be tied to a logic 0 or logic 1. MOS lines will float between logic 1 and 0 due to their high impedance and may actually be damaged by static charge if they are left open. When inputs to MOS devices go to an edge connector of a circuit card, shunt resistors should be connected to V_{DD} or V_{SS} to avoid static damage and noise generation when the inputs become unterminated with the power supply on.

Transmission Line Effects

One of the primary sources of noise in a microcomputer system is transmission-line noise caused by improperly terminated lines and mismatched driver-line impedances. When designing a system, it is important to specify terminations and line impedances according to the manufacturer's recommendations for the logic family being used.

One of the most common misconceptions concerning transmission lines is that low-frequency lines need not be terminated because low-frequency signals generate very little noise. The error in this reasoning is that noise generation depends on waveform as well as frequency. It is *transition time* rather than *frequency* that determines noise generation, and *square waves have fast rise times,* whether they are at 50 MHz or 50 Hz. It is therefore the logic family that determines noise generation, not the frequency at which it is run.

Regular, low-power, and low-power Schottky TTL and CMOS have relatively slow rise times, and even poor impedance matching and the lack of ground planes do not have too great an effect on circuit operation. Generally, obeying good power supply and clock distribution, keeping leads as short as possible, and adequately decoupling TTL circuitry is all that is necessary to keep transmission-line noise at a minimum.

Emitter-coupled logic and Schottky TTL, however, are a different matter. The Motorola MECL 10,000 series of ECL parts are specifically designed to provide low propagation delays as well as slow rise times, and although they can run at higher frequencies than Schottky TTL, they generate less noise. Schottky TTL's noise problem is compounded by totem-pole output spikes. For these two logic families it is necessary to use proper termination resistors and impedance-matched transmission lines as well as good power and clock distribution practices. Manufacturers' literature clearly outlines procedures for working with high-speed logic and should be followed for best results.

Microcomputer backplanes or motherboards are very prone to detrimental transmission line effects due to the large number of signal sources (bus drivers) and stubs (card connectors) on each line. Some buses have provisions to reduce these effects through impedance matching. The PDP-11 *Unibus* and LSI-11 bus are two examples of open-collector buses that have impedance-matched termination resistors.

Memory System Design

Memory system design poses a number of problems not encountered in the design of discrete microcomputer logic. Densely packed arrays of identical memory chips, row after row of parallel address and data lines, and high-voltage, fast-rise-time MOS driver lines tend to cause extensive noise, power-distribution, and crosstalk problems. Memory interface parts add delay and timing uncertainties to memory designs. It is therefore important to take precautions to reduce noise and crosstalk as well as make sure that cumulative propagation delay is taken into account.

The following general rules should be followed in memory system design:

1. Make sure enough drivers are used to drive address and data lines.

2. Use a good power distribution system with heavy grounds and an adequate number of decoupling capacitors.

3. Run high-voltage, high-current MOS driver lines perpendicular to address and data lines to reduce crosstalk. (On two-sided boards this is accomplished by using perpendicular conductors on opposite sides of the board.)

4. Obey all memory timing requirements. Most components are specified quite conservatively, but due to the competition in the memory market, memories are specified right to the limit. A 500 ns memory IC, for example, could start causing problems at 490 ns access times.

A number of books entirely devoted to memory design exist and should be consulted if very large memory systems are to be built. You should consult large, well-known memory manufacturers, such as Intel, for up-to-date memory application information.

Interfacing to Standard Buses and Peripherals

Mass production and standardization are the two factors most responsible for the wide availability and low cost of microcomputers. Mass-produced microprocessors, RAMs, interfaces, and discrete components spread expensive overhead and development costs among millions of economically priced parts, while standardized microcomputer buses encourage the development of peripherals and computer add-ons. Standardization is an evolutionary process. Standards are written and introduced into the electronics industry and marketplace by electronics organizations and individual companies, but it is ultimately the public who decides which standards survive and which die. Many times, well-developed standards have failed to take hold while haphazardly defined ones have thrived. In the end, it is down-to-earth practicality and utility rather than theoretical perfection and years-ahead conceptualization that makes a standard desirable.

A standard's popularity tends to build on itself. As a standard microcomputer bus gets popular, manufacturers develop many peripherals and add-ons to meet the market demand, and the market demand increases because of the wide availability of products.

We will discuss a few of the most popular microcomputer buses in this section. Data communication standards and common peripherals will also be covered.

THE FORMATION OF STANDARDS

There are two types of standards: proclaimed and *de facto*. Proclaimed standards are standards that are reasoned out and officially established by electronics associations such as the Institute of Electrical and Electronics Engineers (IEEE) or the Electronic Industries Association (EIA). These organizations attempt to "design standards to serve the public interest through eliminating misunderstandings between manufacturers and purchasers, facilitate interchangeability and improve products, and assist the purchaser in selecting and obtaining with minimum delay the proper product for his particular needs."* Proclaimed standards tend to be extremely well defined with next to no ambiguities or loopholes. The IEEE 488 instrument bus, EIA RS-232C, and IEEE-583 CAMAC interface system are examples of proclaimed standards. Standardizing associations are at the mercy of the manufacturers in regard to bus implementation, because these organizations do not build computers.

What we refer to as de facto standards are interface methods that gained popularity through widespread use without being officially defined. Whenever a manufacturer introduces a new microcomputer bus, a candidate for a de facto standard is generated. Unlike proclaimed standards, no official definition is available (unless the manufacturer had the foresight to generate one); peripheral device manufacturers do the best they can to figure out how signals are supposed to be used, and use them accordingly. The problem with this interfacing approach is the lack of compatibility of devices designed for the same bus. The S-100 microcomputer bus is a prime example of a de facto standard that has caused many compatibility problems. The Digital Equipment Corporation's PDP-11 *Unibus* and LSI-11 bus as well as Teletype's 60 mA and 20 mA *current-loop* standards are examples of well defined de facto standards.

MICROCOMPUTER BUS STANDARDS

In microcomputing's short history, many bus standards have come and gone. In many cases the buses were found to be cumbersome and hard to work with, and in some cases the company supplying the buses went out of business. A few of these standards, however, have become very popular. The S-100 bus originally appeared on the MITS Altair computer and subsequently on the IMSAI 8080 system. The SS50 bus was originally incorporated in Southwest Technical Products' 6800 system. These and the LSI-11 bus are currently the three most popular microcomputer buses. Three buses that are gaining in popularity at this time are the IEEE 488 bus featured in the Commodore *Pet,* the TRS-80 bus incorporated into the Radio Shack TRS-80 system, and the *Apple*

*Quote from the front page of an EIA RS-232C standard document.

277

II peripheral bus found on the Apple II microcomputer. The high sales volume of these systems is aiding the popularity of these buses.

The S-100 Bus

The S-100 bus is a 100-line bus originally designed to be used with the Intel 8080 microprocessor. Many of the signals are similar in name and function to those coming directly out of an 8080. This bus has gained wide popularity because it was the first inexpensive microcomputer bus, and hundreds of peripheral cards, including memories, terminal interfaces, graphics units, and speech synthesizers, are available for it.

The S-100 bus is very poorly defined. Until recently there was no official definition concerning how the signals were intended to be used. Many compatibility problems between S-100 bus processor cards and peripherals are caused by interface designers' misunderstandings of bus line functions. Status lines as well as control lines are sent along the bus, and many S-100 peripheral cards use the status lines as control signals. The greatest incompatibilities arise when microprocessors other than the 8080 are used with the bus. A wide selection of Z80, 6800, and 6502 processor cards that mimic the 8080's control signals are now available, and most of them cannot produce the 8080's signals completely correctly.

This bus takes the onboard regulation approach to power distribution. Two ground lines (there would have been more on a professionally specified bus), two unregulated 8 V power lines (to supply 5 V regulators), and single unregulated +16 V and −16 V lines (to supply ±12 V regulators) are used.

The S-100 bus has become so popular that an official specification for it is being written by the microprocessor standards committee of the IEEE Computer Society. Perhaps this standard will reduce compatibility problems on future products. There may be a few slight changes in the final specification, but all the signal line functions are quite firmly established and the I/O cycles (Fig. 7-1) will work with most properly designed equipment. (Chapter 4 of this text should be referenced for explanations of I/O terms and methods.)

Table 7-1 lists the S-100 bus signals and their assigned functions and names.

The SS50 Bus

Southwest Technical Products Company's 6800 computer system was one of the first microcomputers to gain wide popularity. This system is based on the 6800 microprocessor and follows Motorola's design suggestions very closely. A few characteristics that helped make this machine popular were: high reliability, low cost, no audible noise (this unit is convection cooled), and good software support.

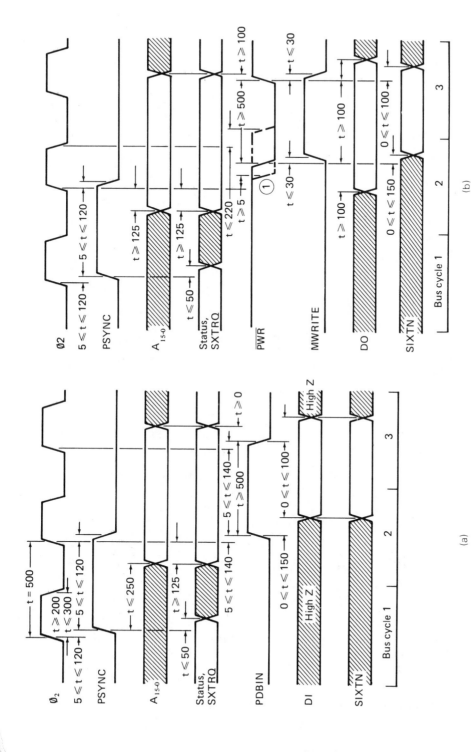

Figure 7-1   S-100 bus input and output timing. (a) Memory or I/O read. (b) Memory or I/O write.

Table 7-1 IEEE S100 Microcomputer Bus Standard (Proposed)

Pin #	Signal Name and Type	Polarity	
1	+8 volts (B)[1]		Instantaneous minimum greater than 7 volts, instantaneous maximum less than volts, average maximum less than volts.
2	+16 volts (B)		Instantaneous minimum greater than 14 volts, instantaneous maximum less than 35 volts, average maximum less than 20 volts.
3	XRDY (S)[1,10]	positive	One of two ready inputs to the current Bus Master. The bus is ready when both these ready inputs are true.
4	$\overline{VI}_0$ (S)[10]	negative	Vectored interrupt line $\emptyset$.
5	$\overline{VI}_1$ (S)[10]	,,	,, 1.
6	$\overline{VI}_2$ (S)[10]	,,	,, 2.
7	$\overline{VI}_3$ (S)[10]	,,	,, 3.
8	$\overline{VI}_4$ (S)[10]	,,	,, 4.
9	$\overline{VI}_5$ (S)[10]	,,	,, 5.
10	$\overline{VI}_6$ (S)[10]	,,	,, 6.
11	$\overline{VI}_7$ (S)[10]	,,	,, 7.
12	—	—	Not specified.
13	—	—	,,
14	—	—	,,
15	—	—	,,
16	—	—	,,
17	—	—	,,
18	$\overline{\text{STAT DSB}}$ (M)[1,10]	negative	The control signal to disable the 8 status signals[2].
19	$\overline{\text{C/C DSB}}$ (M)[10]	,,	The control signal to disable the 6 command/control signal[3].
20	UNPROT	—	Not specified.
21	SS		Not specified.
22	$\overline{\text{ADD DSB}}$ (M)[10]	negative	The control signal to disable the 16 address signals[4].
23	$\overline{\text{DO DSB}}$ (M)[10]	,,	The control signal to disable the 8 data output[5] signals.
24	ϕ_2 (B)	positive	The master timing signal for the bus.
25	ϕ_1		Not specified.
26	PHLDA (M)	positive	A command/control signal used in conjunction with PHOLD to coordinate Bus Master transfer operations.
27	PWAIT (M)	,,	The acknowledge signal to either of the bus ready signals XRDY, PRDY or to a HLT instruction.
28	PINTE	,,	Not specified.
29	A5 (M)	,,	Address bit 5.
30	A4 (M)	,,	Address bit 4.

Table 7-1 (continued)

Pin #	Signal Name and Type	Polarity	
31	A3 (M)	,,	Address bit 3.
32	A15 (M)	,,	Address bit 15 (most significant).
33	A12 (M)	,,	Address bit 12.
34	A9 (M)	,,	Address bit 9.
35	D01 (M)/EA1 (M)/DATA1 (M/S)	,,	Data out bit 1, Extended address bit 1, Bidirectional data bit 1.
36	D00 (M)/EA0 (M)/DATA0 (M/S)	,,	Data out bit $\emptyset$, Extended address with bit $\emptyset$, Bidirectional data bit $\emptyset$ (least significant)
37	A10 (M)	,,	Address bit 10.
38	D04 (M)	positive	Data out bit 4.
39	D05 (M)	,,	,, 5.
40	D06 (M)	,,	,, 6.
41	D12 (M)	,,	Data in[6] bit 2.
42	D13 (M)	,,	Data in bit 3.
43	D17 (M)	,,	Data in bit 7 (most significant).
44	SM1 (M)	,,	The status signal which indicates that the current bus cycly[7] is an op-code fetch.
45	SOUT (M)	,,	The status signal identifying the data transfer bus cycle of an OUT instruction.
46	SINP (M)	,,	The status signal identifying the data transfer bus cycle of an IN instruction.
47	SMEMR (M)	,,	The status signal identifying bus cycles which transfer data from memory to a Bus Master which are not interrupt acknowledge instruction fetch cycle(s).
48	SHLTA (M)	,,	The status signals which acknowledges that a HLT instruction has been executed. that a HLT instruction has been executed.
49	CLOCK	—	Not specified.
50	GND		Signal and power ground.
51	+8 volts (B)		See comments above for pin #1.
52	−16 volts (B)		Instantaneous maximum less than −14. volts, instantaneous maximum greater than −35 bolts, average minimum greater than −20 volts.
53	SSWI	—	Not specified.
54	EXT CLR	negative	A reset signal to reset Bus Slaves. When this signal goes low, it must stay low for at least 3 bus states.
55	—	—	Not specified.
56	—	—	,,
57	—	—	,,

Table 7-1 (continued)

Pin #	Signal Name and Type	Polarity	
58	—	—	Not specified.
59	$\overline{\text{SXTRQ}}$ (M)	negative	Master signal which requests 16 bit wide slaves to respond by asserting SXTN.
60	—	—	Not specified.
61	$\overline{\text{SXTN}}$ (S)	negative	The signal generated by 16 bit slaves in response to the 16 bit request signal SXTRQ.
62	—	—	Not specified.
63	—	—	,,
64	—	—	,,
65	—	—	,,
66	—	—	,,
67	$\overline{\text{PHANTOM}}$ (B)	negative	A bus signal which disables normal slave devices and enables phantom slaves — primarily used for bootstrapping systems without hardware front panels.
68	MWRITE (B)	positive	The logical negation of PWR and SOUT; this signal must follow PWR by not more than 30 ns.
69	$\overline{\text{PS}}$	—	Not specified.
70	PORT	—	,,
71	RUN	—	,,
72	PRDY (S)[10]	positive	See comments above for pin #3.
73	$\overline{\text{PINT}}$ (S)[10]	negative	The primary interrupt request bus signal.
74	$\overline{\text{PHOLD}}$ (M)[10]	,,	The command/control signal used in conjunction with PHLDA to coordinate Bus Master transfer operations.
75	$\overline{\text{PRESET}}$ (B)[10]	,,	The reset signal to reset Bus Master devices. When this signal goes low, it must stay low for at least 3 bus states.
76	PSYNC (M)	positive	The command/control signal identifying BS_1. (See bus states comments.)
77	$\overline{\text{PWR}}$ (M)	negative	The command/control signal signifying the presence of valid data on the DO bus[8].
78	PDBIN (M)	positive	The command/control signal that requests data on the DI bus[9] from the currently addressed slave.
79	A$\emptyset$ (M)	,,	Address bit $\emptyset$ (least significant).
80	A1 (M)	,,	Address bit 1.
81	A2 (M)	,,	,, 2.
82	A6 (M)	,,	,, 6.
83	A7 (M)	,,	,, 7.
84	A8 (M)	,,	,, 8.

Table 7-1 (continued)

Pin #	Signal Name and Type	Polarity	
85	A13 (M)	,,	,, 13.
86	A14 (M)	,,	,, 14.
87	A11 (M)	,,	,, 11.
88	D02 (M)/A8 (M)/DATA2 (M/S)	positive	Data out bit 2, extended address bit 2, & bidirectional data bit 2.
89	D03 (M)/A19 (M)/DATA3 (M/S)	,,	Data out bit 3, extended address bit 3, & bidirectional data bit 3.
90	D07 (M)/A23 (M)/DATA7 (M/S)	,,	Data out bit 7, extended address bit 7, & bidirectional data bit 7 (most significant).
91	D14 (S)/DATA12 (M/S)	positive	Data in bit 4 & bidirectional data bit 12.
92	D15 (S)/DATA13 (M/S)	,,	Data in bit 5 & bidirectional data bit 13.
93	D16 (S)/DATA14 (M/S)	positive	Data in bit 6 & bidirectional data bit 14.
94	D11 (S)/DATA9 (M/S)	positive	Data in bit 1 & bidirectional data bit 9.
95	D1∅ (S)/DATA8 (M/S)	positive	Data in bit ∅ & bidirectional data bit 8.
96	SINTA (M)	,,	The status signal identifying the instruction fetch cycle(s) that immediately follow and accepted interrupt request presented on PINT.
97	$\overline{\text{SWO}}$ (M)	negative	The status signal identifying a bus cycle which transfers data from a Bus Master to a slave.
98	SSTACK		Not specified.
99	$\overline{\text{POC}}$ (B)	negative	The power-on clear signal for all bus devices; when this signal goes low, it must stay low for at least 3 bus states.
100	GND		Signal and power ground.

Adapted from table by the IEEE Computer Society Microprocessor Standards Committee.

A number of manufacturers, including Smoke Signal Broadcasting, Midwest Scientific, and Percom, are currently supporting this bus.

The SS50 bus is actually two buses. A large 50-line bus is used for large processor and memory cards, and a smaller 30-line bus (which is a subset of the 50-line bus) is used for peripheral interface cards. All the address lines are removed from the peripheral bus and are replaced by single peripheral select lines driven by a decoder circuit built onto the motherboard.

The SS50 motherboard is unconventional. It consists of rows of 50 vertical Molex-connector pins soldered to the printed-circuit motherboard. In the rear of the 6800 chassis, rows of 30 vertical pins for the peripheral cards run perpendicular to the larger cards. The peripheral selection logic along with a voltage regulator is mounted in the center of the motherboard. The whole motherboard snaps in and out of the 6800's aluminum case.

Electrically, the SS50 bus is nearly identical to the 6800 microprocessor's signals with a few power supply and baud rate clock frequencies thrown in for easy interfacing.

There are no official numbers for the SS50's pins, and the signal names are marked directly on the motherboard.

50-Pin Bus (from left to right)	
Data bus $\overline{D0}$–$\overline{D7}$	—8-bit data bus
Address bus A15–A0	—16-bit address bus
Ground pins	—3 ground pins are used
+8 V unregulated	—3 unregulated power pins are used
−12 V	—Unregulated; can vary from −12 to −15 V
+12 V	—Unregulated; can vary from 12 to 15 V
Index	—Card index pin. Filled with plastic.
$\overline{\text{M.RST}}$	—Master reset. Connected to front panel switch.
$\overline{\text{NMI}}$	—Nonmasked interrupt
$\overline{\text{IRQ}}$	—Interrupt request
UD1 and UD2	—Two undefined lines
phase 2	—6800 clock, $\emptyset2$
$\overline{\text{VMA}}$	—Valid memory address
R/$\overline{\text{W}}$	—Read–write line
$\overline{\text{Reset}}$	—Clean, processed reset signal
BA	—Bus available
phase 1	—6800 clock, $\emptyset1$
$\overline{\text{HALT}}$	—Processor halt
110,150,300,600,1200	—Baud rate output pins

30-Pin Bus (from back to front)	
UD3 and UD4	—Undefined lines
−12 V, +12 V, 2 grounds	—4 power lines
Index	—Card index pin
$\overline{\text{NMI}}$, $\overline{\text{IRQ}}$	—Interrupt request lines
RS0, RS1	—2-bit register select code
D0–D7	—8 data lines
R/$\overline{\text{W}}$	—Read–write
8 V unregulated	—2 power lines
1200,600,300,150,110	—Baud lines
$\overline{\text{RESET}}$	—Interface reset lines
I/O #	—I/O device select line (decoded by motherboard)

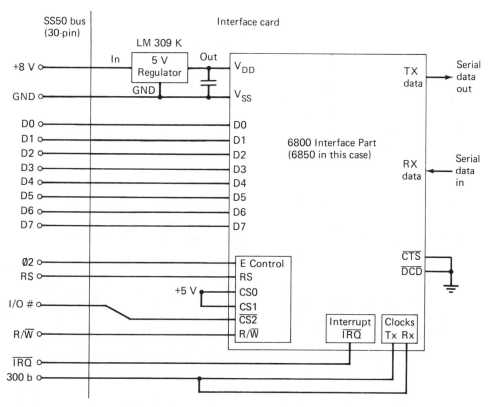

Figure 7-2   SS50 bus interface.

Interfacing to the 50-pin bus is nearly identical to interfacing to a 6800 microprocessor bus. A 6800 microprocessor application manual can be used as a timing guideline. The baud lines can be used whenever data communication frequencies are called for.

Interfacing to the 30-pin bus is even simpler than interfacing to the 50-pin bus because the address decoding is already performed by the motherboard. A serial interface, for example, can consist of just two parts: an ACIA and a voltage regulator. Figure 7-2 illustrates an SS50 interface.

The LSI-11 Bus

The Digital Equipment Corporation's LSI-11 series of microcomputers is based on the PDP-11 minicomputer system that preceded it. The LSI-11 is very much like a PDP-11 in its register and memory operational formats, and the LSI-11

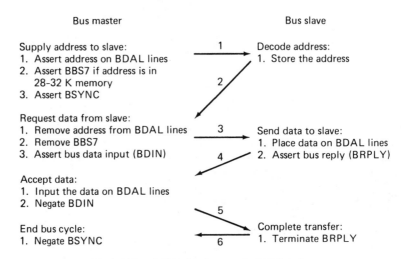

Figure 7-3   LSI-11 data input cycle (DATI cycle).

can even be equipped with an extended instruction set and floating-point instruction set option. The LSI-11 bus (sometimes called the Q-bus) is quite a bit different from the PDP-11's Unibus, however. The general philosophy of the Unibus remains the same, but the number of bus lines has been greatly reduced through the use of a multiplexed address and data bus.

The LSI-11 bus is an asynchronous, 16-bit transfer-oriented bus. Data transfer is based on handshaking between devices, and no master clock lines are used. This feature allows a wide range of different-speed peripherals to be placed on the bus. The bus also has a number of sophisticated features not normally found in a microcomputer. A *power available* (BPOK H) and *dc power available* (BDCOK H) line from the power supply are meant to automatically reset the processor as power is applied and to initiate a power failure routine (save registers in nonvolatile memory such as core) when the power gets too low. This power fail–restart is a standard feature on most large mainframes.

The LSI-11 bus uses central voltage regulation. Regulated +5, +12, and −12 V are available, and 8 ground pins are allocated to each card.

The LSI-11 system uses very sophisticated bus communication methods, card mounting methods, signal pin labeling, and card designs that are carried down from DEC's larger computers. Anyone who is used to working with DEC hardware will feel comfortable with the LSI-11. The 800-page *Microcomputer Handbook,* published by DEC, is a good source of information concerning DEC design philosophy and LSI-11 particulars.

Figure 7-3 shows a typical LSI-11 bus input transfer. The master device (processor or DMA device) is reading data from a slave device (memory or input interface). The address and data are sent over the same set of signal lines

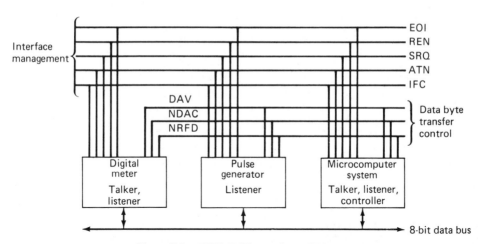

Figure 7-4 IEEE 488/Commodore PET bus.

(BDALO-15). The handshaking on the bus insures that data is received, but it also slows down the data transfer. The LSI-11 bus is therefore not a very fast communication bus.

The IEEE 488 Bus

The IEEE 488 bus was initially designed to be an electronics instrument interface bus. This bus has been used extensively by electronics instrument manufacturers, and Hewlett-Packard makes extensive use of it in computers as well as instruments. The IEEE 488 bus is sometimes called the HPIB (Hewlett-Packard interface bus).

The IEEE 488 bus is of considerable interest in the microcomputer field because of its use in the *Pet* microcomputer by Commodore. This microcomputer is destined to become one of the most popular microcomputers, and many peripherals will eventually be built around it. Interface users should be cautioned that the 488 bus interface handshaking protocol is patented by Hewlett-Packard and a license is required to manufacture devices incorporating it.

The 488 bus is an asynchronous, handshaking-oriented bus and uses communication protocols that are similar to the LSI-11 bus. Instead of master and slave devices, however, "talkers," "listeners," and "controllers" are used. Devices can each contain talker or listener circuitry, and one controller is enough for a whole system. Talkers send data to listeners under control of the controller. A microprocessor card can act as a controller, talker, and listener and can send data to listener-controlled pulse generators or read data from a listener-controlled digital meter, for example. Figure 7-4 illustrates a typical IEEE 488 bus configuration.

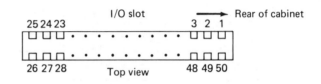

Pin	Signal	Pin	Signal
1	I/O SELECT	30	IRQ
18	R/W	31	RES
19	n.c.	32	INH
20	I/O STROBE	33	−12 V
21	RDY	34	−5 V
22	DMA	35	n.c.
23	INT OUT	36	7M
24	DMA OUT	37	Q3
25	+5 V	38	Phase one
26	GND	39	User one
27	DMA IN	40	Phase zero
28	INT IN	41	Device select
29	NMI	50	+12 V

Figure 7-5   Apple II I/O slot signals.

The Apple II Bus

The Apple II microcomputer does not have a full-featured bus as do the LSI-11, SS50, and S-100 machines. Because this microcomputer is essentially a one-card microcomputer with built-in memory, keyboard interface, audio interface, and video generator, it does not really need one. A row of eight 50-pin connectors for external peripherals is incorporated into the system card, however, to add expandability to the system. Printers, disk drives, and other peripherals can be interfaced to the Apple II using these interface slots. Figure 7-5 shows the pinout for an I/O slot.

Interfacing to the I/O slot is quite simple. Synchronous bus transfers using 16 address, 8 data, and a few control lines are performed in typical microprocessor fashion. The I/O slot closely resembles the 6502's bus that drives it. An interface can easily be built by reading the signal descriptions and using the proper signals to perform the required I/O functions.

Power lines   —The Apple II can supply small amounts of +5, −5, +12, and −12 V for interface use. In large peripherals it is advisable to have a separate power supply, however, because current is limited.

Address lines	—A0–A15; a 16-bit address becomes valid on these lines 300 ns after the beginning of the ∅1 clock. Each address line can drive 16 TTL loads.
Data lines	—D0–D7; during write cycles data is available 300 ns after the beginning of the ∅2 clock. Data must be ready 100 ns before the end of the ∅2 clock during reads. These lines can drive 8 low-powered Schottky loads.
Device select	—A read or write to one of 16 peripheral addresses assigned to a slot will assert this signal during clock ∅2. Up to 4 standard TTL loads per I/O socket are allowed.
DMA	—This direct memory access control output should be driven with an open-collector driver.
DMA IN and DMA OUT	—A DMA priority system uses these lines in a daisy-chain fashion. DMA IN accepts signals from higher priority devices, while DMA OUT sends to lower priority ones.
INH	—This line can be pulled low by an open-collector driver to inhibit all internal ROMs.
INT IN and INT OUT	—Interrupt daisy-chain lines that follow the same convention as the DMA lines.
I/O select	—This line will go low during clock ∅2 if data is written to or read from any of the 256 addresses assigned to the peripheral connector.
I/O strobe	—This line goes low during ∅2 if memory locations C800 to CFFF are accessed.
IRQ	—This line will halt the microprocessor when driven low with an open-collector driver. This line should be submitted during ∅1 time.
RES	—Goes low when the keyboard's reset button is pushed.
R/W	—This line means read when high and write when low.
∅0	—Microprocessor "phase zero" clock.
∅1	—Complement of ∅0.
7M	—General-purpose 7 MHz clock.

Further information concerning the Apple II bus can be obtained from the Apple II reference manual. Literature pertaining to the 6502 is also helpful when working with this bus.

The TRS-80 Bus

The TRS-80 microcomputer, sold by Radio Shack, is the best-selling microcomputer in the world. Its wide success is attributed to its low cost, vast media exposure, and large distribution network. The TRS-80, like the Apple II, is basically a single-board microcomputer, but an expansion bus connector is built into the TRS-80 instead of many peripheral interface slots. This 40-pin bus is designed to plug into the nearest peripheral, which in turn plugs into yet another peripheral. The bus therefore daisy-chains itself between peripherals.

Figure 7-6 depicts the TRS-80 bus pinout. Because the TRS-80 uses dynamic memory and the Z80 microprocessor's automatic RAM refreshing system, bus lines for row and column select lines on dense 16K RAMs are provided.

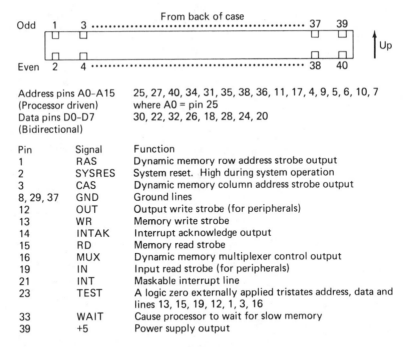

Address pins A0–A15   25, 27, 40, 34, 31, 35, 38, 36, 11, 17, 4, 9, 5, 6, 10, 7
(Processor driven)   where A0 = pin 25
Data pins D0–D7   30, 22, 32, 26, 18, 28, 24, 20
(Bidirectional)

Pin	Signal	Function
1	RAS	Dynamic memory row address strobe output
2	SYSRES	System reset. High during system operation
3	CAS	Dynamic memory column address strobe output
8, 29, 37	GND	Ground lines
12	OUT	Output write strobe (for peripherals)
13	WR	Memory write strobe
14	INTAK	Interrupt acknowledge output
15	RD	Memory read strobe
16	MUX	Dynamic memory multiplexer control output
19	IN	Input read strobe (for peripherals)
21	INT	Maskable interrupt line
23	TEST	A logic zero externally applied tristates address, data and lines 13, 15, 19, 12, 1, 3, 16
33	WAIT	Cause processor to wait for slow memory
39	+5	Power supply output

Figure 7-6   Radio Shack TRS-80 bus signals.

SERIAL DATA COMMUNICATION STANDARDS

Although most peripherals such as terminals, line printers, and modems are designed to transfer characters of data in the form of the American Standard Code for Information Interchange (ASCII), data is rarely sent to these peripherals as parallel bytes. Due to the slow-speed nature of these devices and the long cable requirements for remote peripherals, serial data transfer is used almost exclusively. Two very popular standards are used in nearly every computer terminal that uses serial communication: the EIA RS-232C standard and the 20 mA current-loop standard, the latter of which is a de facto standard that gained popularity due to the widespread use of Teletype printers.

The RS-232C standard is a more official standard derived from the C.C.I.T.T. telecommunications standard. Most computer terminals have inputs for both RS-232C and current-loop serial I/O; interface cards that provide either or both standards are widely available.

The EIA RS-232C Standard

The EIA RS-232C standard defines the interfacing between data terminal equipment and data communications equipment employing serial binary data interchange. Electrical signal and mechanical aspects of the interface are well

Table 7-2   RS-232C Interface Signals

Pin	Description
1	Protective Ground
2	Transmitted Data
3	Received Data
4	Request to Send
5	Clear to Send
6	Data Set Ready
7	Signal Ground (Common Return)
8	Received Line Signal Detector
9	(Reserved for Data Set Testing)
10	(Reserved for Data Set Testing)
11	Unassigned (See section 3.2.3)
12	Sec. Rec'd. Line Sig. Detector
13	Sec. Clear to Send
14	Secondary Transmitted Data
15	Transmission Signal Element Timing (DCE Source)
16	Secondary Received Data
17	Receiver Signal Element Timing (DCE Source)
18	Unassigned
19	Secondary Request to Send
20	Data Terminal Ready
21	Signal Quality Detector
22	Ring Indicator
23	Data Signal Rate Selector (DTE/DCE Source)
24	Transmit Signal Element Timing (DTE Source)
25	Unassigned

specified. The complete RS-232C interface consists of 25 data lines. This would seem to be enough signals for a complex parallel communication line, but many of the 25 lines are very specialized and a few are undefined. Most computer terminals only require from 3 to 5 of these lines to be operational. Table 7-2 briefly describes all 25 of the defined lines.

Figure 7-7 illustrates an RS-232C data communications system. Because RS-232C was originally intended for data communications equipment, a few lines must be swapped between a computer and terminal if no modem or other data communications equipment is used. These wires are swapped within the cable connecting the two devices. This line is called a *null modem* cable.

The five signals shown in Fig. 7-7 are the most commonly used RS-232C signals. Bidirectional data lines are provided (transmit and receive data) and a handshaking system consisting of the *request to send* and *data set ready* line are used to control data transfers.

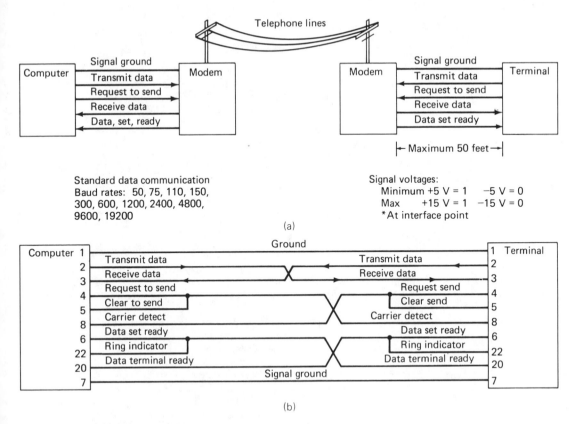

Figure 7-7   RS-232C data communications. (a) RS-232C interface with data communication equipment. (b) Direct-to-computer RS-232C wiring.

The RS-232C electrical specification calls for a number of voltage and current limitations:

1. Drivers must be able to withstand open or short circuits between any pins in the interface.

2. Voltages below -3 V shall be called *mark* potentials; above 3 V, called *space* voltages.

3. Maximum transfer rate is 20,000 bits per second.

4. The load impedance of the terminator side of the interface must be between 3000 and 7000 ohms, and not more than 2500 pF.

The 20 mA Current-Loop Standard

This standard is much simpler than the RS-232C interface standard and consists of only four basic wires: transmit plus, transmit minus, receive plus, and re-

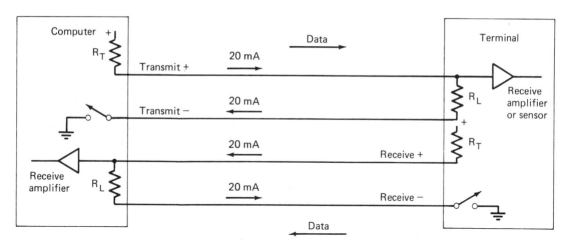

Figure 7-8   20 mA current-loop interface.

ceive minus. As Fig. 7-8 illustrates, four lines form two 20 mA current loops. Logical 1s and 0s are sensed by opening and closing the current loop. When the current loop was first used in teletypewriters, the loop was connected and broken by actual rotating switch contacts within the teletypewriter sending the data, and the 20 mA signal drove a print magnet in the receiving teletypewriter. Today, most 20 mA current loops electronically mimic the opening switch and magnet arrangement.

It is important to note where the current is generated. Voltage is applied to a current-limiting resistor at the data sending end (the end with the switch). Voltage is dropped across current-limiting resistor R_T and also across load resistor R_L. The values of the transmit resistor and positive voltage applied to it must provide a 20 mA current flow. Although a low-voltage and a low-value resistor can be used, a high voltage and a high-value resistor are usually chosen. One of the big advantages of a current-loop communication system is that wire resistance has no effect on a constant-current communication loop. Voltage does not drop across it as it does in a voltage-oriented interface such as RS-232C. For this advantage to be realized, however, a constant-current source, instead of just a resistor and voltage, are needed to generate the 20 mA. A high-voltage and a high-value resistor are less affected by line resistance variations and essentially act as a near-constant current source.

In many systems a mixture of EIA RS-232C interfaces and 20 mA current-loop interfaces is unacceptable. Standardization to the more modern RS-232C standard is usually the recommended course of action. This conversion can be simply performed by using an RS-232-level receiver to drive a switching transistor on the transmit end, and an optoisolator and load resistor to drive an RS-232C driver on the receive end.

PARALLEL DATA
COMMUNICATIONS STANDARDS

Parallel data communications over microcomputer buses is satisfactory for short interconnecting distances within microcomputer enclosures, but parallel communication over long distances is often required as well. High-speed disk drives, tape transports, and even powerful terminals outrun the common serial interface standards. It would seem appropriate to start describing the common standardized parallel interfaces at this point; but the fact is, there are no common standardized parallel interface formats. This situation has been brought about by (1) the lack of a popular device that uses a parallel interface from which a de facto standard might have been derived, and (2) the lack of an industry standard such as EIA RS-232C.

Most parallel communications buses do follow a general pattern, however. There are usually two parallel data buses: an input and an output. There are also handshaking signals indicating when data is ready and when it can be sent. The input/output section of this text describes typical parallel data transfers, and the explanations given apply to most parallel interfaces.

MATCHING NONSTANDARD
TO STANDARD INTERFACES

A completely standardized I/O system can improve a system's flexibility and expandability enormously. If all microcomputer inputs are designed to handle RS-232C, for example, off-the-shelf peripherals can be bought, plugged in, and operated without any redesign or new interface work. In a completely I/O-standardized microcomputer system, all the peripherals must be converted to the chosen standard as well (with the exception of high-speed system devices such as disks and tapes). This procedure adds versatility to the peripherals as well as the overall system, for the peripherals then become compatible with other systems using the same interface standards.

Parallel-to-Serial

Because there are no common parallel standards, it is usually necessary to convert devices to *serial* data communications standards. A keyboard that is connected to a parallel interface, for example, should be converted to a serial device with an RS-232C driver. Converting to serial standards has the added benefit of increasing equipment mobility. A parallel keyboard requires about ten lines, for instance, while an equivalent serial keyboard requires but two. It is simpler and less expensive to route a 2-conductor wire than a 10-conductor ribbon cable. Figure 7-9 illustrates a sample parallel-to-standardized-serial conversion.

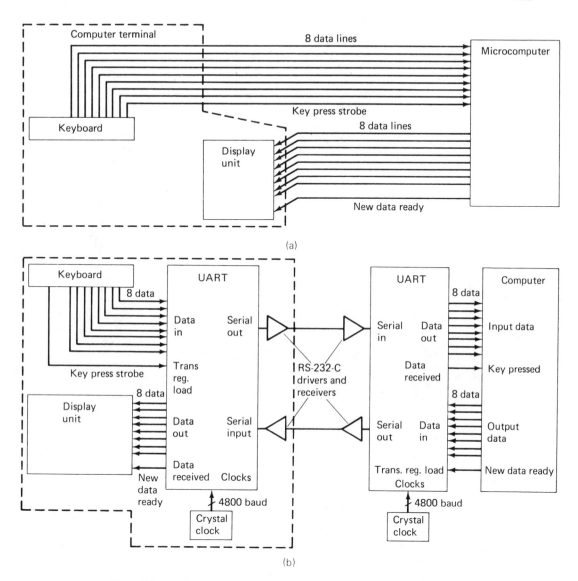

Figure 7-9 Conversion of a nonstandard parallel terminal. (a) Nonstandard parallel interface. (b) Standardized serial terminal interface.

Interfacing Common Peripherals

The number of types of peripherals a computer can have is nearly limitless, ranging from light pens to joysticks. With nearly all of these peripherals, however, there is usually some way to put the input into a standardized form. Table 7-3 lists some common peripherals and offers suggestions concerning possible interface methods.

Table 7-3 Popular Device Interface Methods.

Device	Purpose	Interface
Terminal	Data entry and read-back. Simple terminals have alphanumeric capability only. Complex terminals have graphics.	Serial interfaces of the 20 mA or RS-232C type are adequate in most cases. Slow speed 110 to 1200 baud rates are usually necessary in hard-copy terminals, while video terminals can usually accept 9600 to 19,200 baud.
Disk drive	High density, low access time data storage.	Due to the high data transfer rates and disk drive control functions, unique parallel interfaces are practically the only way to interface these devices.
Magnetic tape drive	Very high density, sequential data storage.	Like the disk drive, high data transfer rates and control functions necessitate the use of parallel interfaces.
Cassette tape drive	Medium density, sequential data storage.	Cassette data transfer rates are low enough to allow serial data transfers. Control functions require either the use of reserved characters that are sent over the serial line, or discrete control lines.
Image sensor	Device that converts images into a computer-readable form.	Because data is usually scanned out in these devices, serial interfaces are adequate, but RS-232 is much too slow. Special drivers, receivers, and lines that operate in the MHz range are required.
Plotter	Hard copy device that draws images, graphs, and alphanumerics with a moving pen. Line drawings are generated with plotters.	Due to the mechanical motion involved, plotters require low data transfer rates. Serial data transmissions over RS-232C lines is often used.

Table 7-3 (continued)

Device	Purpose	Interface
Data tablet	A device that translates operator pen motions into computer data. Data tablets are essentially the opposite of a plotter.	Data tablets can generate low- or high-speed data, depending on their operation. Serial data transfer for "end point only" data tablets is adequate, while parallel transfer is required for continuous sample models.
Joystick	A control stick with X and Y axes of control. Two potentiometers connected to a gimbal are usually used.	Joysticks are basically analog devices and require A/D conversion before data can be used. Analog data transmission to an interface at the computer is popular, but conversion at the joystick and serial or parallel transmission is better.
Light pen	A device that translates operator pen movements on a CRT into computer data. Similar to a data tablet in function.	Conversion circuitry is required at the light pen. Data can be sent serially. Light pens are often part of terminals and blend into the terminal's serial or parallel communication format.
Speech synthesizer	A device that mimics human speech under computer control.	There are two basic types of generators and interfaces. Computer-controlled waveform generators require parallel interfaces due to their high data rate. Word- or phoneme-oriented generators require simpler commands and serial interfaces can be used.
Card reader/punch	A unit that reads or punches 80-column "IBM cards."	Most card readers transfer data slowly enough for a serial RS-232C interface to handle. Vacuum-actuated high-speed readers require parallel interfacing due to high data rates and many control functions.

Table 7-3 (continued)

Device	Purpose	Interface
Line printer	A hard-copy device that prints alphanumeric copy on a line rather than a character basis.	Line printers with print rates up to about 600 lines per minute can be interfaced serially at RS-232C data rates. High-speed line printers require parallel interface. Nearly all commercial line printer interfaces are parallel in nature.

8 Interface Layout and Construction

The design is finished. All interface components have been chosen, the circuits have been carefully planned following the design rules, and timing diagrams and logic design have been double-checked to insure that the circuit will work. The final steps of system hardware development must now be taken: fabrication and testing. Even logic circuits built in a haphazard manner will probably work, especially if good design practices were followed and low-speed logic such as TTL is used. A little care in the layout and construction, however, will vastly improve the reliability, testability, and appearance of the final product and is certainly preferable to haphazard construction.

For a small single-board microcomputer system, circuit board layout, enclosure selection, and external interface wiring must be performed. With larger multicard systems, a universal card mounting method, commonly known as a backplane or motherboard, must also be chosen. A topdown approach should be taken in large systems. The card mounting method and enclosure must first be selected, followed by logic card layout and construction. In many cases it will be necessary to iterate the enclosure and board layouts a few times to come up with the optimum system configuration. A 10-card backplane may be initially chosen and eventually changed to a 20-card backplane to accommodate all circuit modules, for example. It is therefore a good idea to have fairly firm board layouts and enclosure selection before parts procurement.

CHOOSING AN ENCLOSURE

The type of enclosure ultimately chosen for a microcomputer system is dependent on system complexity, system application, and component constraints.

The Integrated Enclosure

A metal or plastic box containing one circuit card, a built-in power supply, and possibly a few status lights, switches, or a keyboard is a popular enclosure for single-card microcomputer systems. Figure 8-1 depicts such an enclosure. A single circuit board is mounted in the box with spacers, and a power supply is mounted next to it. There are a few important features to note about this box.

1. Five spacers (one in each corner and one in the middle of the circuit card) are used to hold the card in position. It is important that the card be rigidly supported and that the exposed conductors on the back of the card do not touch the metal case.

2. Connectors are used on all board-to-case and board-to-power-supply connections. This feature allows easy board removal and installation for servicing.

3. The power supply is mounted rigidly on spacers; care is taken to make sure the parts will remain mounted. Power supplies contain many big components such as resistors and transformers that require more than solder to keep them in place. Lockwashers are used on the transformer, and capacitor clips are used on the filter capacitors.

4. A fan keeps the circuit cool. This fan is optional if enough air circulation can be generated by ventilation slots. It is important to remember that even low-power devices can build up heat in a sealed enclosure. There should always be some sort of ventilation. Another point of interest concerning the power supply is the direction of air flow. The air flows over temperature-sensitive logic circuitry before cooling the power supply. Power supplies are less sensitive to heat and tend to preheat the air if air is used to cool them before it reaches the logic.

5. Cables and wiring are protected against strain. Individual wires are bound with cable ties and the power cord has a strain relief.

6. Components are mounted only on the bottom of the enclosure. This allows the cover to be taken off for testing and servicing without being inconvenienced by dangling wires. If parts must be mounted on the cover, it is wise to use a connector or at least to leave a long length of wire so the cover can be set aside.

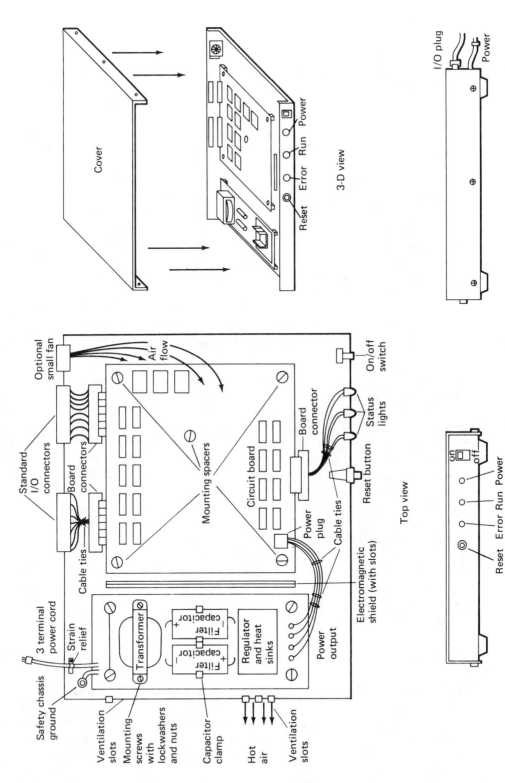

Cover

Power
Run
Error
Reset

3-D view

I/O plug
Power

Side view

Optional
small fan

Air
flow

Standard
I/O
connectors

Board
connectors

Board
connector

Status
lights

Cable ties

Circuit board

Reset button

Mounting spacers

On/off
switch

Top view

Cable ties

Power
plug

3 terminal
power cord

Strain
relief

Transformer

Filter
capacitor
−
+

Filter
capacitor
+
−

Regulator
and heat
sinks

Electromagnetic
shield (with slots)

Power
output

Safety chassis
ground

Ventilation
slots

Mounting
screws
with
lockwashers
and nuts

Capacitor
clamp

Hot
air

Ventilation
slots

off

Reset   Error Run Power

Front view

Figure 8-1   Integrated enclosure.

301

7. A metal shield between the power supply and the circuitry protects analog components on the circuit card from power supply noise. This is particularly important when switching-type power supplies are used.

A few additional ideas concerning integrated enclosures should be noted. In many cases integrated enclosures will be sitting next to a microcomputer user. Convection cooling or a low-noise fan should be used to cut down on annoying fan noise. Fans such as Rotron's *Whisper Fan* are ideal in these applications. When a keyboard is incorporated into an enclosure, it is sometimes a good idea to put the on–off switch and reset button (in the case of a reset-and-go microcomputer) on the back of the enclosure. It may be more difficult to turn the microcomputer on and off, but the risk of accidentally resetting the microcomputer or turning it off in the middle of a program while reaching for the keyboard is eliminated.

Finally, safety should be considered. A three-terminal power plug should be used and the case should be grounded to the protective ground. Any high-voltage points should be insulated or marked, and the cover should be firmly fastened.

Modular Card Cages

Most large computers and many microcomputers use a modular card cage to house system logic. Figure 8-2 illustrates the modular card cage. In this case, 12 connectors are provided for plug-in cards. The connectors are wired in a parallel-bus format (in this case, the S-100 bus is being used). A separate circuit card, called a motherboard, is used to carry power and signals to the connectors. Motherboards are available for most of the common standard buses (S-100, SS50, IEEE 488).

Most of the features that applied to the integrated enclosure also apply to the modular card cage. The main difference is the way in which cards are mounted. Each card simply slides into place and is usually held in by the connector's insertion force. Because this force is substantial on large cards, small levers that aid in inserting and pulling the card are often incorporated. Figure 8-2 shows a card with built-in card extractors.

Rack Mounting

Before microcomputers were invented, computers took up so much volume that integrated enclosures and modular card cages were not even considered in the enclosure decision. One of the largest available enclosures of the times, the 19-inch relay rack (used in telephone switching and industrial equipment), became the de facto standard for computer construction. Figure 8-3 illustrates a 19-inch relay rack.

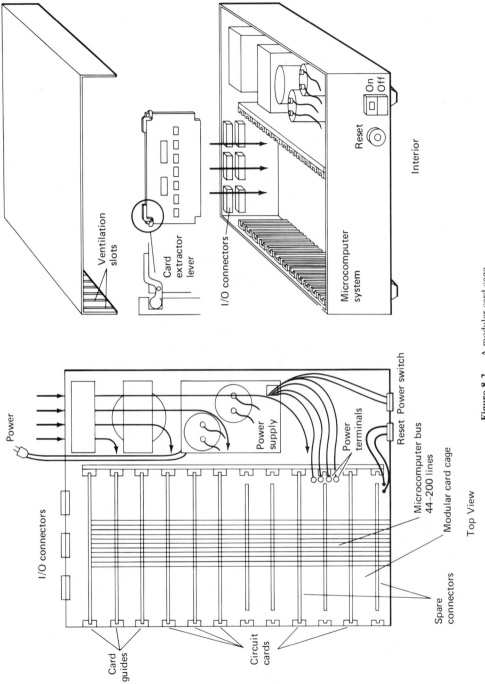

Figure 8-2 A modular card cage.

Ventilation slots

Card extractor lever

I/O connectors

Microcomputer system

Interior

On
Off

Reset

Power

Power supply

Power terminals

Reset Power switch

Microcomputer bus
44-200 lines

Modular card cage

Top View

Spare connectors

I/O connectors

Card guides

Circuit cards

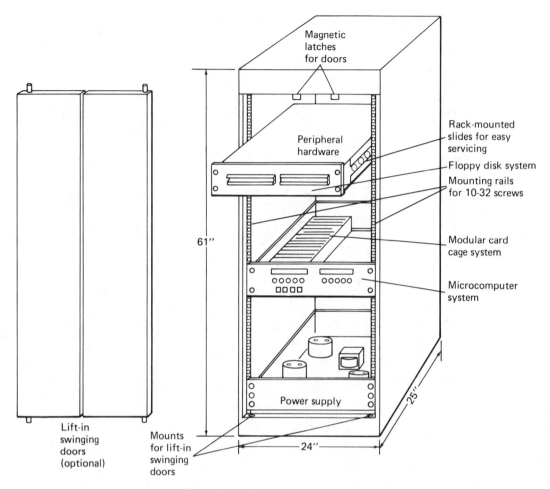

Figure 8-3   19-inch relay-rack mounting system.

The relay rack still offers some advantages not found in other enclosures. Many peripherals are designed to be mounted directly into relay racks, and a microcomputer or minicomputer system along with a rack-mounted disk, tape drive, and modular power supplies can fit in one nice enclosure. Power supplies are traditionally mounted on a separate relay rack plate (usually at the bottom of the rack to lower the center of gravity).

The relay rack also increases serviceability. Rack slides allow circuitry to pull out of the rack like drawers out of a filing cabinet.

Custom Enclosures

In some cases the enclosure choice does not have to be made at all because the enclosure already exists. Mounting a small microcontroller inside another piece of equipment is a good example of this situation. In these cases you must do the best you can to follow good mounting, wire securing, and noise shielding practices.

If an existing enclosure must be used, and the environment inside that enclosure is not well suited to microcomputer circuitry, an integrated enclosure housing the microcomputer circuitry should be built into the existing enclosure. This "box inside a box" approach can greatly increase reliability.

CHOOSING A CONNECTOR SYSTEM

Virtually no microcomputer is a "sealed box." There are always connections to peripherals and external power. As systems grow more complex, the number of interconnections increases. It is therefore important to choose a good, standardized connector system for external as well as internal microcomputer connections.

The crudest approach to interconnections, aside from soldering wires directly into place, is the *direct* card-connector method. Wires from external peripherals, as well as card-to-card connections not connected on the motherboard, are terminated with connectors that plug into the tops of cards or into sockets on the cards. Holes in the back of the enclosure are used to pass cables leading to peripherals. Two problems with this method include strain on the cards caused by external cable tension, and cable clearance problems for large peripheral cables. A clamp at the back of the enclosure is often used as a strain relief, as shown in Fig. 8-4.

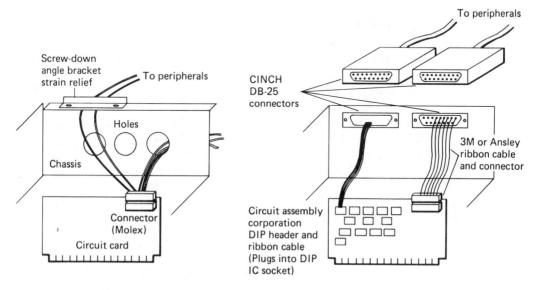

Figure 8-4 Connector systems. (a) Simple, inexpensive connector system. (b) Rugged, professional connector system.

More sophisticated is the use of enclosure-mounted connections. Standard-ized I/O connectors such as the DB25/EIA RS-232C connector are mounted to the back of the microcomputer and separate two-sided connector cables are used to connect cards to the connectors. Ribbon cable is used to keep cables organized and flat, which allows good cover clearance. Figure 8-4(b) shows the ribbon cable connector method.

Cables used to connect microcomputers to external devices are one of the weakest links in a microcomputer system. The use of quality wire with strong insulation and firmly mounted plugs and sockets helps reduce problems in this area. Strain reliefs should be used on cable ends to keep tension off actual electrical connections.

CIRCUIT CARD LAYOUT AND CONSTRUCTION

A few tradeoffs must be made when choosing a circuit board for a logic circuit. Ruggedness, ease of servicing, and packaging density requirements must be weighed and the best card for the job chosen. Let's turn now to look at a few common circuit board construction techniques and their advantages and disad-vantages.

Circuit Boards

Double-sided circuit boards are the most common production-type logic cards. These cards are usually made of fiberglass-epoxy with copper-clad printed circuitry on both sides of the card. Plated throughholes connect the circuit paths between the two sides. Generally, double-sided circuit cards are laid out with parallel conductors running in one direction on the top of the card and in a perpendicular direction on the bottom of the card. This simplifies layout and helps avoid crossover problems. If a data bus or single line must cross another bus, it can do so by "jumping over it" on the opposite side of the card.

Single-sided printed circuit boards are seldom used in digital logic due to the crossover problem and the complexity of logic circuits. It takes jumpers to jump over other circuit etches, and the installation time is prohibitive on large circuits. Layout is also trickier with single-sided boards.

Single- and double-sided circuit boards have the advantage of low cost, relatively simple fabrication, and easy servicing, because conductors are ex-posed. The major disadvantage of single- and double-sided boards is packaging density. Room must be left around ICs for data buses and power buses, and only about a quarter of a circuit board's area is covered by components.

Multilayer Boards

The multilayer board is a stack of very thin printed circuit boards, each with a circuit pattern on one side. The multilayer board overcomes most of the disad-vantages of double- and single-sided circuit boards. Packaging density can be increased, because many circuit levels are available for complex interconnections, and whole layers of a multilayer board can be dedicated to ground and power planes.

While the multilayer board overcomes packaging density problems, it creates two new problems. Multilayer boards are expensive to produce due to the precision required to fabricate them, and circuit tracing and repairing are very difficult due to the hidden layers between the board.

Wire-Wrap Boards

Wire-wrap boards consist of firmly mounted integrated circuit sockets or socket pins inserted into a fiberglass board material. Square, plated (or tinned) posts protrude from the back of the card. Thin (typically 30-gage) silver-plated wires are wrapped around these posts (about 5 to 10 times) to make interconnections. The height of the posts determines how many wires can be wrapped to it. A post capable of holding three wires is called a three-level wire-wrap post.

The general first impression of wire-wrap is that it is a shoddy way to build a circuit, but it is in fact one of the most reliable circuit interconnection methods. The tool used for wire-wrapping puts a high tension on the wire as it is wrapped around the posts, so airtight connections are formed at the square post corners. A wire twisted around a post 10 times therefore has 40 connection points. Because the wire-wrap wire is silver-plated, it conducts signals very well at high frequencies.

Circuit packing densities are very high where wire-wrapped construction is used. Integrated circuits can be mounted right next to each other, because circuit-board etches are nonexistent. The surfaces of the circuit board on which the wire-wrap pins are mounted are often used as ground and power planes. Circuitry remains accessible because there are no buried planes (as there are in multilayer boards), and circuit modification is quite simple. Figure 8-5 illustrates wire-wrapped construction and shows the recommended method of stringing buses from pin to pin. Using this method, it is never necessary to remove more than three wires in the replacement or modification of a wire.

Wire-wrap construction has one big disadvantage: board thickness. Wire-wrap posts protrude from the back of a card while socket thickness adds width to the front.

Special Board Wiring Methods

A number of special board wiring methods for special applications exist. One such method is the multiwire method, a type of wiring that consists of insulated wires that connect circuit pins in much the same way wire-wrap does; instead of using square posts, however, wires are terminated directly to the IC leads and are soldered. The wires are applied by a special machine and are adhesively attached to the back of a card. Multiwire boards have all the advantages

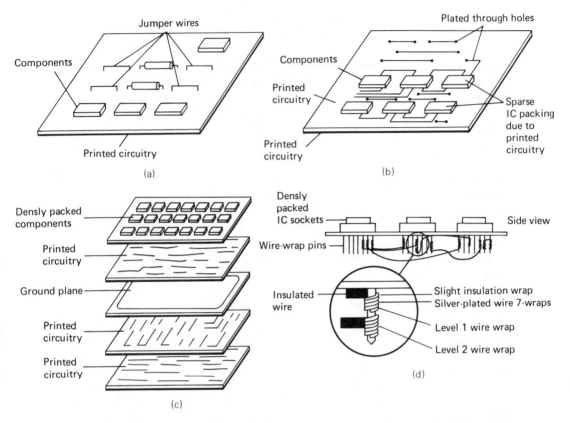

Figure 8-5   Wiring methods. (a) Single-sided board. (b) Double-sided board. (c) Multi-layer construction. (d) Wire wrap.

of wire-wrap, are quite easy to modify (although some soldering is needed), and are as thin as multilayer boards. This method is better suited to large-scale production due to the machinery needed to implement it.

Another method that attempts to overcome the thickness disadvantage of wire-wrap is stitch-weld wiring. This method utilizes point-to-point wiring as wire-wrap does, but instead of using wire-wrap posts, the wires are welded to circuit pads next to the IC pins using a special welding tool. Modification of a stitch-welded board is not as easy as modifying a wire-wrapped board, but the thickness problem is avoided.

Choosing a Circuit Card

The size and thickness of a circuit card should be defined by circuit size and enclosure constraints. Circuit boards for card cages and standardized buses will be predetermined size-wise. The type of wiring method chosen should be

based on individual requirements. If a board is a prototype and modifications are to be made, wire-wrap is the best choice. For large production runs of a finalized design, two-sided boards are the best choice; and if packing density is important in a production environment, multilayer or multiwire are good methods. The advantages and disadvantages of each method should be weighed.

Solder versus Sockets

There are two methods of mounting integrated circuits: sockets and solder. Many people have the idea that the mounting decision resolves to a purely economic question. Sockets cost more than no sockets, so one is led to believe that soldering in ICs is an economizing measure. In reality, there are many factors that must be weighed before deciding where to use and where not to use sockets.

Table 8-1 lists some of the advantages of sockets and soldered construction. It is true that ICs are easier to replace with sockets, and troubleshooting by the chip replacement method (a poor way to diagnose problems, incidentally) is easier, but it should be remembered that modern ICs are very reliable and rarely fail unless they are of the "surplus" variety often used by experimenters. In addition, modern fault isolation tools allow a faulty IC to be spotted quite easily, and special desoldering tools allow ICs to be removed quickly and easily with no board damage.

Table 8-1   Solder versus Sockets

Characteristic	Socket	Soldered
Cost	Higher	Lower
Mechanical integrity	Poor to good	Excellent
Chance of bent-over pins due to poor insertion	High	Extremely low
Replaceability	Easy	Difficult
Thermal shock incurred during installation	None	Moderate

Most mainframe and minicomputer manufacturers have learned that sockets are more of a service problem than a benefit. Due to poor mechanical integrity, the chance of pins getting bent as ICs are inserted, and the possibility of ICs being accidentally pulled out as the circuit card is inserted into a card cage (possibly by rubbing against another card), soldered-in construction is almost exclusively used.

Thermal shock is another item to be considered in the decision between sockets and soldering. The soldering process transfers a lot of heat to an integrated circuit, especially if a wave-soldering machine (a machine that solders all of a card's pins at once by dipping the card surface in a solder bath) is used. Integrated circuits, however, are designed to take soldering stresses of about

300°C (lead temperature) for 10 seconds and should work fine after such soldering unless they were defective to begin with. High heat applied from the outside of an IC tends to cause bond failures due to package expansion and rarely damages the IC chip itself. The thermal shock caused by direct soldering does not have much effect on reliability, and the advantage of greater mechanical integrity far outweighs it.

A mix of soldered-in and socket ICs is often a good idea. Small interface parts such as drivers, receivers, and gates can be soldered into place, while large LSI parts such as microprocessors and UARTs are plugged into sockets. This allows quick replacement of the large, hard-to-remove parts, yet retains the mechanical integrity of solder construction on most of the parts.

Special Board Processing

Complex circuit boards with many parallel buses are prone to solder bridges caused by flux sputtering and excessive solder flow. Solder masks are therefore incorporated into many complex logic cards. A solder mask is a coating (usually transparent green, blue, or pink) that covers the soldered side of the circuit card in all areas not to be soldered. Solder cannot stick to the solder mask, and flux can be removed easily from it. Solder masks are almost always used in wave-soldering production applications.

Circuit cards destined for harsh environments (humid, dusty, greasy) are often completely coated on both sides with a thin plastic protection blanket called a conformal coating. Connectors are, of course, masked from the coating to retain conduction. Circuits going into automative, industrial, and military applications should always be conformally coated.

Circuit Card Layout

Once a board type has been chosen, it is time to lay out the parts on the board. The following tips for laying out boards should be followed.

1. Arrange the logic circuitry as efficiently as possible. Group logical sections with many interconnections close to one another.

2. Place bus transceivers close to the edge connector (assuming a modular card cage and bus are being used). Lines taken from the bus should be as short as possible to reduce bus noise.

3. Keep analog circuitry as far from noise-generating logic circuitry as possible.

4. Place onboard voltage regulators where their heat will cause no problems. Cooling air should blow over logic circuitry first, followed by the voltage regulator heatsink.

5. Allow space for decoupling capacitors and place the input voltage regulation capacitor near the power input point on the board.

6. If there is any space left on the board, arrange it so one or more additional ICs can be added at a future date. Expandability is a desirable feature.

Circuit Board Routing

Whether a circuit board is a printed circuit or wire-wrapped board, there are a few general signal-routing techniques that should be followed. Signal leads should be kept as short as possible. Squared-off wires and etches look nice, but they are electrically inferior to shorter, more direct connections. Signal lengths up to 50 cm perform quite satisfactorily in well designed TTL and MOS microprocessor systems in which good power distribution techniques (ground and power planes or equivalent) are used.

On circuit boards, power and ground planes or etches should be as wide as possible. Signal leads can be as narrow as 0.38 mm (0.015 in.) for TTL circuitry. Signal spacing of 0.38 mm is adequate, but minimum spaced, long parallel lines should be avoided for crosstalk reasons. Parallel bundles of wire-wrap wire should likewise be avoided in wire-wrapped systems.

Circuit Board Assembly

After a circuit board is fabricated, assembly begins. Discrete components, nonsensitive integrated circuits such as TTL drivers and transceivers, decoupling capacitors, and miscellaneous hardware should first be mounted on the board. Sensitive MOS parts, including microprocessors, complex interface parts, ROMs, and RAMs should be mounted or plugged in last.

Care should be taken to avoid exceeding component heat requirements, and grounded soldering equipment should be used to avoid component destruction due to static or power-line voltages.

Finally, when parts are being plugged into IC sockets, care should be taken to avoid bending IC pins. Pins that are bent out sideways are easy to spot, but bent-under pins are nearly impossible to detect without test equipment.

PURCHASING THE PARTS

National parts distributors such as Cramer Electronics and Hamilton/Avnet supply industry with microcomputer and interface parts, and parts obtained from these distributors as well as certified representatives of the semiconductor manufacturers can be assumed to be first-run, prime parts. But you also pay a premium price for parts from these sources.

Slightly lower prices can be obtained by purchasing parts from a surplus or discount parts distributor, but telling good parts from bad is very difficult. Some discount distributors can give low prices because they buy in such large quantities. Parts obtained from these distributors are the same as you would get from a national industrial supplier. In many cases, however, discount distributors buy surplus and marginally rejected lots of parts. There is nothing wrong with true surplus parts, as these are manufacturers' overruns that would have been sold to an industrial customer if one existed. Higher than expected chip yields, canceled orders, and overestimated demand produce surplus parts. The parts to watch out for are the rejected ones. These parts may not work over the full temperature range, may not fall within voltage or current requirements, or may have out-of-spec propagation delays. Using these parts in a well designed circuit will defeat all the carefully performed work that preceded it. Here are a few tips to help identify rejected parts.

1. Suspect the lack of the words *first-run* or *prime* on advertising material.

2. Suspect the lack of official manufacturer markings on the IC package.

3. Suspect the words "100% tested" on advertising—even rejected parts are tested.

4. Suspect obvious defects such as chipped cases and misformed leads.

In experimenter-type applications in which the experimenter is long on time and short on money, rejected and surplus parts may be acceptable. Good troubleshooting experience can be gained from tracing down initially bad and prematurely failed parts. The use of surplus or rejected parts in production applications or by the experimenter who would rather develop software than spend time fixing his computer should be avoided. Overall system cost may be a bit higher initially, but the added reliability will pay back the difference many times over.

CIRCUIT AND SYSTEM TESTING

Even the most carefully designed and constructed system will rarely work properly when first powered up. Component failures, software bugs, wiring errors, unexpected noise interference, or uncaught errors in the design can cause system problems. Fortunately, a wide selection of tools and methods is available to help reduce troubleshooting effort.

The first things to check in a new system are the power forms. It is a good idea to have important chips unplugged (if sockets are used) during the initial power checkout just in case something is wrong. A voltmeter should be used to check voltage levels and an oscilloscope should be used to examine the voltage waveforms. Abnormal voltage levels can be caused by overloaded voltage regulators, voltage drops across power lines, or malfunctioning power supply components. Voltages at all points, including the power supply output, card connections, and IC leads, should be tested.

If all the power forms are within specified limits, an error in the logic circuitry or software is likely to be the problem. The first thing to check is the logic circuitry.

Static testing is a good first step in the logic troubleshooting process. Much of a system's circuitry can be tested with the system clock stopped, using a voltmeter, oscilloscope, or logic probe. Gates, drivers, receivers, static RAMs, and discrete components can be checked for open circuits, short circuits, and defective logical action. One particular problem to watch for is open-circuit enable lines. If problems still exist after static testing is complete, dynamic testing must be performed.

A wide selection of special tools is available for dynamic testing. Oscilloscopes allow actual waveforms to be watched and multi-channel digital oscilloscopes or logic analyzers allow signals to be watched on a 1 and 0 basis. By connecting an oscilloscope's or logic analyzer's trigger and input probes to logic signals, it is possible to trace down a problem to its source. A good place to start tracing down problems is at the master clock oscillator. If the oscillator is working, devices driven by the oscillator should be checked.

Troubleshooting a computer system is unlike simple equipment troubleshooting. Once a computer is debugged to a semioperational point, the troubleshooting becomes easier because the computer can help troubleshoot itself. If a microcomputer is working but one of its interfaces is not, a test program that repeatedly sends data or retrieves data from that interface can be written and run. An oscilloscope or logic analyzer can then be used to watch the input/output interaction and the error can be quickly found.

A microcomputer is well suited to testing its own memory, also. By writing memory test patterns into memory and reading them back under processor control, bad memory bits can be identified, and the diagnostic program can even be written to identify which memory card and IC is at fault.

9 Interface Software Design and Implementation

Before you actually get involved with putting a micro system together, there is a certain tendency to think that once the system is built and tested, what follows is merely that "small matter of programming." This belief, however, will very likely be dispelled the first time you take on the task of software design and implementation in your microcomputer-based project.

It is true that some systems will require considerably less in the way of software than others. A complex controller, for example, may require large amounts of critical real-time software, while a general-purpose computer would not, because in this case the programming burden is placed on the "programmers," whoever they may be. Software design may be likened to hardware design in many ways, but there is no parallel more universally appropriate than that which states "a good design approach and the proper tools can make the development go smoother and faster."

Volumes have been devoted entirely to microcomputer software tools, design, and implementation—and for a complete understanding of the subject, a thorough study of one or more of these books is a virtual necessity. This chapter is not offered to impart a full understanding of micro software; it does, however, address those factors that are most important in microcomputer software design and thus can serve as a guide for topics that merit your further study.

THE ELEMENTS OF SOFTWARE DEVELOPMENT

In a microcomputer magazine article on software development, the author spoke glowingly about the profits to be made by generating software and admonished his readers to get cracking; he wrote, ". . . with the profits which can be made in software, it would be foolish to not immediately run to your computer and start typing in programs." With no intended reflection on the zealous enthusiasm of the author of those words, a modicum of caution is certainly in order. There is no question that the microcomputer software field can offer some very attractive financial opportunities for the specially skilled, but the quoted suggestion could hardly be more foolish than its implications. Software generated in the manner suggested is usually not worth buying.

Jumping directly into computer coding (writing the actual computer instructions) is like developing an interface circuit by beginning with a soldering iron and a bag of integrated circuits. It is of utmost importance to bear in mind that software, like hardware, must be carefully specified, conceptualized, and finally coded. A topdown approach is the key to successful software.

Software development is a process that consists of three discrete phases: software definition, algorithm design, and software coding. And these phases neglect the preliminary steps that involve the weighing of hardware-versus-software tradeoffs, learning what can and what cannot be implemented economically with software, the selection of the "right" computer language, and other such mundane considerations.

Software Definition

Software definition consists of precisely defining the function of the software. In a system programming application, this may mean defining the capabilities of a program such as an editor, assembler, or high-level language. In a control application this step would include specification of all the timing constraints and a listing of the complete sequence of events of the controller.

Algorithm Design

Software algorithm design is the process of choosing a method for accomplishing the task set forth in the specification. There are hundreds of ways to turn a signal on and off with a microprocessor; the method best suited for the application should be found and used. Algorithm design also involves program *partitioning*. Large programs are more easily designed, debugged, and tested if they are broken up into smaller modules or subroutines; and the points at which to break the algorithm into modular elements must be defined. Modules should be small enough so that each module is not too large in itself, and large enough that individual instruction-like modules of a few statements each are avoided.

Coding Prerequisites

Before the actual coding begins, a few important decisions about the coding should be made. The choice between using a high-level language such as BASIC or FORTRAN for high-speed software development, or pure assembly language for the highest possible execution speed, or a combination of both assembly and high-level languages must be made. The documentation methods must also be specified to the person writing the code.

It is especially important to generate good documentation when writing microcomputer software. Flowcharts should be used to represent program control flow, and data flow diagrams should be used to keep track of variables not considered in the flowchart. A description of each module's function should be written and comments should be used extensively within each module.

One of the keys to good programming is the efficient and logical use of variables. Data areas within a program should be well defined, and all variables that affect a particular subroutine should be clearly called out in the documentation. Poorly defined variables and ''under-the-table parameter-passing'' between subroutines should be avoided.

Large systems and microcontrollers will usually contain one or more interrupt-driven processes. Care must be taken in any subroutine called by an interrupt service routine. Reentering a subroutine that has been interrupted can cause unpredictable results upon subroutine return due to destruction of temporary variables. Reentrant subroutines must therefore be used also.

In addition to good software design practices, good software and hardware tools are required for successful software development. We look at some of these requirements in detail in this chapter, but we begin with a cursory examination of the tradeoffs involved in language selection.

THE PROGRAMMING LANGUAGE

The choice of programming language will have a great impact on the support software needed in a development system. The programming language choice should therefore be made before ordering a system or picking a vendor to order from (some vendors are specialized in certain languages).

The choice between assembly language or high-level language is basically a tradeoff between software development cost and processing speed. High-level languages typically require 2–10 times as much memory as optimized assembly language and run 2–100 times slower. Development time can be cut from a half to a tenth of the time required for assembly language programming by using a high-level language.

The choice of languages is itself a tradeoff that must be weighed from a system capability and economic viewpoint. The choice is not strictly a one-or-the-other situation, however. Most high-level languages allow program subroutines to be replaced with equivalent assembly language routines. Studies show that programs spend 90% of their time executing 10% of the program (the commonly used subroutines), so by converting just a small percentage of the program to assembly language, great speed increases can be effected with a minimal software-development investment.

SOFTWARE TOOLS

Software development is a computer-aided design process that requires both hardware and software tools. We will look at the hardware requirements in the next section; here, we will examine some of the important items of development software, which include editors, assemblers, simulators, debuggers, compilers, and interpreters. Compilers and interpreters are less often used than editors, assemblers, and debuggers, but they can serve a useful purpose, particularly in large software development tasks.

Editors

Programs must be "typed into the computer" and put into a computer-readable format that other development software can use. It is the editor program that allows text, mathematical expressions, and anything else to be input from the typewriter keyboard.

Data typed into an editor is usually temporarily stored in microcomputer memory as an "edit buffer." A 16K-byte edit buffer can store about 2600 five-letter words or their equivalent in expressions, and small or medium-sized microcomputer programs can usually fit within the edit buffer. Many editors have a paging feature that allows full data buffers to be dumped onto a data storage device (disk or tape), leaving an empty edit buffer in which to continue the program. A large program may consist of many pages of code. Paging is very seldom an automatic feature. The programmer must decide when to "turn the page."

Because computers have a great memory manipulation capability, editors can incorporate many features that are not found in an ordinary typewriter. These features include text insertion and deletion, character string searching and changing (useful for replacing words or sentences of text), and block movements of text.

There are three basic types of editors: string-oriented, cursor-oriented, and line-oriented. Each type has its own advantages.

String-Oriented Editors. A string-oriented editor treats a whole program (or equivalent text) as one long string of characters. The point at which characters will be added to or deleted from the program is determined by where the "character pointer" is. The user has complete control over where the character pointer moves and what it does, and can insert or delete text from the middle of lines as well as at their beginnings and ends. Moving blocks of characters from one location to another is not usually possible with simple character editors found on microcomputers.

Line-Oriented Editors.   In a line-oriented editor, a line number is assigned to and printed at the beginning of every line of text. Line editors have the advantage of simple character block movement but require that line numbers be specified when editing text. Smooth text typing is difficult for the occasional typist, because line numbers must be put at the beginning of every line.

Cursor-Oriented Editors.   These are used primarily on video terminals on which the blinking cursor can be moved left, right, up, or down. Editing is accomplished by moving the cursor to exactly the point on the screen where the data is to begin, and then typing the data. Old data at the location is overtyped by new data. This kind of editor is particularly useful when many small changes are required and cursor positioning ease is of prime importance.

Assemblers

Assemblers take microcomputer programs that are in an assembly language or *source code* format (instruction names instead of the 1s and 0s of pure machine code) and convert them to machine language or *object code*. Assemblers automatically associate addresses with variable names and compute numeric offsets commonly found in relative addressing and branching. Assemblers are usually matched to a particular editor format and must therefore be compatible with the editor used on the microcomputer system.

The capabilities of assemblers vary widely. Most assemblers can assign machine-code values to symbolic names and compute addresses. Advanced assemblers have far more than these rudimentary features, however.

Program location control is one valuable feature to look for in an assembler. By changing a start location variable in the submitted program it is possible to have the program assembled to run at any location in memory. An even more powerful feature than program-specific program location control is relocatable object-code generation. Object code created by a "relocating assembler" (often called relocatable object code) can be loaded at any location in memory using a relocatable loader program. No new assemblies are required to make it run at a different address.

Macro capability is another desirable feature in an assembler. Assembly language programs usually end up having certain sequences of instructions that are written over and over again by the programmer. A macro assembler allows a special code word to be assigned to these repeated sequences, essentially turning them into macros. Instead of retyping the sequence of instructions each time it is needed, the programmer merely writes the macro name and the assembler accordingly substitutes the proper code sequence. Macros can help make programming easier and help make documentation more understandable. A descriptive macro name such as SHIFT8 for a sequence of instructions that performs eight shifts in a row is more descriptive than eight shift instructions one following another.

Monitors and Debuggers

A monitor is a small control program from which other, larger programs such as assemblers and editors can be loaded and run by the microcomputer operator. When a program is finished running, or when the microcomputer reset button is pressed (assuming a reset-and-go type microcomputer is being used), control is returned to the monitor for new program selection and execution.

Because monitors are the central operating point for program execution and system operation in general, many useful features are incorporated into them. The ability to examine memory locations and register contents, modify memory locations, and jump to programs is usually included. Monitors with even more convenient functions fall into the "monitor–debugger" class of programs. These programs usually include a breakpoint feature that allows the person executing the program to put a return-to-monitor point at any location in the program. The program's progress up to the breakpoint can be studied and any error-causing conditions can be debugged.

Compilers

It is a well documented fact that programs can be developed with less time and effort if a high-level computer language is used instead of assembly language. Compilers are programs that convert high-level languages such as FORTRAN, BASIC, and PL/M into assembly language and finally into machine code.

Compilers create machine-language programs that perform the specified task, but the programs take longer to execute than hand-optimized assembly language due to the general way in which expressions are handled by the compiler. Most compilers, for instance, would not recognize the fact that a number multiplied by 2 is the same as a simple left arithmetic shift. A full multiply would therefore be performed needlessly.

There are compilers that do their best to recognize candidate program optimization points, but these optimizing compilers are not available for microcomputers at this time. The future will undoubtedly see programs of this type.

Interpreters

High-level lanugages can also be executed by an interpreter. An interpreter does not convert the high-level language program into machine language before executing it as does the compiler, however. Instead, statements are read as the program is executed, each instruction is broken apart and interpreted for its logical or arithmetic meaning, and the calculations are performed. This is a very slow process, because all the statements must be reread every time they are executed.

FORTRAN and PL-type languages (Intel's PL/M, Zilog's PL/Z, and others) are usually *compiled*, while BASIC is usually *interpreted*. An advantage to using slowly interpreted BASIC is that program debugging is very easy. Because the program does not need to be compiled every time a simple program change is made, rapid user feedback of modification effects is possible.

There are a few BASIC compilers available for the most popular microprocessors, and a viable approach to software development is to develop software using interpreted BASIC as a debugging tool and compiled BASIC as the final product.

HARDWARE AIDS

Software-development *hardware* includes such tangibles as development systems, time-sharing mainframe computer systems, minicomputers, in-circuit emulators, evaluation kits, and PROM programmers. The list of hardware that could be used to assist in the implementation of software can be made much longer, but these mentioned items are certainly a cross section of such aids, and it is to these that we now direct our attention.

The Microcomputer Itself

It is desirable to have an interactive computer system to develop microcomputer software. The system can be used for typing in, assembling or compiling, and debugging programs. One prime candidate for this task is another microcomputer system. Nearly any general-purpose microcomputer with a keyboard, data storage medium, fairly large memory, and a hard-copy output device can be used as a system development tool. Of course, there must be development software that runs on the system as well.

An editor and assembler constitute a minimum set of software; compilers, debuggers, and interpreters add to the system's development capabilities.

In a serious software development effort, it is imperative that a hard-copy device such as a line printer or printing terminal be used. Video terminals are fine for program editing, but debugging a program without a hard-copy program listing is at best cumbersome and at worst nearly impossible. It is preferable that the hard-copy device print on paper that you can mark up with ordinary writing tools, because marking up a listing can help significantly in the debugging process.

Development Systems

Microprocessor manufacturers and other companies recognized the need for microcomputer software and hardware development tools and produced micro-computers designed specifically for that purpose. Intel's MDS system, Motorola's EXORciser system, and Tektronix' 8002 system are but a few of the currently available "development systems." Microprocessor manufacturers tend to orient their development systems around their individual products, while instrument companies tend to take the "universal" approach. The best way to get an idea of what a typical development system contains is to examine one.

The American Microsystems Incorporated (AMI) MDC system is a devel-opment system designed primarily for 6800 microprocessor software and hard-ware development. The system includes advanced hardware and software fea-tures that simplify debugging and testing considerably.

The heart of the MDC system is the development station. This device is a modular card cage, keyboard, and CRT display built into one large enclosure that looks like an oversize video terminal. The card cage contains slots for 16 modules, including processor, PROM programmer, dual disk drive, debug, memory (RAM and preprogrammed ROM), and many other optional modules.

While many other manufacturers offer minifloppy disks and cassette tape as storage-device options, AMI offers only a full-size (8-inch) dual floppy-disk system for the MDC. This is a wise choice because the time loss and aggrava-tion caused by the smaller, slower data-storage peripherals is not worth the price savings they would return on this $9000 system. Total data storage capac-ity is therefore 512K bytes, which is adequate for many user programs as well as a good-size library of development software.

A PROM programmer card can be plugged into the MDC card cage, and object files can be transferred directly to PROMs using the MDC's PROM programming software.

Software support for the MDC system includes a disk operating and file management system, resident assembler and loader, resident editor, debug control programs, and trace programs.

A data acquisition module and logic analyzer module are planned expan-sions for the MDC system, and these additions will increase the system hardware's debugging capability.

One feature not found in the MDC is an in-circuit emulator. Many develop-ment system manufacturers produce modules for their development systems that have a 40-pin extender plug that mates with the microprocessor socket of the device being developed. The development system then mimics the micro-processor and simultaneously allows user intervention in the program execu-tion process. In-circuit emulators allow memory locations, external interfaces, and microprocessor registers to be examined, thereby giving the user a good idea of what is happening in a newly built system.

Evaluation Kits and Prototyping Boards

Another way of developing software for a microcomputer is by breadboarding the microcomputer (or a reasonably similar copy of it), and testing it in action. It is not necessary to start the breadboarding process from scratch, however. Many manufacturers make universal breadboards based on their particular processors. These breadboards, which are often called evaluation kids or prototyping kits, are built on double-sided circuit boards and contain enough logic to build a reasonably powerful system. A design can be built up using the board's facilities, and the used portions of the design can be transferred to the final product.

The American Microsystems Incorporated (AMI) EVK200 prototyping kit is representative of a good breadboard that can be used for hardware as well as software development. This breadboard contains:

- 2K ROM
- 512 bytes EPROM
- 1K bytes RAM
- EPROM programmer
- 20 mA current-loop interface
- EIA RS-232C interface
- TTY operating system software in ROM
- ROM subroutine library
- Interval timer
- Tiny BASIC

Assembler and disassembler ROMs are also available for this unit.

TIME-SHARING AND MINICOMPUTER-BASED SOFTWARE DEVELOPMENT

If a small, one-time programming task is all that is going to be undertaken, it is advantageous to avoid purchasing an expensive development system. One alternative to a development system is a time-sharing system. Many national time-sharing services such as National CSS and General Electric have extensive microprocessor support software that can be run from a rented terminal. Cross assemblers (assemblers that assemble programs for another computer) and compilers are used because large time-sharing systems typically use IBM or Control Data mainframes as the main processor. Simulators are used to "run" programs on time-sharing systems and are useful in debugging programs before transferring them to a microcomputer system.

Popular minicomputers can also be used to develop microprocessor software. Microprocessor manufacturers offer broad lines of non-resident software for users who already have their own minicomputers or mainframes. Motorola, for example, offers 6800-compatible cross assemblers, simulators, and high-level language compilers for IBM 360–370, HP 2100, Data General *Nova*, HIS 6000, CDC 6000, PDP-11, and Sigma 9 computers.

OBTAINING SOFTWARE DESIGN INFORMATION

Books devoted exclusively to software development are available and a representative sampling should be consulted before programming a microprocessor. For the engineer with extensive microprocessor experience, a system design data manual and programmer's manual are all that is really required to program a system. Engineers who need some guidance in the area of programming techniques should consult college-level texts concerning programming methods.

It is a good idea to learn good programming techniques from the very beginning, or unlearn bad habits that may have been picked up. The most common bad software habits are poor documentation and unstructured data flow. This is not surprising, because most books that deal with programming techniques concern themselves with program control rather than data flow or style. A good book that can help develop a good programming style is *Program Style, Design, Efficiency, Debugging and Testing* by Dennie Van Tassel.

CONCLUSION

Building a microcomputer system properly is not as simple as many microprocessor manufacturers lead you to believe. As this text has shown, system conceptualization, design, fabrication, testing, software design, and system integration all play an important part in the function and reliability of the final product. In summation, a properly designed and constructed system will take more engineering effort to develop than a poorly designed system, but the rewards in reliability, functional operation, and cost reduction due to logic optimization and lower service requirements more than compensate for the added effort. In regard to microcomputer interfacing, it pays to do it right!

Glossary of Microcomputer Terminology

Absolute address. A location in memory specified by its numerically assigned value.

Absolute loader. A program that loads data or instructions into memory at a fixed absolute address.

Access time. The time required to read a word out of memory.

Accumulator. An internal microcomputer register (or registers) where arithmetic and logical data are stored and manipulated.

ACIA. Abbreviation for *asynchronous communications interface adapter* (used for serial data communication).

Acknowledge. A signal commonly used to signify that data has been received or control information accepted in a handshaking situation.

Acoustic coupler. A piece of hardware designed to connect a telephone handset to a computer system, usually through inductive means.

A/D. Analog-to-digital (as in A/D converter).

Adder. A circuit that performs binary addition in a processor or interface.

Address. A numerical value that identifies word positions in a memory system.

Algorithm A step-by-step procedure that always leads to the solution of a problem.

Alphanumeric Containing potentially both letters and numerals as characters.

ALU Abbreviation for *arithmetic logic unit* (used to perform binary arithmetic and logical functions in a processor).

Analog The property of operating over a continuous, varying range of voltage or current values.

AND A logical operation in which all inputs must be at a logic 1 level for the output to be at a logic 1 level.

ANSI Abbreviation for *American National Standards Institute,* an organization that establishes standards.

Arithmetic logic unit A device used to perform binary arithmetic and logical functions in a processor or interface.

ASCII Abbreviation for *American Standard Code for Information Interchange.* This code is commonly used in data communications.

Assembler A program that takes symbolic instructions and variable names and converts them to a computer-usable program consisting of 1s and 0s.

Asynchronous Signals or device actions that are not synchronized with a master clock frequency.

Backplane A piece of computer hardware that contains the connectors and bus wiring for the system circuit boards.

Bank A large unit of memory.

BASIC Acronym for *beginners' all-purpose symbolic instruction code,* a popular computer language characterized by its ease of use. This language is usually interpreted instead of compiled.

Baud Officially defined as the reciprocal of the shortest pulse width in a data communication stream, but usually taken to mean bits per second.

BCD Abbreviation for *binary-coded decimal,* a limited radix-10 system in which four bits are used to express the numerals 0 through 9.

Benchmark A test program designed to test the performance of a processor in a given application.

Bidirectional The property of handling data flow in two directions.

Bipolar The characteristic of containing NPN or PNP transistors.

Bit A binary digit that can be set to represent a 1 or a 0.

Bit-sliced A system consisting of many identical parallel components, each of which performs operations on only a few bits of the total processed word.

Boolean algebra Binary arithmetic rules that define the logical operations of AND, OR, inversion, and exclusive-OR.

Bootstrap An initialization program that is used to start a computer's operation.

Buffer A circuit that amplifies and restores a signal to a proper drive level. An area of memory where data can be temporarily stored.

Bug An error in a piece of hardware or software.

Burn-in   The act of operating a piece of equipment for a period of time to isolate any early-failing parts.

Byte   A predefined number of parallel bits. In the microcomputer field, a byte is typically 8 bits.

Cache   A high-speed intermediate buffer memory that lies between the processor and main memory in a computer's memory hierarchy.

Carry   An output signal or status bit which is used to indicate positive arithmetic overflow of an adder or left shift overflow of a shift register.

CerDIP   An acronym for *ceramic dual-inline package*.

Checksum   A character residing at the end of a data block that corresponds to the binary sum of all the characters in the block. This is used for error checking.

Chip   Commonly used to describe a monolithic integrated circuit, in or out of a package.

Clock   A master reference waveform used to synchronize all of the logic in a system.

Coaxial cable   A transmission line consisting of a central conductor surrounded by dielectric material and an external conductor, and possessing a predictable characteristic impedance.

Complement   The logical inverse of a signal or bit. The complement of 1 is 0, and the complement of 0 is 1.

Console   The central control terminal in a computer system, or the front panel controls on a computer system.

Core   Commonly used word describing memory, but officially used to define memory built with small magnetic toroids strung together to form memory words.

Crash   The act of losing control of a computer by getting into a loop or executing the wrong program. The situation in which a floating disk head accidentally contacts the disk surface, thereby misreading or destroying the disk.

CRT   Abbreviation for *cathode-ray tube*, a vacuum tube with a viewing screen as an integral part of its envelope.

Compiler   A program that translates a high-level language consisting of arithmetic expressions and character manipulations into assembly language or directly into machine code.

Cycle time   The time it takes a memory to read data and restore itself for the following read operation.

D/A   Abbreviation for *digital-to-analog*.

Daisy chain   An electrical wiring scheme that passes signals through logic in every module to which the signals go.

Data base   A large collection of data files organized for easy access.

Debouncing   The act of removing the intermediate noise states from a mechanical switch.

Debugger   A program that is useful for checking out and developing computer programs.

Decoder   A circuit or array of circuits that converts a few coded inputs into many discrete inputs, of which each corresponds to a unique code.

Dice   Small silicon wafers that contain integrated circuitry.

Diskette   A flexible plastic (usually Mylar) disk coated with magnetic oxide and enclosed in a plastic jacket; also referred to as *floppy disk*.

Direct addressing   An addressing mode that uses a short field in an instruction to signify a portion of the addressed memory's address. The remaining portion of the field is either loaded separately or assumed to be a certain value.

DMA   Abbreviation for *direct memory access*, the process of bypassing the processor and taking data from or putting data directly into memory.

Dot matrix   A square or rectangular field of LEDs or points on a CRT that are selectively turned on or off to form characters and graphics. Printers also use dot matrix methods to form characters.

Double density   Having twice the storage capacity of a standard disk.

Double precision   A method of increasing the range of expressible numbers in a computer by using multiple bytes to represent single numbers.

Driver   A circuit that amplifies and reshapes a waveform for use by many devices or a single high-power device.

Drum   An obsolete memory system consisting of a rotating magnetically coated drum and appropriate magnetic read and write heads.

DTL   Abbreviation for *diode–transistor logic*, the forerunner of TTL.

Dump   The process or printing out or externally storing the contents of a computer's memory.

Duplex   Bidirectional data communication capability.

Dynamic   Refers to circuitry that stores its states as tentative charges and must be refreshed by restoring the charges periodically.

Dynamic memory   Memory constructed of dynamic cells that need refreshing.

Echo   The process of sending an acknowledging character or signal back to the sending peripheral of a computer.

ECL   Abbreviation for *emitter-coupled logic*.

Editor   A program that allows a user to type data into a formatted computer file and to change and manipulate that data.

EIA   The *Electronic Industries Association*, an agency that sets standards.

Emulate   The process of simulating the actions of a device or system in real time.

EOF   The *end-of-file* character.

EOT   The *end-of-transmission* character.

EPROM   Acronym for *erasable programmable read-only memory.*

Error-correcting code   A computer data transmission code that allows one or more bits of data to be in error without resulting in the loss of any information.

FAMOS   Acronym for *floating-gate avalanche MOS*. This device technology is commonly used in PROMs.

Fan-in   The number of inputs a gate or device will accept.

Fan-out   The number of devices or gates a circuit will successfully drive.

Fetch   The act of retrieving an instruction or data from computer memory.

File   A formatted block of data that is treated as a unit.

Firmware   System programs stored in ROM in a microcomputer system. A processor-internal bootstrap program is an example of firmware.

Flag   A status signal in hardware or a bit of memory from the software point of view that holds a status indication until read or reset by the interrogating device.

FSK   Abbreviation for *frequency-shift keying;* a method for using audio signals to operate teletypewriter keys.

Gap   A small amount of unused recording material between tape or disk files and used as file separators.

Glitch   An unwanted transient noise pulse or burst of pulses usually of very short duration and high amplitude.

Ground   A standard potential (usually zero volts) to which all other system voltages are referenced.

Half-duplex   Bidirectional communications in which data can travel in only one direction at a time due to the sharing of a common communication line.

Halt   A digital system's or a computer's stopped state (where no operations are performed).

Hamming code   A common error-correction code that assigns extra parity digits to correct errors in words.

Handshaking   Data communications control technique based on multiple data transfer requests and ready and acknowledge signals between devices.

Hard copy   A physical written or printed record of computer output. Printers are hard-copy devices.

Hard-sectored   The division of a disk into sectors through the use of index holes in the disk.

Hard-wired   A function performed by physical logic and wiring instead of software.

Hexadecimal   Radix-16 arithmetic and numerical representation.

High-order   Refers to the most significant bits of a word.

Immediate   An addressing mode in which data for an instruction immediately follows the instruction in memory.

Impact printer   A hard-copy device that prints letters on paper using a physical hammer motion of some kind.

Indexed addressing   An addressing mode in which data for an instruction is located at the memory location pointed to by an index register plus an offset value contained in the instruction.

Indirect addressing   An addressing mode in which data for an instruction is located in the memory location pointed to by the contents of the addressed word.

Initialization   The process of resetting and preparing an interface or processor for program execution.

Interlace   The technique of creating a raster-scan image by overlaying two scanned fields, with the second field's lines falling between the first's.

Interleaving   A memory addressing scheme based on successive addresses being assigned to different memory banks, and used to increase memory throughput.

Interpreter   A program that executes a high-level language by reading the language statements, interpreting them, and performing the operation in a real-time mode. Statements are not converted to assembly language first.

Interrupt   The act of diverting a program's execution to a more urgent task.

IIL or I²L   Abbreviation for *integrated injection logic*.

Joystick   A manual control device consisting of a vertical stick that can be tilted in any direction, thereby sending the longitudinal and lateral tilt parameters to a computer or other device.

Kansas City standard   A common micocomputer tape format consisting of ones represented by 8 cycles of 2400 Hz and zeros represented by 4 cycles of 1200 Hz.

Kludge   A poorly designed trick or circuit patch used to temporarily correct a circuit error.

LCD   Abbreviation for *liquid-crystal display*.

LED   Abbreviation for *light-emitting diode*.

Light pen   An input "pencil" that a user points at a desired position on a display screen, thereby sending that positional information to the computer.

Linking loader   A program that loads program segments that were assembled separately and generates all the proper jump addresses and variable addresses between segments.

Load   The process of moving data from one peripheral to another, from a peripheral to memory, or from one register to another.

Logic analyzer   A piece of test equipment that is similar to an oscilloscope but that displays strings of 1s and 0s as well as waveforms.

Loop   A sequence of instructions cyclically repeated a number of times.

LSB   Abbreviation for *least significant bit*.

Machine language   A computer program in binary form.

Macro   A sequence of instructions that is so often used that a separate name is given to it. A macro assembler implements the instruction seuqence whenever the name is submitted.

Macro assembler   An assembler capable of handling macro expansions.

Mask   A logical function used to always set certain bits in a word to an established binary state.

Masked ROM   A nonprogrammable ROM that must be programmed at the factory by varying the chip's mask.

Memory map   A diagram showing a system's memory addresses and what programs and data are assigned to each section of memory.

Memory-mapped I/O   A method of interfacing by assigning memory addresses to I/O ports as well as memory. Data is sent to and read from peripherals by simply reading or writing into a certain memory location.

Microcomputer   A completely operational computer system built around a microprocessor.

Microcontroller   A microcomputer designed strictly for control applications.

Microprocessor   A complete processor including arithmetic logic and control logic on one or more LSI chips.

Microprogram   A wide-word-width program that controls the internal workings of a microprocessor.

Mnemonic   A descriptive name given to a computer instruction that makes assembly-language programming easier.

Modem   A device that modulates digital signals and sends them across a telephone line, and that demodulates incoming signals and converts them into digital signals.

Monitor   A program that performs communication between a computer and the console terminal and handles simple system loading and execution commands.

Motherboard   Another name for a backplane, and usually referring to a backplane module.

MSB   Abbreviation for *most significant bit*.

Multiplex   The act of channeling two signals to one source, or sharing a system resource between users.

MUX   Abbreviation for *multiplexer*.

Negative logic   Logic that has 0 assigned to the voltage normally associated with logic 1 and 1 assigned to the voltage normally associated with 0.

Nested   The name given to subroutine calls in subroutines or loops inside loops.

Nybble   Half a byte—typically 4 bits in a microcomputer system.

Noise   Unwanted electrical signals caused by induction, capacitive action, or semiconductor characteristics.

Null modem   A cable that interconnects two RS-232C devices together by acting as a piece of dummy data communication equipment.

Object code   The binary machine-language output of an assembler. Object code can be loaded into a computer and run as-is.

Octal   Representation of numbers in a radix-8 system.

Ones' complement   A binary representation in which the MSB of the word is assigned the negative value of its normal weight minus one. Negative numbers can thereby be expressed and numbers can be negated by simply complementing them.

Operating system   A program that manages software files and hardware functions of a computer system.

OR   A logical function defined as a logic 1 output if any one of the inputs is equal to 1.

Overflow   The act of exceeding an ALU's or adder's numerical capacity in the positive or negative direction.

Paging   The process of breaking memory or files into smaller, more manageable pieces.

Parity   The even or odd characteristic of the number of 1s in a byte or word.

Peripheral   An external device connected to a computer.

Phase   A clock waveform that occurs with a predefined relation to other clock waveforms in a multiphase clock system.

PIA   Abbreviation for *peripheral interface adapter*.

PIO   Abbreviation for *programmable input/output*, an integrated-circuit chip.

Plotter   A device that allows a computer to draw images using a motor-controlled pen.

Polling   The act of determining device or peripheral status by continually interrogating the associated status word.

Positive logic   The normal mode of logic operation and the associated logical functions.

Power-fail restart   The process of saving a computer's execution state in nonvolatile memory as power is failing, and resuming execution when power returns.

Power supply   The unit that supplies the voltage power forms to a system's circuitry.

Priority   The importance of a device or peripheral in an interrupt system. If two devices interrupt at the same time, the higher-priority device will get serviced first.

PROM   Acronym for *programmable read-only memory.*

Propagation delay   The amount of time it takes an electrical signal to go through a logic element or wire.

PSW   Abbreviation for *program status word.*

Pullup or pullup resistor   A resistor that holds a point in a circuit to a logic 1 level. Typically used to hold unused inputs high and to supply current to open-collector gates.

Push   The act of putting data into a stack.

Quad   The characteristic of four units. A quad-gate package has four gates.

Random access   The ability to interrogate any location in a memory without interrogating any others first.

Raster scan   The process of forming an image by scanning a beam of electrons in a multilined pattern on a phosphorescent screen.

Redundant   A signal that is not necessary for a system to perform an identical function under all conditions.

Refresh   The act of replenishing the charge on the MOS data storage transistors in a dynamic device.

Relative addressing   An addressing mode in which data is located at a displacement distance from a base word or instruction.

Relocatable loader   A program that can load object code into memory at any location and retain the functionality of the program. This type of loader must compute new addresses; it offsets corresponding to the load address.

Resident   The property of software residing in the memory of the computer system. If two programs are in memory at once, they are coresident.

Rise time   The time it takes for a waveform to change from its low to high logic state.

Rollover   The action of pressing two or more keyboard keys simultaneously.

RTL   Abbreviation for *resistor–transistor logic.*

Sample-and-hold   A circuit that samples an input voltage and holds an output voltage at that level until resampling occurs.

Scratchpad   A small memory (usually high-speed) used to store temporary results inside a processor.

Second source   An alternate manufacturer of a part.

Sector   A pie-slice shaped section of a disk.

Seek   The act of a disk head moving to a proper disk track to perform a read or write operation.

Serial data   Data broken into single bits and transmitted on a sequential bit-by-bit basis.

Setup time   The time a signal must be stable at an input before another signal (usually a clock signal) occurs.

Simplex   Unidirectional data transfer.

Simulator   A program that acts like the device it is simulating on a nonreal-time basis.

Slew rate   The rate at which voltage rises on a line (expressed as volts per second).

Socket   A mechanical connection device used to connect the pins of an integrated circuit to the circuit board.

Solder mask   A protective coating on a printed circuit card that only allows solder to adhere to areas it is supposed to.

Source code   The user-readable assembly language input file that is read into the assembler.

Stack   A file of hardware registers or an area in memory assigned to act as a last-in–first-out memory. Data is put onto the stack using pushes and is taken off using pops.

Start bit   The first bit in an asynchronous word transmission.

Static memory   Memory that retains its contents without refreshing.

Status   The condition or state of a device.

Stop bit   The last bit in an asynchronous word transmission.

Strain gage   A transducer that varies its resistance depending on the amount of tension applied to it.

Technology   The materials and fabrication method used to manufacture a device. A circuit built from CMOS parts is said to use CMOS technology.

Thermistor   A device that varies its resistance depending on the temperature applied to it.

Throughput   The rate at which data is processed or accessed from a device. It is typically measured as instructions per second or words per second.

Track   A concentric ring on a disk on which data is stored.

Trap   The process of diverting program execution to an error routine if an error condition is detected.

Triac   A thyristor consisting essentially of back-to-back SCRs connected in parallel.

TTL   Abbreviation for *transistor–transistor logic*.

Twos' complement   A numbering system used to express positive and negative binary numbers in which the MSB takes on the negative value of its normal weight.

UART   Abbreviation for *universal asynchronous receiver/transmitter*.

USART   Abbreviation for *universal synchronous/asynchronous receiver/ transmitter*.

Utilities   Short useful programs that are often used in a computer system.

Vectors   Addresses set aside as jump addresses to be used in case of interrupts (interrupt vectors), traps (trap vectors), and other program actions.

Virtual memory   A memory addressing scheme in which hardware completely controls the memory hierarchy and the system appears (to the programmer) to have one huge random-access memory.

VLSI   Abbreviation for *very large-scale integration*.

VMOS   Logic built with V-groove semiconductor technology.

Wire-wrap   A circuit interconnection method incorporating individual silver-plated wires wrapped around square posts.

Word   A predefined field of bits that usually consists of two bytes. Microcomputers typically have 8- or 16-bit words.

Word processing   The field of working with text and manuscripts using computers.

Workspace   An area of memory where user programs are allowed to reside.

XOR   The logical exclusive-OR function defined as a 1 output when either of two inputs is logic 1.

Yield   The percentage of operational chips resulting from the fabrication of an entire batch of chips.

Zener diode   A diode whose reverse breakdown voltage is precisely controlled and can be used to advantage.

Index